ITINERARIES
OF EXPERTISE

Intersections: Environment, Science, Technology

Sarah Elkind and Finn Arne Jørgensen, Editors

ITINERARIES
OF EXPERTISE

Science, Technology, *and the* Environment
in Latin America's Long Cold War

EDITED BY ANDRA B. CHASTAIN
AND TIMOTHY W. LOREK

University of Pittsburgh Press

Published by the University of Pittsburgh Press, Pittsburgh, Pa., 15260
Manufactured in the United States of America
Printed on acid-free paper
10 9 8 7 6 5 4 3 2 1

Cataloging-in-Publication data is available from the Library of Congress

ISBN 13: 978-0-8229-4596-3
ISBN 10: 0-8229-4596-7

Cover art: Rockefeller Foundation agronomist Ulysses J. Grant consulting with an unidentified Colombian agronomist as part of the Rockefeller Foundation's Colombian Agricultural Program (CAP, 1950–1964). Source: Folder 177, Box 7, Series 100, Rockefeller Foundation Photographs, Rockefeller Archive Center, Tarrytown, NY.
Cover design: Melissa Dias-Mandoly

Dedicated to Gilbert M. Joseph

CONTENTS

III. Infrastructures of the Built Environment

IV. Toward New Regimes of Expertise

ACKNOWLEDGMENTS

In a book about the paths traveled by experts and expertise, it is perhaps fitting that this book represents the culmination of the work of many different collaborators whose trajectories connect the United States, Latin America, and the United Kingdom. The itinerary that this volume has taken required the persistence, patience, and commitment of our contributors, and we are deeply grateful for their dedication. Throughout this process, since we began thinking about the themes of this book in 2013–2014, we found support, wisdom, and encouragement from Gilbert Joseph, without whom this project would not have been possible. Gil graciously shared his own expertise with us at critical moments, yet always allowed us to steer the ship.

This volume began as a pair of conference panels at the Latin American Studies Association annual meeting in San Juan, Puerto Rico, in 2015. We thank the participants on those panels for their enthusiasm and role in building momentum for further exploration. In particular, thank you to Julio Moreno, Emilio de Antuñano, Jennifer Hoyt, Taylor Jardno, Tony Andersson, Marco Ramos, and Eric Rutkow.

In October 2016 we hosted the conference at Yale University that resulted in this volume. For conference funding and support, we thank the MacMillan Center for International and Area Studies, the Yale Council on Latin American and Iberian Studies, the Edward J. and Dorothy Clarke Kempf Memorial Fund, the Pontifical Catholic University of Chile, the Yale Graduate School of Arts and Sciences Dean's Fund, the Yale Graduate and Professional Student Senate, Yale Environmental History, the Mellon Fund for Latin American History at Yale, and the Yale Latin American Studies Speaker Series. Paulo Drinot, Marcela Echeverri, Gilbert Joseph, Paul Sabin, Stuart Schwartz, James Scott, and Susan Stokes offered critical counsel, support, and intellectual engagement with this project. We also thank Tricia Connolly, Lourdes Haynes, Marilyn Wilkes, Lisa Brennan, Marcy Kaufman, and the Yale Program in Agrarian Studies for the logistical support, without which the conference would not have been possible.

All those who presented at the conference deserve recognition for their generous and insightful contributions that propelled this project forward.

Beyond those whose work appears in this volume, we thank Gabriela Soto Laveaga, Margarita Fajardo, María Alejandra Pérez, Javier Puente, Rebecca Tally, Manuel Rodríguez, and Ricardo Salvatore. Scott D. Crago deserves special recognition for his role as not only a conference presenter but one of the original architects of this idea long before it became a reality.

A faculty grant from Washington State University Vancouver significantly aided in the publication of this book. Andrew Chastain provided important technical assistance throughout this process, not least in creating the map of Latin America. We are also grateful to the various presses and academic journals that permitted portions of previously published work to appear here. We also acknowledge the many archivists and institutions that facilitated the research projects contained herein and granted permissions for the use of images from their collections.

We are grateful to our supportive editor, Sandra B. Crooms, who championed this project early on and shepherded it through the long and winding publication process. Two anonymous readers for the University of Pittsburgh Press provided incisive comments that significantly improved the final product. Any mistakes or errors that remain are exclusively our own.

MAP OF
LATIN AMERICA
AND FEATURED
SITES OF EXPERTISE

Tepalcatepec
Valley

Mexico
City

Papaloapan
Valley

CUBA

PUERTO RICO

Bogotá

Bajo Anchicayá
Dam

Cali

Cañón del Pato
Dam

Manu National
Park

Rio de Janeiro

Rapel Dam

Santiago

ITINERARIES
OF EXPERTISE

INTRODUCTION

Andra B. Chastain and Timothy W. Lorek

We contend that, beneath the conflicts waged by diplomats and militaries, the Latin American Cold War was conducted by experts. Scientists and engineers, doctors and social workers, agronomists and architects—as well as the webs of expertise they wove—made material the political ideologies of the era. Indeed, the intertwined dreams of development and modernization that animated the Latin American Cold War relied on an army of highly specialized experts whose influence reverberates across the hemisphere and around the globe. The advent of new crop varieties and animal breeds, new houses and transportation systems, and new infrastructures of energy and tourism intimately changed the way millions of Latin Americans ate, worked, lived, and played. Around the globe, how many billions continue to feel the effects of the Green Revolution or, alternately, rally around or condemn new ways of knowing such as biodiversity conservation or neoliberal political economy, all of which germinated in Cold War Latin America? Perhaps because the technologies associated with these developments were often mundane or invisible to the naked eye—the genetics of seeds and cattle, the invisibility of electrical currents, radio waves, or market trends—they have too often been overlooked by historians of the Cold War in Latin America in favor of more dramatic moments of conflict and confrontation.

The roles of conventional Cold War actors such as diplomats, intelligence agencies, revolutionaries, political parties, and militaries have been the focus of traditional histories of the Cold War in Latin America.[1] More recently, scholars have shown how culture, broadly conceived, became an instrument in the Latin American Cold War, as artists, writers, intellectuals, and stu-

dents helped to shape the contours of conflict.[2] Yet the experts who constitute the focus of this volume have escaped these categories: they often portrayed themselves as removed from politics, even as their work directly and
indirectly contributed to the key geopolitical agendas of the day. Moreover,
whereas social scientists have written extensively about development projects
in Latin America, the individual actors behind that work too often evade direct historical analysis.[3] The experts behind the region's Cold War projects of
modernization and development are too easily taken for granted, rather than
examined as complex historical actors in their own right. In this volume, we
intend to pull back the curtain to reveal a set of individuals and institutions,
trace their physical and intellectual itineraries across time and space, and dis-
sect their roles in the on-the-ground negotiation of the Cold War.

This book sets out to answer the following questions: In the Latin American Cold War, who constituted an expert, and why? Where did experts originate, how did they travel, and who funded their work? How did local, national, and international actors negotiate expertise on the ground? Readers
acquainted with US-led Cold War development projects will encounter some
familiar names: the Rockefeller Foundation, the World Bank, David Lilienthal of the Tennessee Valley Authority, and Norman Borlaug of Green Revolution fame all make appearances in the following pages. However, none of
the essays focus primarily on these figures. Although such individuals and
institutions played critical roles in the circulation of technical knowledge
and the implementation of development projects in Cold War Latin America, our intent is to dig deeper and uncover the national and transnational negotiation of expertise, including the role of Latin American experts in these
processes.[4]

The task of historicizing experts and expertise is particularly relevant
now, as global events have cast doubt on the onetime aura and authority of
experts. The ideas presented in this volume emerged out of a conference held
at Yale University in October 2016. Months before our event, in the United
Kingdom, a chorus of economic experts urging voters to remain part of the
European Union seemed to do little to sway the opinion of the electorate.
The shock caused by Brexit was met or exceeded by the election of Donald
Trump in the United States just weeks after our conference, where all the apparently expert polling promised that he would be roundly defeated. While
explanations for Brexit and Trump continue to be hotly contested years later,
increased skepticism toward urban elites and experts is undoubtedly a factor.
And the erosion of trust in expert authority is by no means confined to the
ideological Right, as measles outbreaks caused by low vaccination rates and
antivaccination propaganda have demonstrated. Indeed, some have warned
that we are witnessing the "death of the ideal of expertise itself," with alarm-
ing consequences for science, the environment, and democracy.[5]

It is hardly this volume's intention to promote a blind trust of scientific and governmental authority. Nevertheless, as we began to assemble the book, the fury galvanized by the Trump administration against journalists, intellectuals, scientists, and political bureaucrats seemed determined to unravel both the internal mechanics of US federal agencies and US-shepherded global order. The president's political appointments to head federal agencies, including the Environmental Protection Agency, the Department of Energy, and the Department of Housing and Urban Development, to name a few, exhibited a critical lack of experience with the work of the agencies in question and often an outright hostility. Meanwhile, key sources of federal funding threatened to dry up as the new administration's initial budget proposal slashed the National Endowment for the Arts, the National Endowment for the Humanities, the Institute of International Education and other programs supporting the circulation and exchange of knowledge and expertise.

Diverse resistance fought off some of these measures, including science and expertise in its intersectional outrage. Groups of rangers with the National Park Service opened a renegade Twitter handle. Signs reading "Science Is Real" appeared alongside those championing the rights of women, people of color, undocumented immigrants, sexual minorities, and other marginalized communities. By the time this volume went to press, it was clear that the administration that had labeled falsehoods "alternative facts" had deepened a cultural chasm regarding the validity of knowledge. Out of the culture wars giving rise to populist neonationalist movements, a sharpening war on expertise has emerged.[6] Yet as Javiera Barandiarán reveals in this volume's penultimate chapter, the contemporary breakdown emerges from the late–Cold War ascendance of free-market ideology, which undid the formerly close relationship between expertise and the state. The first nationwide experiment with neoliberal shock treatment occurred under Pinochet's military dictatorship in Chile and, as Barandiarán writes, set the stage for a new era of conflict between a reoriented power structure and scientific experts.[7] In this way, and in many other ways described in these pages, the Latin American experience in the Cold War continues to resonate in our contemporary moment. The ongoing transformation of the role of experts in government demands new histories of expertise, specifically ones that focus on the Latin American laboratories where Cold War knowledge was generated, applied, and contested.

As this volume shows, the politicization of expertise is nothing new. However, we argue that the Cold War raised the stakes of expert knowledge in concrete ways. From iconic Cold War technologies such as atomic bombs and satellites to social scientific knowledge about strategic peoples and places, experts seemed to hold the secrets to state security and prosperity. The

United States sought to prevent the spread of communism in Latin America through the deployment of experts and funding tied to technical aid missions, including those in Truman's Point Four program and, later, Kennedy's Alliance for Progress. Many Latin American leaders, for their part, embraced the promise of the expert—first through efforts at import-substitution industrialization and state planning, and later through authoritarian, technocratic projects to dismantle the state's role in the economy. The thorniest sociocultural problems posed by the Cold War—such as how to feed, shelter, and educate a rapidly growing population—seemed to offer a carte blanche for the intervention of a host of experts. The embrace of technical solutions to solve complex sociocultural challenges was a hallmark of Cold War modernization projects, as Mary Roldán notes in her chapter. "Hungry? Produce more food. Low yields? Apply fertilizer or selective breeding. Too many children, unable to feed, clothe or educate them? Control your fertility. Longing to escape the shackles of ignorance, poverty, and subordination? Plagued by clientelism, paternalism, or oppressive government? Learn to read." As Fernando Purcell argues in this volume, the politicization of expertise during the Cold War in Latin America became a "revolutionary phenomenon."

Merging Science and Technology Studies with Environmental History

This volume grows out of a conviction that the perspectives of two important and growing subfields—science and technology studies (STS) and environmental history—can help us rethink the Latin American Cold War in productive ways. Both fields have grappled with how to understand increasing human control over nature and the consequences this has wrought for both the natural and built environment over the course of the twentieth century. Indeed, both STS and environmental history have posed new questions about the relationship between human and nonhuman actors, the intersection of technology and power, and the often-unseen processes by which individuals and communities produce new knowledge. As the environmental historian Richard White and the historian of science Gabrielle Hecht have shown for different contexts, the invisibility of power does not signify that it is uncontested or without material consequences.[8] In this volume, we intend to illuminate how "technologies of power" traveled and became negotiated along circuits of expertise in Latin America during the Cold War.

We follow other scholars who aim to advance dialogue and scholarship at the nexus of these two fields.[9] We also build on the growing literature that examines histories of Cold War science and technology in the United States and the world, as well as the Cold War's impact on the environment.[10] Yet, with some notable exceptions, Latin America has been relatively absent in these accounts.[11] Our volume aims not only to bring Latin American perspectives to bear on Cold War "envirotech,"[12] but to probe the interactions between "high" and "low" expertise, between state officials and the grassroots, and between national or international actors and local forms of knowledge. All our authors are specialists in Latin America, many of them particularly versed in its cultural and social histories, which comes through in their studies of science, technology, and the environment.

This collection also builds on dynamic new scholarship in the field of Latin American environmental history. Until relatively recently, some environmental historians characterized scholarship on Latin America in terms of one-sided narratives of degradation, declension, and exploitation while increasingly robust historiographies in the United States and other regions dissected nature, culture, and the state through complex webs of interaction. J. R. McNeill, for example, observed an earlier generation of Latin Americanist environmental historians inspired by dependency theory to produce large-scale narratives in which individuals and individual agency could sometimes get clouded.[13] More recently, Mark Carey picked up on these assertions and advocated for further integration between Latin American environmental history and the field's signature social histories. Historians of science, he argues, have offered more sophisticated analyses linking science and scientific actors to social relations, nation-building, and state formation.[14] To be fair, some of these critiques of Latin American environmental history evaluated the field according to parameters developed in the United States for US historical contexts. They also tended to focus on major works by US-based authors. In fact, as Carey notes, the strong tradition of scholarship on agrarian and natural resource issues in Latin America predates the popularity of "environmental history" in the United States. Yet it can hardly be denied that a new wave of scholarship has complicated and elevated Latin American environmental history in the international arena. This is evident in recent collections that highlight the diverse interpretations of Latin American environmental history and explore the concept of the "nature state" within and beyond Latin America.[15]

Rather than offering a definitive statement on how these various fields coalesced in the Latin American Cold War, this collection seeks to open new avenues and provoke new research on the role that experts played, both in relationship to political processes broadly conceived and to their own fields of expertise. We thus highlight the role of certain experts more than others, with an emphasis on individuals whose work touched on the natural or built environment, such as engineers, environmental scientists, agronomists, and architects. We conceive of technology broadly, taking it to include infrastructures such as dams, housing, transportation systems, and radio, as well as technologies modified from the natural world such as hybrid seeds and animals. We trace these experts in their individual and institutional itineraries and their engagement with technologies, environments, and state projects in an era of intensified international political pressure and exchange.

We draw significant inspiration from an increasingly sophisticated literature on medicine and public health in Latin America, which offers a roadmap for the type of scholarship we seek to expand for other arenas of expertise. Bridging histories of medicine and the larger historiographies of social and cultural relations and state formation in Latin America, Marcos Cueto and Steven Palmer depict public health as "contested by a wide variety of actors (including the sick) through complex local processes of reception, adaptation, eclectic redeployment, and hybridization." The resultant "polycentric networks" and "creative interplay" between centers and peripheries in the realm of public health expertise might be adopted as a template for other forms of expert circulation and interaction across borders.[16] Indeed, Stuart McCook recast Palmer's description of a "republic of rational health" as a "republic of rational agriculture" in order to describe the growing professionalization and internationalization of another type of expert.[17]

By focusing on case studies of individual experts and the localized application *and* generation of knowledge, we find that itineraries of expertise were more varied and complex than modernization orthodoxies of the Cold War era would make them out to be. That is, specialized knowledge and technologies did not always flow from the Global North to the Global South, or from the United States and Europe to Latin America; the center–periphery model of development is insufficient to account for the transnational exchange of expertise within Latin America and between Latin America and the world. As we see in the contributions by Thomas Rath and Tore Olsson, Latin American veterinary scientists and hydroelectric engineers shaped the way their counterparts in England and the United States fought hoof-and-mouth disease and promoted rural development, respectively. Expertise also traveled through unexpected and even South–South networks. In this volume we see Mexican experts in the US South, Puerto Ricans working in Colombia, and Japanese experts in Chile, among others. By tracing the itineraries of Latin American Cold War expertise, these studies help us reconsider well-worn binaries: they explore how traveling experts traversed the boundaries between the rural and the urban; how networks of expertise strengthened or undermined the North–South and East–West axes imposed by Cold War geopolitics; and how experts reinforced or defied other binaries, such as developed–developing, First World–Third World, and Global North–Global South. Throughout the book, we highlight the multiple levels of expertise at play and show how it was not always easy to disentangle "local" or "domestic" from "global" or "foreign" knowledge.

Expertise and the State from the Eighteenth Century to the Cold War

The study of expertise and state power is not limited to the Cold War era, of course, and the figures studied in this volume emerged out of a longer tradition of scientific governance reaching back at least to the eighteenth century. It is important to recognize that this long process predated the onset of the Cold War and modernization theory in order to account for the Cold War's continuities as well as accelerations, not to mention the preexisting traditions of expertise in Latin America.

Historical frameworks of expertise and governance grew out of associations between science and natural law. In tracing a "genealogy of technologies of power," Foucault argued that eighteenth-century physiocrats, or those who believed in the "rule of nature" in economics and government, were crucial in establishing a close connection between the state and expertise. Physiocrats, he noted, emerged from the prestige carried by the scientific study of economics and its association with physics in eighteenth-century Enlightenment circles. Physiocrats and their governing patrons thus believed that politics should function according to the strict application of perceived natural law to society.[18] Governance, like physics, drew its authority from the inalienable truths of science, best interpreted and applied by experts.

For our purposes, Foucault's analysis of the naturalizing of economics in the eighteenth century has provided foundations for contemporary scholars to trace the history of capitalism.[19] When viewing capitalist development through a historical lens, the Cold War's practitioners of modernization theory and, later, those of neoliberalism, grow out of this tradition of merging the laws of the market with the laws of nature. The literature critiquing the self-assurance of expertise in pursuit of naturalized notions of modernization and twentieth-century development schemes is vast but fundamental to the framing of our studies of expertise in Latin America.[20] These works question the seemingly natural, universal logic of capitalism and thus serve as a useful model for this volume's critique of the universalizing logic of Cold War modernization.

Historically, the example of Europe's physiocrats touched Latin America in a variety of ways. European colonial powers sent engineers and botanists, among others, to construct and collect in their overseas territories. During the independence era of the early nineteenth century, Latin America hosted numerous transnational scientific expeditions, most famously those of the Prussian Alexander von Humboldt.

Humboldt's travels in Latin America would inspire both international and domestic itineraries of expertise in Latin America during the nineteenth century. Among these, Darwin's voyage of the *Beagle* to the Americas launched the study of evolutionary biology and influenced both scientific theories and racist social dogmas in Latin America and beyond. Yet, as Jorge Cañizares-Esguerra has argued, both the colonial expeditions sent from the metropole and their nineteenth-century republican descendants masked the parallel existence of a domestic Latin American scientific tradition. European transplants, such as Claudio Gay in Chile and José Celestino Mutis in Nueva Granada; homegrown Latin American scientists and intellectuals; and the countless denizens of "local knowledge" influenced the work of their more famous European counterparts.[21] New scholarship on domestically funded surveys and cartographic expeditions in nineteenth-century Mexico, Chile, and Colombia, for example, trace Humboldt's legacy in the Americas while shifting the focus to national actors and often racialized projects of state formation and imagined communities.[22]

The prestige of physiocrats in the European Enlightenment tradition spread to muscular and sometimes authoritarian Latin American projects of modernization in the late nineteenth century. The *científicos* employed under the Porfirio Díaz regime in Mexico resembled Foucault's physiocrats in name and deed. Blending science and governance, *científicos* employed interpretations of rational and natural law based on Comtean Positivism. With the blessing of the Díaz regime, *científicos* sought to modernize Mexican infrastructure and prepare the natural and social landscape for the reception of foreign capitalist investment.[23] Positivism spread throughout Latin America, with many governments turning to meritocratic expertise in an effort to modernize their growing state bureaucracies.[24] European expertise was especially prominent in the modernization campaigns of the late nineteenth and early twentieth centuries, with British and German influence in fields such as railroad construction, electrification, and the professionalization of national militaries. Overall, the rich literature on nineteenth-century expertise in Latin America reveals the importance of local citizen-experts, including women and people of color, in building what Stuart McCook calls "creole science."[25]

With the Spanish–American War at the close of the nineteenth century, the United States' power and interest in shaping networks of expertise in Latin America grew dramatically. As Greg Grandin and Gilbert Joseph have argued, the decades-long rise of US hegemony was deeply intertwined with a long Latin American Cold War, and many of the traveling experts discussed in this volume emerged out of US initiatives that predated World War II.[26] In the 1920s and 1930s, for example, US financial experts facilitated the extension of new banking and currency systems through "dollar diplomacy," while labor and social welfare policies in Latin America also reflected transnational currents.[27] Meanwhile, and as recent work by Ricardo Salvatore demonstrates, Cold War academic interest in Latin America built on the networks established by scholars during the New Deal and World War II.[28] Gilbert

M. Joseph's essay in this volume further explores the vexed origins of Latin American studies in the United States and its connection to the Cold War.

The Progressive movement and New Deal in the United States each cast ripples across Latin America, serving as the training ground for the experts who would later travel abroad in the context of World War II and the Cold War.[29] Some of the circulation of ideas and expertise in these earlier eras filtered through the US territory of Puerto Rico, which positioned itself as an intermediary in a "cultural triangle" connecting the United States and Latin America. Puerto Rico served as a convergence zone and training ground for both US and Latin American professionals, while Puerto Rican experts like Carlos Chardón influenced significant national development campaigns in multiple countries. Significantly, Puerto Rico's early role in the hemispheric circulation of expertise would blossom into the Alliance for Progress. The Puerto Rican governor Luis Muñoz Marín served as a key adviser to Kennedy on Latin America, and the head of Puerto Rico's Operation Bootstrap, Teodoro Moscoso, became the inaugural coordinator of the Alliance for Progress.[30]

After World War II, these preexisting foundations for an international order of expertise gained funding and a renewed ideological mission. From Truman's Point Four program to Kennedy's Alliance for Progress, and from the Bogotá-based Inter-American Center for Agrarian Reform (CIRA, sponsored by the Organization of American States) to the UN's Economic Commission for Latin America and the Caribbean (CEPAL), experts of different nationalities and backgrounds constructed blueprints for development programs in Latin America and beyond. After the watershed victory of the Cuban Revolution in 1959, the urgency of state expertise and modernization schemes intensified, even as US–Latin American partnerships foundered amid the rise of more radical—and less expert-oriented—solutions to underdevelopment.

In tracing this relationship between experts and Latin American states, we focus most intently on several locations that, we argue, constituted particularly fertile sites in not only the application but also the generation of Cold War expertise. Because of domestic factors as well as their strategic importance for the United States—in which friendly diplomatic relations, economic ties, and the potential for communist influence combined in a potent mix—we find that the Caribbean, Mexico, Colombia, and Chile served as crucial laboratories of Cold War expertise in the region.[31] Puerto Rico and Mexico, for example, became early sites of experimentation that previewed and catalyzed what would become broader hemispheric programs for Cold War development and science, as the chapters by Olsson, Lorek, and Rath describe here. Colombia and Chile, as well, attracted a density of experts in many fields, a fact that was tied to their strategic potential during the Cold

War. Taken together, the locations studied in this volume became important Cold War centers in what the Cuban historian Leida Fernández-Prieto calls the "global archipelago of knowledge."[32] Our focus on specific convergence zones opens an opportunity to critique the notion of Latin America as peripheral either to the Cold War struggle or to global knowledge production. In focusing in depth on these particular sites, we follow the historian of science and medicine Julia Rodríguez in pursuing the "smart centering of Latin America."[33]

Our centering of these convergence zones of expertise contributes to a growing scholarship reorienting the Latin American Cold War experience. Such new histories of the Cold War in Latin America, in part, reflect a broader scholarly commitment to expanding the historiography of the global Cold War to account for archives and actors in so-called developing or Third World countries.[34] However, as recent edited volumes have effectively modeled, a Latin American perspective is cast from not only the use of Latin American archives but also the incorporation of nontraditional actors, interactions between state actors and the grassroots, and an expansive periodization that brings to light long-running national projects of state formation and modernization. Drawing from Greg Grandin's seminal *The Last Colonial Massacre*, Joseph describes this move as a need to "take discussion of the Latin American Cold War in a different direction, beyond—or better *beneath*—the great diplomatic debates that have particularly stunted the region's Cold War historiography."[35] As Joseph observes in his contribution to this volume, new research that goes beneath superpower conflict to examine grassroots encounters highlights "a history of the *Latin American* Cold War—rather than just a history of the Cold War *in* Latin America."

Over the past two decades, historians of Latin America have emphasized cultural politics and state formation in order to showcase the locally or nationally situated contingencies of the Cold War.[36] Building on these contributions, the chapters in this volume examine how state formation conditioned the way Cold War experts could do their work. Although the United States is a crucial part of this story, it cannot be explained as merely an enforcer of a one-dimensional "enterprise of knowledge" in support of an "informal empire" in Latin America.[37] We need an analysis that entangles experts and expertise in webs of power, what William Roseberry described as social fields, placing "the local within larger networks." "The local is global," he wrote, "but the global can only be understood as always and necessarily local."[38] We seek to incorporate a multiplicity of locally situated *and* internationally traveling experts, highlighting moments of interaction among experts, state actors, and the grassroots in twentieth-century Latin America.

We therefore propose "itineraries" as a conceptual framework for analyzing Cold War expertise both spatially and chronologically. Spatially, "itineraries" refer to pathways of negotiated knowledge, similar to Neil Safier's use of the term in his discussion of European and Amerindian knowledge in the Amazon.[39] Chronologically, the concept of "itineraries" also underpins our argument for a "long Cold War" periodization that predates World War II. Several chapters demonstrate how Cold War transformations such as the Green Revolution (Lorek) or the "concrete revolution" (Purcell and Olsson) were rooted in local forms of expertise prior to 1945.[40] Itineraries, conceptually, help us expand traditional Cold War spatial relationships and historical periodizations.

The histories in these chapters deepen international histories of the Cold War and development to introduce critical actors previously invisible to non–Latin American specialists: actors motivated by long-standing domestic political concerns but operating in an international context of bipolar ideological struggle. In this volume, knowledge moves along an alternative itinerary wherein Havana, San Juan, Mexico City, Bogotá, Santiago, and even the Peruvian Amazon join New York, London, and Moscow as intellectual centers and generative laboratories of Cold War expertise, not as mere receiving locations or proxies on the Cold War geopolitical map.

Everyday Forms of Expertise

The chapters that follow employ an expansive definition of experts and expertise. For our purposes, an expert is someone with specialized knowledge whose identity is strongly shaped by his or her profession, whether or not he or she possesses specific educational credentials. Many of the experts discussed in the following chapters attended prestigious institutions, whether in their home countries or abroad. But others acquired their expertise through hands-on experiments, practical experience, and other forms of local knowledge beyond the bounds of elite university training. Rather than presuming that expertise was necessarily outside or foreign, or that experts arrived in Latin America from the Global North, the following chapters trace how the ideals of development and modernization were negotiated on the ground by local, national, and transnational actors. Similarly, we aim to question the assumption that experts came into conflict with local people and values. Although some high-modernist development schemes and the experts who promoted them did clash with local populations, expert visions at times aligned in unexpected ways with local worldviews.[41] As Eve Buckley describes in her study of technocrats in the Brazilian Northeast, individual experts could often express deep solidarity and empathy with their subjects, despite "the frequent tensions between a universalizing technocratic vision of progress and the particular cultural and political contexts in which scientific reformers operated."[42]

Methodologically, we contend that the study of Cold War expertise in Latin America ought to be grounded in the histories of specific people and places. Certainly, the trajectories of individual experts cannot be understood without having a firm grasp on the histories of key international institutions that shaped much of the Cold War–era development landscape, such as the World Bank, the Rockefeller Foundation, or the UN's Economic Commission for Latin America and the Caribbean. The chapters that follow are indebted to the work of scholars who have charted these institutional histories and revealed the funding and policy networks that shaped Latin American development initiatives.[43]

Yet this volume seeks to ask other questions—such as what motivated individual experts, including the complex mix of personal, professional, and political motives that conditioned the work they did; how their expertise was negotiated in local contexts; and how their itineraries were influenced by, or helped to influence, the unfolding of Cold War conflicts in the region. We treat expert knowledge not as a pure, disembodied set of principles that travel from "a point A of high expertise, to a point B of low expertise," but as evolving knowledge practices that are deeply informed by the personal backgrounds of experts and their own identities. In some cases, it may even make sense to speak of the "hybrid nationalities of experts," as these individuals often belonged to multiple communities—not only their countries of birth and the nations where they practiced but also the international communities that shaped their professional identities.[44]

Indeed, an important theme that runs through these studies is that the use of science and technology in pursuit of development transcended geopolitical divides. Despite the fact that modernization theory has garnered significant attention in the Global North's waging of the Cold War in the Global South, the United States and its allies did not have a monopoly on the dream of development. Indeed, as Reinaldo Funes-Monzote and Steven Palmer point out for the Cuban case in these pages, "the idea of scientific development, progress, and expertise cut across political and economic systems." The application of science and technology for human betterment was pursued by those on both sides of the East–West and North–South divide, as well as those in the interstices of the conflict. We contend that experts played a key role in the Cold War precisely because they could adapt their knowledge and skills to different political regimes and diverse global audiences. As Mary Roldán puts it in her chapter, Cold War experts could adjust their "discursive framing" to suit different political agendas both at home and abroad.

The ideological flexibility of expertise did not mean that experts escaped the sway of politics, however. In this regard, another important theme in this volume is that Cold War politics did shape the spread of expertise. Indeed, we contend that certain kinds of expertise held concrete political significance in

that they aligned with particular moments in Latin American state formation. For example, as Mark Healey shows, the focus on "aided self-help" rural
housing at the Inter-American Housing and Planning Center in Colombia
paralleled a broader shift in Colombian political culture after 1958. Tore
Olsson, likewise, demonstrates how the United States' New Deal model for
rural development, the Tennessee Valley Authority, inspired two dramatically contrasting dam projects in rural Mexico, each sponsored by presidents
with ideologically distinct visions of development. As Javiera Barandiarán
shows, the consolidation of neoliberalism in Chile's transition from an anticommunist military regime to the democratic Concertación government
deeply shaped the work that environmental scientists could do. As these authors and others show, politics shaped expertise to fit particular ideological
frameworks.

We also argue that the geopolitics of the Cold War shaped the way experts
and expertise traveled. Programs such as the Alliance for Progress opened
up funding channels that influenced the circulation of experts, but in other
cases, Cold War rivalries (such as the US embargo against Cuba) foreclosed
some avenues of knowledge exchange while opening up others. On this latter point, Funes-Monzote and Palmer demonstrate how the US embargo
led Cuba's revolutionary regime to look to Canada for collaboration in livestock breeding and dairying. A Cuban stockyard even emerged at the port
of Saint John, New Brunswick, to further the project of supplying purebred
temperate cattle for the tropical island. At times, the influence of geopolitics
on expertise was more subtle. As Pedro Ignacio Alonso and Hugo Palmarola
show, NASA officials portrayed their agenda as scientific (and thus outside
of politics) partly in order to cover up their military and intelligence aims in
Latin America.

Finally, we contend that many of today's global knowledge systems owe
substantially to everyday forms of expertise that originated in Latin America's long Cold War. As Fernando Purcell argues in chapter 9, on hydroelectric
dams, US institutions accumulated a "dense internalization of local knowledge" around the world and applied this to broader development initiatives
through technical assistance. Similarly, Emily Wakild, in her contribution
here, examines the creation of local or "residential" knowledge in the Peruvian Amazon and shows how it contributed to biodiversity science and the
global conservation movement. And, not least, recent work by Tore Olsson,
Gabriela Soto Laveaga, Netzahualcóyotl Gutiérrez, and Timothy Lorek reveals how the Rockefeller Foundation's agricultural programs in Mexico and
Colombia—which would go on to lay the institutional foundations for the
Green Revolution—owed substantially to prior domestically funded, locally
oriented centers of expertise.[45] One of the key aims of this book is to unearth
the local and regional Latin American roots of Cold War technical expertise

that informed, influenced, and catapulted would-be global movements from the "concrete revolution" to the Green Revolution. Via "itineraries of expertise," the Cold War not only entered Latin America; Latin America's internal historical struggles also entered global circulation.

Chapter Outline

In his essay following this introduction (chapter 1), Gilbert M. Joseph situates this volume's focus on experts and expertise within the expanding field of Latin American Cold War studies. As Joseph demonstrates, the conflict was "cataclysmic" for the region not just because of the scale of violence unleashed by anticommunist dictatorships and civil wars, but because of the way broader ideological struggles and the dialectic of radical reform and repression resulted in the profound "politicization and internationalization of everyday life." His essay reveals how recent scholarship probes beneath and beyond the high politics of superpower rivalry, opening up rich new veins of research on the cultural encounters of the Latin American Cold War and the ways that it fused with longer cycles of revolution reaching back at least to the Mexican Revolution of 1910.

In this volume's first section, "Agrarian Antecedents and Rural Development," Tore C. Olsson , Timothy W. Lorek , and Mary Roldán examine individual experts' ideological formation in the 1940s, as well as in pre–World War II historical contexts, including the Mexican Revolution, the Progressive movement, the New Deal, and interwar Europe. In Olsson's chapter 2, we travel with Mexican dam engineers to the US South, where they viewed the Tennessee Valley Authority as a shining example of rural modernization. Yet the two Mexican river valley commissions inspired by the TVA were not simple "transplants"; they instead demonstrated the multiple meanings of national development projects that were, paradoxically, born of transnational comparisons. In the following two chapters, we move south to Colombia. In chapter 3, Lorek examines the localized roots in the Cauca Valley of what would become the Green Revolution. He excavates the worldviews of three experts—two from Colombia, and one from Puerto Rico—whose partnership in the 1920s and 1930s would create a foundation for agricultural research in the postwar world. In Roldán's chapter 4, we meet an altogether different kind of expert, the Catholic priest, Father José Joaquín Salcedo, who used a different kind of technology—radio networks—to promote rural literacy and development. Roldán demonstrates how Salcedo's Catholic development organization nimbly adjusted to different contexts and modified its message for different funders.

The second section, "Cold War Scientific Exchanges," extends the first section's focus on agriculture and rural development to the politics of animal genetics, veterinary science, and aeronautics. In response to concerns about the mid-twentieth century's demographic growth, national leaders on both sides of the Cold War divide enlisted livestock experts to boost the production of protein, both to feed their own growing populations and to remain competitive in global markets. In chapter 5, Reinaldo Funes-Monzote and Steven Palmer reveal how, in postrevolutionary Cuba, the reform of the cattle ranching industry was a top priority, as the shift toward an intensive dairy industry promised to provide protein to the people. We see in their account how a famous dairy cow, Ubre Blanca (White Udder), became a symbol of the revolution's success—and became, in the words of Fidel Castro, a "machine for producing milk." In chapter 6, Thomas Rath examines a transnational network of veterinary labs in Mexico, Brazil, the United States, and the United Kingdom that together sought to eradicate foot-and-mouth disease. The scientific exchanges studied here were multidirectional, as outbreaks of the disease in Latin America affected institutional structures in the United States. Guiding our shift from the natural to the built environment, chapter 7, by Pedro Ignacio Alonso and Hugo Palmarola examines the visual politics of the Cold War, showing how NASA used graphic design to brand itself as scientific (and thus apolitical) partly in order to obscure its military and intelligence aims in Latin America.

The third section, "Infrastructures of the Built Environment," probes the role of traveling experts in the fields of housing, hydropower, and urban transportation. In chapter 8, Mark Healey traces the emergence of Bogotá as a center for training and experimentation in "aided self-help housing," as key housing experts from elsewhere in Latin America developed new technologies for rural housing. In chapter 9, Fernando Purcell charts the circulation of hydropower expertise in Chile, Peru, and Colombia and argues that technological imaginaries were crucial in fostering wide public acceptance of dams and electricity. Finally, in chapter 10, Andra Chastain's study of the Chilean urbanist Juan Parrochia emphasizes the flow of expertise between Chile and France during the planning and construction of the Santiago metro system. She demonstrates how the Cold War raised the stakes of expertise in the late 1960s, as the Christian Democratic government that spearheaded the metro was roundly attacked by both the Right and the Left for the way it planned the project.

As in the first section, our final section, "Toward New Regimes of Expertise," similarly stretches the periodization of the "long Cold War" in Latin America. Here our authors complicate the logic of the Cold War's sudden end between 1989 and 1991. We emphasize new regimes of expertise that emerged in the Cold War cauldron but have reoriented global knowledge systems in the twenty-first century. Focusing on case studies in environmental science, we offer two essays that introduce the contrasting knowledge systems of biodiversity and neoliberalism in formation in their respective Latin American laboratories. In chapter 11, Emily Wakild's examination of conservation, biology, and national parks in the Peruvian Amazon during the 1970s foreshadows the international scientific ascendancy of biodiversity that emerged parallel to heightened conservation efforts and national campaigns for ecotourism. Continuing the theme of environmental science, in chapter 12 Javiera Barandiarán explores the paradoxes of Chile's transition to democracy and the consequences this had for environmental scientists and their relationship to the state. Neoliberalism, she shows, threatened to privatize environmental expertise, with sobering consequences for twenty-first-century Chile and beyond. It is worth noting that the "new regimes" examined here are commonly understood in opposition to one another: biodiversity arguably suffers from the triumph of unbridled capitalism and the lack of state regulations under neoliberal models. Yet, in this section, we ask readers how these might instead be viewed as entangled processes, not diametric opposites.

Finally, the volume ends with a collaborative essay joining leading figures in Latin American science and technology studies and environmental history. In the Conclusion, Eden Medina and Mark Carey begin with a story of national technological prominence on display at the 2016 Olympics in Brazil. Challenging the embedded meanings of this display, the authors launch a conversation about changing depictions of science, technology, and environment in Latin America. In particular, they highlight four themes through which the chapters in this book engage with this changing historiography. First, Medina and Carey outline how this volume's authors build on the project of dismantling simplistic core–periphery frameworks and the directional flow of expertise. Second, they describe how the various authors redefine technology, nature, and expertise in these pages. Third, Medina and Carey suggest that the volume contributes to historiographies that decenter the state and state-centric periodization. Instead, they show how the authors here examine regional and transnational dynamics and alternative chronologies. Finally, they note how each chapter in this collection contributes to an emphasis on diverse and changing forms of expertise and multiple knowledges, especially including Latin American voices often overlooked in grand Cold War narratives of development.

As noted above, our chapters engage most with certain regional centers that acted as convergence zones in the circulation of expertise. Mexico City, Bogotá, and Santiago, for example, played significant roles within Latin America as both host sites for international agencies and senders in intraregional circuits of expertise and development. Moreover, Cuba served as an engine for the generation and dissemination of alternative varieties of expertise. Our efforts to foster dialogue between chapters necessarily overlooks other important sites and forms of expertise.[46] Connections between Latin America and Soviet models of expertise, for example, represent a compelling avenue for further research.[47] Brazil and Argentina, as well, played influential roles in the hemispheric circulation of Cold War development schemes, yet each remains largely absent from this volume.[48]

Similarly, although the experts presented in these chapters are heterogeneous, we deliberately narrow our gaze on select fields of expertise to enhance the volume's cohesiveness. Many forms of expertise beyond our purview likewise deserve mention as subjects of current and future research—including, but not limited to, the work of anthropologists, economists, doctors and public health officials, nuclear scientists, and teachers.[49] Across the varying professions of Cold War experts in Latin America, more attention is needed on how expertise intersected with racialized and gendered understandings of the nation-state and constructions of citizenship.[50] Astute readers will note that our experts are a fairly narrow group: largely white or mestizo, middle or upper-middle class, and mostly men. We acknowledge that while we have pushed the boundaries beyond the Global North in terms of who gets to count as an expert, there is still much more work to do to uncover the role of marginalized actors in developing and spreading Cold War expertise in Latin America. To a certain extent, we think that this limitation in our volume reflects an important historical theme: our experts were largely linked to the state, and their knowledge was validated by specialized training in universities and institutes. This does not mean that the specialized knowledge of women, people of color, workers, and other marginalized actors was insignificant, but that they often had more limited access to the official halls of power—such as universities, institutes, and government ministries—where knowledge was deemed policy-relevant expertise. Our aim is for this volume to provide a base from which current and future scholarship on non-elite and otherwise silenced forms of knowledge might connect to foreign relations and transnational histories of the Cold War that have hitherto largely marginalized Latin American contexts altogether. We hope this volume will provide a platform for important questions and stimulate future research in these areas.

Although the Berlin Wall fell three decades ago, the legacies of the Cold War in Latin America are present now as much as ever. From Cuba to Nicaragua, onetime revolutionaries have become reactionaries, refusing to concede power to a younger generation. In Colombia, the state and the Revolutionary Armed Forces of Colombia (FARC) negotiated a long and difficult peace accord in 2016, though a turn toward the political Right in 2018 chipped at the cracks in a fragile peace. Meanwhile, in Brazil, the far-right Jair Bolsonaro was elected on a platform of hate and violence toward women, people of color, the LGBT community, indigenous people, and the poor. He not only speaks in favor of torture; his administration has also sought to rewrite history to glorify the country's Cold War–era military dictatorship. Recent trials of Chilean and Argentine military officials for abuses committed during those countries' dirty wars likewise reveal the continuing challenges of rendering justice for victims of the Cold War.

But we also note less obvious continuities with Cold War expertise in Latin America. The persistence of neoliberal policies in Chile, for example, has sparked mass protests over income inequality, with experts and citizens alike wrestling with the long-term consequences of the Pinochet regime. Moreover, the dream of modernization through large-scale infrastructure investment remains alive and well, with China displacing the United States in funding many ambitious ventures, including a transoceanic canal in Nicaragua, lithium mining in the Andes, and a space station in Argentina.[51] As the following chapters show, new dams, seeds, cows, vaccines, houses, subways, and parks gave material expression to the Cold War and its driving aspiration of development. Throughout Latin America and beyond, the itineraries of Cold War expertise reverberate in the ways citizens eat, work, and play. The sweeping implications of these transformations live with us still.

NOTES

1. For a provocative assessment of the foreign relations literature on the Latin American Cold War, see Gilbert M. Joseph, "What We Now Know and Should Know: Bringing Latin America More Meaningfully into Cold War Studies," in *In From the Cold: Latin America's New Encounter with the Cold War*, ed. Gilbert M. Joseph and Daniela Spenser (Durham, NC: Duke University Press, 2008), 3–46. Recent scholarship in the vein of diplomatic and international history has shown that the Latin American Cold War was more than a one-sided conflict with the United States, with the diplomatic agency of multiple countries highlighted. See Tanya Harmer, *Allende's Chile and the Inter-American Cold War* (Chapel Hill: University of North Carolina Press, 2011); Virginia Garrard-Burnett, Mark Attwood Lawrence, and Julio E. Moreno, eds., *Beyond the Eagle's Shadow: New Histories of Latin America's Cold War* (Albuquerque: University of New Mexico Press, 2013); Hal Brands, *Latin America's Cold War* (Cambridge, MA: Harvard University Press, 2012); Piero Gleijeses, *Conflicting Missions: Havana, Washington, and Africa, 1959–1976* (Chapel Hill: University of North Carolina Press, 2002); and Tanya Harmer and Alfredo Riquelme Segovia, eds., *Chile y la guerra fría global* (Santiago: RIL, 2014).

2. See, for example, Joseph and Spenser, *In From the Cold*; Benedetta Calandra and Marina Franco, eds., *La guerra fría cultural en América Latina: Desafíos y límites para una nueva mirada de las relaciones interamericanas* (Buenos Aires: Biblos, 2012); Victoria Langland, *Speaking of Flowers: Student Movements and the Making and Remembering of 1968 in Military Brazil* (Durham, NC: Duke University Press, 2013); Patrick Iber, *Neither Peace nor Freedom: The Cul-*

tural Cold War in Latin America (Cambridge, MA: Harvard University Press, 2015); and Renata Keller, *Mexico's Cold War: Cuba, the United States, and the Legacy of the Mexican Revolution* (New York: Cambridge University Press, 2015).

   3. We are not alone in our project to further contextualize and historicize knowledge production and expertise in Latin America. For one example from Europe, see Stefan Rinke and Delia González de Reufels, eds., *Expert Knowledge in Latin American History: Local, Transnational, and Global Perspectives*, Historamericana 34 (Stuttgart: Heinz, 2014).

   4. In this way we differ from scholarly treatments of international development centered on the United States, such as David Ekbladh, *Great American Mission: Modernization and the Construction of an American World Order* (Princeton, NJ: Princeton University Press, 2009), as well as popular narratives of individual experts such as Charles C. Mann's recent and acclaimed book about Norman Borlaug and William Vogt, *The Wizard and the Prophet: Two Remarkable Scientists and Their Dueling Visions to Shape Tomorrow's World* (New York: Alfred A. Knopf, 2018).

   5. Tom Nichols, "How America Lost Faith in Expertise," *Foreign Affairs*, March/April 2017, and *The Death of Expertise: The Campaign against Established Knowledge and Why It Matters* (New York: Oxford University Press, 2017).

   6. In addition to the recent articles cited above, there is growing academic literature on the demise of expertise in US politics and culture. See, for example, Katherine J. Cramer's *The Politics of Resentment: Rural Consciousness in Wisconsin and the Rise of Scott Walker* (Chicago: University of Chicago Press, 2016).

   7. See Javiera Barandiarán's essay in this volume (chapter 12). On neoliberal economics and the remaking of the global political order, including the seminal role of Chile in this process, see David Harvey, *A Brief History of Neoliberalism* (New York: Oxford University Press, 2005).

   8. Richard White, *The Organic Machine* (New York: Hill and Wang, 1995); Gabrielle Hecht, *The Radiance of France: Nuclear Power and National Identity after World War II* (Cambridge, MA: MIT Press, 1998); and Michael Thad Allen and Gabrielle Hecht, *Technologies of Power: Essays in Honor of Thomas Parke Hughes and Agatha Chipley Hughes* (Cambridge, MA: MIT Press, 2001); and Gabrielle Hecht, "The Work of Invisibility: Radiation Hazards and Occupational Health in South African Uranium Production," *International Labor and Working Class History* 81 (Spring 2012): 94–113.

   9. Dolly Jørgensen, Finn Arne Jørgensen, and Sara B. Pritchard, eds., *New Natures: Joining Environmental History with Science and Technology Studies* (Pittsburgh: University of Pittsburgh Press, 2013).

   10. See Gabrielle Hecht, ed., *Entangled Geographies: Empire and Technopolitics in the Global Cold War* (Cambridge, MA: MIT Press, 2011); Naomi Oreskes and John Krige, eds., *Science and Technology in the Global Cold War* (Cambridge, MA: MIT Press, 2014); and J. R. McNeill and Corinna R. Unger, eds., *Environmental Histories of the Cold War* (Cambridge: Cambridge University Press and German Historical Institute, 2010). There is a rich and extensive literature on the history of US science and technology during the Cold War. For an outstanding recent study of the political uses of US science and scientific freedom in the Cold War, see Audra

J. Wolfe, *Freedom's Laboratory: The Cold War Struggle for the Soul of Science* (Baltimore: Johns Hopkins University Press, 2018).

11. For a pathbreaking collection on science and technology studies in Latin America, see Eden Medina, Ivan da Costa Marques, and Christina Holmes, eds., *Beyond Imported Magic: Essays on Science, Technology, and Society in Latin America* (Cambridge, MA: MIT Press, 2014). In addition, there seems to be growing interest in the role of science and technology in the Latin American Cold War, as evidenced by a panel organized by the historians Barbara Silva and William San Martin at the 2017 conference of the Society for the Social Studies of Science (4S).

12. Scholars working at the intersection of environmental history and the history of science and technology have recently adopted the term *envirotech*. For Latin America in the period preceding the Cold War, Mikael D. Wolfe recently made strong use of the concept in his book, *Watering the Revolution: An Environmental and Technological History of Agrarian Reform in Mexico* (Durham, NC: Duke University Press, 2017).

13. J. R. McNeill, "Observations on the Nature and Culture of Environmental History," *History and Theory* 42, no. 4 (December 2003): 5–43.

14. Mark Carey, "Latin American Environmental History: Current Trends, Interdisciplinary Insights, and Future Directions," *Environmental History* 14, no. 2 (April 2009): 221–252.

15. John Soluri, Claudia Leal, and José Augusto Pádua, eds., *A Living Past: Environmental Histories of Modern Latin America* (New York: Berghahn Books, 2018); and Wilko Graf von Hardenberg, Matthew Kelly, Claudia Leal, and Emily Wakild, eds., *The Nature State: Rethinking the History of Conservation* (New York: Routledge, 2017).

16. Marcos Cueto and Steven Palmer, *Medicine and Public Health in Latin America: A History* (New York: Cambridge University Press, 2015), 9. See also Gabriela Soto Laveaga, *Jungle Laboratories: Mexican Peasants, National Projects, and the Making of the Pill* (Durham, NC: Duke University Press, 2009).

17. Steven Palmer, "Central American Encounters with Rockefeller Public Health, 1914–1921," in *Close Encounters of Empire: Writing the Cultural History of U.S.-Latin American Relations*, ed. Gilbert M. Joseph, Catherine C. LeGrand, and Ricardo D. Salvatore (Durham, NC: Duke University Press, 1998), 311–332; and Stuart McCook, *States of Nature: Science, Agriculture, and Environment in the Spanish Caribbean, 1760–1940* (Austin: University of Texas Press, 2002), 3. Rebecca Tally emphasized this concept in her contribution to the October 2016 conference: "The Body of Experts: Masculinity, Agronomy, and the Rockefeller Foundation in Colombia," paper presented at the conference "Traveling Technocrats: Experts and Expertise in Latin America's Long Cold War," Yale University, October 14–15, 2016. The intersection of public health expertise and the Latin American Cold War is coming under increased scrutiny; see Anne-Emanuelle Birn and Raúl Necochea López, eds., *Calenturas! Health and Medicine in Cold War Latin America* (under contract with Duke University Press).

18. Michel Foucault, "Lecture 18 January, 1978," in *Security, Territory, Population: Lectures at the Collège de France, 1977–1978* (London: Palgrave MacMillan, 2009), 29–53.

19. For example, see Steven Stoll, "A Metabolism of Society: Capitalism for Environmental Historians," in *The Oxford Handbook of Environmental History*, ed. Andrew C. Isenberg

(Oxford: Oxford University Press, 2014), 369–397. Stoll's advocacy for using Braudel and the Annales School to trace the history of capitalism likewise fits with this volume's objective to merge local, regional, and global scales in studying the circulation of experts and expertise.

20. See, for example, Bruno Latour, *We Have Never Been Modern* (Cambridge, MA: Harvard University Press, 1993); James Ferguson, *The Anti-Politics Machine: Development, Depoliticization, and Bureaucratic Power in Lesotho* (Minneapolis: University of Minnesota Press, 1994); Arturo Escobar, *Encountering Development: The Making and Unmaking of the Third World* (Princeton, NJ: Princeton University Press, 1995); James C. Scott, *Seeing Like a State: How Certain Schemes to Improve the Human Condition Have Failed* (New Haven, CT: Yale University Press, 1998); Timothy Mitchell, *Rule of Experts: Egypt, Techno-Politics, Modernity* (Berkeley: University of California Press, 2002); and Tania Murray Li, *The Will to Improve: Governmentality, Development, and the Practice of Politics* (Durham, NC: Duke University Press, 2007).

21. Jorge Cañizares-Esguerra, *Nature, Empire, and Nation: Explorations of the History of Science in the Iberian World* (Stanford, CA: Stanford University Press, 2006).

22. See, for example, Daniela Bleichmar, *Visible Empire: Botanical Expeditions and Visual Culture in the Hispanic Enlightenment* (Chicago: University of Chicago Press, 2012); Raymond B. Craib, *Cartographic Mexico: A History of State Fixations and Fugitive Landscapes* (Durham, NC: Duke University Press, 2004); Patience A. Schell, *The Sociable Sciences: Darwin and His Contemporaries in Chile* (New York: Palgrave Macmillan, 2013); Rafael Sagredo Baeza, "Ciencia, historia y arte como política: El Estado y la *Historia física y política de Chile* de Claudio Gay," in *Ciencia-Mundo: Orden republicano, arte y nación en América*, ed. Rafael Sagredo Baeza (Santiago: Editorial Universitaria y Centro de Investigación Diego Barros Arana, 2010), 165–234; and Nancy P. Appelbaum, *Mapping the Country of Regions: The Chorographic Commission of Nineteenth-Century Colombia* (Chapel Hill: University of North Carolina Press, 2016).

23. Craib's *Cartographic Mexico* connects the *científicos* of the Porfiriato to earlier histories of cartographic expertise in the nineteenth century, whereas Christopher Boyer's work on forestry links the transitional period of the Porfiriato and its *científicos* to a later history of expertise in the twentieth century. Christopher R. Boyer, *Political Landscapes: Forests, Conservation, and Community in Mexico* (Durham, NC: Duke University Press, 2015).

24. Ivan Lins, *História do positivism no Brasil*, 2nd ed. (São Paulo: Companhia Editora Nacional, 1967); Patricio Silva, *In the Name of Reason: Technocrats and Politics in Chile* (University Park: Pennsylvania State University Press, 2008); Todd A. Diacon, *Stringing Together a Nation: Cândido Mariano da Silva Rondon and the Construction of a Modern Brazil, 1906–1930* (Durham, NC: Duke University Press, 2004); and Teresa Cribelli, *Industrial Forests and Mechanical Marvels: Modernization in Nineteenth-Century Brazil* (Cambridge: Cambridge University Press, 2016).

25. McCook, *States of Nature.*

26. Greg Grandin, "Living in Revolutionary Time: Coming to Terms with the Violence of Latin America's Long Cold War," and Gilbert M. Joseph, "Latin America's Long Cold War: A Century of Revolutionary Process and U.S. Power," in *A Century of Revolution: Insurgent and Counterinsurgent Violence during Latin America's Long Cold War*, ed. Greg Grandin and Gilbert M. Joseph (Durham, NC: Duke University Press, 2010), 1–43 and 397–414, respectively.

27. On financial missions, see Paul Drake, *The Money Doctor in the Andes: The Kemmerer Missions, 1923–1933* (Durham, NC: Duke University Press, 1989), and Emily S. Rosenberg, *Financial Missionaries to the World: The Politics and Culture of Dollar Diplomacy, 1900–1930* (Durham, NC: Duke University Press, 2003). On labor policies, see, for example, Paulo Drinot, *The Allure of Labor: Workers, Race, and the Making of the Peruvian State* (Durham, NC: Duke University Press, 2011).

28. Ricardo D. Salvatore, *Disciplinary Conquest: U.S. Scholars in South America, 1900–1945* (Durham, NC: Duke University Press, 2016). For further references on the origins of Latin American studies in the United States, see Gilbert Joseph's essay in this volume (chapter 1).

29. Tore Olsson, *Agrarian Crossings: Reformers and the Remaking of the US and Mexican Countryside* (Princeton, NJ: Princeton University Press, 2017); Nicole Sackley, "Cosmopolitanism and the Uses of Tradition: Robert Redfield and Alternative Visions of Modernization during the Cold War," *Modern Intellectual History* 9, no. 3 (November 2012): 565–595; Sarah T. Phillips, *This Land, This Nation: Conservation, Rural America, and the New Deal* (Cambridge: Cambridge University Press, 2007); Deborah Fitzgerald, "Exporting American Agriculture: The Rockefeller Foundation in Mexico, 1943–1953," in *Missionaries of Science: The Rockefeller Foundation and Latin America*, ed. Marcos Cueto (Bloomington: Indiana University Press, 1994), 72–96. For a counterexample wherein economic development initiatives hatched in Latin America during the 1930s, see Christy Thornton, "'Mexico Has the Theories': Latin America and the Invention of Development in the 1930s," in *The Development Century: A Global History*, ed. Stephen Macekura and Erez Manela (Cambridge: Cambridge University Press, 2018), 263–282.

30. See Timothy Lorek's chapter 3 in this volume as well as Timothy W. Lorek, "The Puerto Rican Connection: Recovering the 'Cultural Triangle' in Global Histories of Agricultural Development," *Agricultural History* 94, no. 1 (January 2020): forthcoming; Manuel R. Rodríguez, *A New Deal for the Tropics: Puerto Rico during the Depression Era, 1932–1935* (Princeton, NJ: Markus Wiener, 2010); Darryl E. Brock, *Botanical Monroe Doctrine and American Empire: The Scientific Survey of Puerto Rico* (Tuscaloosa: University of Alabama Press, forthcoming); Geoff Burrows, "Rural Hydro-Electrification and the Colonial New Deal: Modernization, Experts, and Rural Life in Puerto Rico, 1935–1942," *Agricultural History* 91, no. 3 (Summer 2017): 293–319; and McCook, *States of Nature*. See also see Manuel R. Rodríguez and Silvia Álvarez Curbelo, *Tiempos Binarios: La Guerra Fría en Puerto Rico* (San Juan: Ediciones Callejón, 2017).

31. On "laboratories," see Michael Lapp, "The Rise and Fall of Puerto Rico as a Social Laboratory, 1945–1965," *Social Science History* 19, no. 2 (Summer 1995): 169–199. On colonial, racial, and gendered laboratories in Puerto Rico, see Laura Briggs, *Reproducing Empire: Race, Sex, Science, and U.S. Imperialism in Puerto Rico* (Berkeley: University of California Press, 2003), and Daniel Immerwahr, *How to Hide an Empire: A History of the Greater United States* (New York: Farrar, Straus and Giroux, 2019). On another framing of the laboratory beyond Puerto Rico, see Nicole Sackley, "The Village as Cold War Site: Experts, Development, and the History of Rural Reconstruction," *Journal of Global History* 6, no. 3 (2011): 481–504.

32. Leida Fernández Prieto, "Islands of Knowledge: Science and Agriculture in the History of Latin America and the Caribbean," *Isis* 104, no. 4 (December 2013): 797.

33. Julia Rodríguez, "Beyond Prejudice and Pride: The Human Sciences in Nineteenth- and Twentieth-Century Latin America," *Isis* 104, no. 4 (December 2013): 807–817.

34. For example, Odd Arne Westad, *The Global Cold War: Third World Interventions and the Making of Our Times* (Cambridge: Cambridge University Press, 2007), offers a survey drawn from this growing body of scholarship. A helpful introduction to the methodologies of this expansive archival movement is Cindy Ewing, "Cold War Archives in the Third World," Wilson Center Sources and Methods blog, March 13, 2017, https://www.wilsoncenter.org/blog-post/ cold-war-archives-the-third-world. For a reflection of this movement in Latin America, see Brands, *Latin America's Cold War.*

35. Joseph, "What We Now Know and Should Know," 16. See also Greg Grandin, *The Last Colonial Massacre: Latin America and the Cold War* (Chicago: University of Chicago Press, 2004).

36. See Daniela Spenser, ed., *Espejos de la guerra fría: México, América Central y el Caribe* (Mexico City: Ciesas/Porrua, 2004); Grandin, *Last Colonial Massacre*; Joseph and Spenser, *In from the Cold*; Greg Grandin and Gilbert M. Joseph, eds., *A Century of Revolution: Insurgent and Counterinsurgent Violence during Latin America's Long Cold War* (Durham, NC: Duke University Press, 2010); Calandra and Franco, *La guerra fría cultural en América Latina.*

37. Ricardo D. Salvatore, "The Enterprise of Knowledge: Representational Machines of Informal Empire," in Joseph, LeGrand, and Salvatore, *Close Encounters of Empire*, 69–104.

38. William Roseberry, "Social Fields and Cultural Encounters," in Joseph, LeGrand, and Salvatore, *Close Encounters of Empire*, 521.

39. Neil Safier, "Global Knowledge on the Move: Itineraries, Amerindian Narratives, and Deep Histories of Science," *Isis* 101, no. 1 (March 2010), 133–145.

40. In chapter 9 in this volume, Fernando Purcell borrows the phrase "concrete revolution" from Christopher Sneddon, *Concrete Revolution: Large Dams, Cold War Geopolitics, and the US Bureau of Reclamation* (Chicago: University of Chicago Press, 2015).

41. On high modernism, see Scott, *Seeing Like a State*. On low modernism, see Jess Gilbert, *Planning Democracy: Agrarian Intellectuals and the Intended New Deal* (New Haven, CT: Yale University Press, 2015).

42. Eve E. Buckley, *Technocrats and the Politics of Drought and Development in Twentieth-Century Brazil* (Chapel Hill: University of North Carolina Press, 2017), 3.

43. See, for example: Cueto, *Missionaries of Science*; Marcos Cueto, *The Value of Health: A History of the Pan American Health Organization* (Rochester, NY: University of Rochester Press, 2007); Jeremy Adelman, *Worldly Philosopher: The Odyssey of Albert O. Hirschman* (Chapel Hill: University of North Carolina Press, 2012); Nick Cullather, *The Hungry World: America's Cold War Battle against Poverty in Asia* (Cambridge, MA: Harvard University Press, 2013); Daniel Immerwahr, *Thinking Small: The United States and the Lure of Community Development* (Cambridge, MA: Harvard University Press, 2015); Amy C. Offner, *Sorting Out the Mixed Economy: The Rise and Fall of Welfare and Developmental States in the Americas* (Princeton, NJ: Princeton University Press, 2019); Amy L. S. Staples, *The Birth of Development: How the World Bank, Food and Agriculture Organization and the World Health Organization Changed the World, 1945–1965* (Kent, OH: Kent State University Press, 2006); Jeffrey F. Taffett, *Foreign Aid as*

Foreign Policy: The Alliance for Progress in Latin America (New York: Routledge, 2007); and two papers presented at the conference "Traveling Technocrats: Experts and Expertise in Latin America's Long Cold War," Yale University, October 14–15, 2016: Javier Puente, "'Tierra para el que la trabaja': Rural Expertise and Agrarian Technocracy in Cold War Peru, 1960–1970," and Margarita Fajardo, "Autonomy in Question: How Latin American Economists Made ISI History."

44. Thanks go to Paulo Drinot and Gilbert Joseph, respectively, for these turns of phrase.

45. See Purcell (chapter 9), Olsson (chapter 2), and Lorek (chapter 3) in this volume, as well as Gabriela Soto Laveaga, "Traveling Seeds, Stationary People? Contesting Narrative of Agricultural Expertise in the Era of the Green Revolution." paper presented at the conference "Traveling Technocrats: Experts and Expertise in Latin America's Long Cold War," Yale University, October 14–15, 2016; and Netzahualcóyotl Luis Gutiérrez Núñez, "Cambio agrario y revolución verde: Dilemas científicos, políticos y agrarios en la agricultura mexicana del maíz, 1920–1970" (PhD diss., Colegio de México, 2017). Theresa Ventura examines this theme for the Philippines in a forthcoming monograph titled "Empire Reformed: The United States, the Philippines, and the Practices of Development." In the same vein, Megan Raby, in her book *American Tropics: The Caribbean Roots of Biodiversity Science* (Chapel Hill: University of North Carolina Press, 2017), astutely traces the Cold War roots of "biodiversity" in US-operated Latin American field stations.

46. In fact, a wider assortment of expertise may be discerned in the original impetus for this volume: two panels organized for the Latin American Studies Association Annual Congress in San Juan, Puerto Rico in 2015. Presentations on these panels included Emilio de Antuñano, "Mexico City's Mid-Century Housing Crisis: Conceptualizations of Urban Poverty for a Shifting City"; Taylor H. Jardno, "Counterrevolutionary Consultations: The Politics of Private Education in Cold War Mexico"; Jennifer T. Hoyt, "More Like the West: The Last Military Dictatorship, Urban Reforms, and Professional Protest in Buenos Aires, Argentina (1976–1983)"; Marco A. Ramos, "Cold War Violence and Psychoanalysis in Buenos Aires"; Anthony W. Andersson, "Trees, Beans, and Bullets: Forestry, Development, and Counterinsurgency in Northern Guatemala, 1960–1970"; and Eric Rutkow, "The Mountain of Death and the Selegua Gap: The United States, Highway Engineers, and the Early Cold War in Central America." There is also growing interest in histories of expertise and technology and how these underpin economic globalization; see David Pretel and Lino Camprubí, eds., *Technology and Globalisation: Networks of Experts in World History* (Cham, Switzerland: Palgrave Studies in Economic History, 2018).

47. On Soviet as well as US influences in public health in the Latin American Cold War, see the chapters in Birn and Necochea López, *Calenturas!* On the circulation of concrete-block housing technologies from the Soviet Union to Cuba and Chile, see Pedro Ignacio Alonso and Hugo Palmarola, *Panel* (London: Architectural Association, 2014).

48. The rich historiography on experts and expertise in Brazil may be glimpsed in Thomas D. Rogers, *The Deepest Wounds: A Labor and Environmental History of Sugar in Northeast Brazil* (Chapel Hill: University of North Carolina Press, 2010); Buckley, *Technocrats*; and Regina Horta Duarte, *Activist Biology: The National Museum, Politics, and Nation Building in Brazil*

(Tucson: University of Arizona Press, 2016), among others. See the following two footnotes, as well.

49. For anthropologists and sociologists, see Diana Schwartz, "Transforming the Tropics: Development, Displacement, and Anthropology in the Papaloapan, Mexico, 1940s–1970s," (PhD diss., University of Chicago, 2016); Joanne Rappaport, "Beyond Participant Observation: Collaborative Ethnography as Theoretical Innovation," *Collaborative Anthropologies* 1 (2008): 1–31; Mónica Moreno, "The Relationship between the Sociology Program at the Universidad Nacional de Colombia and the Rockefeller Foundation and the Ford Foundation: A Preliminary Description of Its Dynamics," Rockefeller Archive Center Research Report (2013). On medical expertise, see Josh Mentanko, "Development, Tradition, and Decolonization: Racial Thought and Reproductive Politics in post-1950 Mexico" (PhD diss., Yale University, in preparation); Marco Ramos, "Making Disappearance Visible: Psychoanalysis, Trauma, and Human Rights in Cold War Argentina" (PhD diss., Yale University, 2017); Jelke Boesten, *Intersecting Inequalities: Women and Social Policy in Peru, 1990–2000* (University Park: Pennsylvania State University Press, 2010); and the essays in Birn and Necochea López, *Calenturas!.* For public health, see Marcos Cueto, *Cold War and Deadly Fevers: Malaria Eradication in Mexico, 1955–1970* (Baltimore: Johns Hopkins University Press, 2007) and Eric D. Carter, *Enemy in the Blood: Malaria, Environment, and Development in Argentina (Tuscaloosa: University of Alabama Press, 2012).* For economists, see Adelman, *Worldly Philosopher*; Offner, *Sorting Out the Mixed Economy*; Christy Thornton, *Revolution in Development: Mexico and the Governance of the Global Economy* (Berkeley: University of California Press, forthcoming); and Margarita Fajardo, "The Latin American Development Experience: Social Sciences, Economic Policies, and the Making of Global Order, 1944–1971" (PhD diss., Princeton University, 2015). For nuclear science and security experts, see Manuel Rodríguez, "Radioactive Designs: Expertise and Fallout Shelter Programs in Puerto Rico, 1960–1968," paper presented at the conference "Traveling Technocrats: Experts and Expertise in Latin America's Long Cold War," Yale University, October 14–15, 2016; Raby, *American Tropics*; and Christopher Dunlap, "Parallel Power Play: Nuclear Technology and Diplomacy in Argentina and Brazil, 1945–1995" (PhD diss., University of Chicago, 2017). For additional work on Cold War housing and urbanism, see Leandro Benmergui, "The Alliance for Progress and Housing Policy in Rio de Janeiro and Buenos Aires in the 1960s," *Urban History* 36 (August 2009): 303–326; Helen Gyger, *Improvised Cities: Architecture, Urbanization, and Innovation in Peru* (Pittsburgh: University of Pittsburgh Press, 2019); Mark A. Healey, *The Ruins of the New Argentina: Peronism and the Remaking of San Juan after the 1944 Earthquake* (Durham, NC: Duke University Press, 2011); Jennifer T. Hoyt, "Clean, Fast, and Green: Urban Reforms in Buenos Aires and Cold War Ideologies, 1976–1983," *Urban History* 42, no. 4 (November 2015): 646–662; Marcio Siwi, "Making the Modern and Cultured City: Art, Architecture, and Urbanism in Postwar São Paulo, 1945—1969" (PhD diss., New York University, 2017); and Adrián Lerner Patrón, "Jungle Cities: The Making of Urban Space in Twentieth-Century Amazonia" (PhD diss., Yale University, forthcoming).

50. The work of Scott Crago, one of the 2016 conference participants, is especially instructive on these points. See Scott D. Crago, "Perquenco's Travelling Guitarists and the Administrative Inconsistencies of the Pinochet Dictatorship's Indigenous Policies," *Journal of Latin*

American Studies 50, no. 1 (February 2018): 59–86. For hydroelectric projects, dictatorship, and indigenous politics in Brazil, see Jacob Blanc, *Before the Flood: The Itaipu Dam and the Visibility of Rural Brazil* (Durham, NC: Duke University Press, 2019).

51. The trans-Pacific connections between Latin America and Asia offer an important arena for future research. On Taiwanese experts in Latin America and beyond during the Cold War, see the work of James Lin, including "Sowing Seeds and Knowledge: Agricultural Development in the US, Taiwan, and the World, 1949–1975," *East Asian Science, Technology, and Society* 9 (June 2015): 127–149.

1

BORDER CROSSINGS AND THE REMAKING OF LATIN AMERICAN COLD WAR STUDIES

Gilbert M. Joseph

Few periods in Latin America's history have been as violent and turbulent, and some would argue, transformative, as the half century that ran roughly from the end of World War II through the early 1990s and constituted the Cold War. This is because, as in other regions of the Global South, Latin America's Cold War was rarely cold. In fact, you would have to go back to the early nineteenth-century Wars of Independence to find the same level of mass mobilization, revolutionary upheaval, and counterrevolutionary repression. Yet the international connections, organizational capacities, and technologies of death and surveillance at work in the late twentieth-century Cold War render that earlier cycle of violence almost quaint by comparison. Latin America's great novelist Gabriel García Márquez graphically evoked this "outsized" and "unbridled reality" in his 1982 Nobel acceptance speech. Conjuring up a litany of grisly and apocalyptic events—the dirty wars, disappearances, and displacements of the 1970s and early 1980s that had turned Central America and South America's Southern Cone into killing fields and barrios—he told his Nobel audience that he had been obliged to develop a new literary genre, "magical realism," to assimilate the period's mind-boggling occurrences and, as he put it, "render our lives believable."[1]

How do we account for such cataclysmic violence? To be sure, Latin America's past is characterized by alternating cycles of social reform and intense conservative reaction, in which the influence, aid, and intervention of imperial powers have figured prominently. Even so, the dynamics of the Latin American Cold War are embedded in a particularly ferocious dialectic linking reformist and revolutionary projects for social change and national

development, with the excessive counterrevolutionary responses they triggered, in the decades after World War II. This dialectic, which shaped Latin
American life in the late twentieth century and carried legacies into the new
millennium, played out in intertwined domestic and international arenas
of political, social, and cultural power. At a macro level the Cold War was a
struggle between superpowers—the United States and the Soviet Union—
over shifting geopolitical stakes and ideological visions of how the world
should be organized.[2] But what ultimately gave the Latin American Cold War
its "heat"—what Greg Grandin terms its "transcendental force"—were the
politicization and internationalization of everyday life. On a variety of fronts
across several decades, Latin American elites and newly expanded and empowered popular classes participated in local and national political contests
over land, labor, and the control of markets and natural resources—contests
that rarely escaped the powerful undertow of the larger superpower conflict.[3]

This chapter seeks to provide a broad orientation to the global Cold War
and especially to its distinctive Latin American variant. It also focuses attention on two of the more fertile veins in a burgeoning historiography: first,
the notion that the region's Cold War should be placed in a broader historical
context, which scholars are increasingly referring to as Latin America's "long
Cold War," and second, an analysis of the long Cold War's multivalent cultural dimension. If study of the Latin American Cold War has become something of a growth industry in the past fifteen years, its leading edge may well
be efforts to tease out the complex, power-laden *cultural* processes, relationships, exchanges, and institutional forms that antedated and shaped Latin
America's Cold War proper (ca. 1947 to the early 1990s), and had legacies beyond the conflict's denouement. *Itineraries of Expertise* is certain to advance
these discussions, insisting as it does that although foreign diplomats and
grand strategists, military juntas and intelligence apparatuses, leftist guerrillas and right-wing paramilitary forces, CIA-backed coups and covert operations have remained at the center of traditional accounts of the Cold War
in Latin America, beneath or in the wake of the conflicts they orchestrated,
the Latin American Cold War was waged by technocrats and experts. Thus,
according to Andra Chastain and Timothy Lorek, "scientists and engineers,
doctors and social workers, agronomists and architects—as well as the webs
of expertise they wove—made material the political ideologies of the era."
This volume argues that the appeal of the mass utopias of the superpowers
was predicated on "intertwined dreams of development and modernization"
that underwrote a political and cultural struggle likely just as consequential
as the paroxysms of insurgent and counterinsurgent violence the period witnessed. And this political, cultural, and technological struggle "relied on an
army of highly specialized experts" whose role in the conflict has not yet been
well apprehended.[4]

To date, most studies of the region's cultural Cold War have focused on the usual subjects of cultural history—the intellectuals, students, artists, writers, and social thinkers who aspired to a higher profile in the conflict.[5] Similarly, several studies of certain signature projects of "development," and critiques of the vexed concept itself, have emerged and narrowed the gap between Latin Americanist scholarship and more robust interdisciplinary work on this theme for other areas of the Global South.[6] But what this volume's contributors argue so compellingly is that the experts and technocrats, the cultural and political intermediaries behind these projects, have routinely been elided and deserve attention in their own right. In fact, it is only by examining their role in various infrastructural and environmental projects, educational and housing missions, biological research and agricultural experiment stations—in short, their concrete plans, movements, networks of collaboration, and the manner in which they negotiated their work at both higher levels and at the grassroots (with national leaders, US agencies, transnational foundations and think tanks, and, not least, with the local populations they studied and served)—that we can develop a more nuanced history of Cold War Latin America. Such fine-grained analysis over decades of experts who were both peripatetic and locally situated, who often presented themselves as removed from politics, even as their work fed directly or indirectly into prevailing geopolitical agendas, contributes to a Cold War history that is multistranded, attentive to history's contingencies, and capable of transcending frayed, dichotomizing paradigms of interpretation. These essays showcase how traveling experts traversed a variety of boundaries: between the city and the countryside, between northern and southern countries, and albeit less frequently, between southern and eastern bloc destinations and within the Global South. They demonstrate how experts' itineraries and collaborations tended to strengthen, but occasionally undermined and complicated the imperatives dictated by Cold War geopolitics. In the process, the volume's contributors force us to reconsider other binaries in conventional Cold War studies: between "developed" and "developing" nations, the First World and the Third World, and the Global North and Global South. Congruent with recent turns in transnational studies, by highlighting multiple agents, sites, and scales of expertise during the Cold War, the contributors accentuate a blurring of the "local" and the "foreign," especially where the production of knowledge is concerned.

These essays and the new cultural history of Cold War Latin America that the volume advances underscore an ascendant "expansionist" sensibility where cultural history is concerned: a recognition that cultural phenomena are inextricably bound up with political and social forces.[7] Thus, as Chastain and Lorek observe in the introduction to this volume:

[The] Cold War raised the stakes of expert knowledge in concrete ways. From iconic Cold War technologies such as atomic bombs and satellites to social scientific knowledge about strategic peoples and places, experts seemed to hold the secrets to state security and prosperity. The United States sought to prevent the spread of communism in Latin America through the deployment of experts and funding tied to technical aid missions, including those in Truman's Point Four program and, later, Kennedy's Alliance for Progress. Many Latin American leaders, for their part, embraced the promise of the expert—first through efforts at import-substitution industrialization and state planning, and later through authoritarian, technocratic projects to dismantle the state's role in the economy. The thorniest sociocultural problems posed by the Cold War—such as how to feed, shelter, and educate a rapidly growing population—seemed to offer a carte blanche for the intervention of a host of experts. The embrace of technical solutions to solve complex sociocultural challenges was a hallmark of [the] Cold War.

In from the Cold: Toward a New Historiography of the Latin American Cold War

Itineraries of Expertise reflects the kind of intellectual border crossings that have remade the historiography of the Latin American Cold War. It promotes a unique discursive community that brings historians of science and technology, environmental historians, and students of the Cold War into conversation with one another. Over the past fifteen years or so, our understanding of Latin America's distinctive variant of the Cold War has repeatedly benefited from similar attempts to talk across fields and disciplines. Because the literature is vast, the following review must paint in broad strokes, focusing on what I regard to be pivotal themes and watersheds.[8]

The first major attempt at cross-fertilization sought to bring students of Latin America's tumultuous twentieth century, particularly its political and social movements, into conversation with foreign relations scholars. Thus, Latin Americanists who studied the Cold War from the inside out and often "from below," using tools and concepts from area studies, social and cultural history, anthropology, political science, and cultural studies, hoped to foment a more sustained engagement with diplomatic historians and international relations scholars of the Cold War. The latter had largely been preoccupied with grand strategy and US policy, drawing mostly on US archives. Sadly, although foreign relations scholars and Latin Americanists *should* share fraternal relations, they have more often remained, in the words of the foreign relations scholar Max Paul Friedman, "polyglot distant cousin[s]."[9] But beginning roughly with the new millennium, through a series of international conferences, volumes, debates, and exchanges, a widening network of Latin

American specialists have identified kindred foreign relations scholars who work across the methodological, interpretive, and linguistic divides that previously had separated their respective fields, in an effort to encourage a more vital cross talk between them. These collaborations, galvanized initially by historians based at Yale University, New York University, CIESAS-Mexico City, and the Woodrow Wilson International Center for Scholars' Cold War History Project, have reverberated internationally in the decade and a half since, triggering new rounds of specialized conferences, high-profile publications, and research clusters at the London School of Economics, the Woodrow Wilson Center, the University of Wisconsin, Madison, the University of Texas, Austin, the Universidad Torcuato Di Tella in Buenos Aires, Argentina, the University of Bergamo in Italy, the Universidad de Puerto Rico, and the Pontificia Universidad Católica in Santiago, Chile, to name but a few.[10]

This first major effort of Latin American specialists to engage foreign relations scholars about their mutual research interest in the Cold War was certainly overdue. No field of foreign relations history was as well studied as the Cold War, and interest in the global conflict showed no signs of abating. A broad consensus had emerged regarding the global Cold War within the foreign relations literature by the late 1990s.[11] Scholars generally concurred that in global terms the conflict was a complex phenomenon that turned on the rivalry of two powerful states, each a "rookie superpower" possessing a universalizing ideology and a distinct system of political economy. The rivalry between them led to the division of Germany and Europe, an intense, often violent competition in the southern peripheries, and a strategic arms race. Although the superpower belligerents were careful not to engage in direct hostilities with each other, they consistently eschewed serious negotiation of their disputes—in effect seeking a diplomacy based on their own terms. The conflict took place in the wake of World War II, when an unsettled international system posed unprecedented threats and opportunities for many leaders, but especially those of the United States and the Soviet Union. As the leading foreign relations historian Melvyn Leffler has put it: "Interpreting those threats and opportunities through ideological lenses, cultural traditions, and cognitive habits of mind, American and Russian officials had the incentive and power to pursue their strategic and economic goals in ways that accorded with their understanding of national interest and ideological predilections. Their actions triggered reactions in a spiraling model of distrust and recrimination. Meanwhile, other governments (and parties and groups within those nations) sought to exploit the rivalry to enhance their own interests."[12]

Finally, the consensus held, one of the belligerents, the United States, was far more powerful and wealthy throughout and enjoyed a political-economic system that was vastly more productive, flexible, and technologically responsive. "The wonder," Leffler observed, is that the other side imploded without precipitating a major conflict."[13]

Intellectual historians of foreign relations had contributed important insights into the intensely ideological character of this "abnormal war." This was no ordinary state conflict, and geopolitical analysis does not suffice to explain the cruel and brutal form it took, especially in the Global South. Indeed, geopolitics may enrich our understanding of the military-political domain of the global conflict, but it has little to say about the ideological-cultural realm. The irony of the Cold War was that it represented, in the words of Anders Stephanson, "an extreme polarity organized around the total annihilation of the opponent in a period of ostensible peace."[14] Before 1963 and the resolution of the Cuban Missile Crisis, annihilation *literally* seemed a distinct possibility. Thereafter, neither side appeared to require or seriously risk the actual destruction of the other. In theory, each could have gone on indefinitely without having to change its system as a result of the other's existence (hence, the rather Eurocentric notion of a "long peace," as John Lewis Gaddis has termed it), since open conflict was deterred by the nuclear reality of "mutually assured destruction," and displaced and managed on the so-called Third World periphery.[15] Yet in another sense, the Cold War remained systemic and total. It was waged in fiercely doctrinal terms as an "invasion" or delegitimization of the other's social order, replete with a demonology of the other and a mythology of one's own eternal virtues. No doubt, argues Stephanson, the rigid *territorialization* of systems, beginning in 1947 in Europe, only intensified the mutually exclusive ideological aspect of the war, propelling it into its most primitive forms. The intensification of ideology assisted in securing, in different ways and contexts, each side's socioeconomic systems in the two halves of Europe and in spheres of influence such as Latin America.[16] Yet, in whatever context, the domestic social order could never be taken for granted; repression of internal dissent was axiomatic: red-baiting and worse in the United States and Mexico; wholesale purges in the Soviet Union; ethnocide in the western highlands and northern jungles of Guatemala.

For their part, at the turn of the new millennium, foreign relations historians of Latin America had largely accepted this prevailing consensus centered on bipolar superpower conflict. They had scrutinized the United States' and the Soviet Union's strategic stakes in Cuba, Central America, and the Caribbean. They had debated the psychology and personal style of Fidel Castro; sought to gauge the ebb, flow, and relative autonomy of Castro's relationship with the Soviets, and the consequences this had for Cuban and Soviet intervention abroad. They had also examined US polices to contain that intervention. But, in the words of Mark Gilderhus, a senior US foreign relations scholar who took stock of this field in the late 1990s, the Latin Americanist

literature, despite some impressive pieces of work, remained "narrowly focused, and largely dependent upon the records of the United States."[17] Greg
Grandin, who was soon to produce *The Last Colonial Massacre: Latin America
and the Cold War*, a major study of the Guatemalan Cold War that attempted a
provocative new synthesis of the broader Latin American conflict, also chid-
ed foreign relations historians for their myopic concerns. He wrote:

> Poets may see the world in a grain of sand ... but only diplomatic historians could
> reduce the Latin American Cold War to a Cuban beach. The Cold War radically
> transformed Latin America, yet historians of US policy toward the region inevi-
> tably focus on the period's most rousing events. These episodes more often than
> not have to do with Cuba—the 1959 Revolution, the Bay of Pigs, the Missile Cri-
> sis, and plots to murder Fidel Castro. Yet just as Fidel eventually made it off the
> beach and into the mountains, the time has come for US historians to assess the
> Latin American Cold War from [another] vantage point, one less preoccupied
> with what motivated United States policymakers and more concerned with iden-
> tifying what was being fought over in Latin America itself.[18]

No doubt these critiques accounted in part for the fact that, as of 2000,
the region had rarely been incorporated into the great historiographical debates about the character of the Cold War, and remained disproportionately
underrepresented in journals specializing on the conflict. But this was not
the *only* reason. For many years—indeed, through the mid-1990s at least—
Cold War debates centered excessively on the *origins* of the conflict—effectively on *who was to blame*. For heuristic purposes, we might boil the two
sides down to two contending master narratives: "Realism" and "Revision-
ism."[19] The Realists were largely concerned with geopolitics and grand strategy; some of Realism's most influential statements hark back to the point of
view of America's early cold warriors. Thus, Realists like John Lewis Gaddis
find in the plethora of new documents from Russian, East European, and
Chinese archives clear-cut substantiation that the authoritarian Soviet state
not only started the Cold War but, in concert with junior partners like the
Cubans, determined its trajectory. In contrast, New Left Revisionists emphasize the logic of US economic domination. Thus, an inexorable need for the
US economy to expand into new areas and create a new world system after
World War II, and the muscular liberal capitalist ideology that guided US
policymakers, were regarded to be largely responsible for the character of the
global struggle between East and West.

No doubt the Revisionists have carried the day where foreign relations
studies of the Cold War in Latin America are concerned. Latin America represented something of an "Achilles' heel in the hard armor of U.S. virtue":
even the most triumphal Cold War scholars associated with Realism were
hard-pressed to explain away US actions that brought about the toppling of

popularly elected regimes and contributed to the murder and torture of hundreds of thousands of people.[20] It is hardly surprising, therefore, that aided by the increased declassification of US security documents, there was a steady stream of monographs critiquing US involvement in Latin America from the late 1940s through the end of the twentieth century (and beyond)—even as some synthesizers of the larger conflict continued to declare an unshakable faith in American righteousness and exceptionalism. New Left scholarship and dependency theory came together most forcefully in Walter LaFeber's *Inevitable Revolutions: The United States in Central America*. Appearing in 1984, as Guatemala, Nicaragua, and El Salvador had become the Cold War's final killing zone, the volume highlighted the contradiction created by a US development model that generated poverty and insurgency and a regional diplomacy that enforced political stability at tremendous human cost.[21]

Nevertheless, at least as far as many area specialists were concerned, a veritable obsession with first causes, with blame, and with the motives and roles of US policymakers often served to join Realist historians and their New Left Revisionist critics at the hip, and preempted other intellectual agendas for examining the Latin American Cold War. Shortly after 2000, the efforts to bring Latin Americanists and "new" foreign relations scholars together began to take discussion of the region's Cold War in different directions, to bring it "in from the cold," as it were. Following a major international conference in Mexico City in 2002, two volumes—*Espejos de la guerra fría: México, América Central y el Caribe*, edited by the Mexican historian Daniela Spenser in 2004, and a much expanded, substantially revised English-language volume, *In from the Cold: Latin America's New Encounter with the Cold War*, edited by Gilbert Joseph and Spenser in 2008—argued that scholars should go beyond or beneath dichotomizing currents of interpretation that *themselves* appeared to be artifacts of the global conflict. While agreeing that the state and its agents played a preponderant role in the history of the Latin American Cold War, contributors to this project contended that the manner in which conventional foreign relations accounts had assessed the conflict almost exclusively in terms of national interest, state policy, and the broad imperatives of the international economy had often *marginalized human subjects*, particularly women and members of the poorer and middle sectors—peasants, workers, intellectuals, students, religious workers, and indigenous and ethnic groups. The prevailing literature had also ignored a serious examination of their social and cultural identities and political agency. Finally, it had largely neglected other political-cultural realms in which the state's power was brought to bear (and challenged) through a series of representations, symbolic systems, new technologies, and transnational collaborations involving agents that engaged with but often transcended the state.

Starting with the border crossings reflected in *Espejos de la guerra fría* and *In from the Cold* and continuing in a raft of subsequent volumes, articles, and forums, new understandings of Cold War in the region have emerged. In scholarship produced in the United States and Latin America, but also in Europe, the transnational and cross-border dimensions of Cold War struggles have been fleshed out, as well as the local and national ones—and not just for states but for everyday people. The result has been the elaboration of a more decentered and more grassroots and subject-oriented understanding of the deployment and resistance of power in the Latin American Cold War— but one that is always embedded in overlapping domestic and international social fields. Rather than give rise to a definitively "new" Cold War history for Latin America (in the sense of a manifesto, as some authors have characterized their new interpretative volumes on the broader global struggle[22]), we have witnessed an effort to seek *new intellectual encounters* with the Latin American Cold War, ones that might move the discussion beyond the machinations of the contending superpowers, the international determinants of their policies, and broad-brush treatments of the "collateral damage" these wrought upon Latin America roughly between 1947 and 1990. Indeed, up until the early 2000s, the term *Cold War* had been used as a kind of "shorthand to describe either direct U.S. or Cuban [or Soviet] intervention in Latin American politics, or the collateral damage from superpower conflict."[23] What was lacking was a framework for understanding the *grassroots* dynamics, motivations, and meanings of the Latin American Cold War, one that would enable us to better integrate the conflict's domestic and foreign—and transnational and transcultural—dimensions.

In keeping with the best new international history, recent scholarship has made an effort, on the one hand, to leaven Latin American social, cultural, and political history by "bringing the interstate system back in," while also complicating bipolar grand strategy narratives by "transnationalizing" and "Latin Americanizing" them.[24] In the process the new watershed of scholarship has begun to produce a history of the *Latin American* Cold War—rather than just a history of the Cold War *in* Latin America—by documenting in concrete terms and in multiple sites how an "international civil war" (the phrase is Arno Mayer's), which involved fluctuating geopolitical stakes and contending visions of how society and its benefits should be organized, intensely internationalized and politicized everyday life. It was this internationalization and politicization that gave the Latin American Cold War its often incandescent heat, calling into question notions of a "long peace" propounded by Eurocentric observers of the global conflict.

As local conflicts throughout the region (some of which had *extensive* antecedents, issuing as they did from the social contradictions of long-running processes of capitalist development) were subsumed in this intensely polarizing global struggle, opposition movements, like the governments they opposed, received ideas, inspiration, and material and technological support from afar. Not infrequently, Latin American states used a Cold War rationale and scientific and technological capacity, often but *not always* generated from outside the region, to wage war against their citizens, to gain or perpetuate power, and to create or justify authoritarian military regimes.[25]

At certain junctures—most notably, the triumph of the Cuban Revolution in 1959 and the strategy of international armed struggle that it supported in the 1960s and 1970s, or the hemispheric anticommunist crusade of the 1970s and 1980s that linked South America's brutal military regimes in a joint effort to track down and liquidate communist subversives—these struggles and the leftist and rightist ideologies that fueled them, transcended national borders and significantly influenced the relationship between the superpowers themselves. In the process, the stakes rose precipitously and the potential for violence and terror could escalate to brutal, even genocidal proportions—as in the Maya communities of Guatemala's western highlands—or in the roundup of "subversives" in the Southern Cone, orchestrated by Operation Condor with US assistance or acquiescence.[26] The threat of almost inconceivable violence rose to the highest level during the international Cuban Missile Crisis. The oral testimonies in a scene from CNN's documentary series on the Cold War starkly and eerily illustrates this point. A Cuban campesino reminisces: "I saw these weird weapons [rolling by my house]. I said to my friend Pablo, 'Pablo, how powerful *are* these weird weapons? And he answered 'these are nuclear missiles.' So I thought, 'oh, really powerful.' And they just put them here [pointing to his field], right out in the open."[27]

The rise of ambitious transnational and transregional analysis, steeped in multisited, multiarchival (and often oral history) research strategies, is one of the hallmarks of the new Cold War literature. Much of this scholarship has been undertaken by a new generation of international relations scholars and historians of Latin America.[28] For example, Piero Gleijeses has published extensively on the international and transnational dimensions of Cuba's Marxist revolution, which went well beyond the Fidelistas' unsuccessful support of guerrilla insurgencies in a number of Latin American countries.[29] The more successful international revolutionary mission that the Cubans mounted was in Africa, in the 1960s, 1970s, and 1980s. Here was a front in the global Cold War in which Cuba's military and social intervention—with doctors, teachers, and aid missions, as well as troops—really mattered in liberating a series of black African countries, such as Angola and South Africa, and in turning the tide against apartheid regimes. For the Cubans, these African struggles for social and racial equality resonated with the goals of their own revolution and the injustices of their prerevolutionary past. At the same time, their involvement in Africa kept the United States preoccupied on another front; thus, fighting abroad helped the Fidelista regime defend its revolution at home.

Another graphic case of the Latin American Cold War flowing across national borders is Argentina's still understudied Central American crusade against communism. This episode receives important treatment in the scholarship of the Argentine political scientist Ariel Armony.[30] For the leaders of that Southern Cone military dictatorship, Central America represented yet another front in what they actually believed constituted a "Third World War"—one they had to wage *everywhere* against the spread of communism, in order to preserve Western civilization. What Armony demonstrates convincingly is that Argentina was not merely a puppet or client of the US superpower. To be sure, the United States was actively training Latin America's right-wing militaries in counterinsurgency and supporting them with unprecedented levels of aid. Yet what Armony shows is that, in Central America, Argentina's generals and their hyperdeveloped intelligence branch acted with a substantial degree of autonomy from the United States—just as Cuba acted at certain junctures against the preferences of the Soviet Union.

Tanya Harmer's meticulously researched transnational account of the rise and fall of Allende's Chile also opens up fresh perspectives.[31] Not only does it provide the fullest account we have of the Vía Chilena's engagements with a dynamic inter-American system and global Cold War milieu, drawing on untapped archives in Brazil, the Eastern bloc, and the Vatican, as well as declassified documents in the United States. It also valorizes the previously underappreciated roles of Cuba and Brazil in the defense and destabilization of Allende's Popular Unity regime, respectively.[32] Like Argentina in Central America, Cuba and Brazil operated with a substantial degree of autonomy from their superpower patrons; indeed, the Soviet Union remained lukewarm about supporting Allende's Chile, "increasingly reluctant to let a Latin American revolutionary process spoil its new understanding [of détente] with the United States." Moreover, the Chilean Armed Forces that carried out the coup against Allende, perceived themselves to be the guarantors of national political stability going well back into Chile's past; they never saw themselves as instruments of the United States and international capitalism. Although supported, prodded, and ultimately lauded by Nixon and Kissinger's rabidly anticommunist administration, the Chilean military always regarded themselves first as national crusaders against the *foreign* doctrine of Marxism.[33]

The Uruguayan historian Aldo Marchesi's *Latin America's Radical Left: Rebellion and Cold War in the Global 1960s* is a similarly ambitious, multisited transnational history, one steeped in archival repositories and oral testimonies from several countries.[34] His is the first account of the of the peripatetic militant generation that embraced organized violence and transnational strategies as the only means of achieving meaningful structural change in South America's Southern Cone. Although Marchesi is attentive to world historical forces and ideas that inspired the routinely under-thirty generation of revolutionaries that galvanized radical urban groups like the Tupamaros (Uruguay), the Montoneros and the ERP (People's Revolutionary Army, Argentina), and the MIR (Revolutionary Left Movement, Chile), who challenged the rise of military authoritarianism in the Cono Sur, he places greater emphasis on their movements and encounters within the region. Examining key events and watersheds of mobilization and exile, which over the course of the 1960s and 1970s led successively from Montevideo, through Havana, Bolivia (the site of Che's disastrous *foco* campaign), and Santiago, to Buenos Aires, Marchesi charts the rise, fall, and political legacies of this clandestine variant of the New Left. Their trajectory from groups with diverse ideological origins into a militant network possessing a common repertoire of practices, a shared political culture, and a basically unified interpretation of the events unfolding in the region sheds new comparative light on the global 1960s, the consolidation of the Southern Cone's military dictatorships via Operation Condor, and the nature of its postconflict political arenas.[35]

The new transnational scholarship has also contributed importantly where studies of Cold War Mexico are concerned. As astonishing as it seems, before 2000 the country had received little attention in Cold War studies; indeed, Mexico was typically celebrated by apologists of the long-running official Institutional Revolutionary Party (or PRI) for having avoided the cold and dirty wars that ravaged much of the hemisphere. The failure to problematize Mexico's distinct Cold War past was even more striking considering that Mexico (with Brazil) constituted one of the region's two "middle powers," and also because it was the ally and southern neighbor of the hemisphere's Cold War hegemon, with whom it has shared a historically volatile border.

Scholars have done much over the past decade to address this lacuna. There are a brace of essays in *Espejos de la guerra fría* and *In from the Cold*, as well as the historian Renata Keller's recent monograph, *Mexico's Cold War: Cuba, the United States, and the Legacy of the Mexican Revolution* (2015), that further our understanding of the motivation and capacity of the Mexican state to skillfully balance between the superpowers.[36] Like the cases of Cuba, Argentina, and Chile, the Mexican case also points up often-ignored, *ambivalent* relationships between Cold War allies. In the Mexican government's tourist promotions for a US audience during the Cold War decades, Mexico presented itself—much as it does today—as an exotic but familiar "amigo country"; but in its foreign policy, Mexico remained publicly committed to nonintervention and "Third Worldism," and never severed relations with Castro's Cuba. Indeed, it supported Cuba and remained the island's most consistent friend throughout the Cold War proper—even as it also spied on

Cuba for the United States. At the same time, Mexico traded with Red China but voted with the United States on important questions; it maintained correct but extremely cautious relations with the Soviet Union; it permitted the Mexican Communist Party to operate but harassed, surveilled, jailed, and occasionally disappeared its leaders. Ever Janus-faced, Mexico consistently sought to reassure US policymakers and investors that, despite its inconsistencies, at core it remained a reliable Cold War ally of the United States.

The PRI state's reassurances were particularly compelling in view of its series of campaigns against civil society radicals and rural revolutionaries in the decades after World War II. We now have a robust literature on the co-optation and coercion of radical students, teachers, railroad and auto workers, miners, and peasants in the decades leading up to the Tlatelolco Massacre in October 1968.[37] This literature is complemented by excellent treatments of the state's unremitting but relatively hushed dirty war against Marxist revolutionary groups in the predominantly indigenous southern state of Guerrero and elsewhere in the 1970s.[38]

The paradox of Cold War Mexico makes more sense if we factor in its complicated relationship to revolutionary Cuba. As Eric Zolov, Keller, and others have demonstrated, the Fidelistas' glittering new revolution was a destabilizing force in Mexican affairs. In 1959 the young Cuban *barbudos* (bearded revolutionaries) were utterly committed to many of the same nationalist and radical causes that, decades earlier, had fired Mexico's own revolutionary compact with its people in the wake of the tumultuous decade-long upheaval unleashed in 1910. By the early 1960s, however, it seemed obvious to Mexicans that the sclerotic PRI had long since abandoned these revolutionary principles.[39] Thus, a dynamic combination of domestic challenges and Cold War geopolitics would shape the Janus-faced policies of Cold War Mexico.

Such cases underscore the new scholarship's broader contention that the texture of the Latin American Cold War emerged out of widening processes of social conflict *in* Latin America and the Global South—processes that should not be subordinated to the grand strategies or machinations of the superpowers.[40]

The Long Cold War

The notion of a "long Cold War" (rather than a "long peace"), which influences the chronologies of many of the essays in *Itineraries of Expertise*, should be understood in the same spirit. The concept was introduced by Greg Grandin and Gilbert Joseph in their 2010 collection *A Century of Revolution: Insurgent and Counterinsurgent Violence during Latin America's Long Cold War*. They contended that the concept facilitated an examination of both the patterns and intricacies of the region's violent politics *and* the imperial dynamics of

Cold War *within the same conceptual frame.* Thus, "a long Cold War" provided a reasonably coherent interpretation of the contours of Latin America's twentieth-century political history, suggesting broader regional conclusions based on the histories of individual countries that had typically been viewed alone. Simultaneously it drew attention to the long-term material and ideological stakes—the "hegemonic presumption"—of the United States, which both preceded and transcended the Cold War proper and had significant consequences for Latin America early in the twenty-first century.

Building on their own earlier work, Grandin and Joseph argued that the 1947–1990 conjuncture was part of a longer, arguably more consequential epoch: Latin America's revolutionary twentieth century, which "proceeded on parallel tracks" with the United States' rise to hemispheric and global preponderance, with "each greatly informing the shape the other took."[41] Running at least from the Mexican Revolution of 1910 (if not the political and social repercussions of the wars of 1898) to the Central American insurgencies of the 1980s, this period in Latin America was defined by sequential attempts to transcend what had become an unsustainable model of exclusionary nationalism, restricted political and social institutions, persisting rural clientelism, and dependent export-based development. The volume's contributions make clear that the experience of each country's involvement in this nearly century-long cycle of insurgent politics aimed at reform and liberalization, as well as each nation's relationship with the imperial hegemon, was distinct, though many shared similar patterns of radicalized reform, followed not infrequently by revolution, civil war, and state terror. Moreover, each successive bid to transform society generated domestic experiences and international responses that shaped subsequent attempts.[42]

Let me summarize the progression of this centennial cycle of reform and revolution in broad strokes.[43] In 1910, Mexico's epic revolution signaled the first sustained assault on a US-backed, modernizing, nineteenth-century oligarchical regime, putting agrarian reform and social rights fully on the policy agenda. Of course, Mexico's revolution played out against the backdrop of the institutionalization of the Soviet Bolshevik regime and the onset of Comintern activity in the Western hemisphere. In the 1920s and early 1930s, in a variety of settings, miners, factory workers, and some campesinos organized, joined unions, mounted strikes of unprecedented militancy, supported new democratic parties, and injected strength into existing communist, socialist, and radical movements. In some countries, such as Mexico, El Salvador, and Chile, these Old Left formations had galvanized local rebellions and popular struggles, which were targeted by repressive oligarchical states during virulent Red Scares that some scholars now refer to as the "first Cold War."[44] In the 1930s and 1940s, populism and popular front regimes, most notably in the Southern Cone, sought to extend rights, supersede the patronage relations of local powerholders with national institutions, and articulate a more inclusive national-popular identity. In the 1940s, socialists, nationalists, and liberals tried to make good on the promise of antifascist social democracy, which for a brief time received both the blessing and inspiration of a Pan Americanist, Good Neighborly United States. In the 1950s, a sharper and more radical nationalism gained ground, with a defined program of import-substitution, particularly in revolutionary Guatemala and Bolivia. By the 1960s, even more dissident paradigms of development had emerged, most notably a full-fledged dependency theory pitting the imperial core against the Latin American periphery.[45]

Again, Grandin and Joseph emphasize the powerful dialectic that governed this process. Imperial dominance and intervention both responded to the immanent threat of postwar structural change and, in turn, provided the impetus for new revolutionary movements and initiatives. In this sense, the Cuban Revolution may be seen as an important fulcrum in Latin America's "century of revolution": the frustration and anger engendered in the region by Latin America's failed democratic spring—which in Guatemala included the overthrow of Jacobo Arbenz's popular social democratic regime in 1954 and later, the virtual liquidation of the Old Left that was attempting to rekindle it—produced a radicalization of the Left's political agenda in one nation after another—as well as a resolve to avoid the fate of Guatemala.[46] In this sense, the Cuban case served "both [to crystallize] decades of regional experience and [to link] that experience to a broader, global crisis of legitimacy that by the late 50s [and 1960s] threatened to overwhelm both the West and East alike."[47]

What makes the Cuban conjuncture particularly consequential is that revolution's capacity to fully understand itself as a "world historical" project and thus attempt to "externalize" itself in the empire's backyard as well as in Africa. In the process it fractured sclerotic Old Left groupings and inspired New Left activists even after the limitations of its *foco* strategy became painfully obvious. The subsequent revolutionary initiatives in Chile, Guatemala, and Nicaragua in the 1970s and 1980s, for example, all of which were predicated on New Left political identities and the merits of *concientización* (consciousness-raising), were as much *reactions* to the Cuban model as they were *products* of it. The Vía Chilena's experiment with political pluralism; the attempt by Guatemala's Guerrilla Army of the Poor to incorporate entire indigenous communities into the insurgency; the Sandinistas' efforts to harness radical Christian currents with an undogmatic Marxism in Nicaragua—*all* reflect some level of engagement (positive and negative) with the Cuban experience.[48]

These dialectical elements came together in their fullest expression in Central America in the 1980s. A brutal (and often misnamed "low intensity") conflict that articulated both East–West and North–South dynamics, it ultimately gave way, amid the carnage of the Cold War's final killing fields and barrios, to the Central American Peace Accords that ended Latin America's "century of revolution" (if not its concomitant "long Cold War," which, as developments in the new millennium suggest, possibly knows no end, both in this hemisphere, Europe, and elsewhere in the Global South).

The legacies of these brutal decades are with us still. Certainly the Cold War is still palpable in Central America and the Southern Cone, the Andean nations, and even Mexico, as relatives of the victims of terror continue to protest past atrocities, exhume graves, and actively press legal claims against the perpetrators, with increasing success. Nor has the violence subsided: lynchings and other episodes of extrajudicial violence continue to bubble up in countries like Guatemala, Nicaragua, Honduras, El Salvador, and Mexico. Such local violence frequently maps onto the fault lines and frustrations of recent Cold War pasts, and in many cases intersects with newer manifestations of banditry, gang-fueled narcoviolence, and arms and human smuggling. Indeed, the *maras* who have wreaked such violence in the Northern Triangle of Central America, fueling unprecedented new waves of youthful undocumented migration to Mexico and the United States, are now regarded to be among the most sinister forms of blowback from the Cold War.[49]

Yet within this longue durée of US hemispheric hegemony and resistance to it, the Cold War proper (ca. 1947–1990) represented a *particularly consequential* juncture. This was evident in terms of the massive infusion of counterinsurgent aid and expert personnel, the dramatic narrowing of political space and options, and the manner in which a deadly combination of rational, precise counterinsurgent technologies (typically imported from the United States and its allies), *and* more atavistic local sentiments and tactics honed the new internal security state and the bureaucratic strategies of terror that undergirded it. Although the present volume has chosen not to focus on the specialized technologies and experts associated with these regimes of surveillance and torture, they have been amply studied in the literature on the dirty wars and represented in its popular culture and literature.[50]

In social and cultural terms, more was at issue here than a Cold War *ideological veneer and discourse*—the language with which people, often leaders, described their struggles during the second half of the twentieth century (and even before). What the contributors to *A Century of Revolution* attempt to convey (and is evident more generally in the new watershed of Latin American Cold War scholarship) is a reality that goes much deeper than the ideological veneer, a struggle in which forms of discourse and representation, often (but not always) generated outside the region, became imbricated in, and constitutive of, the lives people lived. In this sense, the Cold War, as Greg Grandin puts it, was "a powerful integrator," and local and national political, social, and cultural fabrics often had less to do with the strategies, ideologies, and discourses of the superpowers, and more to do with the manner in which these *mapped onto* and were *mediated by* local values and aspirations: *for or against* democratization, a leveling of class or ethnic or racial distinctions, and a liberalization of gender relations.[51] And, whether we like it or not, we have to recognize that many poor and middle-class Latin Americans were not proponents of greater freedom and opening. Not only did some members of middling and subaltern classes nurture personal rivalries and other discontents with leftist reformers and revolutionaries but others were also driven by status anxiety, racial hatred, or the fear of losing patriarchal privilege, which for some women meant a loss of protection. Grandin and others have shown, for example, that, in the main, the fight against Guatemala's burgeoning revolutionary challenge was directed not by those at "society's commanding heights" but by middle-class ideologues, often anticommunist Catholic students who fancied themselves in the vanguard of a worldwide movement of the Right. "It was this impassioned middle sector that functioned as a broker between the upper echelons, both domestic and foreign, of reaction and street thugs and paramilitary forces responsible for some of the worst acts of counterinsurgency."[52]

We might see the anthropologist Carlota McAllister's recent writings on peasant mobilization in a rural Guatemalan hamlet, which combine archival research and ethnographic techniques (the methodological pluralism that characterizes much of the new work in Latin American Cold War studies), as among the new watershed's signature contributions.[53] McAllister relates how, in the highland community of Chupol, Maya campesinos *and campesinas* sought to implement contemporary western developmental prescriptions (in effect W. W. Rostow's "modernization theory") according to their own lights, against a backdrop of generations of class and racial repression. Their efforts ushered in a species of petty market capitalism, political mobilization, and women's empowerment that, in short order, provoked a genocidal response from the hypervigilant, anticommunist military state. In reflecting on McAllister's work, we might keep in mind Pope Paul VI's 1967 encyclical, "On the Development of Peoples," which speaks to the multilayered approach to Latin American Cold War history that many of us have sought to advance, and is perhaps as good a handy definition as any that can be found on what constituted the Latin American Cold War. "Social conflicts, the Pope wrote, "have taken on world dimensions."[54]

The Cultural Cold War

Thus, it is not surprising that a particularly fertile vein in the new scholarship on the Latin American Cold War, especially for the conflict's later decades (the 1960s to the 1990s) has been the reconstruction of the experiences and memories of the followers of both revolutionary and counterrevolutionary movements, as well as of men and women on the margins and in the interstices of both. These inquiries represent a species of cultural history that lies at intersections of the political, the economic, and the social. They attend to the complex local processes in workplaces, communities, and households whereby ideas and ideologies were received and appropriated. They shed light on the transformation of Old Left and populist formations into newer incarnations of the Left and populism.[55] More often than not, these studies contain surprises that muddy up master narratives. They suggest that just as workers, peasants, the urban poor, religious workers, and women were not mere creatures of populist and popular-front arrangements at midcentury, so they were not passive instruments in the hands of vanguard Left intellectuals or counterinsurgent states later on. They draw our attention to more autonomous, contingent, and creative uses of socialist ideas by the grassroots Left than model-building social scientists often allow.[56] In some cases the very durability of guerrilla movements had much to do with appeals to more latent but venerable traditions of popular liberalism or to radical, communally driven forms of democracy, *under cover* of more standard Marxist-Leninist discourse (for example, in local formations of the FARC [Revolutionary Armed Forces] in remote regions of Colombia, and perhaps in similarly remote outposts of support for Sendero Luminoso in Peru). Finally this new scholarship, especially on Guatemala and the Southern Cone, gives us greater insight into how people remember and come to grips with the telling of episodes of collective violence and trauma, and how the protagonists in cultural wars over memory use this arena to shape the political and cultural future.[57]

Steve Stern's extensive, award-winning scholarship has been critical in defining questions of memory and repression during and after the Latin American Cold War, especially in the Southern Cone. The three volumes comprising his study of memory politics in Chile over the past four decades are daunting in their simultaneous exploration of the way Chileans experienced the trauma and terror of military rule under the Pinochet regime, as well as the challenges such research poses for historians who must contend with the "tricks" and silences of "emblematic memory."[58] Stern's work is pioneering in its ability to contend with the enormous range of experience and perception under the dictatorship, without shortchanging vivid insights into the ways in which memory works (in Cold War Chile as well as during the Holocaust, for example). In the process, he probes the highly complex relations between individual recollections and the creation of "collective memory." Stern is not only concerned with the memory struggles of the Left, human rights activists, and progressive elites who insisted on a moral reckoning with the past; he also attends to dynamics on the Chilean Right, including those who remember Pinochet's military coup and dictatorship as a "time of salvation." In the third and final volume of his trilogy, *The Memory Box of Pinochet's Chile*, Stern shows how a contested national process of truth and justice has created new spaces for dialogue and dispute.

Stern's ambitious project has been celebrated in Latin American studies for its interdisciplinary methodology, comparative historical implications, and creative narrative structure, but it has also influenced studies of repression, memory, human rights, and political transition elsewhere in the Global South. Significantly, his contributions to these fields both predate and transcend the trilogy of publications. In the late 1990s, collaborating with Latin American and international colleagues such as the Argentine sociologist Elizabeth Jelin, the late Peruvian anthropologist Carlos Iván Degregori, and the US political scientist Eric Hershberg, and backed by funding from the Social Science Research Council and the Ford Foundation, Stern brought together scholars and students from across the hemisphere, creating a discursive community around the memory of repression and the pursuit of social justice in the Americas. In addition to publishing over a dozen edited volumes on these themes over the course of a decade, the project trained a new generation of Latin Americans who have gone on to play critical roles as scholars and public intellectuals in their postconflict societies—and are now training their own students.[59] In addition, Stern's trilogy and the decade of collaborations with the Social Science Research Council (SSRC) and the Ford Foundation paved the way for a book series, Critical Human Rights, co-edited by Stern and Scott Straus for the University of Wisconsin Press, which since its founding in 2010 has published close to twenty-five titles on Latin America and other parts of the world.

The new cultural history of the Latin American Cold War has also accessed other political-cultural realms that engage themes similar to those examined in *Itineraries of Expertise*. We might call these realms transnational "contact zones," drawing on the cultural theorist Mary Louise Pratt's generative formulation.[60] In the context of a long cultural Cold War, the Argentine historian Ricardo Salvatore has done pioneering work on the role of travelers, missionaries, geographers, businessmen, and generations of the North American academy in sustaining a far-flung "enterprise of knowledge" that, he argues, advanced US economic aims in South America before 1945.[61] The contributors to the present volume have done research that usefully advances an understanding of transnational contact zones before and especially during the Cold War proper, via an examination of traveling engineers, agronomists, scientists, educators, conservationists, planners, designers, demographers, and economists. Studying such actors draws our attention to a variety of sites and conjunctures in which US (and other foreign) power has been brought to bear unevenly in Latin America, through diverse transnational and trans-

cultural arrangements. Forms of power are multiple and complex: simultaneously arranged through nation-states and nongovernmental entities; via
business and communications networks and culture industries; through
money doctors and trade delegations; via imported technologies; through
academic collaborations and exchanges, scientific foundations, philanthropic agencies, and agricultural extension services.

Contact zones are not geographic places with stable significations; they
are suffused with diverse constructions of modernization, nationality, race,
ethnicity, gender, and sexuality. They may represent attempts at hegemony,
but are simultaneously sites of multivocality; of negotiation, borrowing, and
exchange; and of redeployment and reversal. An understanding of the kinds
of transnational encounters that underwrite the present volume's agendas of
expertise entails an analysis of institutions and multilayered collaborations,
but also an appreciation of new intellectual and "development" paradigms,
symbol systems, and the representations that convey them.[62]

Thus far, much scholarship on Cold War transnational contact zones has
featured diverse business networks;[63] studies of Cold War films, TV, and
newsreels;[64] other forms of popular culture, leisure, advertising, and consumption;[65] churches and religious workers;[66] progressive human rights and
solidarity movements;[67] and counterinsurgent aid missions.[68] Popular riots
and demonstrations in the public sphere have also been deconstructed—
such as Ernesto Capello's sophisticated examination of Nelson Rockefeller's tumultuous tour of Latin America in 1969 or Eric Zolov's multilayered
analysis of Mexican riots against US–Mexican cultural institutes in the wake
of the Bay of Pigs invasion.[69] We also have fragmentary studies of US government cultural dependencies like the United States Information Agency
(USIA) and the Office of the Coordinator of Inter-American Affairs;[70] professional associations like the Latin American Studies Association (which
succeeded the early pioneers of Latin American Studies whom Salvatore
examines in *Disciplinary Conquest*);[71] philanthropic institutions such as the
Ford and Rockefeller Foundations, whose fingerprints appear on several of
the long-running, collaborative Cold War projects examined in the present
volume;[72] and grassroots development initiatives such as the Peace Corps.[73]

Scholarship on electronic media also has the capacity to bring subtle,
foreign-local dimensions of Cold War power relationships into sharp relief.
The ongoing research of the transnational media historian and videogra-
pher Seth Fein, for example, is concerned with various collaborations that
involved shifting combinations of the Mexican film and television industries,
the Mexican state, Hollywood, and US television, and a variety of dependencies of the US government. These collaborations produced mainstream films
and television shows, propagandistic current events newsreels, and short
films for peasant villagers on what constituted proper citizenship, patriotism,

and modern hygiene. In some cases these US–Mexican collaborations were so well integrated and disguised that it becomes difficult to determine where one Cold War state project began and the other ended, let alone distinguish agents of the state from those of the private sector.[74]

All these cultural approaches suggest that, although the new Cold War history, like the more conventional foreign relations history that preceded it, is concerned with the exercise and contestation of power, that power does not flow only from the policies and interventions of states; nor does it flow only in one direction.

A recent collection published in Italy and then in Argentina in 2013, edited by the Italian cultural historian Benedetta Calandra and her Argentine colleague Marina Franco, attempts to assess the state of scholarship on *La guerra fría cultural en América Latina*. This international volume, which assembles a team of interdisciplinary scholars, mostly from Italy, Spain, and Latin America, builds conceptually on the collaborative Cold War volumes already introduced, and also on a precursor to that cycle of research, the 1998 anthology *Close Encounters of Empire: Writing the Cultural History of U.S.-Latin American Relations*, edited by Gilbert Joseph, Catherine LeGrand, and Ricardo Salvatore. The Calandra and Franco volume also builds on studies that Salvatore and colleagues in Argentina and internationally have published in a volume on *imperial cultures*.[75]

Above all, the Calandra and Franco volume stresses the *emerging* nature of studies on Latin America's cultural Cold War. Unlike the more robust bodies of work on Europe and the United States, studies of Latin America's Cold War cultures remain modest and dispersed, with immense gaps. Nevertheless the collection reinforces the interpretive approaches of work analyzed above. Thus, the editors—and contributors such as Eduardo Rey Tristán and Ixel Quesada Vargas—also argue for a long Cold War in the cultural realm. They suggest that the Cold War proper's pivotal political events and watersheds were not congruent with longer-running cultural and intellectual formations, which date back at least to the positivist and progressive "civilizing" and "modernizing" missions of the early twentieth century and then—as several essays in the present volume similarly attest—take an important turn in the 1940s and 1950s when a more muscular technocratic capacity, influenced substantially by New Deal mindsets and policies, gains ascendance throughout the hemisphere.[76]

There is much discussion in the literature regarding what explicitly political and ideological valences should be attached to notions of a "cultural Cold War." As we have seen, there has been a venerable New Left Revisionist current in foreign relations scholarship, some of whose exponents in the 1960s and 1970s embraced Marxist dependency theory and other "dissident paradigms of development" that were heavily influenced by theorists from

Latin America, Africa, and the Global South.⁷⁷ They were joined in the formative years of Latin American studies by a new generation of Left academics, including many West Coast intellectuals recently trained at Stanford,
Berkeley, and other California campuses who were powerfully shaped by the
antiwar and anti-interventionist movements of the day. These self-avowed
"radical Latin Americanists" identified field research projects that "brought
them into close relationships with Latin Americans struggling for change
and engaging with *radical alternatives* to mainstream thinking."⁷⁸ This transnational academic solidarity, in the words of one of the movement's founders,
Ronald Chilcote, explicitly "rejected the mainstream university-government-
foundation nexus in which academics shared the Cold War assumptions and
goals of U.S. foreign policy and collaborated with government in a variety
of ways."⁷⁹ Over the course of the 1960s and 1970s, these radical academics
and activists created alternative scholarly networks, institutions, and publications in Latin American studies, including the North American Congress
on Latin America (NACLA) in 1966, whose influential *NACLA Report on
the Americas* just celebrated its fiftieth anniversary, and, in 1974, the more explicitly academic journal *Latin American Perspectives* (*LAP*), which Chilcote
has edited from its inception to the present day. Without question this radical
Cold War–era political-cultural formation did much to transform the more
establishment institutions of Latin American studies, like the Latin American Studies Association (LASA) and its official journal the *Latin American
Research Review*, both founded in 1966. This was because many of the radicals and progressives who formed NACLA and *LAP* did not secede from
LASA but worked to change it from within. The committed participation of
radical academics in LASA's early years did much to diversify its membership
and eventually its leadership structure, paving the way for the participation
of women, Latin Americans, and Latinos/Latinas in what began as an almost
exclusively white male association.⁸⁰

There is no question that foundations like Ford and Rockefeller collaborated with Cold Warriors in the US government to fuel the brand of modernization theory and developmentalism that *Itineraries of Expertise* painstak-
ingly fleshes out. Local and transnational projects that fed into the Alliance
for Progress, the Green Revolution, and the Peace Corps sought above all to
contain communism, while forestalling badly needed, but more threatening
structural reforms. According to Chilcote, the least savory episodes of the
Cold War's cultural history, which he and several international scholars examine in a 2018 special issue of *LAP* dedicated to "The Cold War and Latin
American Studies," were no doubt the secretive or semicovert collaborations
between US intelligence and defense agencies and academics who were recruited to use social science research to "predict and prevent advances by the
Left." Such initiatives included Project Camelot, a counterinsurgency study

by the US Army initiated in 1964 (and terminated in 1965) through the Special Operations Research Office located at American University, which surveyed popular attitudes in nine Latin American countries; and the multination Marginality Project, funded by Ford and designed in the mid-1960s by an anti-Marxist European scholar now known to have been funded by the CIA. Another project sponsored by Ford, to "Americanize" the São Paulo School of Business Administration, was directed by a US academic who scholars now believe "secretly engaged with the U.S.-supported Brazilian military dictatorship."[81]

These collaborative research operations were denounced as "imperialist" in one Latin American country after another, and were typically short-lived. But, as Chilcote shows, they did much to discredit US social scientists whose work throughout the region "was widely viewed with suspicion, and caused academics to limit their fieldwork abroad and work with colleagues and professional associations to denounce and ban clandestine research."[82] For many years, the Ford Foundation and LASA, whose founding president, Kalman Silvert, was himself a longtime stalwart at Ford, were at pains to distance themselves from what came to be known as the "Camelot syndrome."[83]

Chilcote also recalls that simultaneously in the North American academy, university and foundation administrators sought to co-opt leftist scholars and, if that failed, to discourage and even prevent their field research. In several high-profile cases, university administrations denied these "radical Latin Americanists" reappointment or tenure.[84] Investigative reporting at the height of the Cold War in the mid-late 1960s (most notably by the *New York Times* and the radical, countercultural magazine *Ramparts*) revealed that the CIA exerted substantial influence on academic and intellectual endeavors, not least through its funding of the Congress for Cultural Freedom (CCF) and the latter's extensive international network of anticommunist periodicals, conferences, and cultural events. In 1966, the CCF established a front organization, the Instituto Latinoamericano de Relaciones Internacionales, to organize congresses in Latin America and do outreach among high-profile Latin American intellectuals. When the CCF was exposed as a CIA front in 1967, it morphed into the International Association for Cultural Freedom, now funded entirely by Ford, but closed its doors for good in 1977.[85] The leading scholar of the CCF, Patrick Iber, writes its epitaph as follows: "By its work, it had discredited communism; by its existence and exposure as a CIA front, it discredited anti-communism."[86]

Without neglecting "scandalous" episodes like the US Department of Defense's manipulative, counterinsurgent use of social science research in Project Camelot (and presumably some of the other initiatives referenced above in the special issue of *LAP*), the contributors to the Calandra and Franco volume prefer to tease out nuances in the deployment of and resistance to imperial cultural power. They eschew just-so stories of hegemony and broad instrumentalist applications of "soft power," arguing instead for historicized, case-specific analyses of imperial contact zones, agents, and more contingent, even ambiguous forms of local reception. The essays by Fernando Purcell on the Peace Corps, Capello on the Nelson Rockefeller tour, and Calandra on the metamorphosis of the Ford Foundation's commitments in the face of increasing persecution of social science disciplines and scholars in the Southern Cone during the dirty-war years, particularly stand out in this regard.[87] Chilcote himself offers nuanced treatment of the Peace Corps, which, he emphasizes, produced a stream of former volunteers who went on to long careers in Latin American studies that were characterized by a principled critique of US foreign policy, interventions, and the concept of "development" itself.[88]

Of course, in a broader sense, all the cultural processes, relationships, and exchanges that played out during the Cold War—including those examined in this volume—were suffused by power and politics. Chastain and Lorek point out in their introduction that "an increasingly sophisticated literature on medicine and public health in Latin America . . . offers a roadmap" for the kind of Cold War scholarship this collection seeks to advance for other areas of expertise. Another important collaborative project, currently in press, *Calenturas! Health and Medicine in Cold War Latin America*, edited by two historians of science and public health, Anne-Emanuelle Birn and Raúl Necochea López, showcases the new directions that literature is taking. Not only does the forthcoming anthology provide an interdisciplinary set of case studies in the domains of health and medicine that, like contributions to the present volume, demonstrate how Latin American actors exercised a substantial degree of agency in the ways they "used, rejected, and reshaped U.S. preferences and interventions,"[89] but it is also especially pioneering in revealing a range of encounters between Latin American health professionals and their Soviet and Eastern bloc counterparts (e.g., in the areas of disease prevention and parasitology, pharmaceutical production, and psychiatry). Finally, it inquires into the kind of relations that Latin American doctors and health workers had with colleagues in other Third World countries within and beyond the region (e.g., in studies of fertility and population control, and in the development of comprehensive health-care programs). All these transnational *encuentros* (and some rather negative *desencuentros* in the field of Cold War psychiatry), did much to define and transform health policy and medical practice in the region.[90]

The new cultural history of the Cold War that volumes like *Calenturas!* and *Itineraries of Expertise* represent is distinguished, above all, by their ability to interrogate and cross the temporal, spatial, and methodological boundaries that conventional diplomatic and foreign relations scholarship set in place. The peripatetic experts and technocrats under scrutiny here spanned generations of knowledge production, mediated "high" and "low modernisms," traversed multiple levels and ideological divides of the world system, and in many instances themselves came to embody transnational identities and "hybrid nationalities of expertise." (Consider, for example, the careers and trajectories of experts such as Ciro Molina Garcés and Carlos Chardón that are showcased in Lorek's chapter 3.) In this regard, an interesting feature of several of the essays is the role that certain sites in the Global South, such as Mexico and Puerto Rico, and to a lesser extent, Colombia, played in the creation of such hybrid identities, typically in the context of transitions from revolutionary and liberal welfare states to the neoliberal regimes that succeeded them. Mexico, Puerto Rico, and Colombia served as intermediary spaces and proving grounds for the kind of biological, agronomic, and hydrological research, and the type of social policies, that would, in time, give rise to institutional hallmarks of the regional and global Cold War such as the Green Revolution and the Alliance for Progress.[91]

Much more can be done by scholars to internationalize cultural (and political-economic) studies of the Latin American Cold War. Like many other countries belonging to the Global South, Latin American states frequently sought to balance between the First and Second Worlds, defying bipolar imperatives (and occasionally constructions of the Monroe Doctrine) when they could and, in the process, entertaining for a time the possibilities of an incipient Third World project. The rise and fall of *Tercermundismo* in Mexico in the 1970s under the populist president Luis Echeverría was emblematic of various ill-fated Latin American attempts, by governments and popular movements alike, to identify with a distinct Third World experience during the Global Cold War. A new collective volume in press, *Latin America and the Global Cold War*, edited by the international historians Thomas Field, Stella Krepp, and Vanni Pettinà, argues that, along with more recently decolonized nations in Africa, Asia, and the non-Hispanophone Caribbean, "Latin America must be treated as a fundamental participant in the Third World project," incorporating perspectives for understanding the region that have often been foreclosed by "the traditional Western Hemispheric or regional framing." In this respect, the volume seeks to break out of what Tanya Harmer has recently termed "the historiographical Monroe Doctrine."[92] This, the editors and contributors demonstrate, entails deeper research into Latin America's political-economic and cultural relations with the Socialist Second World and more attention to political and cultural formations like the 1966 Tricontinental Conference in Havana, Cuba, and the Organization of Solidarity with the Peoples of Asia, Africa, and Latin America (OSPAAAL), founded in its wake.[93] It also entails examination of economic anti-imperialist projects such as the Organization of Petroleum Exporting Countries and the New International Economic Order, created in the 1960s and 1970s, respectively.[94]

The outlook for future work in Latin American Cold War studies is quite promising. As some wounds heal, and as a horizon of life replaces one of death in the region's former killing zones, a greater variety of studies reconstructing the social and cultural histories and memories of the Latin American Cold War is possible. As forensic and truth-telling processes play out, the climate for new encounters with the Cold War, undergirded by a windfall of declassified documents and oral sources, warms. Recent international symposia and a steady stream of publications in the United States, Latin America, and Europe, with still others in production, have underscored the manner in which Latin America is being reintegrated into global Cold War studies and is no longer perceived as peripheral to it, apart from the high-profile struggles around Cuba, such as the Bay of Pigs and the Missile Crisis, which long dominated studies by diplomatic and foreign relations scholars. Projects like the present volume on experts and expertise, technology, science and the environment, augur the possibility of further dialogue between more traditional and newer approaches to the regional and broader conflict, including the burgeoning scholarship on the cultural Cold War that harnesses dynamic currents in Latin American and international history. With the historical record increasingly accessible at a variety of global locations, and with historical amnesia challenged at the international and national levels, as well as at the grassroots, Latin American and US students are rediscovering new aspects of their countries' political, social, cultural, and transnational histories during the second half of the twentieth century and beyond. This development has enlivened our calling as teachers as well as scholars, both in the North and the South.

NOTES

This chapter is derived in part from an article published in *Cold War History* 19, no. 1 (2019), copyright © Taylor and Francis, http://www.tandfonline.com/10.1080/14682745.2 019.1557824.

1. Gabriel García Márquez, "The Solitude of Latin America (Nobel Lecture, 1982)," in *Gabriel García Márquez and the Powers of Fiction*, ed. Julio Ortega and Claudia Elliott (Austin: University of Texas Press, 1988), esp. 81.

2. In 1967 David Horowitz aptly observed: "The very term cold war may be a misleading description, for unlike its prototype, this war has no centrality in terms of geopolitical space. ... Its contested areas are themselves shifting and non-delimitable." David Horowitz, ed., *Containment and Revolution: Western Policy towards Social Revolution, 1917 to Vietnam* (London: Anthony Blond, 1967), 9. The phrase "Cold War" is generally attributable to George Orwell, who used it in 1945 to describe the competition between the United States and the Soviet Union in Europe following the defeat of Nazi Germany.

3. For a fuller discussion, see my introduction, "What We Now Know and Should Know: Bringing Latin America More Meaningfully into Cold War Studies," in *In from the Cold: Latin America's New Encounter with the Cold War*, ed. Gilbert Joseph and Daniela Spenser (Durham, NC: Duke University Press, 2008), 3–46, esp. 3–8. I am grateful to Greg Grandin and Arno Mayer for this dialectic of revolution and counterrevolution in twentieth-century Latin America. See Greg Grandin, *The Last Colonial Massacre: Latin America and the Cold War* (Chicago: University of Chicago Press, 2004), which draws provocatively on Mayer's model for understanding European cycles of violence, elaborated in Arno Mayer, *The Furies: Violence and Terror in the French and Russian Revolutions* (Princeton, NJ: Princeton University Press, 2000). Grandin and I use this dialectic to structure our collection, Greg Grandin and Gilbert M. Joseph, *A Century of Revolution: Insurgent and Counterinsurgent Violence during Latin America's Long Cold War* (Durham, NC: Duke University Press, 2010), which is discussed at length below. For an effective global synthesis that evokes the heat of the conflict in the Global South (though minimally for Latin America), see Odd Arne Westad, *The Global Cold War: Third World Interventions and the Making of Our Times* (New York: Cambridge University Press, 2005).

4. See the editors' introduction to this volume.

5. See, e.g., Patrick Iber, *Neither Peace Nor Freedom: The Cultural Cold War in Latin America* (Cambridge, MA: Harvard University Press, 2015); Enrique Krauze, *Redeemers: Ideas and Power in Latin America* (New York: HarperCollins, 2011); Jean Franco, *The Decline and Fall of the Lettered City: Latin America in the Cold War* (Cambridge, MA: Harvard University Press, 2002); Aldo Marchesi, *Latin America's Radical Left: Rebellion and Cold War in the Global 1960s* (New York: Cambridge University Press, 2018); Jorge Castañeda, *Utopia Unarmed: The Latin American Left after the Cold War* (New York: Vintage Books, 1993); Ronald Chilcote, "The Cold War and the Transformation of Latin American Studies in the United States," *Latin American Perspectives* 45, no. 4 (July 2018): 6–41; Victoria Langland, *Speaking of Flowers: Student Movements in the Making and Remembering of 1968 in Military Brazil* (Durham, NC: Duke University Press, 2013); Jaime Pensado, *Rebel Mexico: Student Unrest and Authoritarian Political Culture during the Long Sixties* (Stanford, CA: Stanford University Press, 2013); Heather Vrana, *This City Belongs to You: A History of Student Activism in Guatemala, 1944–1996* (Berkeley: University of California Press, 2017); Abraham Lowenthal and Martin Weinstein, eds., *Kalman Silvert: Engaging Latin America, Building Democracy* (Boulder, CO: Lynne Rienner, 2016); Daniela Spenser, *En combate: La vida de Lombardo Toledano* (Mexico City: Penguin Random House, 2018); Andrew Kirkendall, *Paulo Freire and the Cold War Politics of Literacy* (Chapel Hill: University of North Carolina Press, 2010); Todd Hartch, *The Prophet of Cuernavaca: Ivan Illich and the Crisis of the West* (New York: Oxford University Press, 2015); Jeremy Adelman, *Worldly Philosopher: The Odyssey of Albert O. Hirschman* (Princeton, NJ: Princeton University Press, 2013); and Mary Kay Vaughan, *Portrait of a Young Painter: Pepe Zúñiga and Mexico City's Rebel Generation* (Durham, NC: Duke University Press, 2014).

6. See, e.g., Arturo Escobar, *Encountering Development: The Making and Unmaking of the Third World* (Princeton, NJ: Princeton University Press, 1995); Mark Berger, *Under Northern Eyes: Latin American Studies and U.S. Hegemony in the Americas, 1898–1990* (Bloomington: Indiana University Press, 1995); Charles Bergquist, ed., *Alternative Approaches to the Prob-*

lem of Development: A Selected and Annotated Bibliography (Durham, NC: Carolina Academic Press, 1979); and Jeremy Adelman and Margarita Fajardo, "Between Capitalism and Democracy: A Study in the Political Economy of Ideas in Latin America, 1968–1980," *Latin American Research Review* 51, no. 3 (2016): 3–22. For more general, comparative studies by a US foreign relations scholar, see Michael Latham, *Modernization as Ideology: American Social Science and "Nation Building" in the Kennedy Era* (Chapel Hill: University of North Carolina Press, 2003), which analyzes how modernizationist assumptions influenced the Alliance for Progress in Latin America, and Latham, *The Right Kind of Development: Modernization, Development, and U.S. Foreign Policy from the Cold War to the Present* (Ithaca, NY: Cornell University Press, 2011).

7. This is certainly a trend that has transformed foreign relations history over the past decade—witness the enhanced profile of cultural history in the field's flagship journal *Diplomatic History*, in forums and debates on *H-Diplo*, and in sessions at the annual meetings of the Society for Historians of American Foreign Relations.

8. For a valuable recent review of the literature that is stronger on its foreign relations and political-economic dimensions than its cultural ones, see Andrew Kirkendall, "Cold War Latin America: The State of the Field," *H-Diplo*, essay 119, November 14, 2014.

9. Max Paul Friedman, "Retiring the Puppets, Bringing Latin America Back In: Recent Scholarship on United States–Latin American Relations," *Diplomatic History* 27, no. 5 (November 2003): 621–636, quote on 625.

10. As best I can determine, the initial catalyzing event for this cross-fertilization of area studies and foreign relations approaches was a major conference held in Mexico City in 2002, which was sponsored by Yale University, CIESAS-Mexico City, and the Cold War International History Project of the Woodrow Wilson International Center for Scholars. The three-day event, which followed two years of planning by Gil Joseph (Yale), Daniela Spenser (CIESAS-Mexico City), and Christian Ostermann (the director of the Cold War International History Project), assembled scholars and archivists across several disciplines and continents, and ultimately generated two volumes, *Espejos de la guerra fría: México, América Central y el Caribe,* ed. Daniela Spenser (Mexico City: CIESAS, 2004) and Joseph and Spenser, *In from the Cold,* which, along with a series of ensuing publications over the course of the next decade, are discussed below.

11. For a fuller discussion of trends in foreign relations scholarship on the Cold War, both internationally and for Latin America, before 2000, see Joseph, "What We Now Know," 8–16.

12. Melvyn Leffler, "Bringing It Together: The Parts and the Whole," in *Reviewing the Cold War: Approaches, Interpretations, Theory,* ed. Odd Arne Westad, 43–63 (London: Frank Cass, 2000), 56–57. Westad's collection is particularly useful in articulating the scholarly consensus on the Cold War's broad contours; see also Michael Hogan, ed., *America in the World: The Historiography of American Foreign Policy since 1941* (New York: Cambridge University Press, 1995).

13. Leffler, "Bringing It Together," 57.

14. Anders Stephanson, "Ideology and Neorealist Mirrors," *Diplomatic History* 17 (Spring 1993): 285–295, quote on 293.

15. John Lewis Gaddis, "The Long Peace: Elements of Stability in the Postwar International System," *International Security* 10 (Spring 1986): 99–142; later reprinted as the final chapter in Gaddis, *The Long Peace: Inquiries into the History of the Cold War* (New York: Oxford University Press, 1987). However, see Gaddis's more recent synthesis *The Cold War: A New History* (New York: Penguin Press, 2005), which stresses the agency of "visionaries" such as Ronald Reagan and Margaret Thatcher, who set about "sabotaging" the East–West stalemate by exploiting Soviet weaknesses and asserting the West's strengths. Since 9/11 and the reality of endless war in the Middle East, it has almost become fashionable in European and American circles, Left and Right alike, to feel a twinge of nostalgia for the Cold War—when James Bond and his adversaries at least played by some set of rules. James Buchan has written: "Those were the days: political caution and circumspection, the survival (as if in ice) of old institutions and manners, history so slow you could even become tired of it." Buchan, "The Superpowers' Balance Sheet," *The Guardian*, January 28, 2006. Of course, in Latin America and other parts of the Global South, where the Cold War was so much hotter, residents would be less prone to engage in such nostalgia.

16. Stephanson, "Ideology and Neorealist Mirrors," 294–295.

17. Mark T. Gilderhus, "An Emerging Synthesis? U.S.-Latin American Relations since the Second World War," in Hogan, *America in the World*, 424–461, quote on 424.

18. Greg Grandin, "Off the Beach: The United States, Latin America, and the Cold War," in *A Companion to Post-1945 America*, ed. Jean-Christophe Agnew and Roy Rosenzweig, 426–445 (New York: Blackwell, 2002), 426.

19. For a more nuanced discussion of these historiographical currents, see Joseph, "What We Now Know," 11–16.

20. Grandin, *Last Colonial Massacre*, xii.

21. Walter LaFeber, *Inevitable Revolutions: The United States in Central America* (New York: Norton, 1984). For subsequent strong Revisionist treatments, see William LeoGrande, *Our Own Backyard: The United States and Central America, 1977–1992* (Chapel Hill: University of North Carolina Press, 2000), and Stephen Rabe, *The Killing Zone: The United States Wages Cold War in Latin America*, 2nd ed. (New York: Oxford University Press, 2013). For a would-be corrective that seeks to balance Realist and Revisionist sensibilities, and ultimately depicts Latin America as caught between the two fires of Cuban revolutionary insurgency and a resulting orgy of US-supported counterinsurgent violence, see Hal Brands, *Latin America's Cold War* (Cambridge, MA: Harvard University Press, 2010).

22. For example, see John Lewis Gaddis, *We Now Know: Rethinking Cold War History* (New York: Oxford University Press, 1997) and Gaddis, *Cold War*.

23. Grandin, "Off the Beach," 430; see also Grandin, *Last Colonial Massacre*, 17.

24. Joseph, "What We Now Know," 7.

25. See, for example, Greg Grandin, "Living in Revolutionary Time: Coming to Terms with the Violence of Latin America's Long Cold War," in Grandin and Joseph, *Century of Revolution*, 1–42, esp. 11–18; Cecilia Menjívar and Néstor Rodríguez, eds., *When States Kill: Latin America, the U.S., and Technologies of Terror* (Austin: University of Texas Press, 2005); Martha Huggins, *Political Policing: The United States and Latin America* (Durham, NC: Duke Universi-

ty Press, 1998); Marguerite Feitlowitz, *A Lexicon of Terror: Argentina and the Legacies of Torture* (New York: Oxford University Press, 1998); and Leslie Gill, *The School of the Americas: Military Training and Political Violence in the Americas* (Durham, NC: Duke University Press, 2004).

26. J. Patrice McSherry, *Predatory States: Operation Condor and Covert War in Latin America* (Boulder, CO: Rowman and Littlefield, 2005); John Dinges, *The Condor Years: How Pinochet and His Allies Brought Terror to Three Continents* (New York: New Press, 2004); and Peter Kornbluh, *The Pinochet File: A Declassified Dossier on Atrocity and Accountability*, rev. ed. (New York: New Press, 2004). The now-published Truth Commission report and the Catholic Church's Recovery of Historical Memory report are invaluable sources for the escalation of violence in Guatemala, particularly in the western highlands. "Truth commission" reports, based on varying mandates, have also been published for El Salvador, Argentina, and Chile.

27. CNN *Cold War* documentary series, episode 10 (1999), "Cuba, 1959–1962," cited in Grandin, "Living in Revolutionary Time," 2.

28. In addition to the scholars whose work is discussed in the remainder of this section, see, e.g., Brands, *Latin America's Cold War*, and the 2018 Yale dissertations of the editors of this volume, Andra Chastain and Timothy Lorek, which are previewed in their individual chapters here. See Andra B. Chastain, "Vehicle of Progress: The Santiago Metro, Technopolitics, and State Formation in Chile, 1965–1989" (PhD diss., Yale University, 2018) and Timothy W. Lorek, "Developing Paradise: Agricultural Science in the Conflicted Landscapes of Colombia's Cauca Valley, 1927–1967" (PhD diss., Yale University, 2019).

29. Piero Gleijeses, *Conflicting Missions: Havana, Washington, and Cuba, 1959–1976* (Chapel Hill: University of North Carolina Press, 2002, and Gleijeses, *Visions of Freedom: Havana, Washington, Pretoria, and the Struggle for Southern Africa, 1976–1991* (Chapel Hill: University of North Carolina Press, 2013). Cuba's support of the armed Left in Latin America is evocatively treated in two biographies of Che Guevara: Jorge Castañeda, *Compañero: The Life and Death of Che Guevara* (New York: Vintage Books, 1997), and Jon Lee Anderson, *Che: A Revolutionary Life*, rev. ed. (New York: Grove Press, 2010), as well as in the second part of Steven Soderburgh's heavily researched film *Che*, which deals with the disastrous insurgency in Bolivia that cost Che his life in 1967.

30. See especially Ariel Armony, "Transnationalizing the Dirty War: Argentina in Central America," in Joseph and Spenser, *In from the Cold*, 134–168, which builds on his earlier monograph *Argentina, the United States, and the Anti-Communist Crusade in Central America, 1977–1984* (Athens: Ohio University Press, 1997).

31. Tanya Harmer, *Allende's Chile and the Inter-American Cold War* (Chapel Hill: University of North Carolina Press, 2011).

32. In these respects Harmer goes beyond Jonathan Haslam, *The Nixon Administration and the Death of Allende's Chile: A Case of Assisted Suicide* (New York: Verso, 2005), which is itself an example of effective analysis integrating international and domestic fields of power.

33. Harmer has also collaborated with the Chilean historian Alfredo Riquelme Segovia on a collection *Chile y la Guerra Fría global* (Santiago: RIL Editores, 2014), which deepens our understanding of the Cold War's impact on Chile by examining specific events, institutions, and parties in a variety of countries (e.g., Italy) that had relations bearing on Chilean affairs or

were influenced by them. For the previously neglected role of Chilean-French relations during the Cold War, see Chastain's essay in chapter 10 of this volume.

34. Marchesi, *Latin America's Radical Left*.

35. Marchesi's translocal discussion of the New Left nicely complements Raymond Craib's narrative history of Chile's generation of anarchists and a "capacious" Old Left during the tumultuous 1920s, a period that some now term the "first Cold War," discussed in the next section, "The Long Cold War."

36. For example, see Lorenzo Mayer, "La guerra fría en el mundo periférico: El caso del régimen autoritario mexicano. La utilidad del anticomunismo discreto," in Spenser, *Espejos de la guerra fría*, 95–118, and Jürgen Buchenau, "Por una guerra fría más templada: México entre el cambio revolucionario y la reacción estadounidense en Guatemala y Cuba," in Spenser, *Espejos de la guerra fría*, 119–149; Seth Fein, "Producing the Cold War in Mexico: The Public Limits of Covert Communications," in Joseph and Spenser, *In from the* Cold, 171–213; Eric Zolov, "Cuba sí, Yanquis no! The Sacking of the Instituto Cultural México-Norteamericano in Morelia, Michoacán, 1961," in Joseph and Spenser, *In from the Cold*, 214–252; Steven Bachelor, "Miracle on Ice: Industrial Workers and the Promise of Americanization in Cold War Mexico," in Joseph and Spenser, *In From the Cold*, 253–272; and Renata Keller, *Mexico's Cold War: Cuba, the United States, and the Legacy of the Mexican Revolution* (New York: Cambridge University Press, 2015. See also Seth Fein, "Myths of Cultural Imperialism and Nationalism in Golden Age Mexican Cinema," in *Fragments of a Golden Age: The Politics of Culture in Mexico since 1940*, ed. Gilbert Joseph, Anne Rubenstein, and Eric Zolov, 159–198 (Durham, NC: Duke University Press, 2001); Eric Zolov, "Discovering a Land 'Mysterious and Obvious': The Renarrativizing of Postrevolutionary Mexico," in Joseph, Rubenstein, and Zolov, *Fragments of a Golden Age*, 234–272; and Steven Bachelor, "Toiling for the 'New Invaders': Autoworkers, Transnational Corporations, and Working-Class Culture in Mexico City, 1955–1968," in Joseph, Rubenstein, and Zolov, *Fragments of a Golden Age*, 273–326.

37. See, for example, the essays in Paul Gillingham and Benjamin Smith, eds., *Dictablanda: Politics, Work, and Culture in Mexico, 1938–1968* (Durham, NC: Duke University Press, 2014); Elena Poniatowska, "El movimiento estudiantil de 1968," in *Fuerte es el silencio* (Mexico City: Ediciones Era, 1980), 34–77; Bachelor, "Miracle on Ice" and "Toiling for the 'New Invaders'"; Pensado, *Rebel Mexico*; Tanalís Padilla, *Rural Resistance in the Land of Zapata: The Jaramillista Movement and the Myth of the Pax Priísta* (Durham, NC: Duke University Press, 2009); Robert Alegre, *Railroad Radicals in Cold War Mexico: Gender, Class, and Memory* (Lincoln: University of Nebraska Press, 2014); Gladys McCormick, *The Logic of Compromise in Mexico: How the Countryside Was Key to the Emergence of Authoritarianism* (Chapel Hill: University of North Carolina Press, 2016); John Mraz, "Today, Tomorrow and Always: The Golden Age of Illustrated Magazines, 1937–1960," in Joseph, Rubenstein, and Zolov, *Fragments of a Golden Age*, 116–157. See also Eileen Ford, *Childhood and Modernity in Cold War Mexico City* (London: Bloomsbury Academic, 2018), which complements studies of the history of Cold War youth in the United States and the Soviet Union by examining the impact on children and families of the changing power relations brokered by Mexico's modernizing, increasingly exclusionary postrevolutionary state from World War II to 1968.

38. See, e.g., Alexander Aviña, *Specters of Revolution: Peasant Guerrillas in the Cold War Mexican Countryside* (New York: Oxford University Press, 2014); Adela Cedillo and Fernando Herrera Calderón, eds., *Challenging Authoritarianism in Mexico: Revolutionary Struggles and the Dirty War, 1964–1982* (London: Routledge, 2012); Marco Bellingeri, *Del agrarismo armado a la guerra de los pobres: Ensayos de guerrilla rural en el México contemporáneo, 1940–1974* (Mexico City: Ediciones Casa Juan Pablos, 2003). For a disturbing first-person testimony, see Alberto Ulloa Bornemann, *Surviving Mexico's Dirty War: A Political Prisoner's Memoir* (Philadelphia: Temple University Press, 2007).

39. Zolov, "Cuba sí, Yanquis no!"; Keller, *Mexico's Cold War.*

40. A recent anthology that is similarly dedicated to bringing Latin Americanists and foreign relations scholars together to showcase "the enormous complexity of the Cold War in the Western Hemisphere" and to "locate and explore a fertile middle ground" between narratives of rigid US repression and hegemony and scenarios of local agency and contingency, is Virginia Garrard-Burnett, Mark Atwood Lawrence, and Julio Moreno, eds., *Beyond the Eagle's Shadow: New Histories of Latin America's Cold War* (Albuquerque: University of New Mexico Press, 2013), which focuses on the 1960s, 1970s, and 1980s. On widening processes of social conflict emanating in the Global South, see Westad, *Global Cold War,* and Grandin, *Last Colonial Massacre.*

41. Grandin, "Living in Revolutionary Time," 29; see also Greg Grandin, *Empire's Workshop: Latin America, the United States, and the Rise of the New Imperialism* (New York: Metropolitan Books, 2005).

42. Grandin, "Living in Revolutionary Time," esp. 29; Gilbert M. Joseph, "Latin America's Long Cold War: A Century of Revolutionary Process and U.S. Power," in Grandin and Joseph, *Century of Revolution,* 397–414.

43. For a fuller discussion, see Joseph, "Latin America's Long Cold War," 400–411.

44. Joseph, "What We Now Know," 20. See the essays by Jocelyn Olcott (Mexico), Jeffrey Gould (El Salvador), and Thomas Klubock (Chile) in *A Century of Revolution,* Part I: "The First Cold War": Jocelyn Olcott, *"Mueras y matanza*: Spectacles of Terror and Violence in Postrevolutionary Mexico," 62–87; Jeffrey R. Gould, "On the Road to 'El Porvenir': A Revolutionary and Counterrevolutionary Violence in El Salvador and Nicaragua," 88–120; Thomas Miller Klubock, "Ránquil: Violence and Peasant Politics on Chile's Southern Frontier," 121–161."

45. Adelman and Fajardo, "Between Capitalism and Democracy"; Bergquist, *Alternative Approaches.*

46. Grandin, *Last Colonial Massacre.*

47. Grandin, "Living in Revolutionary Time, 31.

48. Grandin, "Living in Revolutionary Time," 31–32; Joseph, "Latin America's Long Cold War," 407–408.

49. Joseph, "What We Now Know," 5–7; Joseph, "Latin America's Long Cold War," 408–411.

50. For example, see Sergio Aguayo Quesada, *La charola: Una historia de los servicios de inteligencia en México* (Mexico City: Grijalbo, 2001); Feitlowitz, "Lexicon of Terror"; Menjívar and Rodríguez, *When States Kill*; Gill, *School of the Americas*; Florencia Mallon, *Courage Tastes of Blood: The Mapuche Community of Nicolás Ailío and the Chilean State, 1905–2001* (Durham,

NC: Duke University Press, 2005), esp. chap. 5; Ulloa Bornemann, *Surviving Mexico's Dirty War*; Jacobo Timmerman, *Prisoner without a Name, Cell without a Number* (Madison: University of Wisconsin Press, 1981); Rigoberta Menchú, *Me llamo Rigoberta Menchú y así me nació la conciencia* (Barcelona: Editorial Argos Vergara, 1983); Ariel Dorfman, *Death and the Maiden* (New York: Penguin Plays, 1994); Marjorie Agosín, *Tapestries of Hope, Threads of Love: The Arpillera Movement in Chile*, 2nd ed. (Boulder, CO: Rowman and Littlefield, 2008).

51. See the forum of commentary and debate that was generated in 2009 in *H-Diplo* by Joseph and Spenser's volume *In from the Cold*, especially the exchange between William LeoGrande and Joseph and Spenser regarding the popular appropriation of Cold War ideologies. *H-Diplo Roundtable Reviews* 10, no. 23 (2009), ed. Thomas Maddux and Diane Labrosse, with reviews by Max Paul Friedman, Greg Grandin, William M. LeoGrande, Alan McPherson, and Richard Saull, www.h-net.org/~diplo/roundtables.

52. Grandin, *Last Colonial Massacre*, 185–186.

53. Carlota McAllister, "Rural Markets, Revolutionary Souls, and Rebellious Women in Cold War Guatemala," in Joseph and Spenser, *In from the Cold*, 350–377; McAllister, "A Headlong Rush into the Future: Violence and Revolution in a Guatemalan Indigenous Village," in Grandin and Joseph, *Century of Revolution*, 276–308; McAllister, *The Good Road: Conscience and Consciousness in a Post-Revolutionary Mayan Village in Guatemala* (Durham, NC: Duke University Press, forthcoming).

54. I am indebted to Greg Grandin for bringing the papal encyclical to my attention.

55. See especially Grandin, *Last Colonial Massacre*, 181–184. Evoking the shifting struggles of mostly Q'eqchi' Maya peasants and plantation workers from the coffee-producing region of Alta Verapaz, he develops the concept of an "insurgent individuality," which always existed "in relation to more encumbered social and cultural identities," to show how Guatemala's homegrown Communist Party (the PGT) was able to bridge "the fault lines of modernity, linking nation and world, community and state, and self and society." In effect, Guatemala's Old Left PGT, its class-based, male, modernist, urban bias notwithstanding, allowed itself to be driven by particular grievances , past struggles (especially access to land and an end to forced labor going back generations), and diverse identities in the countryside. This enabled it to encompass a multitude of experiences and subjectivities on the ground. The PGT's leader alluded to the party's bridging mission when he wrote: "To be universal, one has to be from somewhere." After the 1954 coup against Arbenz's social democratic regime, a new generation of vanguardist revolutionaries dismissed the PGT's attempt to usher in progressive capitalism as misguided, in view of US intervention, and irrelevant, in the wake of the Cuban Revolution. Banned and persecuted by the military-led state, but still influential in its highland centers of strength, the PGT ultimately, and only grudgingly, allied with these New Left rebels. Later, in 1966, when its leaders were executed by a US-trained elite counterinsurgency unit, and the PGT was obliterated, Grandin chronicles the transition at the grassroots level of the Old Left into the New Left, examining mobilizations in the face of a particularly intense form of terror that peaked in the Scorched Earth campaign of the early 1980s.

56. A debate exists in the literature between scholars like Grandin, McAllister, and Florencia Mallon (e.g., in *Courage Tastes of Blood*), who historicize subaltern participation, con-

sciousness, and agency in Cold War armed struggles and others, such as David Stoll and Jorge Castañeda (*Utopia Disarmed*), who reduce grassroots episodes of armed struggle to a more formulaic (and ultimately tragic) equation in which romantic, Guevarist (or Maoist) elite intellectuals-turned-vanguardist revolutionaries ran amok, manipulating and coercing desperate and repressed campesinos into their ranks and then reaping a whirlwind of violence at the hands of homicidal military regimes. For the classic formulation of this thesis in which Guatemalan indigenous peasants are caught between "two fires" or armies (often rendered as the *dos demonios* thesis in Spanish), see David Stoll, *Rigoberta Menchú and the Story of All Poor Guatemalans* (Boulder, CO: Westview Press, 1999), and its predecessor *Between Two Armies in the Ixil Towns of Guatemala* (New York: Columbia University Press, 1993), which sparked an acrimonious international debate with Menchú, an icon of the indigenous Maya and international Left and the recipient of the Nobel Peace Prize in 1992. See, e.g., Arturo Arias, ed., *The Rigoberta Menchú Controversy* (Minneapolis: University of Minnesota Press, 2001). For a state-of-the art collection on the Maoist Shining Path (Sendero Luminoso) movement, which is particularly strong in explaining the dynamics of participation in and opposition to it by local Andean communities in the 1980s and early 1990s, see Steve J. Stern, ed., *Shining and Other Paths: War and Society in Peru, 1980–1995* (Durham, NC: Duke University Press, 1998). The volume includes a distinguished cast of Peruvian and international scholars and commentators who skillfully position this heterodox movement within the context of the Latin American and global Cold War. Also see Gerardo Rénique, "'People's War,' 'Dirty War': Cold War Legacy and the End of History in Postwar Peru," in Grandin and Joseph, *Century of Revolution*, 309–337, for a discussion of Sendero within a broader context of insurgent and counterinsurgent politics in Cold War Peru.

57. For a pioneering article by the director of the National Security Archive at George Washington University, on how forensic approaches and a dramatically increased corpus of declassified archives have revolutionized this research, see Thomas Blanton, "Recovering the Memory of the Cold War: Forensic History and Latin America," in Joseph and Spenser, *In from the Cold*, 47–73. On how Cold War "archives of violence" themselves serve as a power point of mobilization around questions of truth, justice, and reconciliation, see Kirsten Weld's pathbreaking study of the recently discovered Guatemalan Police archives, *Paper Cadavers: The Archives of Dictatorship in Guatemala* (Durham, NC: Duke University Press, 2014); for a similar inquiry using a different set of archives for Argentina, see Marco Ramos, "Making Disappearance Visible: Psychoanalysis, Trauma, and Human Rights in Cold War Argentina" (PhD diss., Yale University, 2017). For a bold new treatment of memory politics on both sides of the Florida Straits, see Michael Bustamante, "Cuban Counterpoints: Memory Struggles in Revolution and Exile, 1959–1980" (PhD diss., Yale University, 2016). The main contributions to this literature engage political and memory struggles in Chile, most notably the scholarship of Steve Stern, discussed immediately below. See also recent contributions by Marian Schlotterbeck, *Beyond the Vanguard: Everyday Revolutionaries in Allende's Chile* (Berkeley: University of California Press, 2018); Alison Bruey, *Bread, Justice, and Liberty: Grassroots Activism and Human Rights in Pinochet's Chile* (Madison: University of Wisconsin Press, 2018); and Mario Garcés Durán and Sebastián Leiva, *Golpe en La Legua: Los caminos de la historia y la memoria* (Santiago: LOM, 2005).

58. Steve J. Stern, *Remembering Pinochet's Chile: On the Eve of London 1998* (Durham, NC: Duke University Press, 2004); Stern, *Battling for Hearts and Minds: Memory Struggles in Pinochet's Chile, 1973–1988* (Durham, NC: Duke University Press, 2006); and Stern, *Reckoning with Pinochet: The Memory Question in Democratic Chile, 1989–2006* (Durham, NC: Duke University Press, 2010).

59. See the series of books (Memorias de la Represión), edited beginning in 2002 by Elizabeth Jelin and others, which emerged out of SSRC's long-term project "Collective Memory of Repression in the Southern Cone." The series, published by Siglo XXI Editores, started with a volume edited by Jelin and Ludmila da Silva Catela, *Los archivos de la repression: Documentos, memoria y verdad* (Madrid: Siglo XXI Editores, 2002), which was inspired by the intensely collaborative Memoria Abierta project in Argentina. For a discussion of Memoria Abierta, see Blanton, "Recovering the Memory of the Cold War, " 64–65.

60. Mary Louise Pratt, *Imperial Eyes: Travel Writing and Transculturation* (New York: Routledge, 1992). Also still useful for understanding transnational and transcultural realms and processes are William Roseberry, "Americanization in the Americas," in *Anthropologies and Histories: Essays in Culture, History, and Political Economy,* ed. Roseberry (New Brunswick, NJ: Rutgers University Press, 1994), 80–124; and Amy Kaplan and Donald Pease, eds., *Cultures of United States Imperialism* (Durham, NC: Duke University Press, 1993).

61. See, e.g., Ricardo Salvatore, "The Enterprise of Knowledge: Representational Machines of Informal Empire," in *Close Encounters of Empire: Writing the History of U.S.-Latin American Cultural Relations,* ed. Gilbert M. Joseph, Catherine C. LeGrand, and Ricardo Salvatore (Durham, NC: Duke University Press, 1998); and Salvatore, *Disciplinary Conquest: U.S. Scholars in South America, 1900–1945* (Durham, NC: Duke University Press, 2016). See also Gerard Colby with Charlotte Dennett, *Thy Will Be Done: The Conquest of the Amazon: Nelson Rockefeller and Evangelism in the Age of Oil* (New York: HarperCollins, 1995).

62. For a fuller discussion, see Gilbert M. Joseph, "Close Encounters: Towards a New Cultural History of U.S.-Latin American Relations," in Joseph, LeGrand, and Salvatore, *Close Encounters of Empire,* 3–46. On the relevance of "contact zones," see also "The Nation and Beyond," a special issue of the *Journal of American History* (December 1999), especially David Thelan's essay, "The Nation and Beyond: Transnational Perspectives on United States History," 976–986. Thelan gives particular attention to "how people and ideas and institutions and cultures move above, below, through, and around, as well as within the nation state" (976).

63. See, e.g., Julio E. Moreno, "Coca-Cola, U.S. Diplomacy, and the Cold War in America's Backyard," in Garrard-Burnett, Lawrence, and Moreno, *Beyond the Eagle's Shadow,* 21–50; Bachelor, "Toiling for the 'New Invaders'"; Jason Colby, *The Business of Empire: United Fruit, Race, and U.S. Expansion in Central America* (Ithaca, NY: Cornell University Press, 2013); Andrew Paxman, *Jenkins of Mexico: How A Southern Farm Boy Became a Mexican Magnate* (New York: Oxford University Press, 2017).

64. See, e.g., Fein, "Myths of Cultural Imperialism"; Seth Fein, "Everyday Forms of Transnational Collaboration: U.S. Film Propaganda in Cold War Mexico," in Joseph, LeGrand, and Salvatore, *Close Encounters of Empire,* 400–450; Fein, "New Empire into Old: Making Mexican Newsreels the Cold War Way," *Diplomatic History* 28, no. 5 (November 2004): 703–748; Jessi-

ca Stites-Mor, *Transition Cinema: Political Filmmaking and the Argentine Left since 1968* (Pittsburgh: University of Pittsburgh Press, 2012); Alison Greene, "Cablevision(nation) in Rural Yucatán: Performing Modernity and *Mexicanidad* in the Early 1990s," in Joseph, Rubenstein, and Zolov, *Fragments of a Golden Age*, 415–451; Omar Hernández and Emil McAnany, "Cultural Industries in the Free Trade Age: A Look at Mexican Television," in Joseph, Rubenstein, and Zolov, *Fragments of a Golden Age*, 389–414.

65. See, e.g., Julio Moreno, *Yankee Don't Go Home: Mexican Nationalism, American Business Culture, and the Shaping of Modern Mexico, 1920–1950* (Chapel Hill: University of North Carolina Press, 2003); Heather Levi, "Masked Media: The Adventures of Lucha Libre on the Small Screen," in Joseph, Rubenstein, and Zolov, *Fragments of a Golden Age*, 330–372; Victoria Langland, "Birth Control Pills and Molotov Cocktails: Reading Sex and Revolution in 1968 Brazil," in Joseph and Spenser, *In from the Cold*, 308–349.

66. See, e.g., Susan Fitzpatrick-Behrens, *The Maryknoll Catholic Mission in Peru, 1943–1989: Transnational Faith and Transformation* (Notre Dame, IN: University of Notre Dame Press, 2012); Christian Smith, *Resisting Reagan: The U.S Central American Peace Movement* (Chicago: University of Chicago Press, 1996); Susan Bibler Coutin, *The Culture of Protest: Religious Activism and the U.S. Sanctuary Movement* (Boulder, CO: Westview Press, 1993); Virginia Garrard-Burnett, *Protestantism in Guatemala: Living in the New Jerusalem* (Austin: University of Texas Press, 1998); and Garrard-Burnett, *Terror in the Land of the Holy Spirit: Guatemala under General Efraín Ríos Montt,1982–1983* (New York: Oxford University Press, 2010).

67. See, e.g., James N. Green, *We Cannot Remain Silent: Opposition to the Brazilian Military Dictatorship in the United States* (Durham, NC: Duke University Press, 2010); Jessica Stites-Mor, ed., *Human Rights and Transnational Solidarity in Cold War Latin America* (Madison: University of Wisconsin Press, 2013); William Schmidli, *The Fate of Freedom Elsewhere: Human Rights and U.S. Cold War Policy towards Argentina* (Ithaca, NY: Cornell University Press, 2013); Smith, *Resisting Reagan*; Margaret Keck and Kathryn Sikkink, *Activists beyond Borders: Advocacy Networks in International Politics* (Ithaca, NY: Cornell University Press, 1998); James Jenkins, "The Indian Wing: Nicaraguan Indians, Native American Activists, and U.S. Foreign Policy, 1979–1990," in Garrard-Burnett, Lawrence, and Moreno, *Beyond the Eagle's Shadow*, 175–199. Lars Schoultz, *Human Rights and United States Policy toward Latin America* (Princeton, NJ: Princeton University Press, 1981 [repr. 2016]), remains an enduring classic.

68. See, e.g., Armony, "Transnationalizing the Dirty War"; Peter Kornbluh and Malcom Byrne, eds., *The Iran-Contra Scandal: The Declassified History* (New York: New Press, 1983); Christopher Dickey, *With the Contras: A Reporter in the Wilds of Nicaragua* (New York: Simon and Schuster, 1985); Thomas Walker, ed., *Reagan vs. the Sandinista: The Undeclared War in Nicaragua* (Boulder, CO: Westview Press, 1987); Philip Williams and Knut Walter, *Militarization and Demilitarization in El Salvador's Transition to Democracy* (Pittsburgh: University of Pittsburgh Press, 1997).

69. Ernesto Capello, "Imaginaciones hemisféricas: La misión presidencial a América Latina de Nelson Rockefeller en 1969," in *La guerra fría cultural en América Latina: Desafíos y limites para una nueva mirada de las relaciones interamericanas*, ed. Benedetta Calandra and Marina Franco (Buenos Aires: Editorial Biblos, 2012), 181–194; Fernando Purcell, "El Cuerpo de Paz

y la guerra fría global en Chile (1961–1970)," in Calandra and Franco, *La guerra fría cultural*, 167–180.

70. See, e.g., Seth's Fein's articles "Producing the Cold War in Mexico"; "Myths of Cultural Imperialism"; "Everyday Forms of Transnational Collaboration"; and "New Empire into Old," which tease out the critical role of the USIA and the Office of the Coordinator of Inter-American Affairs in the politics of culture in Cold War Mexico; also see Francisco Rodríguez Jiménez, "'Maquinaria imperfecta': La United States Information Agency y el Departamento de Estado en los inicios de la Guerra Fría," in Calandra and Franco, *La guerra fría cultural*, 97–113.

71. See, e.g., the essays in Lowenthal and Weinstein, *Kalman Silvert*, esp. the editors' introduction and Gilbert M. Joseph, "Kalman Silvert and Latin American Studies Today," 175–180; Chilcote, "Cold War"; and Berger, *Under Northern Eyes*.

72. See, e.g., Robert Arnove, ed., *Philanthropy and Cultural Imperialism: The Foundations at Home and Abroad* (Bloomington: Indiana University Press, 1980); Edward Berman, *The Influence of the Carnegie, Ford, and Rockefeller Foundations on American Foreign Policy: The Ideology of Philanthropy* (Albany: State University of New York Press, 1983); Elizabeth Cobbs, *The Rich Neighbor Policy: Rockefeller and Kaiser in Brazil* (New Haven, CT: Yale University Press, 1992); and Marcos Cueto, ed., *Missionaries of Science: The Rockefeller Foundation in Latin America* (Bloomington: Indiana University Press, 1992).

73. See, for example, Fernando Purcell's insightful research, previewed in "El Cuerpo de Paz," on the multivalent encounters and often autonomous identities that US Peace Corps volunteers forged with their host communities.

74. See, e.g., Fein, "Myths of Cultural Imperialism"; Fein, "Everyday Forms of Transnational Collaboration"; and Fein, "New Empire into Old." Fein's ongoing research looks at the use of transnational television programming in the selling of solidarity and neighborly constructions of the Alliance for Progress. He is also experimenting with interdisciplinary, multimedia installations to evoke cultural linkages between Cold War–era New York City and Latin America.

75. See Ricardo Salvatore, ed., *Culturas imperiales: Experiencia y representación en América, Asia y África* (Buenos Aires: Beatriz Viterbo Editora, 2005). The volume grew out of an international conference at the Universidad Torcuato Di Tella in 2000 that was sponsored by Di Tella and Yale University and assembled a diverse group of scholars dedicated to rethinking imperialism and foreign relations comparatively and over a long duration.

76. See especially Calandra and Franco's introduction, "Desafíos y limites para una nueva mirada de las relaciones interamericanas," in *La guerra fría cultural*, 9–32; Eduardo Rey Tristán, "Estados Unidos y América Latina durante la Guerra Fría: La dimensión cultural," in Calandra and Franco, *La guerra fría cultural*, 51–65; and Ixel Quesada Vargas, "Los orígenes de la presencia cultural de Estados Unidos en Centroamérica: Fundamentos ideológicos y usos políticos del debate sobre los trópicos (1900–1940)," in Calandra and Franco, *La guerra fría cultural*, 67–77.

77. See, e.g., Berger, *Under Northern Eyes*; Joseph, "Close Encounters," esp. 10–13; Bergquist, *Alternative Approaches*.

78. Chilcote, "Cold War," 6 (emphasis added). Chilcote's engrossing account provides document-based analysis and occasionally doubles as a memoir of the radical Latin Americanist Left in the 1960s and 1970s.

79. Chilcote, "Cold War," 7.

80. Chilcote, "Cold War," 7–35. Chilcote's recollections of LASA's early years are corroborated by my reading of the association's early newsletters, which are housed at its headquarters at the University of Pittsburgh.

81. Chilcote, "Cold War," 13. On Project Camelot, see Irving Louis Horwitz, ed., *The Rise and Fall of Project Camelot* (Cambridge, MA: MIT Press, 1967); on the "Marginality Project," see Mariano Ben Plotkin, "U.S. Foundations, Cultural Imperialism, and Transnational Misunderstandings: The Case of the Marginality Project," *Journal of Latin American Studies* 47, no. 1 (2015): 65–92; on the São Paulo Business School, see Bill Cooke and Rafael Alcadipani, "Towards a Global History of Management Education: The Case of the Ford Foundation and the São Paulo School of Business Administration," *Academy of Management Learning and Education* 14 (2015): 482–499.

82. Chilcote, "Cold War," 13.

83. Plotkin, "U.S. Foundations," 73. For Silvert's promotion of Latin American studies through Ford, see Lowenthal and Weinstein, *Kalman Silvert*.

84. Chilcote, "Cold War," 19–22; see also Jawdat Abu-El-Haj, "Latin American Perspectives: A Progressive Collective Intellectual and Its Social Knowledge," *Latin American Perspectives* 40, no. 6 (2013): 11–55; Donald Bray, *The Korean War and Aftermath: A Personal Story* (Bloomington: Indiana University Press, 2011), 58–59.

85. Chilcote, "Cold War," 21–22; see also Sol Stein, "A Short Account of International Student Politics and the Cold War with Particular Reference to the NSA, CIA, etc." *Ramparts* 5 (March 1967): 29–38; Frances Stoner Saunders, *The Cultural Cold War: The CIA and the World of Arts and Letters* (New York: New Press, 1999); and Karen Paget, *Patriotic Betrayal: The Inside Story of the CIA's Secret Campaign to Enroll American Students in the Crusade against Communism* (New Haven, CT: Yale University Press, 2015). On the CCF and its development, see Iber, *Neither Peace nor Freedom*.

86. Iber, *Neither Peace nor Freedom*, 243. Iber's insightful discussion of debates among intellectuals and contests between their principal periodicals in "the cultural Cold War" emphasizes its long trajectory, which predated the Cuban Revolution by as much as four decades and included extensive debates within the Left itself.

87. The essays in Lowenthal and Weinstein, *Kalman Silvert*, about his work at Ford, as well as Ford's subsequent sponsorship, with SSRC, of the lengthy hemispheric project on memory and repression, led by Steve Stern and several Latin American colleagues, bear out Ford's metamorphosis as the Cold War lengthened and got hotter.

88. Chilcote, "Cold War," 22–23.

89. Anne-Emanuelle Birn and Raúl Nechochea López, "Introduction," in *Calenturas! Health and Medicine in Cold War Latin America* (Durham, NC: Duke University Press, forthcoming).

90. For a discussion of these "desencuentros," see Marco Ramos, "'Pyschotherapy of the Oppressed': Anticolonialism and Psychoanalysis in Cold War Buenos Aires," in Birn and Necochea López, *Calenturas!,* forthcoming, and Ramos, "Making Disappearance Visible."

91. A new volume, Manuel R. Rodríguez Vázquez and Silvia Álvarez Curbelo, eds., *Tiempos binarios: La Guerra Fría desde Puerto Rico y el Caribe* (San Juan: Ediciones Callejón, 2017), establishes Puerto Rico's distinctive mediating position in the Cold War between the United States and the greater Caribbean region. It is particularly insightful in terms of the period's cultural history, interrogating reductive binaries and fleshing out more complex Cold War mindsets and attitudes. The volume includes an essay by editor Rodríguez Vázquez, "Imaginar el desastre: Aprensiones nucleares, desvaríos radiactivos y Defensa Civil en Puerto Rico, 1960–1965," which he presented at the 2016 Yale conference that gave rise to *Itineraries of Expertise.*

92. Tanya Harmer, "Review of *The Ideological Origins of the Dirty War* by Federico Finchelstein," *Cold War History* 15 (2015): 419; Thomas C. Field, Stella Krepp, and Vanni Pettinà, Introduction to *Latin America and the Global Cold War* (Chapel Hill: University of North Carolina Press, 2020).

93. The hundreds of distinctive, brilliantly colored, multilingual posters designed by international artists for OSPAAAL, from the organization's origins in 1966 until the mid-1980s, and then intermittently afterward, are themselves a valuable source for Cold War cultural history.

94. See the essays in Field, Krepp, and Pettinà, *Latin America and the Global Cold War*; for precursor initiatives in Mexico, see Christy Thornton's volume, *Revolution in Development: Mexico and the Governance of the Global Economy* (Berkeley: University of California Press, forthcoming).

PART I

AGRARIAN ANTECEDENTS AND RURAL DEVELOPMENT

2

TRANSPLANTING "EL TENESÍ"

Mexican Planners in the US South during the Cold War Era

Tore C. Olsson

In May 1947, Mexico's president Miguel Alemán made the first public state visit to the United States since the outbreak of the Mexican Revolution. The visit was a momentous one, intended to showcase the two countries' warming relationship after decades of tension and distrust. Alemán was greeted by crowds and confetti. In Washington, he addressed the US Congress; in New York, he rode in a parade given in his honor. But after these expected visits to the political and economic capitals of the United States, Alemán surprised observers with an unexpected detour: he set course for northern Alabama and eastern Tennessee. What guided Alemán to this improbable corner of the US South was not whim or coincidence—it was a pilgrimage to observe the works of the Tennessee Valley Authority (TVA), the massive, multistate experiment in hydraulic social engineering undertaken by Franklin D. Roosevelt's New Deal of the 1930s.

Alemán's first stop was Chattanooga, Tennessee, where he toured the concrete leviathan of Chickamauga Dam on the Tennessee River. The president was stunned by the panorama before him, and he eagerly listened to his hosts describe how science and state planning had harnessed the river's wild energy to reverse the region's poverty and desperation. Standing before the dam, Alemán pondered this "great experiment, of which [Mexico] can and will take the greatest advantage." The next day, in Muscle Shoals, Alabama, the president met a family of former cotton sharecroppers who spoke of becoming independent landowners through TVA fertilizers and electricity. "We have much land in my country which is as worthless as that which you have improved," gushed Alemán to the family, and "what you have shown me

FIGURE 2.1. President Miguel Alemán with a family of former sharecroppers in Muscle Shoals, Alabama, May 6, 1947. Image no. KX-02828-A1. Courtesy of the Tennessee Valley Authority.

here today will be most valuable to us in planning the same kind of program in Mexico."[1]

The visit made big news at home; as a headline in Mexico City declared the following day, "Alemán observed yesterday in Tennessee what he proposes to do in Mexico." Such proclamations were not merely rhetorical bluster, but would provide the spark for one of the largest state-led development projects in twentieth-century Mexico. Soon thereafter the federal government broke ground on two river valley commissions, the Comisión del Papaloapan and the Comisión del Tepalcatepec, targeting coastal southeastern and southwestern Mexico, respectively. Both were vast campaigns to engineer rivers into motors of economic and demographic growth through dam building, electrification, road construction, and sanitation programs. These projects marked the apex of nationalist state-led development in postrevolutionary Mexico, yet paradoxically, their genesis was transnational.[2]

This essay probes that contradiction. What follows is not a comparative history of hydraulic social engineering in the United States and Mexico, but instead a *history of comparisons*—a history of how experts and politicians imagined long-distant places as sources of inspiration and legitimacy. Curiously, it is also a story about the collision of Latin American and US

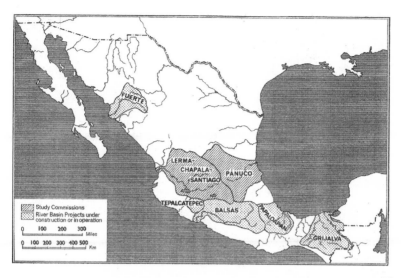

FIGURE 2.2. Mexican river valley commissions by 1963. The Papaloapan and Tepal-catepec commissions predate the rest, both founded in 1947. From David Barkin and Timothy King, *Regional Economic Development: The River Basin Approach in Mexico* (New York: Cambridge University Press, 1970), 95.

southern history—a collision that is rarely acknowledged. Nevertheless, the twentieth-century South—with its history of plantation agriculture, uneven land tenure, racial stratification, and one-party politics—might well represent the northernmost reach of Latin America. Indeed, scholars of US-Latin American relations would benefit much by grappling further with how the complexities of US regionalism mediated those uneven encounters. Too often, we imagine the United States as a monolithic industrial juggernaut, eager to impose a singular model of economic development on incompatible Latin American societies. Yet in the middle of the twentieth century, the United States was a patchwork nation of rich and poor, rural and urban, whose complex history of growth *and* stagnation informed those who hoped to translate its lessons abroad.[3]

If there were a multiplicity of US models that Latin American experts selected from during the Cold War, there were also a multiplicity of meanings that any model might take upon transplantation. This essay examines two Mexican river valley commissions born from paeans to the TVA. Despite their common parentage, however, the two were a striking study in contrasts. Indeed, their divergence reflected Mexico's turbulent turn from a revolutionary to postrevolutionary regime during the transitional decade of the 1940s. On the one hand, the Papaloapan Commission of Veracruz and Oaxaca was Alemán's pet project, a quixotic, grandiose, and ill-conceived effort to remake the landscape and society of the Papaloapan River basin while simultaneously monumentalizing the ruling party's power and legitimacy. Alemán, president from 1946 to 1952, symbolized the rightward turn of Mexico's ruling party away from revolutionary redistribution, and his coastal undertaking followed suit. On the other hand, the Tepalcatepec Commission of Michoacán was proposed and led by none other than Mexico's most renowned champion of campesino interests, the former president Lázaro Cárdenas (1934–1940), who believed that his commission should buttress the cooperative agricultural system enshrined by his administration's program of land reform. The contrasting careers of the Papaloapan and Tepalcatepec projects, alongside their successes and failures, reveal that lessons drawn from the US South could be reinvented to justify wildly diverse political agendas in Mexico.

The Tennessee Valley Authority and Rural Development

In the US South, the Tennessee River is rivaled in historical significance only by the Mississippi. With its headwaters in the Appalachian mountain valleys of northeastern Tennessee, the river flows 650 miles into northern Alabama and middle Tennessee before emptying into the Ohio River in Kentucky. Along that winding path, dozens of tributaries reach out like capillaries, creating a river valley basin that encompasses more than 40,000 square miles. Yet despite the wealth of land, water, and timber resources within the river's basin, the region was one of the poorest in the United States at the beginning of the twentieth century. This poverty was born in part from the scarcity of cash and credit that plagued the entire post–Civil War South, but it was exacerbated by the extractive, semicolonial industries that dominated the valley, particularly mining, logging, and cotton monoculture. Most of the valley's residents were farmers in 1930. White smallholders dominated the more mountainous northeastern portions, whereas northern Alabama and western Tennessee more closely resembled Deep South plantation counties. In total, 11 percent of the valley's population was African American, although most black residents were concentrated in western plantation regions. On the eve of the Great Depression, rates of farm tenancy in some of the valley's cotton-growing zones neared 70 percent, and soil erosion was rampant. To many contemporary observers, the Tennessee Valley was a symbol of deprivation and backwardness.[4]

During World War I, government bureaucrats and business boosters first targeted the fickle wildness of the Tennessee River as a primary obstacle to regional growth. In 1918, the US federal government began constructing a hydroelectric dam in northern Alabama, but once completed in 1925 it languished as private and public forces battled over its control. It was only with

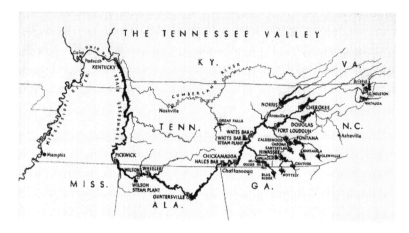

FIGURE 2.3. The Tennessee River and TVA dams along its course. Courtesy of Tennessee Valley Authority.

the political ascendance of Franklin D. Roosevelt in 1933 that the Tennessee Valley would see a dramatic infusion of federal antipoverty spending. Entering the White House with a popular mandate to combat the Depression by any means necessary, Roosevelt unveiled a bewildering array of experimental programs during his first months in office. Few were more ambitious than his vision for the Tennessee River. In April 1933, Roosevelt presented a bill to Congress to charter a government corporation that he dubbed the Tennessee Valley Authority. The authority, in Roosevelt's proposal, would transcend traditional geopolitical boundaries and address the problems of a "complete river watershed involving many States and the future lives and welfare of millions." It would construct more than a dozen hydroelectric dams and administer a distribution of their fruits to local people. The TVA was to be a showcase of the possibilities of state planning: it centralized power in an autonomous agency that answered only to the president, and made that agency responsible for remaking a vast multistate region.[5]

In Mexico during the 1940s, pundits and politicians often referred to a singular "TVA idea" when invoking the promise of US rural development. In reality, the TVA's first decade was marked by radically competing visions regarding the agency's goals. The language of Roosevelt's 1933 bill was deliberately vague, and it was left up to a three-member board of directors to determine exactly what sort of change the TVA would pursue in the valley. The chair of that board, and the most significant policymaker during the agency's first years, was Arthur E. Morgan. Trained as a hydraulic engineer, Morgan was deeply influenced by the utopian socialism of the writer Edward Bellamy and believed that small, self-sustaining agrarian communities coupled with localized industry could serve as an antidote to the chaos of urban civiliza-

tion. Morgan's romantic idealism was balanced out by his two colleagues on
the board: Harcourt A. Morgan and David Lilienthal. Harcourt Morgan—of
no relation to Arthur—was the board's agricultural expert, trained as an en-
tomologist and far more comfortable in partnering with the valley's larger
and wealthier farmers. But Arthur Morgan's most formidable counterweight
on the TVA board was Lilienthal, an Indiana lawyer. To Lilienthal, electrification was the panacea for the valley's ills, but unlike Arthur Morgan, he
saw it as a means to the ultimate goal of urbanization, industrialization, and
creating consumers who would participate in a national market. Lilienthal
entertained few of Morgan's sympathies for agrarian subsistence.[6]

Despite feuds and rivalries, in its heady first years the agency made a profound impact on the Tennessee Valley. Within a decade, the TVA had built
sixteen new multipurpose dams on the Tennessee River and its tributaries,
moving more than a hundred million cubic yards of concrete, rock, and soil.
Dams created massive reservoirs, which both tamed the river for navigabil-
ity and evicted tens of thousands of former residents. But dams represented
only the tip of the iceberg. The agency complemented dams with hundreds
of miles of highways and railroads, alongside thousands of miles of electrical
line. Fertilizer plants powered by hydroelectricity synthesized nitrogen from
the atmosphere and sold their products at low prices to local farmers, in an effort to revive exhausted and eroded soils. TVA public health employees also
penetrated rural communities to wage war on malaria and other preventable
diseases.[7]

But as the TVA gathered momentum, the contradictory philosophies of
its leaders threatened to tear it asunder. During the first few years of the agency's operation, Arthur Morgan had largely attempted to run the authority on
his own, ignoring or silencing the voices of his two colleagues on the board.
The imprints of Morgan's developmental vision were most prominently displayed in the model community of Norris, Tennessee, which he designed to
balance subsistence agriculture with decentralized home industry. By 1935,
however, Lilienthal and Harcourt Morgan had begun to actively resist their
marginalization, and to Arthur Morgan's great frustration, Lilienthal proved
to have far more political acumen than the chair. Publicly ridiculing Morgan's emphasis on community and cooperation as "basket-weaving," Lilienthal went on the offensive in 1937. In time, the vicious battle for the TVA's future erupted beyond the agency's boardrooms, threatening to humiliate the
entire Roosevelt administration. In 1938 the president decided to fire Arthur
Morgan, who had become a political liability.[8]

Once in the driver's seat, Lilienthal began to expunge Morgan's legacy
from the operation and memory of the TVA. In 1944, he solidified his position as the intellectual architect of his agency when he penned *TVA: Democracy on the March,* a work that would be instrumental in forging its lasting

myth. Marked by bold, audacious rhetoric, *Democracy on the March* was Lilienthal's epic tale of the TVA's accomplishments. Propelling the agency, in his telling, was a unified and coherent ideology: "the TVA idea" was singular rather than plural. Its mission was apolitical because "rivers have no politics" and their development should be determined by "dependable technical decisions." Above all, it was transformative: just over a decade after the agency began to excavate rock and pour concrete, the Tennessee Valley's "worn-out cotton fields and rows of tenant shacks" were replaced by "the undulation of neatly terraced hillsides" and booming industry.[9]

Although it was seductively persuasive, *Democracy on the March* was hardly an accurate depiction of the agency's first decade. Instead, Lilienthal simplified and streamlined a history far more ambiguous. Arthur Morgan appears nowhere in the text, and Morgan's emphasis on fostering autonomous agrarian communities is similarly absent. The social, economic, and racial context of the Tennessee Valley is barely broached. The bitterness and frustration of the nearly 130,000 residents displaced by dam reservoirs are given two scant pages of recognition. Perhaps most problematically, though, *Democracy on the March*'s rapturous portrayal of the Tennessee Valley's metamorphosis in the course of one short decade far exaggerated the TVA's actual accomplishments. By the late 1930s the agency had made an insubstantial impact on income and wages, and though wartime spending dramatically improved the socioeconomic index of the valley, it did so equally in regions of the South removed from TVA investment.[10]

Two primary ambitions motivated Lilienthal to write the book. First, he sought to defend an increasingly besieged liberalism at home, sustaining the New Deal into the postwar era. But most important, Lilienthal looked beyond the United States to a larger global task that he called "world reconstruction." Anticipating the growing geopolitical importance of the decolonizing states of Asia, Africa, and Latin America, he believed that US technical assistance to these nations might aid their leaders as they navigated between the political extremities of right and left. In hopes of neatly packaging the TVA for export, Lilienthal distilled a decade of competing visions into a single sentence: his TVA stood for the conquest of nature through the marriage of centralized planning, technical know-how, and democratic rhetoric.[11]

In predicting that the future of the TVA lay beyond the United States, Lilienthal proved prescient. Even as the authority substantially scaled back its domestic social agenda after World War II, becoming—in the words of one observer—little more than a "glorified Power Company," both Lilienthal and the TVA's international reputations ballooned during the early Cold War. As several recent studies have detailed, the TVA became one of the United States' most significant intellectual exports after World War II, when countries as far-flung as Afghanistan, China, Colombia, India, and Vietnam each sought to replicate an imagined TVA blueprint, often with unpredictable consequences. Whether its residents knew it or not, the Tennessee Valley and its image would touch the lives of countless millions worldwide.[12]

Of all the world's observers who turned their eyes to this New Deal experiment in the US South, few came earlier, more frequently, or with more enthusiasm than those from Mexico. Beginning not long after water flowed through the first TVA dam in 1936, Mexican observers charted the agency's successes and failures and considered the potential value of its technosocial engineering. The meanings they drew from such lessons, however, were many and varied.

Paths to Mexico

The desire to manipulate water resources was hardly new to twentieth-century Mexico. Although mid-nineteenth-century liberals had begun efforts to rationalize and order the natural landscape, it was especially during the Porfiriato (1876–1911) that the government undertook projects to turn natural resources to national advantage. Mexico City received particular attention, where engineers sought to drain surrounding lakes to expand residential areas, yet equally important was the arid North. Fearing US encroachment and domination in sparsely populated border states, Porfirians hoped to use irrigation as a way to develop cultivable land and attract commercial farmers to settle the region. Therefore, by the turn of the century, canals, dikes, wells, and small dams became increasingly common in northern states like Sonora, Sinaloa, Coahuila, and Durango.[13]

The coming of the Mexican Revolution brought a renewed faith in hydraulic development, but the political meaning of those projects would prove quite flexible. For some early revolutionary leaders, dam projects were attractive because irrigation and land reclamation might forestall more radical approaches to the smoldering problem of landlessness. When in 1926 President Plutarco Elías Calles founded the Comisión Nacional de Irrigación (National Irrigation Commission), he hoped to create a productive agrarian middle class that would defuse tensions between hacendados and landless laborers. However, at the high tide of peasant activism during the 1930s, President Lázaro Cárdenas oversaw a dramatic shift in the revolutionary rhetoric of water control. When in 1936 Cárdenas expropriated productive cotton estates in La Laguna, the most sweeping exercise in agrarian reform during his presidency, he simultaneously unveiled plans for a high dam on La Laguna's Nazas River to democratize its waters. The Lázaro Cárdenas Dam, claimed the president, would provide the "indispensable hydraulic complement" to the cooperative *ejidos*—state land grants—being deeded to former tenants and wageworkers.[14]

The political meaning of hydraulic engineering in twentieth-century Mexico, therefore, was as fluid as water itself. Yet if there was one common current that linked water management projects from the nineteenth century onward, it was nationalist rhetoric. Dams, canals, and drainage were consistently promoted as monuments to Mexican greatness, fostering national pride and independence. Such pronouncements were deeply ironic, though, because foreign capital and expertise often underwrote these projects. US and British corporations bankrolled countless works during the Porfiriato; even in the heat of Cárdenas's land reform the president chose a New York engineer to oversee La Laguna's dam construction. Many leading Mexican engineers, too, had US experience: Adolfo Orive Alba, a key figure who would later lead the National Irrigation Commission, had trained with the Bureau of Reclamation in the US West. However, these early exchanges were almost exclusively technical, steering clear of human and social problems. Likewise, they were rarely publicized or acknowledged, as most Mexican leaders in the revolutionary era avoided public homage to US models.[15]

The dialogue between the United States and Mexico on hydraulic development shifted dramatically in scope and tone during the 1930s. In that decade, two nationalist, populist presidents pledged to expand state power toward the goal of undoing poverty and inequality. Though ideologically distinct, Roosevelt's New Deal and Cárdenas's Plan Sexenal both rallied massive support among the dispossessed and downtrodden, particularly in the countryside. At this moment of convergence, Mexican attention to US programs of rural transformation predictably increased. Cárdenas's government sent numerous bureaucrats to tour the Tennessee Valley, and federal reports noted the TVA as one of the New Deal's primary successes. In the last year of Cárdenas's term, the Mexico City newsmagazine *Nuevo Orden* sympathetically deemed the TVA a "lesson in socialism," suggesting that "the future of civilization" could well "depend on the possibility of transforming the social tangle of the private corporation [and] developing it socially by democratic means."[16]

The Cárdenas administration's interest in the Tennessee Valley, however, was overshadowed by that of the incoming regime of Manuel Ávila Camacho (1940–1946), which not only oversaw a significant escalation in missions to the TVA but also began to consider a direct application of its lessons to Mexican river valleys. Yet, for Ávila Camacho, the political impulses behind river basin development differed significantly from those motivating Cárdenas. In La Laguna and elsewhere, Cárdenas had seen hydraulic engineering as complementary to his strategy of resolving agrarian strife by redistributing land to the rural population. For Cárdenas's successor, however, river control made possible an entirely different solution: redistributing rural population across the land, especially to sparsely settled regions in

FIGURE 2.4. Engineers Armando Bravo and José Yépez at Fort Loudoun Dam, Lenoir City, Tennessee, in August 1942. Image no. KX-01839. Courtesy of the Tennessee Valley Authority.

coastal southern Mexico. In spring 1941, Ávila Camacho announced plans for a national "march to the sea," which sought to relocate farmers from the crowded central plateau to the "fertile lands of the coast." As he slowed land redistribution, Ávila Camacho envisioned tropical settlement as an alternative safety valve to agrarian discontent.[17]

In pursuing a "march to the sea," the TVA would serve the Ávila Camacho regime as a powerful rhetorical symbol. In November 1941, not long after announcing plans for coastal settlement, the president commissioned a study of the "works being undertaken by the Tennessee Valley Authority," as there "exists a special interest in knowledge of this particular topic." It was not long before the previous trickle of Mexican state visitors to the Tennessee Valley grew to a flood. More than twenty pilgrims representing five wings of government made the trip between 1940 and 1946, usually staying several days in either Tennessee or Alabama. Ávila Camacho also orchestrated an intensive study of the TVA's accomplishments by six engineers, who stayed in Knoxville, Tennessee, for six months during 1942 to study the history, culture, and recent transformation of the Tennessee Valley. In conversation with David Lilienthal, the six engineers were frank about their purpose: their months in the valley were to "equip them for similar work the Mexican government is projecting."[18]

The Tennessee and the Papaloapan

How—and just as important, where—would such "similar work" be undertaken? The first laboratory of New Deal hydraulic development would be the Papaloapan River valley of southeastern coastal Mexico. With its upper basin in mountainous Oaxaca and lower basin in tropical Veracruz, the Papaloapan Valley encompassed nearly 18,000 square miles and contained 1.1 million residents in 1950—about half the size of the Tennessee Valley with a quarter of its population on the eve of the New Deal. Like the US southern valley to which it was often compared, the Papaloapan region saw stark contrasts between lowland plantation economies and autonomous subsistence agriculture in its higher altitudes. Yet the two were undeniably distinct in their history. Peasant radicalism had reshaped lowland politics since the revolution, and communal landholding by indigenous Mixtecs and Mazatecs characterized much of highland Oaxaca. In 1944 a massive flood on the Papaloapan that claimed hundreds of lives focused national attention on the valley. In the eyes of many observers, it seemed ripe for transformation by a sweeping federal program.[19]

Selecting the Papaloapan and providing the political momentum for its transformation was not Ávila Camacho but his secretary of the interior (*secretario de gobernación*)—and future president—Miguel Alemán. Alemán was a native of Veracruz, born in the town of Sayula, on a tributary of the Papaloapan River. A pivotal political figure, Alemán was a key architect of the increasingly conservative postrevolutionary Mexican state. Like Ávila Camacho, Alemán believed that opening lowland southern Mexico for settlement promised a conservative alternative to the long-stewing agrarian problem. He was confident that science and state planning could tame the hot, humid, and disease-prone Papaloapan lowlands—and he was unabashedly cosmopolitan in seeking such a solution. In 1945, when Alemán unveiled his own presidential campaign and promised a campaign of coastal colonization in Veracruz and Oaxaca, he admitted that he was "taking advantage of the experience of the United States, where with much success was realized the program known as the System of the Valley of Tennessee."[20]

Following his inauguration as president in December 1946, Alemán took rapid steps to realize such a transplantation. First, he overhauled the federal bureaucracy of water management, merging the older National Irrigation Commission into a more muscular Secretaría de Recursos Hidráulicos (Secretariat of Hydraulic Resources), which mimicked the TVA in its jurisdictional supremacy over individual states and other government bureaus. Second, within that secretariat, Alemán created the Comisión del Papaloapan, which would coordinate and realize the president's ambitious plans for remaking the river valley of his home state. As the bill creating it proclaimed, the commission would employ "its broadest powers [to] serve as a solid foundation for the progress of this vast region, promoting agriculture through irrigation and the generation of energy through utilization of the [Papaloapan] river's great volume and power." Third—as this essay's introduction explored—Alemán made his own personal visit to the TVA in May 1947.[21]

While in the US South and upon returning to Mexico thereafter, Alemán and his cadre of engineers and planners pontificated on the similarities between the Tennessee Valley and the Papaloapan. "Mexico has a problem similar to the one facing the Tennessee Valley before TVA developments came," the president told reporters in Chattanooga, and his administration hoped to solve those problems "the same way you did." Adolfo Orive Alba, the newly appointed chief of the Secretariat of Hydraulic Resources, was similarly eager to compare the two river valleys. "Look," he declared to Mexican reporters, "at the Tennessee Valley before the initiation of these works, fourteen years ago—there too were sparsely populated areas like those in the Papaloapan; they grew and formed the foundation for new farms."[22]

In truth, the juxtaposition of these two valleys was rather specious. The Tennessee Valley prior to the TVA was hardly underpopulated—it was in fact densely settled, more closely resembling central Mexico with its endemic landlessness and economic stratification. Its primary environmental problem was soil erosion, not flooding. But the Alemán administration persisted in these sweeping comparisons. Why? First, the TVA lent the Mexican state legitimacy, reassuring a skeptical public that it had a successful and replicable precedent. Second, the TVA's rhetoric of social reform provided Alemán a convenient cover for rolling back Cárdenas's land reform agenda. During the 1940s, the ruling party had to tiptoe around the legacy of social revolution, and the adopted New Deal rhetoric performed important ideological work.

Ultimately, the Comisión del Papaloapan would fall far short of its millennial promises. The project poured the lion's share of its resources into constructing one showcase dam, named—unsurprisingly—the Presa Miguel Alemán. Completed in 1955, the dam minimized flooding for lowlands residents, but at the expense of tens of thousands of indigenous peoples uprooted by the dam's massive reservoir. Unlike the TVA, the primary purpose of the dam was not the generation of electricity, which only began haltingly in 1960. Indeed, the Papaloapan Commission departed from its New Deal inspiration in many ways. Of the TVA's two key architects, neither Arthur Morgan nor Lilienthal would have been comfortable with the Papaloapan's transformations. Morgan, insistent on the value of preserving small-scale communities that balanced industry and agriculture, would have been repelled by the commission's persistent dedication to an ideal of bigness, and the greatest beneficiaries of the Papaloapan project were large-scale agribusinesses in the lower basin. Lilienthal might have applauded the project's success in integrating isolated rural communities into a national market, but he would have seen little evidence that it was done in a democratic or participatory manner. Like other wings of the burgeoning one-party state in Mexico, the Papaloapan Commission had little room for citizen input. Orive Alba himself later confessed that his commission was ultimately "a state within a state" that "really ruled" the region.[23]

In the end, the similarities between the Papaloapan project and its New Deal predecessor were largely rhetorical and cosmetic. What Alemán and Orive Alba directly borrowed from the TVA was its autonomous bureaucratic apparatus along with its mandate that regional development be a coordinated campaign to reinvent economy, ecology, and society. Beyond that, the two projects were largely distinct. Yet Alemán's pet project in Veracruz and Oaxaca was not the only river basin commission born from juxtapositions of the TVA. Mexico's most renowned champion of the campesino, Lázaro Cárdenas, also spearheaded efforts to undertake a sister project in the Tepalcatepec river basin of Michoacán. The surprisingly distinct program that he pursued reveals that Mexican river valley development was just as diverse and contradictory as in the United States.

A Cardenista Tennessee Valley Authority?

For decades after leaving the presidency in 1940, Cárdenas cast an unmatched shadow on Mexican politics. Unlike the popular heroes of the revolution's violent years, Cárdenas survived his historical moment and refused to retreat from the public eye, often to the irritation of his successors. In the years following his presidency, Cárdenas performed an awkwardly dual role. On the one hand, he sought to preserve the legitimacy of the one-party state that he had done so much to enthrone during his years in the presidency. On the other hand, he served as the veteran sage of the Mexican Left, nudging party rhetoric toward campesino and worker interests, and not infrequently playing the role of gadfly to the Mexico City political elite.[24]

In April 1947, on the heels of Alemán's unveiling of the Papaloapan Commission, Cárdenas wrote the new president with a bold proposal: he offered his "personal effort" to establish and oversee a similar program in Michoacán's Tepalcatepec basin. The Tepalcatepec River, which drains the southwestern corner of Mexico's central plateau into the Pacific Ocean, somewhat resembled the Papaloapan. Both valleys were marked by a contrast between mountainous, densely settled upper basins and fecund lower basins home to large haciendas, but otherwise underpopulated, rife with disease, and lacking in infrastructure. Yet the two also differed significantly. While Veracruzan peasant leagues in the Papaloapan had been largely unsuccessful in their attempt to break up large plantations, in Michoacán their equivalents found a welcome ally in native son Cárdenas. In 1938, Cárdenas expropriated the productive estates of the Italian Cusi family at Nueva Italia and Lombardía, and subdivided them among nine thousand ejidatarios, marking the low-lands of the Tepalcatepec Valley as one of the most prominent national ex-amples of land reform.[25]

As his proposal to Alemán attested, Cárdenas's commitment to the Tepal-catepec basin endured long after his presidency. His 1947 prescriptions for remaking the valley showcased their author's longtime commitment to cam-pesino interests. Primarily, Cárdenas recommended a unified public health and road construction program to colonize tropical lowlands and relieve the "overpopulation that exists in ejidal centers" elsewhere in Michoacán. But Cárdenas also believed a river valley commission on the Tepalcatepec could bolster earlier land reform gains. As a lack of federal investment and short-age of credit had "made more difficult the situation of the campesino class," Cárdenas implored that the Tepalcatepec Valley receive an infusion of fund-ing from the National Bank of Ejidal Credit, and a new legion of teachers to staff rural schoolhouses. Alemán, likely weighing the political clout of the former president, in May 1947 approved the creation of a second river valley program, the Comisión del Tepalcatepec, and appointed Cárdenas as its *vo-cal ejecutivo*, or chairman.[26]

In drafting and administering the project in Michoacán, how much did Cárdenas rely on comparisons with the Tennessee Valley? There is no doubt that the former president admired the TVA. In 1945 he had corresponded with the agency's chairman David Lilienthal about the "important work in the Tennessee Valley." To his young son Cuauhtémoc, Cárdenas often spoke sympathetically of the TVA's effort to "bring better living conditions and pro-vide opportunities." But unlike the sensationalist Alemán, Cárdenas avoided talk of Mexican replicas. Indeed, Cárdenas managed the Tepalcatepec Com-mission in a strikingly different manner. In contrast to the Papaloapan Com-mission's gigantism, Cárdenas oversaw the building of smaller irrigation dams paired with canals to extend water to distant farms. By 1961, the Te-palcatepec Commission claimed to have opened irrigation to more than two hundred thousand acres, benefiting primarily ejidal farmers. Accompanying infrastructure investments was one of the most sweeping public health cam-paigns in Mexican history, an effort that largely eradicated tropical diseases such as malaria and tuberculosis. As Cárdenas frequently claimed to visitors, his commission's work held the "key to the future of the ejidos," and if its lessons were nationalized, "sooner or later all agriculture of Mexico would be managed cooperatively."[27]

Cárdenas's stewardship of the Tepalcatepec commission also renewed his interest in the US South. In 1954, he wrote to the TVA's leadership to no-

FIGURE 2.5. Cuauhtémoc Cárdenas and Lázaro Cárdenas with TVA chair Herbert
Vogel in Knoxville, Tennessee, February 1959 ,3. Image no. KX03914-. Courtesy of
the Tennessee Valley Authority.

tify them of plans to visit Tennessee as soon as possible. Ultimately though,
it was the enthusiasm of his son Cuauhtémoc that pushed him to finally visit
the TVA. The younger Cárdenas had trained as a civil engineer and traveled
to the Tennessee Valley shortly after his graduation in 1955. To Cuauhtémoc,
the journey was an eye-opener. Writing to the TVA's chair Herbert Vogel after his trip, the young engineer described his awe at the "magnificent
work you are developing and in which you have been successful." Privately,
though, Cuauhtémoc was shocked by the system of racial segregation he witnessed in Tennessee, remembering well the "signs saying 'Entry of Negroes
Prohibited.'"[28]

Nevertheless, Cuauhtémoc's enthusiasm about the project compelled
his father to make his own pilgrimage. In February 1959, Lázaro Cárdenas
and his son arrived in Knoxville, Tennessee, where they were welcomed by
the TVA's leadership. They toured the region, visited dams and farms, and
screened a documentary film detailing how the authority had rescued "a neglected people living in a ruined land." The visit made a deep impression.
Writing in his diary, Cárdenas decided that the "system of the Tennessee has
demonstrated with its affirmative results the beneficence of its organization."
Yet in drawing such a conclusion, the director of the Tepalcatepec project
was looking more toward the future than the past. "If the same system were

introduced in [Mexico] and other countries, on a national scale, it would take a definitive step toward the solution of the social-economic problems that affect each one," aiding the impoverished "who lack that which is most indispensable for their subsistence."[29]

Such declarations were of particular importance because Cárdenas's prominence in Mexican regional development was then waxing, not waning. In 1961 President Adolfo López Mateos merged the Tepalcatepec Commission into a newly founded Comisión del Balsas, a far larger agency that sought to address the economic problems of the entire eight-state Balsas River region, within which the Tepalcatepec was merely one of many tributaries. López Mateos, judging Cárdenas's popularity in Michoacán as an asset in bolstering the project's legitimacy, appointed him as chair of the new venture. In the nine years before Cárdenas died in 1970, he and Cuauhtémoc, who served as a chief engineer, directed the economic development of a region that included millions of inhabitants.[30]

Considering Cárdenas's highly prominent role in Mexico's agrarian reform, many looked hopefully to the Tepalcatepec and Balsas experiments for evidence that the ejido could represent a viable future for the nation's agriculture. They would be largely disappointed. Despite continued efforts by both commissions to ensure that the fruits of federal investment went to ejidatarios, the biggest beneficiaries of the agricultural boom were private owners. Because most ejido farmers were dependent on the state for capital and technical instruction, they were obliged to plant the crops prescribed for them. In the Tepalcatepec basin as elsewhere nationally, that meant a primary emphasis on export crops, particularly limes, melons, and cotton, whose acreage skyrocketed in Michoacán's lower basin during the 1950s and 1960s. But the ecology of the lowlands, favorable to countless insect and disease threats, ensured that such crops would require intensive chemical pest management and mechanized cultivation. Although many ejidatarios attempted to adapt to this changing world, credit and institutional support were rarely sufficient, and most could not compete with private commercial farmers. Therefore, in Michoacán, the Cardenista dream of a productive and contented rural proletariat would slowly perish, neglected and starved by an apathetic federal state.[31]

During and after the Great Depression, both the US and Mexican governments diagnosed the river valley as a basic geographic container for overcoming poverty and underdevelopment in regions believed to be internal economic peripheries. With a near-utopian faith in the union of hydraulic science and centralized state planning, they poured untold resources into remaking these vast regions. Roosevelt's New Deal empowered the muscular TVA to intervene in the culture, economy, and society of the US South. Born

from conflicting ideologies, in its first decade the TVA struggled to define
its social mission while simultaneously overseeing one of the most transformative construction projects of the twentieth century. After the war, an
increasingly hostile US political atmosphere ensured that the TVA would
assume a defensive stance at home. But its apostles, particularly its former
chair Lilienthal, took their evangelism abroad to Cold War battlegrounds in
the nascent Third World. As TVA leaders believed, the fruits of integrated
rural development in the US South had matured, and now their seed must be
cast to the wind.

Postrevolutionary Mexico would provide fertile soil for those seeds to
sprout, where heads of state both before and after the revolution had considered hydraulic engineering as a solution to social and political problems.
But if TVA evangelicals like Lilienthal imagined that a transplanting of US
southern solutions in southern Mexico would be neat or linear, they would
be consistently frustrated. Figures across the Mexican political spectrum
considered the utility of the TVA blueprint after 1933, but ultimately those
most attracted to it were conservatives who hoped to turn a corner from the
agrarian redistribution and radicalism of earlier decades. In the "TVA idea,"
politicians like Alemán saw an alternative solution to the enduring dilemma of rural poverty and insecurity, and one that also promised to strength-
en state power and legitimacy. Their plan, which they believed would satisfy
land hunger in much of central Mexico, was to colonize and populate the
sparsely settled lowlands of the tropical South. Although this goal departed
dramatically from that of the TVA, Mexican leaders in the 1940s consistently
drew reference to that agency to silence critics as well as reassure skeptics.
But as shown by the Papaloapan project, the state's best-funded and most renowned attempt at rural development, that effort hardly proved a workable
solution to the tensions and inequalities within the Mexican countryside. Ultimately, the Papaloapan experiment evidenced all the stereotypical patterns
of *proyectismo*, that development cycle common to Latin America—and the
United States—that saw sanguine early pronouncements followed by costly
mistakes, waning state interest, and ultimate abandonment.[32]

Yet the Mexican Right was not the only political wing that looked to the
Tennessee Valley for lessons in rural reconstruction. Lázaro Cárdenas, the
most prominent advocate of agrarian social justice in midcentury Mexico,
spearheaded his own river valley project in Michoacán beginning in 1947.
In stark contrast to the gigantism of the Papaloapan Commission, Cárdenas
sought to build infrastructure to foster the growth and productivity of land
reform plots granted during the 1930s. Quite frequently, his Michoacán project resembled the early but often-forgotten aspirations of the TVA under Arthur Morgan. Yet in an era when the Mexican state pursued industrialization
and increased production at whatever cost, boasting on the global stage of a

Mexican Miracle, such efforts were ultimately shunted to the political margins. Mexico's countryside in the twenty-first century testifies to the human
impact of such failings.

NOTES

This chapter is from *Agrarian CrossingS: Reformers and the Remaking of the US and Mexican Countryside* by Tore C. Olsson. Copyright © 2017 by Princeton University Press. Reprinted by permission.

1. "Aleman Says Mexicans Will Copy TVA, Build Dams on the Papaloapan," *Chattanooga Times*, May 7, 1947, clipping from folder titled "Pres. Aleman's Visit to TVA and US," Tennessee Valley Authority Corporate Library, Knoxville (hereafter TVA Library); "Enthusiastic Aleman Views TVA Projects," *Nashville Tennessean*, May 7, 1947, clipping from folder titled "Pres. Aleman's Visit to TVA and US," TVA Library. On the essay title: the Hispanicization of "Tenesí" was fairly common in describing the state and river in Mexico. For an example, see David F. McMahon, *Antropología de una presa: Los mazatecos y el proyecto del Papaloapan* (Mexico City: Instituto Nacional Indigenista, 1973), 51.

2. "'Esto es lo que México necesita,' dijo el señor Presidente frente a las obras de Tennessee," *Novedades*, May 7, 1947 (accessed at the Biblioteca Miguel Lerdo de Tejada, Mexico City).

3. I am not the first to acknowledge the significance of historical comparisons between the TVA and the Mexican river valley commissions of the 1940s and 1950s. In previous scholarship, however, this transnational exchange is treated peripherally or in passing, and no other work has grappled seriously with both national historiographies or consulted archival collections in both countries. See Diana Schwartz, "Transforming the Tropics: Development, Displacement, and Anthropology in the Papaloapan, Mexico, 1940s–1970s" (PhD diss., University of Chicago, 2016); Patrick H. Cosby, "Leviathan in the Tropics: A Postcolonial Environmental History of the Papaloapan Development Projects in Mexico" (PhD diss., University of Florida, 2011); Roberto Melville, "Antropólogos mexicanos en el Valle del Tennessee," *Umbral XXI* 5 (1991): 21–28; Roberto Melville, "TVA y la Comisión del Tepalcatepec: Una comparación tentativa," *Sistemas hidráulicos, agricultura, y migración* (1994): 270–295; William E. Cole, Steven M. Neuse, and Richard Sanders, "TVA: An International Administrative Example," *Public Administration Quarterly* 8, no. 2 (1984): 166–183.

4. For racial demographics, see Nancy Grant, *TVA and Black Americans: Planning for the Status Quo* (Philadelphia: Temple University Press, 1990), xxvii. The tenancy statistic describes the western counties of Alabama's Tennessee Valley; see Matthew L. Downs, *Transforming the South: Federal Development in the Tennessee Valley, 1915–1960* (Baton Rouge: Louisiana State University Press, 2014), 18 (table 1). On the valley's pre-TVA social history, see Downs, *Transforming the South*, 17–21.

5. Philip Selznick, *TVA and the Grass Roots: A Study in the Sociology of Formal Organization* (Berkeley: University of California Press, 1949), 5. On the origins of the TVA, see Sarah T. Phillips, *This Land, This Nation: Conservation, Rural America, and the New Deal* (New York:

Cambridge University Press, 2007), 83–88; Paul Conkin, "Intellectual and Political Roots," in *TVA: Fifty Years of Grass-Roots Bureaucracy*, ed. Erwin C. Hargrove and Paul Conkin (Urbana: University of Illinois Press, 1983), 3–34; Downs, *Transforming the South*, 60–67.

6. On the three board members' contrasting visions, see Phillips, *This Land, This Nation*, 89–92; Erwin C. Hargrove, *Prisoners of Myth: The Leadership of the Tennessee Valley Authority, 1933–1990* (Princeton, NJ: Princeton University Press, 1994), 24–30; Aaron D. Purcell, *Arthur Morgan: A Progressive Vision for American Reform* (Knoxville: University of Tennessee Press, 2014); Steven M. Neuse, *David E. Lilienthal: The Journey of an American Liberal* (Knoxville: University of Tennessee Press, 1996).

7. On the first decade of the TVA's operation, see Phillips, *This Land, This Nation*, 93–107; Richard Lowitt, "The TVA, 1933–1945," in Hargrove and Conkin, *TVA*, 36–66; Hargrove, *Prisoners of Myth*, chap. 5; David Lilienthal, *TVA: Democracy on the March: Twentieth Anniversary Edition* (New York: Harper, 1953), chap. 1.

8. Neuse, *David E. Lilienthal*, chap. 5; Purcell, *Arthur Morgan*, chap. 6; Lowitt, "TVA," 44–46; Thomas K. McGraw, *Morgan vs. Lilienthal: The Feud within the TVA* (Chicago: Loyola University Press, 1970).

9. David Lilienthal, *TVA: Democracy on the March* (New York: Harper, 1944), 215, 179, 180, 8.

10. For a close critique of Lilienthal's book, see Daniel Klingensmith, *"One Valley and a Thousand": Dams, Nationalism, and Development* (New Delhi: Oxford University Press, 2007), 53–64. On the slow progress of the TVA during the 1930s, see Bruce Schulman, *From Cotton Belt to Sunbelt: Federal Policy, Economic Development, and the Transformation of the South, 1938–1980* (New York: Oxford University Press, 1991), 35–38. For criticism of the TVA's long-term impact, see William U. Chandler, *The Myth of the TVA: Conservation and Development in the Tennessee Valley, 1933–1983* (Cambridge, MA: Ballinger, 1984); Grant, *TVA and Black Americans*.

11. Lilienthal, *TVA: Democracy on the March* (1944 edition), chap. 19.

12. Schulman, *From Cotton Belt to Sun Belt*, 184. On TVA's postwar globalization, see David Ekbladh, *The Great American Mission: Modernization and the Construction of an American World Order* (Princeton, NJ: Princeton University Press, 2010); Phillips, *This Land, This Nation*, 252–254; Klingensmith, *One Valley and a Thousand*; Daniel Immerwahr, *Thinking Small: The United States and the Lure of Community Development* (Cambridge, MA: Harvard University Press, 2015); Nick Cullather, *The Hungry World: America's Cold War Battle against Poverty in Asia* (Cambridge, MA: Harvard University Press, 2010), esp. chap. 4.

13. On the history of water and dams in Porfirian Mexico, see Luis Aboites Aguilar, *El agua de la nación: Una historia política de México, 1888–1946* (Mexico City: CIESAS, 1998); Clifton B. Kroeber, *Man, Land, and Water: Mexico's Farmlands Irrigation Policies, 1885–1911* (Berkeley: University of California Press, 1983).

14. Mikael Wolfe, *Watering the Revolution: An Environmental and Technological History of Agrarian Reform in Mexico* (Durham, NC: Duke University Press, 2017), esp. chaps. 1–3; Aboites Aguilar, *El agua de la nación*, chaps. 4–5. Mikael Wolfe, "Water and Revolution," in Wolfe, *Watering the Revolution*, chap. 5, 230; Sterling Evans, "La angustia de La Angostura: Consequencias

socioambientales por la construcción de presas en Sonora," *Signos Históricos* 16 (2006): 46–79; Sterling Evans, "Yaquis vs. Yanquis: An Environmental and Historical Comparison of Coping with Aridity in Southern Sonora," *Journal of the Southwest* 40, no. 3 (1998): 363–396.

15. Luis Aboites Aguilar, "The Transnational Dimensions of Mexican Irrigation, 1900–1950," *Journal of Political Ecology* 19 (2012): 70–80; Mikael Wolfe, "Bringing the Revolution to the Dam Site: How Technology, Labor, and Nature Converged in the Microcosm of a Northern Mexican Company Town, 1936–1946," *Journal of the Southwest* 53, no. 1 (2011): 1–31.

16. On TVA visits by Mexican government representatives in the Cárdenas years, see Francisco Gómez-Pérez to Arthur E. Morgan, May 7, 1936, folder titled "184c (Mexico)," box 15, Information Office Correspondence, Records of the General Manager, RG 142: Records of the Tennessee Valley Authority, National Archives Southeastern Division, Morrow, Georgia (hereafter NASE); "Visit of Mexicans," October 4, 1940, folder titled "184c (Mexico)," box 15, Information Office Correspondence, Records of the General Manager, RG 142, NASE. On Cárdenas administration reports on the TVA, see "Los planeamientos económicos en el mundo y sus resultados," July 26, 1938, folder 545.3/220, box 895, Lázaro Cárdenas presidential papers, Archivo General de la Nación, Mexico City. For the newsmagazine article, see J. A. T., "La gran obra del gobierno Roosevelt: Una lección de socialismo—La Autoridad del Valle Tennessee," *Nuevo Orden* 3 (November 1940): 20–22. On the broader dialogue between the United States and Mexico during the 1930s, see Tore C. Olsson, *Agrarian Crossings: Reformers and the Remaking of the US and Mexican Countryside* (Princeton, NJ: Princeton University Press, 2017).

17. Sanford Mosk, *Industrial Revolution in Mexico* (Berkeley: University of California Press, 1950), 220. On Ávila Camacho's "march to the sea," see Luis Aboites Aguilar, "Optimismo nacional: Geografía, ingeniería hidráulica y política en México (1926–1976)," in *Identidades, estado nacional y globalidad: México, siglos XIX y XX*, ed. Brígida von Mentz (Mexico City: CIESAS, 2000), 124–132; Christopher Boyer, *Political Landscapes: Forests, Conservation, and Community in Mexico* (Durham, NC: Duke University Press, 2015), 171–172.

18. For the announcement of the TVA study, see Francisco Castillo Nájera to Ezequiel Padilla, November 12, 1941, III–147–1, Archivo Histórico de la Secretaría de Relaciones Exteriores, Tlatelolco, Mexico City (hereafter AHSRE). On Mexican visitors to the TVA, see "Mexican Visitors," undated, folder titled "030-Mexico," box 20, General Correspondence, David Lilienthal Administrative Files, RG 142, NASE. On the intensive study, see Francisco Castillo Nájera to David Lilienthal, July 29, 1941, III–146–1, AHSRE. On the Lilienthal meeting, see David Lilienthal, *The Journals of David Lilienthal, Volume I: The TVA Years, 1939–1945* (New York: Harper and Row, 1964), 492.

19. Thomas T. Poleman, *The Papaloapan Project: Agricultural Development in the Mexican Tropics* (Stanford, CA: Stanford University Press, 1964), 46–47; Gabriela Soto Laveaga, *Jungle Laboratories: Mexican Peasants, National Projects, and the Making of the Pill* (Durham, NC: Duke University Press, 2009), 27–37; Heather Fowler Salamini, *Agrarian Radicalism in Veracruz, 1920–1938* (Lincoln: University of Nebraska Press, 1978); William W. Winnie, "The Papaloapan Project: An Experiment in Tropical Development," *Economic Geography* 34, no. 3 (1958): 227–248.

20. Miguel Alemán, "Síntesis del Programa de Gobierno," September 30, 1945, quoted in Hugo Rangel Couto, *El sistema del Valle del Tennessee: El desarrollo regional integral en la síntesis del programa de gobierno de Sr. Lic. Miguel Alemán* (Mexico City: unknown publisher, 1946), 7. On Alemán's presidency, see Ryan Alexander, *Sons of the Mexican Revolution: Miguel Alemán and His Generation* (Albuquerque: University of New Mexico Press, 2016).

21. "Acuerdo que crea un organismo técnico y administrativo dependiente de la Secretaría de Recursos Hidráulicos, para planear, diseñar, y construir las obras que se requieren en la cuenca del río Papaloapan," *Diario Oficial*, April 24, 1947, 2–3. On the creation of the Secretariat of Hydraulic Resources, see Martin H. Greenberg, *Bureaucracy and Development: A Mexican Case Study* (Lexington, MA: D. C. Heath, 1970), chap. 3.

22. "Aleman Views TVA Achievements at Chickamauga Dam, Muscle Shoals," *Chattanooga News-Free Press*, May 6, 1947, clipping from folder titled "Pres. Aleman's Visit to TVA and US," TVA Library; "El Tennessee empezará en breve a tener su réplica en el Papaloapan," *El Universal*, May 9, 1947, clipping from file N28074, Archivos Económicos, Biblioteca Miguel Lerdo de Tejada, Mexico City.

23. Orive Alba quotation is from Cole, Neuse, and Sanders, "TVA," 179. On the long-term impact of the Papaloapan Commission, see Schwartz, "Transforming the Tropics"; Cosby, "Leviathan in the Tropics"; Peter T. Ewell and Thomas T. Poleman, *Uxpanapa: Agricultural Development in the Mexican Tropics* (New York: Pergamon Press, 1980); and Poleman, *The Papaloapan Project*.

24. On Cárdenas's postpresidential career, see Marcela Mijares Lara, "Cárdenas después de Cárdenas: Una historia política del México Contemporáneo, 1940–1970" (PhD diss., El Colegio de México, forthcoming); Fernando Benitez, *Lázaro Cárdenas y la Revolución Mexicana* (Mexico City: Fondo de Cultura Económica, 1978), 3:215–252; Roberto Blanco Moheno, *Tata Lázaro: Vida, obra, y muerte de Cárdenas, Múgica, y Carrillo Puerto* (Mexico City: Editorial Diana, 1972), 391–332; Amelia Kiddle, "Lázaro Cárdenas (1895–1970)," in *Iconic Mexico: An Encyclopedia from Acapulco to Zócalo*, ed. Eric Zolov (Santa Barbara, CA: ABC-CLIO, 2015), 105–113.

25. Quotation is from Lázaro Cárdenas to Miguel Alemán, April 21, 1947, 508.1/168, Miguel Alemán presidential papers, Archivo General de la Nación, Mexico City. On the geography and history of the Tepalcatepec basin, see Marco A. Cálderon Mólgora, "Lázaro Cárdenas del Río en la Cuenca Tepalcatepec-Balsas," in *La tierra caliente de Michoacán*, ed. José Eduardo Zárate Hernández (Zamora, Mexico: Colegio de Michoacán, 2001), 233–265; Christopher Boyer, *Becoming Campesinos: Politics, Identity, and Agrarian Struggle in Postrevolutionary Michoacán, 1920–1935* (Stanford, CA: Stanford University Press, 2003), 56–61; David Barkin and Timothy King, *Regional Economic Development: The River Basin Approach in Mexico* (New York: Cambridge University Press, 1970); Elinore Magee Barrett, "Land Tenure and Settlement in the Tepalcatepec Lowland, Michoacán, Mexico" (PhD diss., University of California at Berkeley, 1970).

26. Quotations from the Cárdenas proposal are from Lázaro Cárdenas to Miguel Alemán, April 21, 1947, 508.1/168, Alemán Papers; on the appointment, see Miguel Alemán to Lázaro Cárdenas, June 1, 1947, 508.1/168, Alemán Papers.

27. "Important work" quotation is from Lázaro Cárdenas to David Lilienthal, February 3, 1946, folder titled "CAA-CAR," box 2, General Correspondence, David Lilienthal Adminis-trative Files, RG 142, NASE; author interview with Cuauhtémoc Cárdenas, June 3, 2016 (tran-script in possession of author); Cárdenas quoted in Henrik Infield and Koka Freier, *People in Ejidos: A Visit to the Cooperative Farms of Mexico* (New York: Frederick A. Praeger, 1954), 149. On the commission's accomplishments, see Cálderon Mólgora, "Lázaro Cárdenas del Río," 248–250; Marco A. Cálderon Mólgora, "Desarrollo integral en las cuencas del Tepalcatepec y del Balsas," in *La transformación de los paisajes culturales en la cuenca del Tepalcatepec,* ed. Juan Ortiz Escamilla (Zamora, Mexico: El Colegio del Michoacán, 2011), 227–258; Stephanie Baker Opperman, "Modernization and Rural Health in Mexico: The Case of the Tepalcatepec Commission," *Endeavour* 37, no. 1 (2013): 47–55; Barrett, "Land Tenure and Settlement."

28. On Cárdenas's 1954 plan to visit, see Guillermo Arizcorreta to Raymond Paty, Janu-ary 18, 1954, folder titled "CAR-CARF," box 39, Administrative Files, 1933–57, Records of the General Manager's Office, RG 142, NASE; Cuauhtémoc Cárdenas to Herbert Vogel, Sep-tember 25, 1957, folder titled "Mexico," box 81, Records of the Chairman and the Members of the Board of Directors, 1945–57 (Clapp/Vogel), RG 142, NASE; author interview with Cu-auhtémoc Cárdenas, June 3, 2016 (transcript in possession of author).

29. *The Valley of the Tennessee,* produced by the US Information Agency, 1944; Lázaro Cárdenas, *Obras I—Apuntes, 1957–1966* (Mexico City: Universidad Nacional Autónoma de México, 1973), 3:86–87.

30. Cálderon Mólgora, "Lázaro Cárdenas del Río"; Boyer, *Political Landscapes,* 172–173.

31. Barrett, "Land Tenure and Settlement," chap. 8; Barkin and King, *Regional Economic Development,* 197–200; Melville, "TVA y la Comisión del Tepalcatepec."

32. On "proyectismo," see Poleman, *Papaloapan Project,* 9.

3

STRANGE PRIESTS AND WALKING EXPERTS

Nature, Spirituality, and Science
in Sprouting the Cold War's Green Revolution

Timothy W. Lorek

The year 1948 proved to be critical for Colombia's entanglement in an emerging Cold War. In April, one of the largest urban riots of the twentieth century swept the streets of the capital city as foreign delegates negotiated the formation of the Organization of American States (OAS). The effects of these unrelated but simultaneous events are well-documented. The Bogotazo, a spontaneous burst of collective anger at the sudden assassination of the populist leader Jorge Eliécer Gaitán, served to escalate the bloody conflict known as La Violencia in the Colombian countryside. Meanwhile, the OAS became a key player in negotiating such grassroots conflicts internationally and pursuing anticommunist development partnerships throughout the very hot Cold War in Latin America. The convergences of April 1948 briefly thrust Colombia onto the main stage in international affairs: the first event, a warning about the dangers of rural unrest and the demand for agrarian reform, and the second, a model of international allegiance for dealing strategically with that unrest.

Almost unknown, however, is that a decisive moment in the unleashing of the Cold War's Green Revolution in agriculture also took place that year in Colombia.[1] Significantly, two tours of Colombia by Rockefeller Foundation (RF) scientists on either side of April 1948 paved the way for the internationalization of a model of agricultural experimentation programs pursued in Mexico since 1943 (the Mexican Agricultural Program, MAP). The itineraries of the well-known RF experts Norman Borlaug, E. J. Wellhausen, Paul Mangelsdorf, and Richard Bradfield around the Colombian countryside further linked the country's crisis in rural politics to an international Cold War

agenda. The traveling scientists' observations and subsequent recommendations regarding the political tumult in Colombia urged the Rockefeller Foundation to expand its Mexican project abroad and, by 1951, issue a statement
on the political purpose of agricultural development in stemming the tide of
communist revolution in the global countryside.[2]

But this essay is not about Borlaug and company. Instead, it reveals the
"strange priests" (*extraño[s] sacerdote[s]*) and "walking experts" (*expertos ambulantes*) who designed the set upon which international players like Borlaug
and the Rockefeller Foundation would perform the Cold War in Colombia.
This essay focuses on a group of Colombians, with support from a team of
Puerto Rican scientists, who constructed the institutional capacity that attracted the Rockefeller Foundation and helped launch a global movement.
If a shared intention of this volume is to uncover a contextualized and historically contingent Latin American Cold War, rather than an international Cold
War operating in and upon Latin America, then tracing its intellectual, cul-
tural, and scientific composition expands its dimensions in revealing ways.

A three-way partnership that grew out of the 1920s in Colombia's Cauca
Valley underscores the localized roots and autonomous projects that spurred
the eventual Green Revolution. In 1927 Ciro Molina Garcés, a departmental politician and booster,[3] began collaborating with Carlos Durán Castro,
a homegrown agronomist, to craft the intellectual and institutional foundations for ambitious agricultural science in the Cauca Valley. Together, they
recruited the renowned scientist and reformer Carlos E. Chardón from Puerto Rico, and he visited the Cauca Valley repeatedly over the next decade.

The project site and scientific networks they nurtured during a twenty-
year period caught the attention of a new wave of post–World War II consultants, academics, and scientists traveling to Latin America from the United
States or the ruins of halted development projects in Europe. Significantly,
these traveling experts from the north bought into the specific visions advanced by their Colombian hosts. At least for a time, the North Americans
adopted rather than imposed. Dissecting the cultural components of the visions they echoed back to New York and Washington uncovers critical Latin
American ingredients in Cold War–era international development work.

The literature on the Green Revolution and Cold War international agricultural development projects has, until recently, followed the most accessible document trail to large institutional archives, such as those of the
Rockefeller and Ford Foundations. For Latin America, exclusive or heavy use
of these truly rich materials risks attributing too much innovation to North
Americans active after World War II. Following recent calls for diversified
source bases, longer periodization, and questions specific to local contexts at
the sites of scientific production, my approach here is different. My approach
is similar to that of Gabriela Soto Laveaga, who succinctly writes regarding

her work on Mexico and India, that she is interested in revealing the people shaping the contours of a later Green Revolution as "actors in a long path of attempts to modernize countrysides around the world."[4]

Beginning with the Colombian Cold War convergences of 1948, I look backward to the cultural and political roots of the agricultural science programs to which foreign experts later hitched their funding machines. In this story, individual Latin American scientists and politicians inspired and nurtured the growth of what would come to be known globally as the Green Revolution. Even more surprising, the agricultural visions of these elite men blended ideas about nature and Catholic spirituality to advocate on behalf of their agendas. Today their visions might seem more apropos to ecologists and conservationists, rather than to proponents of a brand of scientific agriculture associated with the Green Revolution and often blamed for soil erosion and leaching, fertilizer runoff, voracious petroleum use, the retreat or destruction of native flora and fauna, the genetic narrowing of crop varieties and landraces, and the nutritional and flavor paucity of its products.

Given the ease with which this Green Revolution is sometimes criticized today, it is tempting to constrict our gaze on the destruction of past landscapes imagined as more sustainable in our contemporary parlance. Indeed, as Shawn William Miller writes in his survey of Latin American environmental history, "if environmental history has an important role to play, it is to remind us of what once was, what has been lost, and whether or not it was worth the price."[5] Yet rather than follow a declensionist narrative of foreign plunder, wherein the Rockefeller Foundation and its representatives pilfered the Latin American landscape to conduct their Green Revolution, this essay explores the particular nature–culture dynamics that motivated Latin American actors in creating the conditions for the Rockefeller Foundation's later arrival. Instead of following the moths and their attraction to the lamp, I pursue the ignition of the lamp. Heeding Mark Carey's suggestions for Latin Americanist environmental history, this essay activates Latin American actors and their culturally constructed mentalities. This move shifts the focus away from the loss of ahistoric Edens to a deeper and more localized appreciation for how Green Revolution agroenvironments were created and negotiated.[6]

Miller goes on to opine that "we should not completely cede that thinkers and actors of the caliber of Thoreau, Muir, and Leopold will never be unearthed (by Latin Americanist historians)." "Environmental heroes," he writes, "are created as much as they are born. . . . Latin America has yet to exhume her environmental prophets, individuals who were ignored by their contemporaries and buried without eulogy or epitaph."[7] My project here, however, is not to ennoble Ciro Molina Garcés, Carlos Durán Castro, or Carlos E. Chardón as Latin American Lorax figures. Nor is it my intention to vilify them (or the Rockefeller Foundation, for that matter) as responsible for environmental and social damages divorced from the initial context of their actions or change over time. Instead, my aim is to offer them a level of historical recognition that they indeed commanded in their time, for their roles as critical and complex players in an international story of science and politics. After all, Molina Garcés's patronage and leadership were celebrated by academics and scientists across the Americas and even eulogized in the *New York Times*. Carlos Chardón has a building named after him at the University of Puerto Rico's land-grant campus and has hundreds of specimens attributed to his collection in the herbarium of the New York Botanical Garden. These men were hardly ignored by their contemporaries or buried without eulogy.

By examining their agricultural visions expressed in the self-conscious representations of their projects in annual reports, I attempt to situate them historically and culturally without the weighty baggage of decontextualized comparisons. In so doing, I hope to illuminate connections between ideas about nature and state formation, parallels in the history of religion and agriculture, and the position of agronomy and other field sciences in the Cold War. The Cauca Valley these individuals helped to construct in fact and in fiction became a critical location in the Cold War's Green Revolution in global food production. As a result, and for better or worse, all of us who eat have some stake in their story.

Ciro Molina Garcés welcomed the first visitor from the Rockefeller Foundation in 1942. Harry "Dusty" Miller recalled his South American reconnaissance tour years later, stating, "On the fingers of one hand could be counted the individual scientists doing work of a level the Foundation could support (and still have a couple of fingers left over)."[8] Throughout most of Colombia, Miller found "no real achievement anywhere."[9]

One significant exception to Miller's prevailing disappointment with the scientific communities of South America, including Colombia, occurred during the very first stop of his continental tour in the city of Cali. Although disheartened by Cali's small agricultural school, outside the city he encountered "a reasonably good, relatively excellent" agricultural experiment station that "a relatively wise State Secretary of Agriculture had founded and given initial support."[10] His hesitant endorsements were for the Palmira Agricultural Experiment Station and Dr. Ciro Molina Garcés, which together composed one of the fingers on Miller's otherwise disappointed hand.

Six years later with the RF considering the expansion of its Mexican Agricultural Program, the future Nobel Peace Prize laureate Norman Borlaug and the maize breeder E. J. Wellhausen followed Miller's itinerary and met Ciro Molina Garcés in Palmira. Borlaug called Palmira "the best agricultural station in Colombia."[11] Four months later, a second set of RF visitors, Paul Mangelsdorf and Richard Bradfield, echoed these positions.

Again and again, Molina Garcés guided his guests on tours of the Cauca Valley. Mangelsdorf and Bradfield reported favorably on Molina Garcés and the staff of the Palmira station. Palmira ranked "much above the average Latin American station," they thought. They described the staff as energetic and motivated, slightly less trained than their counterparts in the United States, but dedicated to their cause. The maize-breeding project overseen by Dr. Fernando Villamil, recently returned from a Rockefeller Foundation fellowship to Iowa State University, and the sugarcane improvement project under Dr. Ramos Núñez in collaboration with the US Department of Agriculture (USDA), each impressed the two RF observers. They described Dr. Rafael Obregón, the station's director and RF fellowship alum, as "an alert, systematic man, willing to give his men a chance to think for themselves." In short, they approved of the job orchestrated by Colombian agronomists at Palmira. Molina Garcés's charms likewise impressed, reflecting "a man of considerable vision who has traveled widely and who is convinced that there is no place in the world which compares with his native Cauca Valley."[12]

Ciro Molina Garcés had sung the praises of his Cauca Valley for two decades when the Rockefeller scientists encountered him in the 1940s. He embodied a long and distinguished tradition of boasting about the beauty and agricultural potential of the Cauca Valley, dating back at least to the early nineteenth century. His overflowing enthusiasm for the Palmira Agricultural Experiment Station and its staff excited his international guests about the prospect of expanding their experimental work in Mexico toward a global project. Molina Garcés and the Palmira staff hooked them on the Cauca Valley.

Located in the hot lowlands of the Cauca River Valley between the western and central chains of the Andes Mountains, the Palmira station had long served as a collaborative project between local growers, the departmental government, and the national government in Bogotá. Founded in 1927, the Palmira station operated for two decades as the embodiment of intellectual and scientific exchanges led by three individuals: Molina Garcés, Carlos Durán Castro, and the Puerto Rican Carlos E. Chardón.

When reflecting on Ciro Molina Garcés and his vision for the station, his allies in the pursuit of scientific agriculture in the valley lined up to sing his praise. Observers called him the "soul," "paladin," "great pioneer," and "guiding genius" of the Cauca Valley's agricultural development.[13] Colombians and foreign experts alike joined the chorus of commendation. The journal of the office of the secretary of agriculture for Valle del Cauca celebrated Molina Garcés as "the apostle of the countryside."[14] The Colombian Association of Agricultural Engineers likewise remembered him as "the most striking and unselfish champion of agricultural progress."[15] The University of Florida geographer Raymond Crist dedicated his book, *The Cauca Valley, Colom-*

bia: *Land Tenure and Land Use*, to Molina Garcés's "genius and devotion."[16] Perhaps the most triumphant accolade of all came from the rural sociologist T. Lynn Smith, who compared him to the mythic founders of the agrarian nation to the north, declaring "truly in the history of agriculture his work in Colombia deserves to be ranked with that of Washington and Jefferson in the United States."[17] Two plants were named in his honor: *Phyllachora molinae Chardón*, a parasitic mushroom in the valley whose name he shared with his Puerto Rican ally, and *Theobroma cirmolinae Cuatrecasas*, a wild cacao of the western cordillera he shared with the esteemed Spanish botanist he recruited to work in Valle del Cauca, José Cuatrecasas.[18] And although he had few actual scientific credentials, the *New York Times* still recognized Molina Garcés's stature in the field and published a short eulogy for "Colombia's leading agricultural scientist" after his passing in 1953.[19]

Ciro Molina Garcés was born into a prominent valley family on December 6, 1891. Like many of his affluent provincial peers, he continued his education in the distant highlands of Bogotá. He shared this trajectory with a certain aspiring agronomist named Carlos Durán Castro, as well as the fictional character Efraín—the protagonist of Jorge Isaacs's romantic novel *María*—who left the Cauca Valley to become a humanist in the capital city. Like Efraín, Molina Garcés ran in the same circles as poets and writers and earned a degree in philosophy and letters on November 14, 1910.[20] His studies yielded his first publication, a study of hexameter verse in the work of a Popayán poet.[21] Besides a self-aware pride in regional literary figures, little of Molina Garcés's formal education in the humanities suggested his later boosterism and determination to advance the agricultural sciences in his native land.

After completing his degree in Bogotá, Molina Garcés returned home to help run the family hacienda with his brother. In the shadows of Jorge Isaacs's legendary hacienda, Molina Garcés extolled the romanticism of genteel country life. Inspired by the idyllic scenes of a peaceful, pastoral life of privilege, buttressed between warm sunrises over the Cordillera Central and breezy sunsets over the Cordillera Occidental, Molina Garcés learned to apply his literary mind to the daily work of hacienda administration. There in the fields north of the city of Palmira, his budding interest in agricultural science began to emerge.[22]

The celebrated romance of the Cauca Valley, of course, concealed a deep and bitter history of social strife, including slavery, racial violence, and, by the 1920s, the increasing mobilization of peasant and landless protest.[23] In this charged atmosphere, Molina Garcés's brand of poetic pastoralism developed a more practical, economically motivated scientific side. He believed modern science and its application to the valley's agriculture offered answers to the social questions of the day.

In his private practice, Molina Garcés experimented with cattle breeding. His initial ventures with imported purebred stock from Panama and the United States all failed, however, as the cattle, European Holsteins and Herefords, died during acclimatization to the new environment. Despite setbacks, stock improvement became a sort of intellectual riddle, to which Molina Garcés dedicated himself as he previously had to the study of hexameter verse. He read scientific journals, concerned himself with pasturage, and began to experiment with chemical compounds, such as trypan blue and sodium cacodylate, to acclimatize and protect imported pedigree.[24] After a two-year diplomatic trip to the United States and Mexico, he returned to the Cauca Valley with an enhanced knowledge of the agricultural and veterinary sciences learned in his excursions to California's irrigated fields. He continued to import livestock to his estate, finally with more success. In July 1925, the Molina Garcés brothers showed two Holstein cows from Holland at an agricultural exposition in Cali, where Ciro had a chance encounter with his old classmate from Bogotá, Carlos Durán Castro, who by then had completed an advanced degree in agricultural engineering from the Universidad Nacional.

Through patronage in the form of the regionally powerful Conservative Holguín political family, Molina Garcés entered the Valle del Cauca Department Assembly. He helped push for Ordinance 21 of 1926, which created a new departmental office, the Secretary of Industries.[25] Designed to improve agriculture, livestock, and industry together, Valle's Office of the Secretary of Industries became the second regional development office of its type in Colombia, following one established in Antioquia. The new office represented the first serious and technical attempt at the departmental level to focus on Valle del Cauca's future economic development through the symbiosis of Cali's aspiring industrial growth and the agricultural production of its rural hinterlands.[26]

Predictably, Governor Manuel Antonio Carvajal appointed Ciro Molina Garcés the first secretary of industries. During his first term, between 1926 and 1930, Molina Garcés had the political platform from which to advance his emerging vision of a coordinated partnership between government institutions, private industry, and the general populace in engineering an economically robust and scientifically oriented future. He created the *Imprenta Departmental*, the provincial government press in Cali that would go on to publish, among other things, agricultural extension brochures and pamphlets. He likewise campaigned successfully for the establishment of a departmental hygiene laboratory and, of course, an agricultural experiment station.[27]

After reconnecting with his old classmate Carlos Durán Castro at the 1925 Cali exposition, Molina Garcés put him to work in the Office of the Secretary of Industries. He enlisted the newly certified agronomist to draft a detailed, technically oriented development plan for Valle del Cauca, a plan that included their shared vision for a new agricultural experiment station.[28] The Palmira Agricultural Experiment Station, affectionately known as *la granja* (the farm), was established in 1927 with joint national and departmental financial support. This institution would become the centerpiece of the two men's coordinated efforts.

The budding experiment station outside Palmira became Molina Garcés's top priority, a site to showcase the cause of integrated economic development and the technical improvement of Valle's agricultural sector.[29] Agricultural development had a profound spiritual resonance for Molina Garcés, one that transcended the economic potential of a region with new transportation infrastructure. Reinterpreting the biblical fall from grace in Genesis, he described rural labor as exalted and redemptive. Toiling in the sun, he said, was not holy punishment, but rather the divine offering for the human "reconquest [*reconquista*]" of the natural world. Eden was a garden, not a wilderness, and agricultural improvement offered a route back to grace. "The study of the natural sciences," he then concluded, "carry us to God through the knowledge of the infinity of His work." The naturalist, the scientific expert, lovingly "collaborates" in the work of the creator as a sort of strange priest (*extraño sacerdote*), uncovering the mystery and rhythms of divine nature.[30] Molina Garcés's vision revealed the influence of a twentieth-century strand of Christian humanism that sought to reconcile science and faith. In its resemblance to the influential Catholic philosophy of the French Jacques Maritain's integral humanism or the poetic theosophy of the Irish nationalist George William Russell, Molina Garcés's brand of advocacy exemplifies a precedent for the later popularity of the Christian Democrat political movement in Latin America, and Catholic social action and community development in Colombia.[31]

Molina Garcés's reports frequently included these justifications for agricultural science (and funding) drawn from philosophies of nature, the role of the scientist as God's intermediary, and the divine communion of labor and agrarian families. In these he eventually became fond of quoting Henry A. Wallace, Roosevelt's rural life spiritualist secretary of agriculture, and his penchant for the "great priest of nature." His concern for harmonious relationships bent him to advocate at times on behalf of small family agriculturalists, often with a strongly gendered interpretation. "Nobody can exploit their own mother," he wrote in one report, "we should confide in her, give back to her the life which she gave us. We should, then, defend the earth like a mother, putting in her defense all the resources of science." Because the woman-derived family is the biblical "vital cell" of all humanity, any "economic or political school that does not base itself in the family sins against nature." When "capitalist industry eliminates family industries" it results in "social disequilibrium," he charged.[32]

A marriage of science and politics offered a protective against both social and ecological disequilibrium. Quoting the valley's own Jorge Isaacs, Molina Garcés underscored "liberty and ignorance equal barbarity."[33] In one example, he wrote an article advocating that the sprawling branches of the samán, or rain tree (*Albizia saman*), gain recognition as the national tree of Colombia. His purpose in publishing such a treatise was ecological and educational. These large trees provided shade for livestock, contradicting the prevailing practice of clear-cutting pasture. They also provided for a properly balanced agroecosystem, offering shade under which smaller coffee, cacao, tea, and nutmeg could flourish. Their roots and leaves regenerated organic life and restored nitrogen to the soil, filtered carbon dioxide from the atmosphere, diminished the risk of plagues, provided habitat for pest-eating birds, and conserved precious rainwater during the dry seasons. The National Federation of Coffee Growers, the country's most powerful agricultural lobbying group, should study the benefits of the samán, he suggested, for reforestation, wood, pulp-derived alcohol, medicine, and forage.[34]

Through the harmony of nature, family, spirituality, and economic production, Molina Garcés envisioned an agriculturally prosperous Valle del Cauca centered on a new research center. "The axis of Valle's economic future will turn around the agricultural industries, cornerstones of our public wealth, and for this reason they have merited preferential attention."[35] The intermediaries to the divine work of God's nature, priests of technical expertise, he charged, would produce a "harmonious plan, scientifically studied ... which will allow us to reach the heights at which we have seen other nations [*pueblos*], less favored by nature than us."[36] Favored by nature, the valley held the promise of a chosen land. State-sponsored agronomists would lead the way to its full realization.

Molina Garcés found his leading *extraño sacerdote* in Carlos Durán Castro. Durán contributed a trained agronomist's technical yin to the yang of Molina Garcés's spiritual poetics and political boosterism. After their Bogotá school days, Durán Castro remained in the capital and graduated with an advanced degree in agronomic engineering from the Universidad Nacional in 1922. His was just the second class of agronomy graduates in Colombia.[37]

Like Molina Garcés, Durán Castro returned to the valley in the 1920s to work on his family's estate. He began his professional career as an agronomist based on his father's property in Bugalagrande, a small town in the north of Valle del Cauca province. On his family land, Durán Castro worked closely with rice and cotton, crops that would later figure prominently in the early years of the experiment station in Palmira. In 1925 he published an article on cotton's potential as an export crop for the province. Despite lukewarm interest from established regional landowners and politicians, Durán Castro used his early work to advocate for an integrated style of scientific agricultural development that could help improve the social and economic conditions of the region.

The new secretary of industries offered Durán Castro the collaboration he had been seeking from regional politicians. Together, they set about planning the new Palmira experiment station. Before Palmira could serve as the beacon of regional agricultural science the two men envisioned, it needed personnel, supplies, contacts, and seeds. The new Palmira station needed to announce itself to the world while simultaneously collecting the acquired institutional knowledge of other similarly focused sites. So the Office of the Secretary of Industries commissioned Durán Castro to take a one-year field trip to study the internal workings of agricultural research stations in the Caribbean and southern United States.

The Secretary of Industries assigned Durán Castro to study the cultivation, organization, and development of agriculture at research sites throughout the greater Caribbean region and to obtain contacts and materials in the process that could be used in establishing the new station at Palmira.[38] Molina Garcés wrote the foreword to Durán's formal report, noting how the agronomist's voyage revealed "the route by which other countries have arrived at the heights we desire for ourselves."[39] The two men identified four primary focus areas of the study: the frameworks by which other nations structured agricultural regulation, experimentation, education, and outreach or distribution of knowledge.[40] During his travels, Durán Castro encountered and studied the site-specific arrangements of these core endeavors that could serve as scientific and political examples for Valle del Cauca.

Durán Castro's itinerary focused on research sites with agricultural environments and socioeconomic conditions that might reflect those of Valle del Cauca. Experiment stations in the cotton, rice, and tobacco regions of the Caribbean and southern United States shared a crop regime and the tropical or subtropical climate that rendered them most valuable and instructive for experimentation aspirations in Valle.[41] A shared history of slavery and plantation agriculture and the effects of these on twentieth-century land tenure, social composition, and economic orientation might similarly underscore the challenges and suggest some of the methods Valle agronomists and politicians might consider when constructing their agricultural agenda. Durán Castro's itinerary therefore revealed an imagination of the Cauca Valley's shared heritage and robust future as an integrated site in a greater Caribbean network of tropical or subtropical agricultural science.[42]

Durán Castro's field work and notes on the US South suggest agricultural experimentation and extension as a state-formation process, a sort of social engineering in the countryside. Agricultural research stations and colleges directed the transfer of state-approved technique and knowledge to men and extended home economics for rural women.[43] He wrote that "the demonstration system is the most effective for defeating farmers' resistance to the changes in the system and the adoption of reform."[44] He witnessed and supported agricultural clubs for children, noting that these were based "on the fact that the child is more susceptible to being influenced by new ideas than the adult." Exhibitions, games, and prizes could help attract rural children, and the conversion of rural children could help bring rural adults into the church of agricultural science.[45] In the US South, the agronomist from Valle del Cauca dissected agricultural bureaucracies and examined their parts. He studied systems and strategies for incorporating the agrarian populace into broader development plans. In short, he learned to see agriculture "like a state."[46]

Significantly, however, the continental United States did not supply the only instruction in the formation and operations of agricultural institutions. Durán Castro began his yearlong voyage with stops in the Panama Canal Zone and Cuba and ended it in Trinidad. But in his report to the Secretary of Industries, he especially cited the methods of agricultural extension and education in Puerto Rico as prime examples that Valle del Cauca might follow.[47]

In Puerto Rico, Durán Castro noted that the island had ten model farms in an area equal to half the size of the Cauca Valley. Each of these served a different crop zone and was well integrated into the lives and routines of neighboring farmers.[48] Further, Puerto Rico faced some of the same challenges as Valle del Cauca, exceeding even the US South in that regard. In Puerto Rico, illiteracy and poor rural roads complicated site visits by extension agents and the distribution of agricultural print and materials. As a result, he wrote, the island's success in agricultural experimentation and extension should serve as "a model and an inspiration for us."[49]

The agronomist returned to Valle in 1928 with the knowledge accumulated during a year of observation and with long lists of field contacts. He also brought material items acquired during his journey: seeds, plants, lab equipment for the new station, and many reels of film on agricultural extension services.[50] Assigned to serve as the first director of the recently opened agricultural experiment station in Palmira, Carlos Durán Castro built on firsthand experiences in the Caribbean and the United States as he began the task of organizing new operations.

The links between Puerto Rico and the Cauca Valley were enhanced after Durán Castro's return home. The director's first order of business in Palmira was to prepare for the extended visit of the famed Puerto Rican mycologist Carlos Chardón and his Puerto Rican Agricultural Mission to the Cauca Valley, invited on behalf of the department's Secretary of Industries. Chardón's resulting report, which Molina Garcés described as "the hotlands farmer's Bible," identified Valle's ongoing land tenure conflicts as a scientific problem: a condition of inefficient cattle grazing and outdated agricultural techniques.[51]

Recommending the more careful importation of hybrid breeds of cattle and grasses, as well as the dissemination of more technically sophisticated agricultural implements and new varieties of seeds, Chardón's mission helped set the agenda for the Palmira station's subsequent agricultural modernization efforts in the 1930s.

Born in Ponce in 1897 and trained at Cornell, Chardón began his professional career as a plant pathologist at Puerto Rico's Insular Experiment Station in Rio Piedras. Early in his career he had already achieved renown in Caribbean scientific circles for his ongoing research there on the devastating sugarcane mosaic disease.[52] In 1923, at the precocious age of twenty-five, Chardón became the island's commissioner of agriculture and labor, a position he would hold until 1930.[53]

Chardón used his government post to advance his focus on biological improvements as a panacea for economic underdevelopment. The onset of the global Great Depression caused him to reflect on and alter these views to further account for the persistent social inequalities that underwrote biological achievements. As economies crumbled and exports declined, Chardón advocated for the integration of science and politics to improve the well-being and self-sufficiency of Latin American nations.[54]

Chardón believed the United States owed much of its agricultural success to its system of experiment stations, which he called "a model for the world" and the "true nervous system and brain of agricultural work."[55] The Cauca Valley region, and Colombia more broadly, could learn from the examples of Hawaii, Java, and especially Puerto Rico in adopting and adapting the United States' model. Using sugarcane as a successful case in point, Chardón described a 70 percent increase in the island's harvest in 1927 without increasing the area of cultivation.[56] This was no overnight success story, however. The mechanics powering the increase lay hidden from public view. For example, Chardón described the island's importation of new varieties of cane in 1919. Although subsequent years brought a decrease in production, by 1925 agronomists in Mayagüez and Rio Piedras had identified several varieties that generated consistently high yields in the island's agroecosystems and began the work of preaching their benefits to growers. These agronomists carried the new varieties to the people, striking a collaborative bargain. The insular government would provide the seed, the agronomists would provide the know-how and instruction, the growers would provide the land, labor, and expenses and, in turn, would enjoy the increased revenue. The benefits of this collaborative model, exemplified in the 1927 figures, had turned the local producer into "a propagandist of the new variety."[57] Given the perceived similarities between Puerto Rico and Colombia, in the latter, Chardón prophesied, experiment stations could lead a similar resurgence in agricultural yields through science and on-the-ground collaboration.

In the early 1930s, the site's leadership saw the Palmira Agricultural Experiment Station as key to an integrated approach to agricultural modernization. The station, funded by a joint effort of the departmental and national governments, worked in close association with the region's producers. This close association with regional producers rested on the station's extension services. Modeled on Durán Castro's field notes on extension services offered by US agricultural experiment stations, *la granja* in Palmira attempted to disseminate its recipes for agricultural improvement during difficult economic times through direct and indirect relationships with people outside its gates.

Published materials and bulletins constituted one mode of dissemination. Just as Molina Garcés had organized a departmental printing press as part of his broader social and agricultural reform efforts in Valle del Cauca, *la granja* likewise made publishing an early priority. The Palmira station began regularly publishing bulletins in the 1930s with updates on its research and experimentation and practical information for regional cultivators.[58]

However, much of the populace of the rural Cauca Valley in the 1930s remained illiterate. Being able to reach a population that some educated officials denounced as backward and primitive emerged as an important obstacle to the success of the station's work. One strategy for accomplishing this task emerged after Carlos Durán Castro's promotion to lead the Colombian Department of Agriculture under the national Office of the Secretary of Industries in Bogotá. In the reformist wing of the Liberal president Enrique Olaya Herrera's administration, Durán Castro sought to reach large and small producers alike through regular radio chats on agricultural issues.

In Durán Castro's hands, the national Department of Agriculture advocated for community-to-community instruction. Similarly, Palmira agronomists, like their allies in Puerto Rico, recognized the power of farmers teaching farmers, of outsourcing the labor of reaching each cultivator to the community level. In this way, each individual agronomist or veterinarian in the station's employ could reach a broader audience through trickle-down instruction. When one literate cultivator executed a practice outlined in a bulletin or attended a workshop, this cultivator was likely to pass this information on to neighbors as *un propagandista de la nueva variedad*, according to the Puerto Rican model introduced by Chardón.[59]

That is, of course, unless their neighbors were their competitors. To overcome the complications that competition and other factors brought to community-to-community methods of dissemination, Palmira agronomists incorporated other more direct methods into their outreach strategies. In particular, they followed another model adapted by Puerto Rico's Insular Experiment Station in Rio Piedras. As Chardón and his team reminded people in Valle, Puerto Rico faced many of the same challenges as southwest Colombia, including poor rural roads and high rates of illiteracy, which rendered

FIGURE 3.1. In the 1950s, advertisements such as this ran in *Agricultura Tropical*, the trade journal of the Colombian Association of Agronomists (Asociación Colombiana de Ingenieros Agrónomos). In this ad, the Colombian Ministry of Agriculture offered "technical services" out of extension centers such as Palmira, reflecting collaborative adaptations such as the *expertos ambulantes* modeled on Puerto Rican programs in the 1920s and 1930s. *Agricultura Tropical* 7, no. 3 (March 1951): 39. Courtesy of the Harry M. Miller Papers, Rockefeller Archive Center. Used with permission of the Asociación Colombiana de Ingenieros Agrónomos-ACIA.

the extension agent's job difficult. Rather than rely exclusively on bringing cultivators to the station site or distributing literature for direct outreach, the Palmira station incorporated the Rio Piedras program of *expertos ambulantes* to canvas the countryside and bring demonstrations to the people.

This model clearly reflected Chardón's philosophy, though it clashed with some of his contemporaries. D. W. May, for example, the director of the USDA's federal experiment station in Mayagüez, Puerto Rico, from 1904 to 1930, expressed frustration with the impositions that extension wrought on scientific achievement. He wrote, "The proper function of an experiment station is research, and instruction should not be expected of it." Science in Mayagüez, according to May, was bogged down by the constant need to "translate its work to a public not familiar with scientific agriculture."[60] Chardón, and later Durán Castro, believed the opposite; that the task of an experiment station was to teach the public about scientific agriculture. Through strategies such as the *expertos ambulantes,* Palmira adopted Chardón's approach.

The Palmira station's reach in the valley grew during the early 1930s, based on imported models of extension from the mainland United States and especially the Rio Piedras Insular Experiment Station in Puerto Rico, the latter seen as particularly relevant to the conditions facing rural Valle del Cauca. As the Palmira site matured, its extension services grew exponentially. In 1930, the young station achieved 167 consultations and distributed 348 seed packets. The next year, it made 952 consultations and distributed 4,028 seed packets. In 1932, the station handled 2,655 consultations and distributed 12,330 seed packets.[61] In the valley's agrarian towns and villages from Florida to Ansermanuevo, a transformation was taking place. In 1915 most of these communities had little state presence or connections to a national Colombia, besides the northward meandering flow of the Cauca River. By 1933, not only did they have access to nearby railroads and highways, they were also visited regularly by agronomist government agents who left behind new forms of knowledge, scientific brochures, and thousands and thousands of seeds.

The three leading champions of the Palmira Agricultural Experiment Station, Ciro Molina Garcés, Carlos Durán Castro, and the Puerto Rican Carlos Chardón, found in each other ready and capable collaborators in their shared vision of agricultural science as a regional fountain of economic prosperity. Through their frequent interactions, they embraced the conjunction of the Cauca Valley to a greater Caribbean scientific network, encompassing Puerto Rico and the Greater Antilles as well as the United States, in particular the economically and climatically similar South. As Juan Pablo Ardilla has wisely observed, US-Colombian agricultural relations in the 1930s reflected *intercambio,* not *imposición,* that is, exchange, not imposition.[62] The partnership outlined here modeled technical collaboration for the region. Personnel both domestic and foreign and representing science and political office, industry and government, made the vital contributions that, together, would reconstruct the agricultural base of the region. This would be a first step in the pursuit of a more dynamic and integrated society and economy. The experiment station they designed would be the engine of this project. Through *la granja*, they hoped the Cauca Valley might finally achieve its celebrated natural potential. Chardón summarized this shared aspiration. "We dare to declare," he wrote, "that the natural conditions of the Cauca Valley are so privileged, that a coordinated force between government and the elements of production based on an aggressive, cooperative, and constant program of agricultural improvement, would finally render material [*daría realización plástica*] the name with which Humboldt baptized it more than a century ago: the Paradise of America."[63]

The Puerto Rican agricultural press suggested, with no small dose of editorial bravado, that the partnership with Palmira would form a metaphorical Mount Nebo from which the promised landscapes of the future, steeped in collaborative scientific agriculture, could be viewed. To carry the metaphor further, Molina Garcés, Durán Castro, and Chardón, like Moses, Joshua, and Caleb, represented different players in the coordinated partnership to deliver this promised land. Spiritually, the tone of their collaboration, poetically expressed by Ciro Molina Garcés in his regular reports, tied their pursuit of the natural sciences to Catholic social doctrinaires. The Palmira project thus represents imaginaries, both spiritual and geographic, that helped establish foundations on which later Catholic community development programs would build in the 1940s, which, in turn, would influence international Cold War community development projects such as the Catholic John F. Kennedy's Alliance for Progress and its embrace by Christian Democratic politics in Latin America (see Mary Roldán's chapter 4 and Andra Chastain's chapter 10 in this volume).[64]

The Rockefeller Foundation visitors in 1948 ingested Molina Garcés's booster optimism directly. "The Cauca Valley has been rated as one of the richest agricultural valleys in the world by students of Colombia since the time of Baron A. von Humboldt," they wrote. Nevertheless, its agricultural potential remained far from realized, even two decades after the establishment of the Palmira station. The station was regularly hamstrung by financial setbacks throughout its early years. The need to secure water for irrigation shifted political attention to the budding Cauca Valley Corporation, a Tennessee Valley Authority–inspired large-scale development project. What is more, an outbreak of the mosaic virus devastated the valley's sugarcane production in the mid-1930s. This crisis led the Colombian national government to buy out the Department of Valle del Cauca in 1937, take over full operation of the station, and rebrand it as a sugarcane research center in close collaboration with neighboring sugar corporations positioning to benefit from large-scale irrigation and partnerships with the USDA. As a result, the 1940s brought a wave of capital accumulation and expansion on the part of the corporate sugar sector while smallholders struggled to hang on amid the murderous threats of La Violencia. This was the Valle del Cauca that the Rockefeller Foundation entered: strong scientific foundations surrounded by violence, inequality, and turmoil. Ciro Molina Garcés was there waiting, ready to receive, hoping a new injection of foreign investment could help rescue the dream of the 1920s.

The discovery of such a place for the Rockefeller Foundation produced a eureka moment for the scientists' evolving interest in how agriculture might alleviate social problems. "Since the problem of food production in many parts of the world has become critical," they warned, "it is important to note that Colombia is one country in which the agricultural resources are still far from being completely utilized"—most especially so, they thought, in the fertile Cauca Valley. This was one place to count on for the necessary expansion of global food production to keep pace with growing populations and stem revolutions.[65] Perhaps the Rockefeller Foundation might be able to provide the technical capacity and financial resources needed to finally push such places to meet their potential. In this way, solving a global food crisis or population crisis depended on finding such promising yet underperforming regions. By adapting a local cultural imaginary of bountiful potential to fit with an emerging global neo-Malthusianism and the politics of communist containment, the Rockefeller Foundation came to *see* the Cauca Valley.

Ciro Molina Garcés and the Palmira station, with their histories and particular agrarian imaginaries, guided the Rockefeller Foundation's vision. As first Miller, and later Borlaug, Wellhausen, Bradfield, and Mangelsdorf marched into South America, the Colombian agronomists in Palmira directed the gaze of their RF guests, as well as RF scholarship and grant allocations. In 1967 the Rockefeller Foundation helped sponsor the creation of the International Center for Tropical Agriculture (CIAT) adjacent to the old Palmira station. CIAT is still in operation as one of fifteen global sites that serve as the institutional engine of the continuing Green Revolution. In this way, histories of Cold War development, the Green Revolution, and the origins of our contemporary global food systems, hinge on the forgotten efforts of regional experts at work recruiting transnational connections.

NOTES

1. The term *Green Revolution*, referring to the intensified use of high-yield seeds, chemical inputs, and mechanization in the growing of staple food and fiber crops like rice, wheat, maize, and cotton, was coined by William Gaud of the United States Agency for International Development (USAID) in 1968 to symbolize an alternative to red revolutions.

2. Rockefeller Foundation Advisory Committee for Agricultural Activities, "The World Food Problem, Agriculture, and the Rockefeller Foundation," June 21, 1951. Folder 23, box 3,

series 915, Record Group (RG) 3, Rockefeller Foundation (RF), Rockefeller Archive Center (RAC), Tarrytown, NY.

3. The Cauca Valley is both a geographic region and a political department in Colombia. In this essay, all references refer to the geographic Cauca River valley within the political boundaries of the department.

4. Gabriela Soto Laveaga et al, "Roundtable: New Narratives of the Green Revolution," *Agricultural History* 91, no. 3 (Summer 2017): 411.

5. Shawn William Miller, *An Environmental History of Latin America* (Cambridge: Cambridge University Press, 2007), 203.

6. Mark Carey, "Latin American Environmental History: Current Trends, Interdisciplinary Insights, and Future Directions," *Environmental History* 14 (April 2009): 221–252.

7. Miller, *Environmental History of Latin America*, 203.

8. *Newsletter of the Rockefeller Foundation* (July 1960): 16.

9. Harry M. Miller Jr. interviewed by William C. Cobb in New York City, February 14, 1967, and May 12, 1967, p. 51, box 19, RG 13: Oral Histories, RF, RAC.

10. Miller interviewed by Cobb, 51.

11. Norman E. Borlaug, "General Notes and Impressions Concerning Agricultural Problems and Agricultural Investigation and Instruction in Central America, Colombia and Venezuela," (February 8–March 7, 1948), p. 1. Folder 3, box 1, series 311, RG 1.2, RF, RAC.

12. Richard Bradfield and Paul C. Mangelsdorf, "Report on a Trip to Colombia and Other South and Central American Countries, June 10–July 8, 1948," 4–6. Folder 7, box 1, series 311, RF, RAC.

13. Carlos E. Chardón, *Reconocimiento Agro-Pecuario del Valle del Cauca: Informe emitido por la Misión Agrícola Puertorriqueña, dirigida por el Hon. Carlos E. Chardón, y presentado al Gobernador del Departamento del Valle en Colombia* (San Juan, 1930), 16; Nelson Delgado M., "La Facultad de Agronomía del Valle," *Agricultura Tropical* 13, no. 11 (November 1957): 669; T. Lynn Smith, "Colombia: Narrative," Folder 17, box 9, T. Lynn Smith Papers, Center for Southwest Research, University of New Mexico (UNM), 2; Raymond E. Crist, Smithsonian Reports: Memorandum to Dr. George M. Foster from Popayán, June 28, 1949, box 8, Raymond E. Crist Papers, Special and Areas Studies Collections, George A. Smathers Libraries, University of Florida, Gainesville.

14. *Boletín de la Secretaría de Agricultura y Ganadería del Valle*, no. 92 (September 30, 1953): 3.

15. "El más gallardo y desinteresado paladín del progreso agropecuario," Delgado M., "La Facultad de Agronomía del Valle," 669.

16. Raymond E. Crist, *The Cauca Valley, Colombia: Land Tenure and Land Use* (Baltimore: Waverly Press, 1952).

17. Smith, "Colombia: Narrative," UNM, 14. On Smith's work in Colombia, see Timothy W. Lorek, "Imagining the Midwest in Latin America: US Advisors and the Envisioning of an Agricultural Middle Class in Colombia's Cauca Valley, 1943–1946," *The Historian* 75, no. 2 (Summer 2013): 283–305.

18. Victor Manuel Patiño, "Esbozo biográfico de Ciro Molina Garcés," *Cespesdesia* 1, no. 3 (Cali: July–September 1972): 159.

19. "Ciro Molina Garces," *New York Times*, September 26, 1953.

20. Patiño, "Esbozo biográfico," 143.

21. Ciro Molina Garcés, *De re metrica, con motivo de los hexámetros de Guillermo Valencia A Popayán: ensayo sobre la evolución de los metros clásicos* (Bogotá: Arboleda y Valencia, 1914).

22. Patiño, "Esbozo biográfico," 144.

23. On the 1920s, see Catherine LeGrand, *Frontier Expansion and Peasant Protest in Colombia, 1850–1936* (Albuquerque: University of New Mexico Press, 1986).

24. Patiño, "Esbozo biográfico," 144.

25. Patiño, "Esbozo biográfico," 145.

26. Eduardo Mejía Prado, "Carlos Durán Castro. Gestor del desarrollo agropecuario del Valle del Cauca," *Credencial Historia*, Nno. 91 (August 1997): 13.

27. Patiño, "Esbozo biográfico," 146.

28. Mejía Prado, "Carlos Durán Castro," 13.

29. Ciro Molina Garcés, "Informe que el Secretario de Industrias rinde al Señor Gobernador del Departamento del Valle del Cauca sobre la marcha del ramo a su cargo" (Cali: Imprenta Departmental, 1928). Reprinted in *Cespesdesia* 1, no. 3 (Cali: July–September 1972): 225.

30. Ciro Molina Garcés, "Informe que el Secretario de Agricultura y Fomento rinde al Sr. Gobernador del Departamento del Valle del Cauca" (Cali: April 1943). Reprinted in *Cespesdesia* 1, no. 3 (July–September 1972): 274.

31. On Christian humanism in rural Colombian community development, see Mary Roldán's contribution to this volume (chapter 4), as well as Mary Roldán, "Acción Cultural Popular, Responsible Procreation, and the Roots of Social Activism in Rural Colombia," *Latin American Research Review* 49, Special Issue (2014): 36, 41.

32. Molina Garcés, "Informe que el Secretario de Agricultura," (1943), 278.

33. Molina Garcés, "Informe que el Secretario de Agricultura," (1943), 282.

34. Ciro Molina Garcés, "Arboles para sombrio y forraje," *Revista de la Academia Colombiana de Ciencias Exactas, Fisicas, y Naturales* 2, no. 6 (April–July 1938): 273–278. Molina Garcés's campaign was not successful. The national tree of Colombia is the wax palm (*Ceroxylon quindiuense*). See S. Madriñán and R. E. Schultes, "Colombia's National Tree: The Wax Palm *Ceroxylon quindiuense* and Its Relatives," *Elaeis* 7, no. 1 (June 1995): 35–56.

35. Molina Garcés, "Informe que el Secretario de Industrias," (1927), 205–206.

36. Molina Garcés, "Informe que el Secretario de Industrias," (1927), 206.

37. Mejía Prado, "Carlos Durán Castro," 12.

38. Secretaría de Industrias del Valle del Cauca, "Informe que el doctor Carlos Durán Castro, comisionado para estudiar la organización de los servicios agrícoles en los Estados Unidos y las antillas, rinde al Señor Secretario de Industrias del Departamento del Valle" (Cali: Imprenta Departmental, no. 9, November 30, 1928): 3. Biblioteca Luis Ángel Arango, Bogotá.

39. Secretaría de Industrias, "Informe que el doctor Carlos Durán Castro," 2.

40. Secretaría de Industrias, "Informe que el doctor Carlos Durán Castro," 3.

41. Molina Garcés, "Informe que el Secretario de Industrias," (1927): 209–210.

42. In this way, his voyage foreshadowed the imagined similarities between the US South and rural Mexico that contributed to the Rockefeller Foundation's investment in the agricultural sciences. See Tore C. Olsson, *Agrarian Crossings: Reformers and the Remaking of the US*

and Mexican Countrysides (Princeton, NJ: Princeton University Press, 2017).

43. Secretaría de Industrias, "Informe que el doctor Carlos Durán Castro," 74.

44. Secretaría de Industrias, "Informe que el doctor Carlos Durán Castro," 77.

45. Secretaría de Industrias, "Informe que el doctor Carlos Durán Castro," 79. On the social engineering and gendered aspects of agricultural clubs for children in the United States, see Gabriel Rosenberg, *The 4-H Harvest: Sexuality and the State in Rural America* (Philadelphia: University of Pennsylvania Press, 2015).

46. See James C. Scott, *Seeing Like a State: How Certain Schemes to Improve the Human Condition Have Failed* (New Haven, CT: Yale University Press, 1999).

47. Secretaría de Industrias, "Informe que el doctor Carlos Durán Castro," 4.

48. Secretaría de Industrias, "Informe que el doctor Carlos Durán Castro," 80.

49. Secretaría de Industrias, "Informe que el doctor Carlos Durán Castro," 79.

50. Mejía Prado, "Carlos Durán Castro," 13.

51. "La Biblia del agricultor de nuestras zonas cálidas." Ciro Molina Garcés, "Informe que el Secretario de Industrias rinde al Señor Gobernador del Departamento del Valle del Cauca, sobre la marcha del ramo a su cargo" (Cali: Imprenta Departmental, 1930), 6.

52. Frank D. Kern, "Dr. Carlos E. Chardon," *Mycologia* 57, no. 6 (November–December 1965): 839.

53. Stuart McCook, *States of Nature: Science, Agriculture, and Environment in the Spanish Caribbean, 1760–1940* (Austin: University of Texas Press, 2002), 75.

54. See McCook, *States of Nature*, 128. Geoff Burrows describes such "Puerto Rican-born, U.S.-educated experts" and their ascension to political prominence, eventually leading the Second New Deal on the island. Chardón represents one particularly strong example of this cohort. See Geoff Burrows, "Rural Hydro-Electrification and the Colonial New Deal: Modernization, Experts, and Rural Life in Puerto Rico, 1935–1942," *Agricultural History* 91, no. 3 (Summer 2017): 293–319; and Manuel R. Rodríguez, *A New Deal for the Tropics: Puerto Rico during the Depression Era, 1932–1935* (Princeton, NJ: Markus Wiener, 2010).

55. Chardón, *Reconocimiento Agro-Pecuario*, 20.

56. According to Chardón's figures, Puerto Rico increased its sugarcane harvest in 1927 by 70 percent over the 1915–1924 period annual average. Chardón, *Reconocimiento Agro-Pecuario*, 21.

57. Chardón, *Reconocimiento Agro-Pecuario*, 26.

58. "Informe del Secretario de Industrias y Agricultura al Sr. Gobernador del Departamento del Valle del Cauca" (Cali: Imprenta Departmental, 1933).

59. This trickle-down practice would later be replicated by community development practitioners in rural Colombia, including the trailblazing work of Acción Cultural Popular (ACPO) after 1947 and, later, the Alliance for Progress and the Peace Corps in the 1960s. In the early 1970s, ACPO partnered with Bogotá-based Profamilia (at that time the largest Planned Parenthood clinic in the world) and the Colombian Federation of Coffee Growers to mobilize rural women in the state of Risaralda to survey and promote health issues. Profamilia's distribution of contraceptives, contingent on the work of these rural women, has been compared to extension agents' distribution of seeds. See Roldán, "Acción Cultural Popular," 37–40.

60. D. W. May, *Report of the Porto Rico Agricultural Experiment Station*, 1.

61. "Informe del Secretario de Industrias y Agricultura al Sr. Gobernador del Departamento del Valle del Cauca" (Cali: Imprenta Departmental, 1933), 36.

62. Juan Pablo Ardila Falla, "Reflexiones sobre el imperialismo norteamericano: La política agraria colombiana y la influencia estadounidense en la década de 1930," *Historia Crítica* 51 (September–December 2013): 171–195.

63. Chardón, *Reconocimiento Agro-Pecuario*, 17.

64. The reverberations of the project in Palmira may be discerned in the Catholic community development described in Roldán, "Acción Cultural Popular"; Mary Roldán, "Popular Cultural Action, Catholic Transnationalism, and Development in Colombia before Vatican II," in *Local Church, Global Church: Catholic Activism in Latin America from Rerum Novarum to Vatican II*, ed. Stephen J. C. Andes and Julia G. Young (Washington, DC: Catholic University of America Press, 2016), 245–274; and Catherine C. LeGrand, "The Antigonish Movement of Canada and Latin America: Catholic Cooperatives, Christian Communities, and Transnational Development in the Great Depression and the Cold War," in Andes and Young, *Local Church, Global Church*, 207–244.

65. Bradfield and Mangelsdorf, "Report on a Trip to Colombia," 2.

4

"COMMUNICATION FOR CHANGE"

Radio Sutatenza/Acción Cultural Popular, the Catholic Church,
and Rural Development in Colombia during the Cold War

Mary Roldán

In 1947 Father José Joaquín Salcedo laid the cornerstone of what would become, until its demise nearly a half century later, Latin America's largest,
Catholic, mass media-based education and community development network, the Radiophonic Schools of Radio Sutatenza and Acción Cultural
Popular (ACPO). Begun as an experiment in rural catechetical outreach using a homemade radio transmitter, three borrowed receivers, and an old film
projector, the radiophonic school system expanded to encompass five radio
stations, state-of-the-art printing and recording facilities, a national circulation newspaper aimed exclusively at rural readers, and Latin America's first
leadership training institutes for peasants. ACPO and its founder achieved
international renown as pioneers in the use of communication technologies
for rural education, acknowledged and celebrated as "experts" by entities as
diverse as UNESCO (US Educational, Scientific, and Cultural Organization), USAID (US Agency for International Development), and the Vatican.[1]

The 1950s witnessed a proliferation of organizations in Latin America
dedicated to training specialists in the implementation of various aspects of
postwar development. Witness the creation of CINVA, the Organization of
American States–supported Inter-American Housing Lab established in Bogotá in 1951 and analyzed by Mark Healey in this volume (chapter 8), and
CREFAL, the UNESCO-sponsored Fundamental Education Center for Latin America established the same year as CINVA to train specialists in the
basics of rural education and community development in Patzcuaro, Michoacán. What set ACPO apart from these initiatives was that it was founded by
a priest, marshaled a widely available popular technology like radio for grass-

114

roots educational purposes, and focused on training individuals to be leaders who had only a few years of primary school education and were drawn from the ranks of the same social strata and rural communities they would one day serve.[2]

The scholarship students selected to attend ACPO's Institutos Campesinos received basic instruction in Catholic catechism and the uses of technology to improve domestic economy, agriculture, sports, health, and community development, the core elements of ACPO's Fundamental Education program. The most promising graduates were hired to work as ACPO's lay apostolate in the countryside, overseeing the management of radiophonic schools and functioning as facilitators similar to extension agents or, later, Peace Corps volunteers. Along with its use of radio-based, nonformal education programs, it was the creation of the rural training institutes that cemented ACPO's reputation and catapulted its founder into the ranks of international education and communication experts. An "itinerant expert" in demand by countries interested in emulating the radiophonic school and rural leadership programs, ACPO's founder flew so often between Bogotá, Europe, the United States, and Latin America, that detractors and admirers alike referred to him as the "airplane monsignor."

A glossy 1959 fund-raising and propaganda brochure produced with the assistance of Madison Avenue's leading advertising and public relations firms and strategically studded with effusive endorsements by international agencies such as UNESCO and statesmen such as Dwight Eisenhower, John Moors Cabot, and Alberto Lleras Camargo, confirmed ACPO's meteoric rise in the 1950s as a radio education pioneer in the global campaign to protect Latin America from the threat of communist subversion. The brochure-cum-manifesto was the product of the American Foundation for Cultural Popular Action, Inc., a nonprofit organization created in June 1958 with headquarters in the offices of the South American Gold and Platinum Corporation in the heart of New York City's financial district. The foundation's ostensible purpose was to publicize and fund-raise for ACPO and to lobby for the replication and adoption of ACPO's radio-based education and community development model in other Latin American countries.[3]

The foundation's board featured prominent members of the US episcopacy such as the auxiliary bishop of Washington, DC, Philip Hannon, and the longtime president of Notre Dame, Theodore Hesburgh; journalists of international stature such as Herbert Matthews of the *New York Times*; politically influential businessmen such as the Democratic Party stalwart and frequent adviser to presidents on matters of business and development from FDR to Ronald Reagan, the conservative Catholic chairman of the W. R. Grace Company, J. Peter Grace; and Phanor Eder, scion of the Valle del Cauca Manuelita sugar conglomerate and legal representative of the South American Gold and

Platinum Company, the largest producer and exporter of platinum in Colombia. The board president was Arthur Dean, the senior partner and managing director of the New York City–based Sullivan and Cromwell law firm where both Dulles brothers (John Foster and Allen) had served as partners before assuming the roles of secretary of state under Eisenhower and CIA director, respectively.[4]

Celebrating ACPO's "proven" expertise in education and mass communications, and the central role assigned these two areas of activity in the global "fight against ignorance and communism," the brochure highlighted ACPO's role in training future leaders in fundamental education by radio for Latin America, as well as the organization's success in reducing adult rural illiteracy in Colombia by 20 percent in twelve years.[5] After five months of training in the Instituto Campesino, the brochure boasted, there was "no stopping them [peasants]; they can take their places with dignity as citizens." What ACPO was doing, moreover, was good for Colombia and for the United States, since "it is to the advantage of Americans as good neighbors, as humanitarians, as hard-headed economists—that illiteracy be wiped out in Latin America." "A red government in the western hemisphere is not beyond the sphere of possibility," the Foundation for Cultural Popular Action warned the American public. The best way to prevent communism was to give peasants a "basic education" so they could achieve their hopes of "individual freedom, a higher standard of living, and democratic institutions," the enviable hallmarks of American life. "Literacy for Democracy," the brochure concluded, was "The Hemisphere's Answer to a Worldwide Challenge."[6]

ACPO embodied the ethos and dynamics of Cold War development experiments focused on rescuing Latin America from the lingering effects of a backward colonial past that stymied the evolution of the region's societies into modern, capitalist democracies and were thought to make them fertile ground for revolution. In the Colombian case, this concern was particularly acute. Protracted civil conflict whose epicenter was located in the countryside and whose primary victims were the rural poor exacerbated long-standing problems around land tenure, poverty, and exclusion, making Colombia an ideal testing ground for novel approaches intended to "modernize" peasants while preempting communist recruitment. ACPO's appeal was due in no small measure to its founder's ability to persuasively suggest that if in a country such as Colombia, radio-based education aimed at rural communities wracked by violence could succeed, then the chances of ACPO being an effective strategy for improving rural life and forestalling revolution elsewhere were high. Indeed, it was the evident transnational appeal of this (unproven) claim that enabled ACPO to grow at an unprecedented pace through the 1950s and 1960s, building new and more powerful radio stations, tripling and quadrupling its output of primers, instructional manuals, recordings, and newspaper circulation, and graduating streams of rural leaders from its three peasant training institutes.

But ACPO also illustrates a dilemma typical of other development projects born within the fairly narrow ideological and financial constraints of the Cold War. Forced to search beyond Colombia for the resources to support the organization's expansion and expenses, not long after its founding, ACPO became dependent on its director's ability to tailor his appeals for support to the agendas of donors whose values and missions did not always coincide beyond a shared antipathy to communism. As the ideological winds or the interests of potential funding agents waned or shifted, ACPO's director adjusted his discursive framing of the organization's mission accordingly. To the Vatican and his Catholic backers in Colombia, Salcedo stressed the catechetical aspect of ACPO's educational work as well as the advantages of a Catholic media network that could be used to counter the threats of Protestant proselytizing and communist propaganda. To foreign businessmen and government-affiliated sources of international assistance, Monsignor stressed the importance of Christian-inspired literacy training that privileged a self-help approach conducive to the promotion of free enterprise and democracy modeled along US lines as a bulwark against the spread of communism.

Indeed, perhaps the most salient feature of Monsignor Salcedo's expertise was his adroit manipulation of anticommunist hysteria, his keen understanding of the importance of public perception, and his considerable salesmanship abilities. These skills, I argue, enabled ACPO's founder to position ACPO's radiophonic schools and peasant leadership training programs as desirable models for export and emulation throughout Latin America and other parts of the developing world even when evidence of the efficacy of technological approaches to the problem of rural underdevelopment proved scant or inconclusive.

Development projects like ACPO's that promised rural peoples a better life through self-empowerment, but ignored or failed to address the structural causes of persistent poverty, disenfranchisement, and illiteracy, ultimately foundered. ACPO shuttered its operations in 1989.[7] But for nearly three decades before that, in a sphere where expertise was normally defined by the engineers, social workers, sociologists, scientists, architects, health professionals, and formal educators who shaped the contours of midcentury modernization and "development" projects examined by other contributors to this volume, a Catholic priest with no technical degree or special training, came to be lauded as "one of the Continent's leading educators" and a renowned expert in the use of communication technologies to address the problem of persistent rural underdevelopment.[8]

Using the case of ACPO as a lens, this essay explores the contested, ideologically inflected ways in which the categories of "expert" and "expertise" were constructed and applied during the Cold War in Latin America, the influence of the Catholic Church in shaping postwar development projects, and the pitfalls and possibilities of relying on technology to effect change.

The Making of a Catholic, Cold War Education "Expert"

The trend of traveling technocrats had become a familiar feature of Latin American life at the turn of the twentieth century, but it accelerated noticeably and expanded to encompass a greater variety of experts including members of the Catholic Church who, as specialists in sociology, labor relations, communications, and social work, played defining roles in the creation of cooperatives and credit unions, the development of workers' circles and agrarian unions, housing activism and urban planning.[9] In the case of Colombia, moreover, the Church had a long history of collaborating with rural modernization efforts and organizations such as the National Federation of Coffee Growers (Federación Nacional de Cafeteros). Priests disseminated seeds, encouraged the adoption of improved cultivation techniques based on scientific experimentation, promoted colonization, brokered community acceptance of extension agents and secular experts, and informed parishioners about relevant agricultural policies, development resources, and the official purchasing price for local grades of the bean on the national market.[10]

Exchanges of experts and expertise in and around the Americas took on new meanings and urgency during World War II, moreover, when securing the cooperation of Latin American nations became a US imperative. In the 1940s the Department of State, the Office of the Coordinator of Inter-American Affairs (OCIAA), and the US bishops' National Catholic Welfare Conference (NCWC) sponsored educational and professional exchange programs in which members of Latin America's clergy, as well as secular professionals in the fields of social work, agronomy, engineering, health and labor, received scholarships for study in the United States while technical specialists and faculty from US academic and scientific research institutions served as visiting professors and consultants to regional and national governments in Latin America.[11] Latin American clergy who took part in educational exchanges in the United States and Canada during the 1940s and 1950s often emerged as important consultants in their respective countries' postwar development efforts.[12]

Wartime exchanges of secular and religious professionals had an important impact in shaping development approaches in countries like Colombia. Influenced by discussions around the relationship between Catholic social doctrine and issues like land tenure, labor, the environment, and the rights of historically disenfranchised indigenous and Afro-descendant populations that took place at Inter-American Seminars sponsored by the US Catholic

Bishops in Washington, DC, for instance, the government of Mariano Ospina Pérez entrusted the task of leading its National Literacy Campaign,
launched in October 1947 over the National Radio broadcasting system,
to a member of the clergy who had recently returned from participating in
an educational exchange at the Catholic University of America.[13] By 1960,
that same clergyman, now the auxiliary bishop of Bogotá, would travel to the
Center for Tropical Agricultural Research and Education in Turrialba, Costa Rica, in search of disease-resistant, inexpensive cattle breeds to promote
smallholder husbandry and take part in promoting Colombia's Land Reform
Law of 1961.[14]

This was the backdrop against which Father Salcedo, as an auxiliary
parish priest appointed to serve in a remote rural village, initiated the radio-based, adult literacy and catechetical experiment that became ACPO in
October 1947. The project might never have taken off as it did, however, had
it not been for the fact that six months later, the popular Liberal leader, Jorge
Eliécer Gaitán, was gunned down on April 9, 1948, in the midst of the Ninth
Pan-American Conference in Bogotá. This prompted a violent outburst of
popular protest that led to considerable destruction, the declaration of a state
of siege, dictatorship, and official denunciations of communist agitation.
Not long after, with the support of Colombia's Catholic Church hierarchy,
ACPO's radio-based education program gained powerful allies within official Colombian circles, cementing its founder's claim to expertise in the areas
of nonformal education and communications.

In October 1949 the Colombian government conferred legal status
on ACPO, a measure that made it possible for ACPO, despite its status as
a religious organization, to negotiate contracts and apply for international
technical assistance funding through the auspices of the Colombian Ministry of National Education. When the twenty-eight-year-old prelate traveled
to New York City in November 1949 to present before the United Nations
and to shop for radio equipment at General Electric, he did so as a budding
Colombian education expert with the help of a diplomatic corps made up of
well-connected members of Colombia's elite, many of whom would continue
to exercise important political and economic influence over national affairs
well into the decade of the 1970s and become known as the architects of Colombian modernization.

In New York City, Father Salcedo first met with UNESCO representatives at the United Nations. UNESCO would later contribute to disseminating ACPO's fame abroad, praising Radio Sutatenza in its international
broadcasts and publications as "the paradigm of what should be realized in
all the countries of Latin America in terms of educational broadcasting."[15]
Devoted to the promotion and dissemination of education, science, and culture and to the use of mass communication technologies to further that goal,

the centerpiece of UNESCO's international program of human development was the Fundamental Education program, an approach that was intended not simply to eradicate the condition of illiteracy that plagued "more than half of the people in the world," but to "help people understand immediate problems and give them the skills to solve them."[16] UNESCO's program became the basis of ACPO's own Fundamental Integral Education program. ACPO's first Instituto Campesino for training male rural leaders, established in Sutatenza in 1954, moreover, was made possible by the direct assistance of two UNESCO-assigned Christian Brothers who were specialists in the technical aspects of radio education.

Every Picture Tells a Story, Especially When Accompanied by a Press Release

Having secured the assistance of UNESCO, Father Salcedo left New York City for the headquarters of the International General Electric Company in Syracuse, where he negotiated the purchase of a transmitter, receiver, and other materials necessary to expand the reach of Radio Sutatenza. Though no mention of communism per se was made in the materials memorializing this encounter or the description of ACPO's objectives, the fanfare expended by General Electric (GE) in response to the "padre's" visit to their offices, including a series of professional photographs accompanying gushing news copy to be broadcast and published in GE media and company bulletins and forwarded for inclusion in the US commercial press, suggest that more might have been at stake than simply selling radios to a young, unknown parish priest from a remote part of Colombia. This meeting would mark Salcedo's first official interaction with corporate America, several of whose CEOs, former presidents, and legal counsel would later be members of the boards of organizations that would assist ACPO such as the American Foundation for Cultural Popular Action, Inc., whose brochure introduced this essay; its successor organization, the Inter-American Literacy Foundation, Inc., founded in 1961; and the Institute for Human Progress, Inc., created in 1963 to facilitate the participation of "grassroots" private sector organizations like ACPO in the competition for Alliance for Progress and USAID development assistance grants.

GE had its own Electronics News Bureau at the Electronics Park in Syracuse where the equipment ACPO would purchase in December 1949—a one-kilowatt shortwave transmitter and seven hundred battery-operated shortwave receivers—was manufactured.[17] In January 1950, a few weeks after Salcedo's visit, the GE News Bureau issued a six-page news story about Salcedo, the radiophonic schools, and the impact of Radio Sutatenza on Colombia's rural population. Described as a "vast network" (at the time this would certainly *not* have been true) dedicated to "providing educational class instruction to thousands of adults and children in Colombia, South America" (an exaggeration), Radio Sutatenza's classes were supposedly held "in public places, in farm houses, or merely by the side of the road" (a feat hard to imagine in the midst of la Violencia).[18]

To give added punch to the news bulletin, a translated copy of an article first published in the Jesuit *Revista Javeriana* written by Francisco Javier Mejía, SJ, and based on his "eye-witness" account of the radiophonic schools, was included in the press packet sent out to different GE offices and the broader commercial media. Mejía began his essay by contrasting life in the United States, where he noted even workers were literate and had the ability to take active part in democratic life by virtue of their education, with the bleak situation of Colombia, where a majority of the poor were illiterate and had little or no access to education, a situation that had negative consequences for both the poor and Colombian society as a whole.[19]

The Jesuit mused that he had often wracked his brains searching for a solution to the dilemma of illiteracy and how best to overcome the challenges posed by Colombia's daunting geography.[20] Mejia recounted with moving eloquence the seemingly insurmountable obstacles that made it difficult to provide education to the country's majority rural population, concluding with an expression of his unstinting admiration for the "dynamic priest of Boyacá" who seemed to have found a solution to the problem of rural illiteracy as he had not.

The heroic myth of the Colombian radio schools and the intrepid and pioneering priest whose vision and tenacity had hit on the brilliantly simple solution of using radio technology to redeem, as a later US propagandist for ACPO put it, the "wretchedness and bleak despair which had made them [peasants] ready prey for atheistic communism,"[21] may be said to have had its origin story with Mejía's tear-inducing account.

"In the patio of a farmhouse," Father Mejía's account began,

> about one hundred men and women were quietly listening to the afternoon lesson. Over there, at the end of the hall, from the radio receiver issued the voice of the teacher while here the assistant teacher used chalk and blackboard to illustrate the points requiring clarification. . . . Book in hand, every pupil followed the lesson attentively, while his [the teacher's] sparkling eyes showed his amazement at the readiness with which the dense wall of ignorance was gradually dropping. Emotions shook me violently and my gaze was lost in the depths of my conception of the Motherland [*Madre Patria*]. I could sense how the marvelous network of the radiophonic schools was extending its reach to the farthest confines of Colombia. I could see how the spiritual reserves of the country—the peasants—revived in the morn of a new day which had ended the dark night of their ignorance.[22]

Father Mejía then went on to detail the equipment used by the radio-phonic schools and that its total cost—estimated at 15,000 Colombian pesos—had been amassed in small donations, many in kind, proffered by the very peasants who were its intended beneficiaries. One peasant was said to have pawned his cattle to help build the station, then presented Salcedo with the deeds to his lands so that the radio priest could use them as collateral for a bank loan. The original equipment, Mejía stressed, had also been made up of GE receivers with three bands that had been "synchronized at the Educational Station at Sutatenza... by the 'teachers of the air,'" whose pupils numbered seven thousand in ninety schools spread over eleven municipalities. Other sources of support for the radiophonic schools, GE's publicity made a point of noting, were provided by the Ministry of National Education, which had donated the primers students used to follow along with the radio instruction, the Ministry of Health, which conducted a sanitation campaign in the towns where radio schools had been established, and various press outlets in Bogotá, which had featured admiring stories about Sutatenza that brought the organization's work to the public's attention in *El Tiempo, El Espectador, El Siglo,* and *Semana.*[23]

Getting by with a Little Help from Friends

Father Salcedo returned to Colombia in January 1950 well-equipped to embark on an ambitious expansion of ACPO and Radio Sutatenza, his reputation as the inventor of an ingenious system for educating the rural poor through the use of radio technology having made him a minor celebrity in certain influential US corporate and official circles. During Salcedo's absence abroad, *The Basis of a Development Program for Colombia,* the result of a 1949 mission led by former New Deal economist, Lauchlin Currie, for the International Bank for Reconstruction and Development (IBRD, later the World Bank), had been completed and published. Two chapters in the report specifically dealt with the topics of what would constitute ACPO's central mission: "Education" and "Training." Both issues were understood by the IBRD analysts as having a "direct bearing on the level of productivity" in society and on human beings' general ability to "appreciat[e]" and "enjoy life,"[24] explicit confirmation of the centrality of ACPO's work to the success of national development aspirations.

Indeed, the 1950s would constitute a kind of "golden era" for ACPO, a time of expansion and growth when the radio schools and their founder enjoyed increasing recognition at home and abroad. Radio Sutatenza, the ACPO broadcasting station, cooperated with the government to develop radio programs for rural schoolteachers, soldiers, and prisoners, expanding its mandate to include broadcasts in urban rehabilitation centers specifically aimed at Bogotá's growing corps of female domestic workers, many of them refugees or migrants displaced from the countryside because of declining economic opportunities or violence.[25] At the same time, through Vatican Radio broadcasts publicizing the Colombian radio schools and the circulation of recommendations made by CELAM (the Latin American Episcopal Conference) at its inaugural meeting in Rio de Janeiro in 1955, word of the radiophonic schools and their success spread, attracting the curiosity and interest of countries in the region facing challenges similar to those in Colombia.

In 1956 the director of ACPO was invited to consult with the cardinal archbishop of Rio de Janeiro and lay educators in Brazil interested in adopting the radiophonic school model for use in the impoverished, overwhelmingly black, northeast. Studies to consider the replication of the ACPO template were also undertaken in mission territories under the direction of Belgian religious orders in Africa, and in select regions of Mexico, the Dominican Republic, Venezuela, Peru, India, and Bolivia. When not traveling to consult abroad, Monsignor Salcedo hosted visitors from other countries at the Sutatenza complex. ACPO also began to offer specialized courses or seminars to educators from Venezuela and elsewhere and to undertake the translation and publication of its educational materials for English-speaking countries. In 1957, when Salcedo was in the midst of preparing a project for the creation of an International Institute of Education with the support of UNESCO, General Gustavo Rojas Pinilla, who had been an important source of financial and political support for ACPO, was forced out of office, ushering in a period of political uncertainty in Colombia and forcing ACPO to recalibrate its approach.[26]

For several years, ACPO had enjoyed the uninterrupted favor of Colombian governments, assuming a quasi-official role in educational matters, its mission no longer limited to addressing the question of *adult* rural literacy, but expanding to encompass the education of rural school-age children as persistent violence in the countryside magnified the deficiencies of an already inadequate rural education system. But "mission creep," the rapidity and scope of ACPO's expansion, its director's frequent, high-profile travel to Washington, New York, Rome, as well as to other parts of Latin America, and ACPO's seeming reliance on the support of a now deposed dictator for its success in soliciting support abroad from foreign governments and private interest groups, began to stir uneasiness among some members of the Colombian episcopacy who worried that ACPO had grown too big, too fast, and that with the fall of its most significant patron might experience difficulties that would reflect badly on the Catholic Church. Was ACPO primarily a "work of the Church" or a government-sponsored rural development agency? The Colombian Bishops Conference insisted ACPO reform its statutes and create a governing body in order to clarify the organization's mission and to bind it more tightly to episcopal oversight.

The seventy-page *Informe de la Dirección General de Acción Cultural Popular a la II Asamblea General de la Institución* summarizing ACPO's work between 1954 and 1957, published in August 1957 shortly after Rojas Pinilla's fall from power, was Monsignor Salcedo's statistical "proof" of the efficacy of the radio school and leadership training model and the organization's emerging regional reputation for technical expertise in the field of communications and community development. An exhaustive enumeration of every aspect of the organization's development, lavishly illustrated with photographs, pie charts, graphs, maps, and lists of participants and beneficiaries, the *Informe* also became an advertisement for ACPO's mastery of the quantitative and public relations skills required of organizations aspiring to be taken seriously by international donors and agencies. By the late 1950s it was no longer enough to have a compelling sob story when requesting foreign assistance; entities like ACPO were expected to demonstrate that they were models of modernizing efficiency and accountability. Already well-acquainted with the extent to which funders in the United States liked to be able to quantify and then advertise the impact of their contributions—the early experience with General Electric and its public relations machine having left a lasting impression on ACPO's director—Monsignor Salcedo understood that the best way to assuage potential critics of the organization at home while convincing prospective supporters abroad that ACPO was up to the weighty task of redeeming rural Latin American society and protecting it from the threat of communism, was to produce a state-of-the-art textual and visual compendium of the organization's achievements framed in uplifting but sober prose, bolstered by abundant graphics, and punctuated with quotes from recognized "experts" attesting to the efficacy and importance of the ACPO project.

Monsignor Salcedo wielded the *Informe* to maximum effect, using it as the equivalent of an annual report for potential investors. Now when he traveled to the United States to lobby corporations, private businessmen, and government agencies and they asked for tangible evidence that ACPO's radio-based rural literacy program worked, the monsignor could point to cold, hard figures: 200,000 illiterates taught to read and write every six months; 13,000 hours of original radio broadcasts logged between 1953 and the end of 1956; half a million pesos' worth of vaccinations, fungicides, drugs, beehives, seeds, pamphlets, chalkboards, paper, pencils, and maps distributed in 1957 alone; 2.5 million pesos' worth of real estate and newly constructed buildings; 1 million dollars' worth of electronic and printing equipment, including 5,000 radio receivers and nearly 40,000 radio batteries; and nearly 1,500 trained male and female peasant leaders graduated from the Rural Training Institutes founded in 1954 and 1956.[27]

Impressed by ACPO's achievements and the extent of its already-developed radio, printing, recording, and training infrastructure, influential

members of the US private sector representing a variety of religious preferences and organizations (education, the press, business, government) formed
the American Foundation for Cultural Popular Action, Inc., in June 1958,
convinced that ACPO was the most effective means of stemming the spread
of communism among Latin America's rural masses and disseminating the
values of entrepreneurship, self-help, capitalism, and democracy. With the
help of the United States Information Agency, the foundation was able to obtain a ruling from the Internal Revenue Service declaring it a charitable organization with tax-exempt status, which in turn enabled it to legally funnel
donations of money and materials to ACPO as well as to fund-raise and lobby
on its behalf in the United States.

Returning to Colombia in August 1958 after his successful fund-raising
trip to the United States, Monsignor Salcedo heard Colombia's newly elected democratic president, Alberto Lleras Camargo, in his sobering inaugural
radio address, allude to the urgent need to adopt a national reconstruction
plan with the help of the "great social forces" (among others, the Church).
Five days later, Salcedo wrote the president offering him the cooperation of
ACPO's extensive rural communications system, more than eight hundred
clergy members at the grassroots level who oversaw the radiophonic school
system, and the lay leaders involved in rural extension and educational activities. The president would accept ACPO's offer of cooperation, inaugurating
what would become over the next decade and a half a partnership between
ACPO and the governments of the National Front (1958–1974) in various
projects focusing on rural community development.[28]

Monsignor Salcedo's role as an acknowledged "expert," moreover, would
only grow. Beginning in 1959, ACPO's director would meet with private-
sector interest groups and State Department officials in the Eisenhower and
Kennedy administrations who were anxious to forestall rural unrest and
secure control of Latin America's natural resources and potential markets,
shuttle back and forth to Venezuela at the request of concerned Christian
Democratic businessmen to advise the cardinal archbishop of Caracas on the
best way to stem the expansion of communism in the wake of the Cuban Revolution, and conduct frequent exchanges with his counterpart in Chile, Roger Vekemans, SJ, even hosting President Eduardo Frei and Chilean lay and
religious rural development experts on week-long visits to ACPO's Sutatenza
educational complex or on field trips to observe ACPO's rural peasant leaders
in action. Little wonder that by 1965, Radio Sutatenza would be considered
"the leading center of radiophonic education in the world" and the object
of yearly pilgrimages by "missionaries and leaders from Asiatic and African
Countries" who visited Bogotá "to learn about the radiophonic schools and
how they c[ould] be made to work among their people."[29]

ACPO in the Wake of the Cuban Revolution

As ACPO and its director scaled the heights of renown, questions regarding the efficacy of radio in boosting literacy rates rarely surfaced. Certainly
it was not in the interests of ACPO's corporate sponsors or the companies
selling ACPO communications equipment to question Salcedo's expertise
or ask if radio actually worked as a method for learning to read and write. As
monsignor, Salcedo dryly noted in a 1965 radio interview with the Spanish
Ministry of Education, he had pitched the radiophonic school idea to General Electric and Philips by saying, "Moving radiophonic merchandise from the
city to the countryside is a good opportunity, a good hope for radio manufac-
turers," adding that "even if we didn't teach reading and writing to peasants
we'd make them buy a lot of radios."[30]

It was the Catholic Church that first commissioned a systematic study
to assess the efficacy of ACPO's radiophonic schools. In 1959 the Swiss-
based Catholic Research Center, FERES, hired Colombia's future "guerrilla
priest" (*cura guerrillero*), Camilo Torres, to evaluate the radiophonic schools
as part of a series of studies analyzing the state of the Catholic Church and
its activities in Latin America.[31] Published in 1961, the study by Torres and
his coauthor Berta Corredor found that the degree to which the radiophonic schools prompted students to improve their education or take part in
community-based, self-help activities aimed at material improvement (home
repair, collaboration to pipe in water, garden/chicken coop adoption) depended largely on the level of commitment and consistent leadership exercised by the parish priest or other ACPO facilitator.[32] In other words, *human intervention* and *leadership*, rather than technology per se, appeared to
be the keys to the radiophonic schools' success. The Colombian sociologist,
Orlando Fals Borda, who evaluated the effectiveness of the government's
secular Communal Action (Acción Comunal) programs around the same
time (1960) arrived at similar conclusions regarding the key elements in successful community development efforts: it was not the materials or machines
donated by the government that made a difference in whether or not Acción
Comunal succeeded, but rather the constant efforts made by local leaders to
model for other peasants the activities to be taken up by the community, and
the stimulus they provided when community enthusiasm waned.[33]

In 1965 Sister Vincent Marie Primrose of Saint Louis University completed a PhD dissertation comparing the reception and effectiveness of
ACPO's radiophonic schools in three different Colombian regions (Antioquia, Valle, and Boyacá).[34] Sister Primrose echoed many of Torres and Corredor's findings, but with considerably more detail. She found that radiophonic schools were most effective when they were neighborhood- rather than
family-centered; that Radio Sutatenza's radiophonic method *had* reduced

illiteracy and been quite influential in galvanizing peasants to adopt techniques for improving their material lives between 1955 and 1960, but interest in the radio schools had since waned; that ACPO's impact was greatest in more remote areas with fewer alternative sources of employment or ways of being exposed to technical skills and "modern" ways of thinking; that lay leaders made the greatest difference in whether communities successfully applied and benefited from ACPO's educational and technical instruction; and that local cultural practices, circumstances, and tastes shaped in fundamental ways whether or not local communities found Radio Sutatenza's programming and teachings appealing.[35] "Personal contact," Sister Primrose concluded, was the key to ACPO's transformative potential: "Radio, even with the supplementary materials, is not enough."[36] In order for ACPO to succeed in the future, the nun concluded, it would need to decentralize its operations and adjust its programming and approach to reflect the very different material and cultural circumstances of its potential rural audience.

In response to changing funding priorities and the critiques offered by studies like Sister Vincent Marie Primrose's, ACPO retooled, incorporating the thinking of a new generation of US rural sociologists who believed that the first step to successful modernization lay in fomenting "a new mentalité and spirit in the peasant milieu" in which exposure to mass media communication alone was insufficient to effect change. New sociological theories espoused by influential US rural sociologists like Everett Rogers of Michigan State University, for instance, posited that in order to "internalize mass media messages," peasants had to be able to "imagine themselves psychologically in the roles" of the modern individuals and situations whose examples they were exposed to in instruction manuals and radio broadcasts.[37] Revisionist thinking on the importance of lay leaders and of peasants modeling change for other peasants actually fit perfectly with ACPO's expanded emphasis on rural leadership training in the wake of the Cuban Revolution, and ACPO beefed up its emphasis on rural leadership training accordingly.

ACPO also restructured its internal organization, creating its own in-house Department of Sociology and entrusting the design of manuals, recordings, radio programming, and rural theater scripts to reflect the varied problems, culture, language, and conditions typical of rural communities in different parts of Colombia to lay professionals, many of whom were sent to obtain graduate degrees at places like the University of Florida (where T. Lynn Smith taught), Michigan State University, and the University of Wisconsin (home of the Land Tenure Center). Priests hired to work in ACPO's administration, moreover, were sent to obtain specialized training in social communications and sociology in Belgium, the Netherlands, Rome, and Germany. These trained "experts" would staff ACPO's newly created Latin American Institute for Rural Leadership Training (1966) and later, ACPO's

International Peasant Institute, designing and producing the educational materials for export that would become the organization's forte in the 1970s and 1980s.

In the 1980s when ACPO was mired in debt and no longer the darling of the Vatican, German bishops, USAID, government or private donors, the efficacy of its "nonformal" education and community development system discredited by some as nothing more than "CIA financed anti-communist propaganda in the countryside under the guise of a Church radio literacy program," and its founder excoriated as a "high-living prelate" who spent more time shuttling around the globe and escorting foreign dignitaries, foundation presidents, and possible donors on specially catered tours of ACPO's impressive, state-of-the-art facilities than tending to the needs of Colombia's peasantry. ACPO nonetheless continued to enjoy an enviable international reputation as one of Latin America's few Cold War development success stories, and its former director was hailed as an early expert in nonformal education and communication technologies for rural development.[38]

Indeed, even the most cursory search on the internet of the name Radio Sutatenza/ Acción Cultural Popular will bring up several glowing references to the organization as the "granddaddy" or precursor of the contemporary community radio movement, and Monsignor Salcedo as the pioneer in the use of media-based technologies for literacy and community development. By the mid-1960s, as one gushing analyst noted, ACPO encompassed "five AM stations . . . [with] the strongest radio signal in Colombia, reaching millions of urban and rural dwellers," two presses, a recording studio for making and distributing printed educational materials nationally and internationally, a weekly newspaper aimed at rural inhabitants with a circulation that rivaled Colombia's largest circulation daily, *El Tiempo*, and three Rural Leadership Institutes for training peasant men and women from Colombia and abroad to become local community leaders.[39]

In this essay I have used the case of Radio Sutatenza/ACPO to explore the politics shaping the motivations, material circumstances, alliances, and expectations that enabled the rise and rapid transformation of a recently ordained, unknown priest assigned to work in a remote rural parish with no credentials to speak of, into a celebrated, transnational, mass communication and education "expert," whose "fundamental integral education" philosophy and radio school approach were enthusiastically embraced and promoted by an eclectic collection of secular, religious, private, and government interests that, superficially at least, defied easy categorization except perhaps for sharing a common interest: defeating communism.

The time frame during which ACPO was founded, flourished, and ultimately foundered almost exactly reproduces the duration many analysts mark as the beginning and end dates of the Cold War, 1947 to 1989.[40] At the same time, the solutions Monsignor Salcedo devised to address the pressing issues of rural education and community development in Colombia faithfully reflected postwar western developmental obsessions with rural communities as "easy targets for Communist infiltration" because of prevailing conditions of "poverty, exploitation and injustice."[41] The ACPO approach, in which literacy formed the linchpin of development, followed up by a training program for rural leaders that emphasized *technical* solutions to address the material *symptoms* of poverty (inadequate housing, poor nutrition, lack of clean water, the absence of collective or communal organization) ultimately left intact the complex social, cultural, and material conditions rooted in structural inequalities of power and material resources that had characterized Colombia's rural society for centuries.

But of course, radical change was exactly what ACPO had been created to avoid and what attracted the significant financial and political support it amassed at home and abroad for the better part of four decades. Like other projects of rural improvement based on an ideology of self-help, moreover, ACPO's one-size-fits-all recipe for raising rural communities out of their supposed lethargy and lack of technical know-how eventually ran up against the realization that while the dearth of schools and general condition of poverty in the Colombian countryside tended to be widespread, the social and geographic situation of the rural poor was varied. Teaching peasants in relatively prosperous coffee-producing regions how to improve their soil with compost, vary their diet by planting a kitchen garden, or reduce bacteria-borne diseases by building a latrine was one thing, but it was quite another to convince those with no access to land, bound in near feudal servitude, to take advantage of ACPO's lessons in how to raise rabbits for extra protein or adopt the use of shoes to avoid hookworm.

ACPO's early and rapid success came at a steep price, moreover, eventually unraveling in the face of controversy over its mission and director, questions about its finances and internal management, political polarization between the Church, the state and Colombian society, and skepticism regarding the efficacy and even the need for education and leadership training aimed at rural adults in an increasingly urbanized country where television and air travel had supposedly supplanted "old-fashioned" technologies like radio in the countryside. Colombia's rural poor were already "modern," ACPO's critics argued by the 1980s, and ACPO's mission and the technologies it deployed, old-fashioned and out of date. Coupled with the organization's inability to continue to reconcile the conflicting agendas and demands of the eclectic patchwork of secular, religious, domestic, and international funders and collaborators that had originally made possible its transformation from a modest, parish-centered catechetical and literacy outreach program to a transnational communications enterprise that exported its products and expertise abroad, particularly once ACPO's Responsible Pro-creation campaign of the early 1970s brought it into direct confrontation with Colombia's conservative, Catholic Church hierarchy, ACPO foundered. In ACPO's demise, as in its rise, parallels may be found with the fate of other ambitious postwar development projects that were once celebrated and now have faded into oblivion, or worse, been delegitimized, as ACPO came to be by critics on the Left, as little more than propaganda or CIA fronts.

Like other iconic development projects targeting "underdevelopment" associated with the Cold War—whether Green Revolution technology to address food scarcity and hunger or family planning to address population growth and maternal mortality—Radio Sutatenza/Acción Cultural Popu-lar's renown was premised on the claim of having identified a chronic, com-mon, unresolved problem, illiteracy; and it pioneered the application of a supposedly straightforward, technical solution—*mass communication tech-nologies*—to address it. A further, usually explicitly articulated claim typical of Cold War development projects like ACPO's was that the problem they tar-geted and the approach they took to solve it, held *the key* to addressing larger, more intractable issues that impeded realizing the postwar Western ideal of stable, prosperous, capitalist democracies. Hungry? Produce more food. Low yields? Apply fertilizer or selective breeding. Too many children, unable to feed, clothe, or educate them? Control your fertility. Longing to escape the shackles of ignorance, poverty, and subordination? Plagued by clientelism, paternalism, or oppressive government? Learn to read. As the final line in one of ACPO's carefully crafted program-justifications-cum-fund-raising-appeals starkly put it, "The activities of the Radio Schools may be summed up in these words: 'BETTER MEN FOR A BETTER WORLD.'"

NOTES

1. The Radio Sutatenza/ACPO Archive, comprising nearly a million documents, includ-ing scripts, peasant correspondence, financial records, educational manuals, recordings, and film, was donated by the ACPO Foundation to Colombia's main public library, the Biblioteca Luis Angel Arango (BLAA) in Bogotá in 2008. The archive is currently in the process of being cataloged but is open for consultation by scholars. The author wishes to thank both the wonder-ful staff in the Sala de Raros y Manuscritos of the BLAA, especially Zulma Abril and Magnolia Hernández, as well as her indefatigable research assistant, Susana Romero Sánchez, without whose research help this essay would not have been possible.

2. There would eventually be three institutes, the first exclusively for men, established in 1954, a training institute for women established in 1956, and a third institute, also for men, established in 1962 in the town of Caldas, Antioquia, near Medellín.

3. Archive of the Catholic University of America (hereafter, ACUA), National Catholic Welfare Conference (NCWC), "International Affairs: Latin America 1960," Box 4, File 43, "Literacy for Democracy" brochure.

4. Stephen Kinzer, *The Brothers: John Foster Dulles, Allen Dulles, and Their Secret World War* (New York: Times Books, Henry Holt, 2013).

5. No consensus exists about Radio Sutatenza's efficacy in the reduction of adult illiteracy, but some agreement exists that rural leadership training could make a difference in peasant acceptance of technology and the encouragement of rural civic participation. See Martin S. Ferrer, *Muestra Piloto de las Escuelas Radiofónicas Rurales* (Bogotá: Acción Cultural Popular, Escuelas Radiofónicas de Sutatenza, 1951); Camilo Torres Restrepo and Berta Corredor Rodriguez, *Las escuelas radiofónicas de Sutatenza-Colombia: Evaluación sociológica de los resultados*. Oficina Internacional de Investigaciones Sociales de FERES, Friburgo y Bogotá (Madrid: Sucesores de Rivadeneyra S.A., 1961); Sister Vincent Marie Primrose, "A Study of the Effectiveness of the Educational Program of the Radiophonic Schools of Sutatenza on the Life of the Colombian Peasant Farmer" (PhD diss., Saint Louis University, 1965); and Everett M. Rogers in association with Lynne Svenning, *Modernization among Peasants: The Impact of Communication* (New York: Holt, Rinehart and Winston, 1969), 78–79.

6. ACUA, NCWC, "International Affairs: Latin America 1960," Box 4, File 43, "Literacy for Democracy" brochure.

7. The reasons that ACPO ended are complex and beyond the scope of this essay to examine in depth. Monsignor Salcedo, however, built on his ACPO experience and considerable international contacts to become a media and educational consultant first in New York City and then in Miami, where he died in 1994.

8. ACPO, *Primer Congreso Latinoamericano de Escuelas Radiofónicas*, 1963, 5.

9. For an excellent introduction to Catholic transnational exchanges and connections in various parts of Latin America before 1962, see Stephen J. C. Andes and Julia G. Young, eds., *Local Church, Global Church: Catholic Activism in Latin America from Rerum Novarum to Vatican II* (Washington, DC: Catholic University of America Press, 2016); for the specific case of Colombia, see chapter 10, Mary Roldán, "Popular Cultural Action, Catholic Transnationalism, and Development in Colombia before Vatican II," 245–274.

10. The Federation of Coffee Growers and ACPO would form a close collaborative relationship promoting various aspects of community development from soil conservation and tree planting to housing, potable water, and family planning campaigns over the long arc of ACPO's existence from 1947 to 1989.

11. "Inter-American Notes," *Americas* 1, no. 2 (October 1944): 237.

12. Catherine C. LeGrand, "The Antigonish Movement of Canada and Latin America: Catholic Cooperatives, Christian Communities, and Transnational Development in the Great Depression and the Cold War," in Andes and Young, *Local Church, Global Church*, 207–244.

13. ACUA, NCWC/USCC Records SAD *Inter-American Seminars*, Washington, DC, 1942, Collection 10, Box 4.

14. ACUA, NCWC, International Affairs: Latin America, 1959–66, Box 43 (2), John Considine, "Working Group on Inter-American Relations," 1.

15. Colombia, Ministerio de Educación, *Memoria* (Bogotá: Imprenta Nacional, 1951), xiii–xiv.

16. UNESCO, *UNESCO Courier,* June 1951, 6.

17. Not included in ACPO's official histories of this visit and the materials purchased, but found in the press booklet GE generated for publicity purposes after Salcedo's visit, is the mention of mobile radio units.

18. GE Electronics News Bureau, Edwin Gurley, "Radiophonic Schools in South America," January 1950, 1.

19. Father Mejía was one of the Colombian priests who benefited from training at the Catholic University of America. With Alliance for Progress and USAID funding, he would go on to work with the Federation of Agrarian Workers in the Valle del Cauca in the 1960s and 1970s. The Javeriana would pioneer social communication studies in Colombia, creating the first degree-granting program in Journalism and Social Communication in the 1950s.

20. Of the several photos that made up the spread for GE's press release on Salcedo's visit, several show GE engineers and managers beaming at Salcedo as he points a bony finger at a map as if to underline Mejía's observations.

21. ACUA, NCWC, International Affairs: 1943–66, letter and outline of a draft appeal for a fund-raising brochure for ACPO sent by John T. O'Brien Associates to Msgr. Carroll, Sec Gen, dated November 2, 1955, Box 36, F. 26.

22. Francisco Javier Mejía, "The Radiophonic Schools," *Revista Javeriana,* republished by *GE Electronics News Bulletin,* 1950, 2.

23. Mejía, "Radiophonic Schools," 3.

24. *The Basis of a Development Program for Colombia.* Report of a Mission sponsored by the International Bank for Reconstruction and Development in collaboration with the Government of Colombia (Baltimore: Johns Hopkins University Press, 1950), 241.

25. ACPO, *Las Escuelas Radiofónicas y su Labor de 1954 a 1957* (Bogotá: 1957), 50–52.

26. ACPO, *Las Escuelas Radiofónicas,* 43.

27. ACPO, *Las Escuelas Radiofónicas.*

28. Archivo General de la Nación (hereafter, AGN), Presidencia; Despacho Sr. Presidente; Acción Cultural Popular, Escuela Radiofónica/Correspondencia; Caja 108; Carp: 2; F:1, August 12, 1958.

29. Primrose, "Study of the Effectiveness of the Educational Program," 2–3.

30. ACPO Archive, Gestión, Ministerio de Educación de España (transcript of radio interview).

31. Eugene K. Culhane, "The FERES Study of Latin America," *America* 111, no. 13 (September 1964): 345–347.

32. Camilo Torres and Berta Corredor Rodríguez, *Las Escuelas Radiofónicas de Sutatenza, Colombia: Evaluación sociológica de los resultados.* Oficina Internacional de Investigaciones Sociales de FERES, Friburgo y Bogotá (Madrid: Sucesores de Rivadeneyra, S.A., 1961).

33. Orlando Fals Borda with Nina Chaves and Ismael Márquez, *Acción Comunal en una vereda colombiana,* Monografías Sociológicas No. 4 (Bogotá: Universidad Nacional de Colombia, Departamento de Sociología, Bogotá, 1960), 11.

34. Primrose, "Study of the Effectiveness of the Educational Program."

35. Primrose, "Study of the Effectiveness of the Educational Program, 158–178.

36. Primrose, "Study of the Effectiveness of the Educational Program, 174.

37. Everett M. Rogers, *Modernization Among Peasants: The Impact of Communication* (New York: Holt, Rinehart and Winston, 1969).

38. Penny Lernoux, *Cry of the People* (New York: Penguin Books, 1991 [1980]), 289.

39. Jorge Pablo Osterling, *Democracy in Colombia: Clientelist Politics and Guerrilla Warfare* (New Brunswick, NJ: Transaction, 1989), 256–257.

40. For an analysis of the development and impact of ACPO's Responsible Procreation campaign, see Mary Roldán, "Acción Cultural Popular, Responsible Procreation, and the Roots of Social Activism in Rural Colombia," *Latin American Research Review* 49, Special Issue (December 2014): 27–44.

41. Chester Bowles, "Administration of Rural Development in the Underdeveloped Countries," Washington, August 17, 1962. National Science Foundation, Ralph Dungan Papers, Box 392, John F. Kennedy Archive.

PART II

COLD WAR SCIENTIFIC EXCHANGES

5

CHALLENGING CLIMATE AND GEOPOLITICS

Cuba, Canada, and Intensive Livestock Exchange in a Cold War Context, from the 1960s to the 1980s

Reinaldo Funes-Monzote and Steven Palmer

From the beginning, the 1959 Cuban Revolution sought to transform an agrarian society dominated by large sugar and cattle estates. Agrarian reform was at the center of Cold War debates about strategies for economic development, and most revolutionary analysts pointed to the need to overcome the huge concentration of land in few hands in order to achieve a more rational exploitation of natural resources and to reverse chronic unemployment.[1] An increase in local food production had become a central goal in almost all evaluations of Cuba's potential economic development on the eve of the revolution, as it was nearly everywhere in the development decades of the 1950s and 1960s. In revolutionary Cuba, this common rhetoric became an immediate target of an agrarian reform highly conscious of how much the Cuban diet relied on imports from the United States.[2] The revolutionary government immediately began planning to diversify domestic sources of animal protein, which, until then, had been overwhelmingly centered on beef and, in smaller measure, milk.

After a brief increase in food imports from the United States in 1959, the growing conflict over the agrarian reform and other revolutionary laws on the island prompted the United States' imposition of an economic embargo on Cuba in January 1961. In response, Cuba urgently sought alternatives to its traditional dependence on US food imports, and in doing so helped to refute the supposed natural order of geography. The opponents of the revolution, especially after the regime's affiliation with the communist bloc, accused the government of "an alteration of the natural and almost spontaneous laws that Cuba's pristine geopolitical factors had imposed," which "are constantly con-

spiring against Castro and his regime."[3] Perhaps one of the best examples
of the revolution's challenge to traditional conceptions of geopolitics and
climatic determinism was its radical shift from patterns of extensive cattle
raising dedicated to beef production to a more intensive model focused on
dairy industries. The catalyst for this shift was the Cuban Revolution's development of a tight relationship with Canada for the massive exchange of
bovine genetic stock and other animal species. Once the doors were closed
to buying breeding animals from the United States, that role was quickly occupied by Canada, which joined Mexico as the only country in the Americas
that did not participate in the US-led hemispheric isolation of Cuba.

The impetus for this partnership came from Cuba, however. Before the
conflict with the United States reached the impasse of embargo, loyal confi-
dantes of Castro's revolutionary leadership, some of them comrades in arms
from the Sierra Maestra, were dispatched to Canada to explore the Canadian government's willingness to welcome Cuban buyers of Canadian animals
and feed. When it became clear that no objection would be raised, a major
program of securing Canadian animal genes was organized, and prized
Canadian livestock were purchased at principal Canadian auction sites. By
May 1963, a total of twenty thousand Canadian Holstein cows and high-
quality breeding bulls arrived in Cuba to transform the island's livestock
herd through direct mating and artificial insemination. To facilitate this relationship, the Cuban government operated a corral in a major Canadian
port to collect and tend to the animals prior to shipment on a fleet of Cuban
vessels. Underscoring the political theater and significance of this relationship, a famous Canadian stud bull was declared a hero of the revolution, and
one of his thousands of descendants, Ubre Blanca (White Udder) would not
only break the world record for milk production, but in a fitting ideological
twist, unseat the reigning champion from the United States in the process.

The shipment of breeding animals would gradually be replaced by importing Canadian materials for artificial insemination. After Canada
launched a more proactive development policy of its own for Latin America
in 1968, full-scale technical assistance and expert scientific exchanges and
training led to an increasingly complex and interwoven program between the
two countries. When the Canadian prime minister Pierre Trudeau became
the second Western head of state to make an official visit to Cuba in 1976, he
noted that, despite the "differences between a Latin American tropical country and a northern continental nation of harsh climate," Canada and Cuba
shared many interests, citing in particular the mutual project of "creating
new breeds of cattle."[4]

The bovine connection between a capitalist, temperate Canada and a
revolutionary, tropical Cuba is poorly treated in studies evaluating the maintenance of diplomatic relations between the two countries.[5] Our research,

based largely on personal interviews with many of the protagonists of the livestock exchange programs between Canada and Cuba, reveals not only the challenge of mutual relations between countries on opposite sides of the ideological Cold War but also the interaction of two countries located in climatic opposition. Notably, Cuba's intensive animal-breeding program generated important exchanges with scientists and experts from several western countries, such as Canada, eclipsing those same scientific exchanges with specialists in the allied countries of communist Eastern Europe and the USSR. The Cuba–Canada cattle exchange is a unique window into the genetic politics of Cold War developmentalism. It further suggests the radical transformations involved in the breeding of "temperate" genetic stock and its acclimation to tropical environments. After the crisis in local food production and the dire scarcities that beset Cuba in 1990 following the collapse of subsidized imports of fuel and fertilizer from the Soviet bloc, the dubious sustainability of such an intensive system of milk production relying on expensive imported inputs reminds us of the vulnerabilities inherent in a scientific and heavily industrialized food system based on the adoption of North American and, ultimately, capitalist agricultural practices.

French Expertise and Revolutionary Cattle

In the 1950s, stock raising appeared to be one of the fields of greatest potential in Cuban agriculture. A 1951 report produced by the so-called Truslow Mission of the International Bank for Reconstruction and Development (IBRD) recognized progress in this area thanks to farmers' energetic efforts in selective breeding. But that change focused on beef cattle and involved the participation of several sugar mills. Stock raising for milk, according to the report, presented a more deficient picture, with a daily production per cow of less than two liters, and only three liters in Havana. As a result, the report stated that "scientific dairymen elsewhere, who consider a cow of dubious value if she cannot give at least sixteen liters and expect twenty to thirty, might feel that it is hardly worth the trouble to milk most Cuban cows."[6] Despite this grim reality, many observers struck an optimistic tone. In 1957, Henry A. Wallace, former vice president of the United States and longtime agrarian commentator in Latin America, visited the agricultural school run by the United Fruit Company's Preston sugar mill, where he noted the island's potential to lead in the continued improvement of tropical varieties of cattle for beef as well as milk production.[7]

Cuba's dairy prospects took on new meaning after 1959. The need to increase local food production to reduce dependence on imports and improve the diet, and especially to diversify the sources of animal protein became a central focus of the new government. In this context, the transformation of

extensive ranching to a more intensive model of stock raising was seen as a
crucial necessity. Many foreign experts sent by international organizations
such as the United Nations Food and Agriculture Organization (FAO), or
invited by the Cuban government, showed a high degree of consensus on
this point. One of these, the French agronomist René Dumont, known for
his studies on agriculture in socialist and tropical countries (including the
USSR, China, Jamaica, and Mexico), became one of the revolutionary government's earliest advisers. His first reports to Cuba's National Institute for
Agrarian Reform (INRA) were presented in May of 1960, and he returned to
the island in 1963 and 1969. He estimated that few countries in the tropics
had such favorable conditions, saying the island "can perfectly well feed 50
million people if it were cultivated like southern China."[8]

Dumont underlined the importance of increased productivity by area
through diversification, water control, and a move toward mixed agriculture.
In his view, milk production was more efficient to the health of young Cubans than beef, since it required 1 to 2 units of fodder per liter of milk against
10 or 20 units per kilogram of meat. Aware that a meat shortage would be
unpopular, he advocated simultaneous increases in the island's hog production and prohibitions on the slaughter of breeding cows.[9] Dumont warned
that the majority of agricultural workers' families were well below his targets for healthy milk consumption. He outlined a plan for national increases
toward 100 liters of annual milk consumption per capita by 1965, followed
by increases to 150 liters by 1970. These targets included the development
of specialized regional processing plants for cheese, butter, and condensed,
evaporated, and powdered milk.

The French agronomist's additional recommendations were to adopt
dual-purpose breeds designed for dairy and beef production; to measure
yields not per head but by area; to phase out the use of comparatively deficient native pasturage except where unavoidable; and to adopt anti-erosion
practices. He warned that if Cuba's livestock sector continued its static practices, the changes to landownership ushered in by the revolution would do
little to improve agricultural output. In this regard, he said, "If sugarcane
demands to be intensified and diversified with other crops, current Cuban
stock raising demands much more, it requires a real technical revolution that
departs completely from the extensive system of grazing and breeding."

In 1960 Dumont was accompanied by his fellow professor at the Agronomy Institute of Paris, Julien Coléou, author of the report, "Animal Production
in Cuba."[10] Coléou warned that the country could not afford to "change its
cattle overnight," given the economic and health risks that this implied. Nevertheless, some pure milk-producing breeds such as the Holstein-Friesen,
the Brown Swiss, and the Jersey could immediately complement a more intensive system. The Holstein historically showcased greater possibilities as

the first internationally coveted breed for milk, and the Brown Swiss had the advantage of resistance to heat. Creole cattle could enhance these foreign breeds' acclimatization through successive crossbreeding, or a process of "grading up." Despite the revolutionary setting, the French experts' recommendations were remarkably conventional and reflected long-standing interest in enhancing nutrition and agricultural production in Latin America through the adoption of foreign breeds and shortcuts to efficiency such as the "dual-purpose" cow, an especially appealing ideal during the lean years of the Great Depression. The significance of their plans lay less in the nuance of the details than in the continuity and adaptation of projects outlined earlier by Henry Wallace or the IBRD for a drastically divergent revolutionary context.

Many of these recommendations were consistent with the ideas of the Chilean agronomist Jacques Chonchol, an Economic Commission for Latin America and the Caribbean-FAO expert. In his August 1960 report, he indicated eight strategies for leveraging progress in the area of Cuban livestock.[11] He recommended the use of quality breeding stock and zootechnical controls. Regional centers could provide breeding males to agricultural enterprises for direct or artificial insemination. He also said that three or four breeds would have to be chosen that proved their ability to adapt to the Cuban environment and that could be further distributed to other countries beyond Cuba.

Assessments such as these of the state of stock raising and its potential coincided with issues being discussed on the island and served to justify a move toward more intensive farming systems. In general, these foreign experts and their Cuban reports channeled a broader discourse on development, including the need to increase animal protein in the human diet.[12]

Furthermore, the foreign experts had Fidel Castro's ear.[13] At the close of the First National Meeting on Agrarian Reform, on August 17, 1961, Castro devoted particular attention to the problems of milk and meat supply. He based his talk on a census conducted by the INRA that showed a dramatic decline in Cuba's livestock herd.[14] His proposed eight-year recovery plan would be based on the specialization of livestock in milk or meat for better production performance. Along with announcing restrictions on the consumption of beef, plans were simultaneously revealed to raise poultry, hogs, and fish as a way to increase protein.[15] Showcasing his personal dedication to this project, Castro spoke at the graduation ceremony of two hundred inseminators at El Chico farm on December 12, 1961. From this early moment, the transformation of Cuban livestock became one of Castro's priorities.

Fidel Castro's enthusiasm set a foundation for the highly publicized visit to Cuba of the famous French scientist André Voisin, the author of several books about pastures, cattle raising, soils and their relationship to human health. He had been invited by Fidel himself to implement his theories of rotating grazing systems. He arrived on the island in late 1964 and followed an intense schedule that included teaching a large class for livestock scientists and technicians, which was attended by Fidel. Voisin rehashed long-standing European assumptions about Edenic tropical nature. "You can do anything you want with this very rich Nature, with this climate," he said. Regrettably, in the middle of his visit, the French scientist died suddenly of a heart attack in Havana on December 21.[16]

Despite Voisin's untimely death in Cuba, Castro's enthusiasm for livestock improvement continued to grow. On many occasions throughout the 1960s, his speeches detailed stock-raising projects, mainly in institutions concerned with these matters or on anniversaries of the National Association of Small Farmers. In those speeches, he spoke of ambitious goals in milk production, cattle population, pasture fertilization through inputs, leguminous cover crops, and irrigation; and of enhancing the dairy industry to produce, for example, dozens of new varieties of cheeses. Castro further outlined the mechanization of milk production, the improvement of living conditions for dairy-farm workers, the concentration of milk production around Havana, and the introduction of mass technical training programs. The basis of this transformative process would be the use of imported Holsteins for crossbreeding with the predominant Zebu cattle, forming a new herd designed for the efficient production of milk and meat by-products.

The most ambitious of these goals never came to fruition, and beef cattle in particular never exceeded the levels achieved at the beginning of the revolution, maintaining a downward trend with small fluctuations thereafter.[17] Yet the country's milk production did increase dramatically during the 1970s and 1980s. The development and consolidation of Cuba's milk program rested on three pillars: genetic improvements of cattle, a productive technical infrastructure, and the promotion of a new food base with the intensive cultivation of pastures, forages, and sugarcane by-products. None of these would have been possible without the extraordinary livestock links forged between Cuba and Canada very early on in the revolution.

Rosafe Signet, the Canadian Father of the Cuban Dairy Industry

The first efforts toward agricultural modernization after 1959 retained the United States and other neighboring countries as main sources for animal genetic stock. But with the breakdown in diplomatic relations with the United States, it was soon clear that the best alternative trading partner was Canada, which for complex reasons maintained diplomatic and commercial links with Cuba despite intense US pressure. The mass importation of animals and genetic material from Canada began between 1960 and 1961, with breeding hogs the primary target at first.[18] The partnership quickly spread to poul-

FIGURE 5.1. Rosafe Signet, Canada 1954—Cuba 1966. Source: Antonio Núñez Jiménez Foundation, photo collection, Album 923. Courtesy of the Antonio Núñez Jiménez Foundation.

try as Cuba imported large quantities of feed and breeding birds from the north.[19] Canada, however, was perhaps best-known internationally for the quality and sophistication of its cattle breeding, and it was free of the foot-and-mouth disease that was rampant in the Americas (see chapter 6 in this volume). Links between Cuban and Canadian cattlemen were not new, but they quickly became key to forming a new genetic base to increase animal protein production in revolutionary Cuba.

The most extensive and complex gene transfer programs between Canada and Cuba involved dairy cattle. The symbolic beginning of a coordinated program to crossbreed Cuban stock with Canadian Holsteins occurred in May 1962 with the arrival in Cuba of a famous stud bull named Rosafe Signet, born in 1954 in Brampton, Ontario.[20] Castro announced the $28,000 purchase of this Canadian bull at the graduation ceremony of the two hundred inseminators at El Chico farm in December 1961.[21] Rosafe Signet, named for his birthplace, Rosafe Farms, was owned by Hector I. Astengo, an Argentine who had come to Canada in 1947 and bought the renowned ABC farm.[22] In the mid-1950s, Rosafe Signet was sold as a calf for $20,000 at the Royal Winter Fair to Jack McCague of Alliston, Ontario. The bull was twice proclaimed Grand Champion Male at the Royal Winter Fair of Canada in 1958 and 1959. He sired twelve daughters who would likewise win international awards.

One of the first Cuban buyers of cattle in Canada during 1963 and 1964 claims that the acquisition of Rosafe Signet owed largely to a veterinarian and former guerrilla soldier named Pío Alvarez Pileta, from the Guáimaro region in Camagüey province. Castro sent Alvarez to Canada with other representatives to accomplish the purchasing mission, and he remained

FIGURE 5.2. Grave of Rosafe Signet at El Dique farm, the former artificial insemination center in Cuba where the bull lived until his death on March 15, 1966. Today
the site is part of the Centro de Investigaciones para el Mejoramiento Animal de la
Ganadería Tropical. Photo by Reinaldo Funes-Monzote.

there until the mid-1960s, buying animals for Cuba's breeding programs. Although Rosafe was already considered an old bull at the time of his purchase
and shipment to Cuba, Alvarez's veterinarian work supposedly prolonged his
breeding vitality.[23] As Castro proclaimed in December 1961, insemination
with the sperm of Rosafe Signet, whom he initially labeled an "aristocratic
bull," could produce offspring in at least five thousand cows a year. Castro
reconsidered Rosafe's revolutionary credentials on these laurels and re-
dubbed him a "worker and producer bull" who should be paired with similarly hardworking cows. As Fidel summarized, in ten years there might well
be fifty-thousand granddaughters or great-granddaughters descended from
Rosafe, and these would in turn be inseminated with proven bulls.[24]

   After four years of service in Cuba, on March 15, 1966, the famous Rosafe
Signet was sacrificed at age twelve due to illness. The news caused great con-
sternation among Cuban leaders and breeders. A monument was later erected at El Dique ranch honoring the famous bull with the inscription, "Here are
buried the remains of the stud of Canadian origins, Rosafe Signet, considered the father of Cuban dairy livestock." A few months later, in April 1967,
his name was given to the largest center for artificial insemination in Cuba,
inaugurated near the El Dique ranch. An article in *Bohemia* explained the
designation as a tribute to the "Father of national stock raising."[25] The author
quoted the testimony of English and French scientists present that day to cel-

ebrate the inauguration of facilities unequaled in the world. At the entrance, a bronze statue would be erected with the imposing figure of Rosafe, who already had his tomb in El Dique. The new center maintained 120 bulls from 6 European breeds, providing enough sperm to inseminate 240,000 cows.

Rosafe's enduring effect on Cuban dairying persisted in other ways as well. In an article dated February 9, 1976, describing the visit of the Canadian prime minister Pierre Trudeau to Cuba, the journalist Robert Lewis wrote about the livestock connections between the two countries:

> The most enduring aspect to the trade in cattle between Canada and Cuba is frozen semen. For example, Rosafe Signet, a Brampton, Ont., bull died in Cuba 10 years ago, but because of the quality of his progeny he is still referred to respectfully as "the genetic giant." So gigantic, in fact, that Gerry Mueller, a chemical engineer at the University of Waterloo, recalls a weekend visit to the deserted Varadero beach, 80 miles east of Havana, in 1973. Down the beach was a group of Canadian cattlemen, who were in Cuba to buy frozen semen produced by Brampton's very own Rosafe Signet.[26]

As the role reversal in this anecdote suggests, Rosafe became a catalyst for a lasting relationship, one that included bilateral and multidirectional exchange of genetic material.

A Cuban Enclave in the Canadian Maritimes

A new era of greater organization in the purchase and transfer of animals from Canada to Cuba started in 1964–1965, when a larger group of Cubans was sent to work on the livestock program in coordination with Cuba's diplomatic representatives. Most of the purchases were made in the dairy heartland of Ontario, but Quebec and the Western provinces were also explored. The buyers visited the farms and established a strong relation with the sellers. The Cuban government decided to open a stockyard in the port of Saint John, New Brunswick, where the animals were concentrated and tended by Cuban cowboys and loaded onto ships specially adapted for them. Groups of young students from the island's new technical school cared for the cattle, pigs, and others animals during the voyage aboard these Cuban merchant vessels.

By the mid-1960s, about 10,000 Holstein bulls had been moved to the island, distributed throughout the country for crossing with Zebu cows, in order to create the so-called F1 (Holstein × Zebu) and other breeds. In addition, Canadian stud bulls like Rosafe were distributed among 19 new artificial insemination centers. In 1962 there was a total of 93 breeding bulls, with an average of 352 cows inseminated per year. By 1970 the figures had grown to 1,383 bulls with 893 inseminations per head.[27] These centers practiced cutting-edge techniques, shifting from insemination via semen in ampoules

to the use of semen tablets or pellets after 1966.[28] To determine the most appropriate technique for Cuban conditions, young graduates from the University of Havana were sent to study in the most modern institutions for artificial insemination in Canada, England, France, Japan, Italy, and Israel.[29]

Often, the Cuban program looked to import semen rather than the bull
itself, as in the case of Seiling Rockman, a great Canadian champion.[30] This
method was more effective, significantly cheaper, and less risky since an expensive stud bull might not meet expectations, as in the case of the bull Black
Velvet International, for which the Cuban government paid $100,000. Born
in 1963 as the great-grandson of the parents of Rosafe Signet, Black Velvet International had been Grand Champion at the International Fair of 1966 and
won the titles All-Canadian and All-American bull.[31] Nevertheless, he died
soon after his arrival in Cuba, possibly due to mistakes with his feeding.[32]

By the late 1960s, Cuba could claim its own stud bulls as well as four
thousand inseminators. Adopting the most modern techniques in semen
conservation, the genetic program was guaranteed for many years. But there
were other concerns. One of these was the effect of weather conditions on
imported Holsteins and their crosses with Zebu and other breeds. Many of
the Canadian cows and bulls became sick and died while acclimating to the
tropical heat and humidity, as had the expensive Black Velvet International. Cuban facilities began to experiment with air-conditioning to study the
effects of tropical heat on milk production capacity.[33] These studies led to experimentation with a small structure in which only the cow's head remained
air-conditioned. Based on the experiences of developed countries and the
understanding that dairy production owed to stresses felt in the head, the
process managed a 25 percent saving in air-conditioning costs.

Due to import costs and acclimatization, Cuba's livestock resurgence
rested on a growing population of specifically Cuban-Canadian hybrids rather than purebred cattle. These included new hybrid breeds with increased capacity for both milk and meat production. The first so-called F1 and F2 (2/3
Holstein × 1/3 Zebu) hybrids grew out of the transnational partnership, later
culminating in the creation of new Cuban breeds with dairy potential that
were christened Mambi (3/4 Holstein × 1/4 Zebu) and Siboney (5/8 Holstein × 3/8 Zebu), names associated with creole patriotism.

An April 1973 article about a visit to Cuba by a group of Canadian Holstein breeders described how 15,500 Canadian Holsteins had been moved
to the island over the previous four years.[34] The visitors were impressed by
the valuable contributions that Canada's Holstein exports were making to
the development of Cuban dairy farming. During their stay, they were able
to visit places that were emblematic of Cuba's stock-raising plans, such as the
Bijirita Genetic Center, the Rosafe Signet Artificial Insemination Center, the
Institute of Animal Science, and the Valle de Picadura dairy, the latter direct-

ed by Ramón Castro, Fidel's older brother. Considering the thoroughgoing transformations of the previous decade, the authors concluded, "As the days passed and we saw the contribution that the Holstein breed is making to provide a better life for the people, it cultivated a sense of pride and satisfaction among the Canadians."[35]

Amid this wave of pride and optimism, Pierre Trudeau came to Cuba in January 1976 for what was only the second official visit of a senior leader of "the West" since 1959.[36] Fidel Castro's speech before his visitor underlined the fact that Canada had been the only country, along with Mexico, that did not join in the US-organized policy of isolating the island. After highlighting the growing trade and economic relations between the two countries, Castro elaborated on the contribution of Canadian techniques, particularly in the area of dairy farming. Trudeau also noted the growing trade between the two countries and the purchase by Cuba of cattle and poultry. Although he did not fail to point out their political differences, he commended the priority given to the development of human resources, and the achievements in agrarian reform, health care, education, sanitation, and food production that were "the envy of many countries." At one point, Trudeau pointedly mentioned the joint Canada–Cuba projects in the field of livestock: "Despite the differences between a Latin American tropical country and a northern continental nation of harsh climate, we see that we share a multitude of interests and benefits. For example, we are working on creating new breeds of cattle."[37] For many in Cuba's scientific community in the mid-1970s, the success of the Cuba–Canada stock-breeding partnership offered a rebuttal to genetic theories about alleged "tropical degeneration" or "maximum production limits." Rather than environment, "it is man and particularly his cultural and political level that is the main determinant in livestock production in our underdeveloped areas," stated one Cuban report.[38]

Following Trudeau's visit, Canada's national newsmagazine, *Macleans*, reported that 3,645 Canadian Holsteins had been imported to the island the previous year. The article focused on Oakridge Farm, north of Toronto, with one of the finest Holstein herds in the world, which shipped cattle to Cuba nearly every month. At the time of writing, the manager, George Darrac, was working with Pastor Santiago, a thirty-three-year-old Cuban farmer, one of a group of ten Cuban farmers sent to Canada under the auspices of the Holstein-Freisian Association and the Ontario Ministry of Agriculture to learn "how to manage a ranch with fewer hands than is customary in Cuba."[39] Science and technical sophistication had begun to eclipse labor.

During the 1970s and 1980s, the links between Cuba and Canada expanded in the area of scientific cooperation, as did trade and political relations. Key to this were loans and grants from the Canadian International Development Agency, which provided $14 million to Cuba in the mid-1970s, as well as Canadian University Services Overseas. For example, the chief of the Cuban livestock program in Canada from 1973 to 1977, Dr. Díaz Mulet, remembered in an interview that between 1976 and 1977 many Cuban engineers and veterinarians were sent to Canada to study the advances in stock raising. He also claimed that Cuban buyers were very aware of market prices and were well-informed through specialized journals and direct participation in fairs and farm site visits.[40] As Holstein genes filtered through Cuban livestock, direct animal imports from Canada decreased. Two specialists in the Ministry of Agriculture's Office of Genetics affirmed that the most important cattle introductions were made from 1964 to 1977, and between 1989 and 1990, when registered Holstein females with valuable and recognized ancestors were purchased for genetic improvement in Cuba.[41]

In this history of intensification of the Cuban livestock economy, one aspect that stands out is the major increase in human capital devoted to agricultural sciences and the wide network of scientific institutions established, such as the Indio Hatuey Experimental Station for Pasture and Forage (1962); the Institute of Animal Science (1965); the National Center for Animal and Plant Health (1969–1980); the Research Center for Animal Improvement of Tropical Livestock (1970); the Swine Research Institute (1972); the Poultry Research Institute (1976); and many schools, such as the Agrarian University of Havana (1976) and other universities in several Cuban provinces.

Important progress was made in animal health and veterinary medicine. Between 1959 and 2007, over 5,000 veterinarians were trained, most of them linked to livestock programs. By 1990 some 400,000 professionals had been trained in areas relevant to stock raising. The national development of animal medicine received great impetus. Modern pasteurizers, refrigeration units, and slaughterhouses were built for Havana and other cities. All this fostered a change in dietary habits, particularly the increase in egg, pork, poultry, and fish consumption.[42] Industrial dairy production rose dramatically compared to 1959: by 2007, Cuba produced 9.2 times more ice cream, 4.4 times more fluid milk, 3.7 times more cheese, and 202 times more yogurt.[43]

The Brief Reign of Ubre Blanca

On July 21, 1981, the front page of the official news sheet *Granma* reported on a cow that had become the national record holder by producing 72.9 liters of milk in a triple milking. Her name was Ubre Blanca, White Udder, already eight years old, and living on La Victoria dairy farm on the Isla de la Juventud. According to the reports, she was the daughter of the famous Cuban stud bull, Naranjo Selling Jupiter, and an F1 female born on the same farm, supposedly the granddaughter by matrilineal descent of Rosafe Signet. From that date, the cow received a special diet on top of her regular pangola pasture grass. Described as "a milk factory," Ubre Blanca had a lineage that traced the history of the Canadian–Cuban dairy partnership.

The veterinarian Jorge Hernandez, who was in charge of the cow, affirmed that her story began in May 1980, when cowboys on her farm found that she produced around sixty-three liters in a day. She received close attention from her milker, the young cowboy Arnorldo Carreno, and a hefty daily diet.[44] After receiving the news about Ubre Blanca's high production, a senior political official in the province called the national authorities, and in particular the head of the Office of Genetics, Merejo Curbelo, who realized that this cow might be the one that Fidel Castro was looking for, with the potential to cross the symbolic threshold of one hundred liters of milk in a day. According to Merejo, he went to the Isla de la Juventud and implemented a plan with nutritionists and other specialists to improve the diet until the cow began to approach eighty liters. After seeing the results, Merejo contacted the comandante, and the next day he visited the cow on the Victoria farm.[45]

Three days after the first news in *Granma*, Ubre Blanca received an official visit from Fidel Castro himself. He declared to journalists that day that the tropical world never had the privilege of breeds capable of supplying the indispensable and valuable food that was milk. For this reason, the Cuban experience could be invaluable to many Third World countries with climatic conditions similar to Cuba's.[46] After that visit, Castro received reports of the cow's work every six hours. On July 29, 1981, on a tour of the eastern provinces, Castro stressed that this "machine for producing milk" was not an isolated phenomenon, but the result of a genetic policy and hard work. He confessed to reporters that he had imagined a cow that could reach 100 liters of milk production in a day with an approximate weight of 1,700 or 1,800 pounds. Ubre Blanca far exceeded his imagination in weighing only 1,100 or 1,200 pounds. "This cow is almost a jersey!" he exclaimed. He believed that if she had been fed well from the start, she could have already surpassed 90 liters and even approached 100 liters. With a change of feed and four milkings, she had already reached 89.9 liters.[47]

Only one day later, Ubre Blanca produced 93.5 liters and by July 31 she exceeded 100 liters (102.5 liters in four milkings). News stories highlighted this as the highest production in world history, and as an unquestionable technical triumph of Cuban stock raising, science, and the revolution. On August 3, the record was surpassed again, reaching 107.3 liters. At the same time, a program was launched to preserve her health because she was pregnant. On August 7, a special television roundtable was dedicated to her, with scientists, technicians, and leaders linked to livestock programs. In conclusion, the experts attributed Ubre Blanca to a successful genetic development policy. The daughter of a Cuban bull and with high-quality milk, "she was capable of feeding more than one hundred children a day."[48]

Fidel Castro returned for a second visit on September 21, in the company of the former president of Venezuela, Rafael Caldera, and the president of the Parliament of India. On Christmas Day, a new record was announced: 97.3 liters in three milkings. On January 5 she gave 104.2 liters in three milkings. The next day, Fidel visited the Victoria farm a third time and predicted Ubre Blanca would break the world record for accumulated milk production. As on other occasions, he insisted that "the results achieved by this cow will be beneficial for all humanity, especially the people of tropical countries."[49] In the face of international disbelief, on January 11, 1982, journalists accredited in Cuba from Agence France-Presse, Reuters, L'Humanite, and other international outlets visited Ubre Blanca, the same day that the cow set a new record of 105.9 liters. Finally, on January 27, Ubre Blanca reached her highest record for three milkings: 110.9 liters. The leader of the revolution returned to the Isla de la Juventud on February 20, on his fourth and final visit to the cow, accompanied by the general secretary of the Yemeni Socialist Party, Ali Nasser Mohamed.

As predicted, Ubre Blanca broke all records for accumulated milk production: 27,674 liters in 365 days of lactation. After this news, her appearance in the media began to decrease.[50] In July 1984, an article explained that she was at the National Center for Animal and Plant Health (CENSA) to recover from old injuries. She had been inseminated by the bull Naranjos Proclamar Brody, from the Rosafe Signet center, in order to effect embryo transplantation, a modern technique introduced a few years earlier in Cuba. Less than a year later, *Granma* announced that on the recommendation of scientists and veterinarians the decision had been made to put Ubre Blanca down because of her age (thirteen) and deteriorating health.[51] A group of taxidermists from the Museum of Natural History undertook embalming, which would show her body and its famous udder to future generations. As a result, she can now be contemplated in the lobby of CENSA.

The note in *Granma* explained that US scientists had predicted, after the records of Beecher Arlinda Ellen (89.9 liters in 1975 from three milkings, and 25,272.4 kilograms in 365 days) and Patzi Bar Pontiac (1,025.8 kilograms of fat), that it would take at least two more decades for females to appear capable of such production. However, in just five years the Cuban cow had surpassed US cows with records of 110.9 liters in three milkings, 27,674.2 liters in a year and 1,051.6 kilograms of fat. The sentiment was expressed that those who could admire the grand champion and her colossal udder would feel grateful for the work of Cuban scientists. Ubre Blanca and her records symbolized dairy's ascension over tropical nature and, with it, the improvement of tropical nutrition. She represented a triumph of the revolution. Ubre Blanca's climatic symbolism could be discerned in her third pregnancy: her calf was named "Tropical."

Ubre Blanca, in life and in taxidermic death, became a symbol of the achievements of Cuban socialism. In this regard, the fact that she broke the records of two US cows outweighed her material milk production in symbolic value. Ubre Blanca's brief reign occurred in the middle of a new chapter of the Cold War between Cuba and the United States, represented by the end of decreased tensions under Carter and the beginning of the hawkish Reagan administration in 1981. In that context, the records of the Cuban cow were also a refutation of reinvigorated US imperialism.

Hopes that the offspring of Ubre Blanca would become like their mother never materialized, yet she did represent a wider boost for dairy farming in Cuba. Her discovery inspired a kind of competition between production centers, as well as advocacy within the movement for model dairy farms and high-producing cows. Interviews with farmers, scientists, veterinarians, and inseminators reappeared, as did news about getting milk outside Havana. The celebrity of Ubre Blanca revitalized the revolution's original enthusiasm for dairying two decades prior.

In the wake of Ubre Blanca's records, there were increases in domestic milk production of 10 percent above planned levels. On August 3, 1982, *Granma* reported that production had reached more than 1 million liters in Havana for 41 consecutive days. This had been achieved the day before with the milking of 95,777 cows with an average production of 10.5 liters. This event would become known as "the one million peak." Over 1.1 billion liters of fluid milk were produced annually between 1981 and 1989,[52] making Cuba the sixth largest producer of milk in Latin America (the others were of much greater size and had climates and geographies more traditionally associated with dairy farming), and first in the Caribbean region, well above Costa Rica with 410–430 million liters and the Dominican Republic with 290 million.[53]

That increase had to do with the policies of livestock intensification beginning in the 1960s, which paired dairy with sugar as the two main axes of national agriculture.[54] The Office of Genetics coordinated the policy responsible for transforming the cattle population, which by 1990 was 63 percent dairy. The Cuban state invested heavily in modern dairy infrastructure, inaugurating thousands of new facilities and the most technologically sophisticated milking machines. It also used organic matter to improve the soil and constructed new roads, water-supply systems, electrified livestock units, fencing with concrete posts and barbed wire, and new towns for workers.

Even modest statistical analyses revealed significant increases in liters of milk produced per hectare in Cuba after 1959. By contrast, beef production showed a clear shift in the opposite direction, declining precipitously between 1960 and 1990. The socialist model of intensive stock raising under the revolutionary government failed to achieve its most ambitious goals, but succeeded in diversifying and increasing local production of animal protein, as well as in achieving a more equitable distribution. The growth of Cuba's dairy industry paralleled demographic increases, including rises in population density and the proportion of urban to rural residents. The success of Cuban dairy likewise proved significant to the revolutionary state as it occurred primarily on second-rate soils, thereby permitting the continued dedication of the most productive land to sugarcane export production.

The Intensive Livestock System in Shock

At the end of the 1980s, Cuba again imported Canadians cows and other animals in an effort to revitalize the genetic stock of the tropical island. It is likely that this was also part of the policies implemented to overcome signs of stagnation in industrial agriculture and livestock programs, which resulted in the so-called Food Program presented to the National Assembly in 1991.[55] In Havana, milk production had grown fivefold over twenty-five years, but the results had not been the same elsewhere due to uneven technical development and less experience in dairy farming. For this reason, new dairy projects were implemented in Camagüey (with three hundred dairy farms and the potential to produce as much milk as Havana), Las Tunas, Granma, Ciego de Ávila, and Sancti Spiritus, along with smaller ones in other provinces. These projects included comprehensive plans for irrigation, micro dams, electricity, paved roads, and new towns. The authorities also experimented with feed based on sugarcane derivatives as well as large-scale vermiculture to produce animal protein and humus for agricultural fields.

All the plans came to nothing with the end of privileged trade relations with the Soviet Union. The collapse of the USSR brought a 75 percent fall in Cuba's foreign trade, and the US economic blockade was reinforced by the Torricelli (1992) and Helms–Burton (1996) acts. As a result, the first half of the 1990s was marked by a sharp 35 percent drop in gross domestic product, with declines in production of sugar, nickel, citrus, seafood, and other industrial and agricultural areas.[56] A sugar harvest that had reached 7.7 million tons in 1991 dropped to an average of 3.9 million tons between 1992 and 2002.[57] The impact of the crisis on the cattle industry was similarly dramatic. The areas most affected were those with a high degree of intensification, especially in the dairy zone around Havana. Milk production fell from 1.132 billion liters in 1989 to 622 million liters in 1992.[58] More than two decades after the onset of the crisis, milk production continued to stagnate below or at less than half of its best years during the Cold War. The daily average milk yield per cow today hovers around four liters, and a steady rise in annual imports of dairy products reflects this trend.[59]

Artificial insemination and milking collapsed along with decreases in fuel and agricultural inputs during the 1990s. A return to traditional methods was imposed and, in fact, areas with less-intensified methods better resisted the crisis.[60] The crisis effected a reorientation in Cuba's livestock sectors. Chicken, eggs, and pork gradually eclipsed the revolution's earlier emphasis on dairy and beef, with significant increases in these former industries visible by the second decade of the new century.[61] State property has gradually shifted to private and cooperative forms, accompanied by the delivery of land in usufruct and massive use of organic fertilizers and silvopastoral systems with trees interspersed in pasture. These changes signal a paradigm shift from intensive "conventional" agriculture to low-input schemes based on agroecology.[62]

The Canadian genetic partnership with Cuba stands as a relic of the celebration of industrial agriculture, as well as a symbol of the will of socialist society to master the forces of nature. It represents a time when the idea of scientific development, progress, and expertise cut across political and economic systems, predicated on the adaptation of temperate patterns of production and consumption to the tropics, widely seen as the solution to the problems of hunger and scarcity. Beyond the achievements or limitations of this policy of large-scale genetic transfer of Canadian livestock to Cuba, this exchange was clearly tied to the Cold War and the conflict with the United States. Notably, early advisers to Cuba's revolutionary program pointed out that more intensive systems of large-scale stock raising should not be copied from North America, or from the United States in particular. Yet in practice, that was largely what occurred, although in a hybrid form relying on Canada, a friendlier though no less capitalist and temperate alternative to the United States.

In 2015 Cuban newspapers announced the unveiling of a sculpture reproducing the physiognomy of Rosafe Signet, a long-standing project that originated at the time of his death fifty years earlier.[63] Whereas some celebrated this event, which owed to a Canadian lawyer's generous donation of $100,000, other voices from the counterrevolutionary side cursed the news. Some articles even affirmed that this bull in particular was the origin of the debacle suffered by the Cuban cattle economy after 1959, though, as we have seen, "debacle" is more appropriate to describe the situation after the Special Period starting in the 1990s.[64] The dispute around Rosafe's sculpture again brings to light discussions about climate and geography, genetics, and the transnational politics of animal protein production. Finally, the monument was placed at the entrance to the National Livestock Fair facilities in the Rancho Boyeros municipality of Havana. Who knows if in the future it might become a symbol for the city, a revolutionary bovine alternative to capitalism's Wall Street Bull unveiled in New York in 1989? For some it will perhaps recall the revolution's mad hubris, while for others it will almost certainly symbolize, as intended, the Canadian friendship with the island in hard times and the remarkable achievements of tropical milk production under Cuban socialism.

FIGURE 5.3. Statue dedicated to Rosafe Signet unveiled at the Rancho Boyeros Live-stock Fair in Havana on May 20, 2015, funded by the Canadian lawyer Gary Linde. The inscription reads: "This is a tribute to Rosafe Signet, the grand champion Cana-dian Holstein breeding bull that Canada sold to Cuba in 1961, and is regarded as the father of Cuba's dairy herd. Rosafe is a symbol of the enduring friendship between Canada and Cuba, a symbol of the Cuban Revolution's commitment to meeting the basic needs of its children, and a proud symbol of Canada's independent foreign pol-icy, based on constructive engagement and respect for the sovereignty of all nations, regardless of political differences." Photo by Reinaldo Funes-Monzote.

NOTES

1. See the numbers dedicated to the topic by the Instituto Nacional de Reforma Económi-ca (INRE) in the *Carta Pública Quincenal, Carta* no. 83, February 1959. "Hacia una Reforma Agraria en Cuba," including the Agrarian Law implemented by the rebels in the Sierra Maestra; *Carta*, no. 91, June 15, 1959, with a study by the agronomist José Arteaga y Ortega, "La cuestión agraria cubana vista en 1950," published originally in the *Revista de la Sociedad Cubana de Inge-nieros*, February 1950. Sessions about the agrarian reform were included in the Primer Simpo-sio Nacional de Recursos Naturales, celebrated in Havana, February 3–14, 1958.

2. Cuba's dependence on the United States was especially evident with regard to the im-port of food and agricultural products. Figures for the period between 1955 and 1959 indicate that 26 percent of the export of agricultural products from the United States to Latin America was concentrated in the Cuban market, followed by Venezuela (16 percent) and Mexico (15

percent). Cuba represented 20 percent of the American purchases of agricultural products in Latin America (mainly sugar), behind Brazil, with 29 percent. But Brazil only received 7 percent of the external sales from the US agricultural sector to Latin America. See Kathryn H. Wylie, "A Survey of Agriculture in Cuba" (Washington DC, US Department of Agriculture: Government Printing Office, 1968). See also José Arteaga, "Estado actual de la agricultura cubana: Informe técnico económico con estadísticas responsables," *INRE, Carta Pública Quincenal*, no. 70, July 30, 1958, which underlined the dependence on the United States for pork products such as lard. Leaders also saw major potential for the development of poultry, eggs, and fish, all of which had been imported. Other components of the Cuban diet that relied heavily on US suppliers were rice and wheat.

3. José Álvarez Díaz et al., *Cuba: Geopolítica y pensamiento económico*. Duplex Paper products of Miami (1964), 33, 531.

4. Pierre Trudeau's speech, reproduced in Spanish in *Bohemia* 68, no. 6 (February 6, 1976): 62–65; original text not available.

5. James Rochlin, *Descubriendo las Américas: La política exterior canadiense hacia América Latina* (Mexico City: Fondo de Cultura Económica, 1999). John M. Kirk and P. McKenna, *Canadá/Cuba: Sesenta años de relaciones bilaterales* (Havana: Editorial de Ciencias Sociales, 2007).

6. Francis A. Truslow, ed., *Report on Cuba* (Washington, DC: International Bank for Reconstruction and Development, 1951), 869–902; quote on 890.

7. Henry A. Wallace, "Ideas para futuros líderes de la agricultura de Cuba," *Revista Ganadera* 8 (September 9, 1957): 20–24. Note that this has been retranslated into English, the original text (likely delivered in English) being unavailable.

8. Wallace, "Ideas para futuros líderes."

9. René Dumont, "Algunas notas rápidas tomadas en el curso de una travesía alrededor de Cuba examinando ciertos problemas agrícolas," unpublished manuscript, May 1960, thanks to J. Peyrellades.

10. Julien Coléou, "La producción animal en Cuba," 1961, unpublished manuscript, thanks to J. Peyrellades.

11. Jacques Chonchol, "La reforma agraria cubana: Realizaciones y perspectivas: Informe final de Misión al Gobierno cubano," Havana, August 1961, unpublished manuscript, thanks to J. Peyrellades.

12. See, for example, Melanie Dupuis, *Nature's Perfect Food: How Milk Became America's Drink* (New York: New York University Press, 2002); Kendra Smith Howard, *Pure and Modern Milk: An Environmental History since 1900* (Oxford: Oxford University Press, 2013); Deborah Valenze, *Milk: A Local and Global History* (New Haven, CT: Yale University Press, 2012); and Wilfred V. Canler and Nalini Kumar, *India: The Dairy Revolution* (Washington, DC: World Bank Publications, 1998).

13. Castro articulated an interest in this area as early as May 1959, in a speech at the cattle fair in Rancho Boyeros, just days before the signing of the first agrarian reform law. See *Revista ganadera*, May–June 1959, 33–45. At the end of May, he visited the El Dique farm, a stud farm for horses for the army, and spoke about ranching projects. There he announced the creation of

an inseminators' school and instructed a veterinarian to travel to the United States and learn the technology of conserving semen in liquid nitrogen. "Cincuenta años de inseminación artificial en Cuba... Testimonio de Jesús Cuétara Veliz," *ACPA* 4 (2009): 32–33.

14. This prohibited the slaughter of cows, and thus increased their number by half a million each year until they reached five million in 1969.

15. For Fidel Castro's speeches, see http://cuba.cu/gobierno/discursos/.

16. See Nidia Sarabia, *Voisin: Viajero de la ciencia* (Havana: Editorial Científico Técnica, 1983).

17. Angel Bu, Pablo Fernández, and Alfredo González Pedraza, *La ganadería en Cuba: desempeños y desafíos* (Havana: Inst. Nacional de Investigaciones Económicas, 2004), 27–30.

18. Carmen Rico, "Genes canadienses en cerdos cubanos," *Revista ACPA* 3 (2006): 52–54.

19. Interview with Jorge Peyrellade, February 26, 2011.

20. The history of the Centro de Investigaciones para el Mejoramiento Animal, created in 1970, claims that Rosafe Signet arrived at El Dique in May 1962, http://www.ecured.cu/.

21. Uncertainty remains about who sold the bull to Cuban representatives, although it is presumed that he still belonged to Jack McCague. Tom Hays, the son of an intermediary who helped to arrange the transaction, speculates that the amount paid may have exceeded $100,000, although the price announced to Cubans by the government was much lower. Regardless, the officially announced amount of $28,000 might be accurate, considering a similar sale that year for $33,000 for a related bull that would later be dubbed "the father of Mexican dairy farming." Stephen Wicary, "Ontario Holstein Bull to Be Honoured with Statue for Role in Cuban History," *Globe and Mail*, March 25, 2017, https://beta.theglobeandmail.com/news/national/ontario-holstein-bull-to-be-honoured-with-statue-for-role-in-cuban-history/article22288218/.

22. ABC farm had previously produced famous stud bulls. Hector Ignacio Astengo, 1895–1981, was the descendant of a wealthy family in Argentina.

23. Interview with Arlen de Arce Roche, August 22, 2014. In the aforementioned article (Wicary, "Ontario Holstein Bull"), we read: "The pedigreed bull seen as near the end of its breeding days received 'amazing, tender loving care' from Cuban veterinarians and remained fertile for another five years."

24. In 1969 Fidel Castro admitted he believed this bull was sold to Cuba because of his old age. Even so, they had drawn from him several thousand vials of sperm to use with selected cows.

25. Rafael Sánchez, "Rosafe Signet, uno de los mejores centros de inseminación artificial del mundo," *Bohemia* 59, no. 14 (April 1967): 20–24.

26. Robert Lewis, "The Cuba Connection," *Macleans*, February 9, 1976, http://www.macleans.ca/archives/the-cuba-connection/. Castro gave Trudeau the largest reception since Leonid Brezhnev, but there was never any doubt as to who the star was—and who the supporting actor was.

27. Lewis, "Cuba Connection," 185.

28. *Avances de la ganadería en Cuba* (Havana, 1975), 181–201.

29. Interview with José Morales, January 14, 2012.

30. See the testimony of the veterinarian Juan Dora Pons in Walfrido López González, *Nosotros los veterinarios* (Havana: Científico Técnica, 2008), 115–122. He was sent to Canada to collect and freeze semen from the best Canadian bulls, especially Seiling Rockman.

31. "Inseminación Artificial: Black Velvet en Cuba," *Bohemia* 59, no. 27, (July 1967): 60–61.

32. This is the opinion of the zoo technician and nutritionist Víctor Rodríguez, in an interview on July 16, 2016.

33. About the debates over red and white Holsteins and associations dedicated to this species in the United States and Canada, see Larry W. Spetch, "Red and White Holstein History," extension.psu.edu/animals/dairy/documents/red-and-white-holstein-history.

34. Peter English, "Cuba's Dairy Herd Improving," *Holstein-Friesian Journal* (April 1973): 24–26.

35. English, "Cuba's Dairy Herd Improving," 26.

36. The first visit of a renowned Western leader was made by Olof Palme, first minister of Sweden, in 1975.

37. Pierre Trudeau's speech, reproduced in Spanish in *Bohemia*, 68, no. 6 (February 1976), 62–65; original text not available.

38. *Avances de la ganadería en Cuba*, 206–207.

39. Lewis, "Cuba Connection."

40. "Una vida profesional con la mochila al hombro: Doctor Ernesto Diaz Mulet," in Walfrido López González, *Nosotros los veterinarios* (Havana: Científico Técnica, 2008), 197. This book offers testimonies from various veterinarians who worked on the livestock plans.

41. Niurka Prada and Alma Fernández, "La raza Holstein y su papel en la ganadería de Cuba," *ACPA* 3 (2006): 38–40.

42. Fisheries increased from 27,000 tons in 1959 to 219,800 tons in 1985. The consumption of eggs in 1989 reached 240 per capita.

43. Asamblea Nacional del Poder Popular, *El Programa Alimentario* (Havana: José Martí, 1991), 107–111.

44. Jorge Hernández, "Ubre Blanca," *Catauro* 25 (2012): 93–102.

45. Interview with Merejo Curbelo, March 22, 2011.

46. Orlando Gómez, "Visita Fidel el distrito ganadero Victoria, en la Isla de la Juventud, para conocer a la campeona lechera Ubre Blanca," *Granma*, July 24, 1981: 1, 3.

47. Julio García, "La visita de Fidel a Las Tunas y Holguín," *Granma*, July 29, 1981: 1, 3.

48. "Ubre Blanca significa la confirmación de una política acertada de desarrollo genético," *Granma*, August 7, 1981: 2–7.

49. "Visitó Fidel la Isla de la Juventud," *Granma*, January 5, 1982: 1, 3.

50. Ariel Rojas, "Una recordista mundial. La asombrosa Ubre Blanca," *Cuba Internacional* 2 (1982): 42–45.

51. Raisa Pages, "Una decisión necesaria para perpetuar la historia de Ubre Blanca," *Granma*, January 28, 1985: 3.

52. A. González et al., *La ganadería en Cuba*, 160.

53. Alfredo Riesco, "La ganadería bovina en el trópico americano: Situación actual y perspectivas," in *Avances de la producción de leche en el Trópico Americano*, ed. Saúl Fernández-Baca (Santiago: FAO, 1992), 15–46.

54. Rafael Hernández, "Azúcar y leche: Dos indicadores de desarrollo económico cubano," *Economía y Desarrollo* (January–March 1977), 418–447.

55. Enrique Pérez and E. Muñoz, "Agricultura y alimentación en Cuba" (Havana: Editorial de Ciencias Sociales, 1991).

56. Carmelo Mesa-Lago, "Historia y evaluación de medio siglo de políticas económico-sociales en Cuba socialista, 1959–2008," in *Historia de las Antillas, vol. 1. Historia de Cuba*, ed. C. Naranjo (Madrid: CSIC-Doce Calles, 2009), 521–523.

57. Brian H. Pollit, "The Technical Transformation of Cuba's Sugar Agroindustry," in *Reinventing the Cuban Sugar Agroindustry*, ed. Jorge F. Pérez-López and José Álvarez (Lanham, MD: Lexington Books, 2005), 55–56.

58. This was due in part to the decrease in milk cows, but above all to the significant decrease in average production.

59. Anicia García and A. Nova, "Food Production and Import Substitution in the Cuban Reform Process," in *No More Free Lunch: Reflections on the Cuban Economic Reform Process and Challenges for Transformation*, ed. Claes Brundenius and Ricardo Torres Pérez (Cham, Switzerland: Springer, 2014), 83–108.

60. Beef cattle were also affected by the urgency of resuming the use of oxen as draft animals. Arcadio Ríos and J. Cárdenas, "La tracción animal en Cuba: una perspectiva histórica," in *La tracción animal en Cuba* (2003), ed. Paul Starkey and B. Sims, http://www.recta.org.

61. Carmen Rico, "Genes canadienses en cerdos cubanos," *Revista ACPA* 3 (2006): 53–54.

62. This system is not without precedent in Latin America; see Lorek's description of advocacy for the presence of the rain tree in Colombian pastures in chapter 3. The Cuban experience became a reference for advocates of alternative agricultural models and is considered the largest attempt at national conversion to organic farming. See Julia Wright, *Sustainable Agriculture and Food Security in an Era of Oil Scarcity: Lessons from Cuba* (London: Earthscan, 2009).

63. Wicary, "Ontario Holstein Bull"; and Valerie Hauch, "Once Upon a City: The Enduring Charm of the Farm," *Star*, October 27, 2016, https://www.thestar.com/yourtoronto/once-upon-a-city-archives/2016/10/27/once-upon-a-city-the-enduring-charm-of-the-farm.html.

64. Rolando Cartaya, "Develan estatua de toro canadiense implicado en la ruina de la ganadería cubana," *Radio Televisión Martí*, May 22, 2015, https://www.martinoticias.com/a/cuba-ganaderia-canada-rosafe-estatua/94867.html; Miguel Sales, "Fidel y Rosafe," *Diario de Cuba*, August 11, 2015, http://www.diariodecuba.com/cuba/1439190980_16240.html; Pablo Alfonso, "El delirio inseminador de Fidel Castro," *Radio Televisión Martí*, November 30, 2016, https://www.martinoticias.com/a/el-delirio-inseminador-de-fidel-castro/127910.html; and Carlos Ferrera Torres, "Rosafe Signet. Dios del semen," *CiberCuba*, June 19, 2017, https://www.cibercuba.com/lecturas/rosafe-signet-dios-semen.

6

A TALE OF FOUR LABORATORIES

Animal Disease, Science, and Politics in Cold War Latin America

Thomas Rath

The French Revolution propelled a tale of two cities. What connected four animal disease laboratories in Mexico, Brazil, the United States, and the United Kingdom? With a bit of conceptual maneuvering, we can keep the literary conceit going: the answer is at least two other revolutions, and perhaps three. The first is a long version of the Mexican Revolution: rebellion and upheaval in 1910–1920, and the process of social reform and nation-building that followed during which the state gradually extended control over a recalcitrant, often rebellious, and frequently illegible countryside, and found ways to coexist with the colossus of the north.[1] The second we could think of as a thick (and also rather long) version of the green revolution: a US project to blaze a path of noncommunist rural modernization using intensively farmed, chemically enhanced, scientifically bred plants, alongside intensively farmed, chemically enhanced, scientifically bred livestock.[2] The third more nebulous revolution is the one that some elites feared might happen if this project of rural modernization was implemented too late, too little, or too inflexibly.

In the 1940s, all three revolutions collided in Mexico. In October 1946, a Mexican veterinarian examined some cattle around Veracruz and found signs of foot-and-mouth disease (FMD). Since the mid-nineteenth century, governments, scientists, and farmers had come to fear the disease for its effects on livestock economies; infected cattle typically lost weight, developed painful ulcers and blisters, and a few died; in the 1940s, US experts estimated that FMD reduced the productivity of livestock and dairy production by 25 percent.[3] In response, US and Mexican governments created a joint commission to eradicate FMD. From 1947 to 1954, the commission inspected, quarantined, slaughtered, and vaccinated millions of head of livestock across the coastal plains and high plateau of central Mexico. Involving thousands of veterinarians and ranchers from both countries, and many battalions of Mexican troops, the campaign against FMD was unprecedented in size and the level of cooperation across borders. The campaign was also very controversial and, in many places, deeply unpopular. Despite this, by 1954 it succeeded in eradicating FMD in Mexico.

The aim of this essay is to use the intertwined histories of four laboratories in four different countries to trace the ramifications of this contentious campaign. There are many ways for social scientists to puncture the aura of timeless objectivity surrounding laboratory work, depending on the sources available to them.[4] Rather than delving into scientists' networks and everyday processes of knowledge production, this chapter uses a more traditional historical approach: an overview of institutional structures and roles and the social, political, and geopolitical context in which they developed. The laboratories are important in their own right, but serve to illustrate broader shifts in policy frameworks and in the circulation of organic material and knowledge—both of the virus itself, and techniques of vaccine production and administration. It argues that the Mexican campaign, by demonstrating the apparent threat FMD posed to national security and the viability of vaccine technology, inspired the creation of the three American laboratories and shaped all four laboratories' roles, resources, and relationship to new US-led international institutions governing animal disease. The conclusion discusses the larger implications of this story for how we write the history of politics and scientific expertise in this period.

Foot-and-Mouth Disease and US Policy

By the early twentieth century, it was common for states and scientists in Europe and the Americas to group FMD alongside rinderpest as one of the two great devastating animal plagues. Yet, little was self-evident or natural about this. FMD was highly contagious, but its clinical symptoms, particularly among low-bred livestock, could be very mild—unlike the highly fatal rinderpest. Only the interplay of several factors through the nineteenth century allowed the idea that the disease was a serious—even existential—problem to gradually take hold: the developing art of statistics to measure and model harm to national well-being, economic interests of elite livestock breeders, and the growth of increasingly professional and ambitious veterinary experts.[5]

Still, consensus regarding what to do about this problem was difficult to achieve. By the early twentieth century, two main policies emerged in Europe and the Americas: the "stamping out" method using quarantine and slaughter to eradicate the virus; and the use of quarantine, serums, and vaccines to restrict and ameliorate it. In some ways the emergence of these protocols in each country is a distinctive national story shaped by a host of different factors: changing perceptions of disease, the relative sophistication of laboratory research, the prestige of veterinarians, state capacity, national identity, and the shifting nature of rural societies and the meat and dairy trade. However, once the contagious (rather than spontaneous) nature of the disease was recognized, geography and the scope of infection imposed a general pattern on policy rationales. In much of continental Europe and South America, where FMD was widespread or enzootic, and particularly where extensive trade or land borders threatened future reinfection, a mix of vaccination and serums proved compelling and cost-effective. By contrast, the United Kingdom—largely free of the disease, and relatively isolated geographically—became the leading exponent of "stamping out."[6]

The US adoption of this "stamping out" model was based less on the prestige of UK scientists or their knowledge of the virus and its stubborn array of types—which was relatively underdeveloped—and based more on these geographical and epidemiological similarities. By the 1940s, the slaughter method was thoroughly institutionalized in the federal Bureau of Animal Industry (BAI), a powerful and autonomous branch of the United States Department of Agriculture (USDA); it had been implemented successfully during US outbreaks in the 1910s and 1920s—many of whose veterans were sent down to Mexico—and the US government (and allied cattle-ranching interests) successfully brought huge pressure to bear on Mexico to adopt it.[7]

In general, across the Americas and Europe, research on the FMD virus has always flowed from state efforts to control it, rather than the other way around. This intimate connection of research and policy ensured another common pattern: veterinarians often found themselves called on to defend the scientific objectivity of state policies, as if they were as natural and self-evident as a microbe discovered under a microscope, but in private recognized that policies were based on a host of decidedly nonscientific interests and assumptions about state, economy, and society. Still, such assumptions were often deeply held. As in the United Kingdom, "stamping out" in the United States also became part of many BAI officials' professional identity, fed by a sense of national superiority; slaughter was not only effective and, in the long term, economic; it proved that the United Kingdom and the United States were the kind of determined, virile, and efficient countries that could wage an outright war against disease and handle the bitter medicine of slaughter, unlike lax Latin countries (or, for that matter, the feckless Irish).[8] In the field, some US veterinarians fantasized about how the FMD campaign might propel broader cultural change among Mexicans, replacing "the word 'mañana' with 'let's do it now.'"[9]

The initial slaughter program also reflected more recent US concerns about what would soon come to be known as the Cold War. The experience of World War II deepened US official understandings of food production as a matter of national security.[10] Indeed, since the late 1930s US military and intelligence services had worried that other states—principally Germany and then the Soviet Union—would weaponize FMD for germ warfare. The German virologist Otto Waldmann's announcement in 1938 that he had produced the first reliable FMD vaccine was particularly troubling, since it raised the possibility that other countries would be able to inflict FMD on enemy territories while protecting their own.[11] In 1951 the Central Intelligence Agency argued that, as far as biological attacks against animals were concerned, "foot and mouth disease constitutes the most serious threat to the country."[12] Officials also hoped that the campaign in Mexico could boost propaganda, providing a compelling example of Pan-American cooperation in the face of communist-sponsored criticism of US imperialism.[13] The initial slaughter program also reflected broader US notions of rural development in the late 1940s. The commission's general blindness to agrarian tensions, the way it calculated costs, and the kinds of compensation it offered—individual indemnities for livestock at market rates, support for mechanization, tractors, meat-processing facilities—all reflected shifts under way in official views of the countryside. As historians of the Rockefeller-funded Mexican Agricultural Program have shown, by the late 1940s earlier concerns with rural distribution, or even justice, had been subsumed by an emphasis on generic and supposedly transferable technical and market-oriented solutions.[14]

Mexico City

The origins of our first laboratory lie in the enormous difficulties the US–Mexico Commission for the Eradication of FMD had implementing the policy of mass slaughter. Resistance in Mexico was varied, broad, and deep. Some narratives at the time (and since) shoehorned protest into a familiar dichotomy: modernizing US and Mexican elites against peasants.[15] This certainly captures some key dynamics. Many Mexican and US officials blamed peasant resistance on their ignorance and supposedly "sentimental" attachment to livestock.[16] Of course, this masked the distinctive rationality of small and peasant farmers: just as in mid-nineteenth-century Britain, the farmers who were engaged in small-scale, multiple-use animal husbandry, who were less integrated into markets, and whose low-quality *creole* breeds suffered mild clinical symptoms—and who, besides, had ample experience of venal federal officials—found the economic rationality generated by aggregate national statistics less than compelling. Moreover, the ashes of rural Mexico still smoldered with the heat of social revolution and Catholic counterrevolution. As recent research has shown, despite ebbing autonomy, in the 1940s rural communities were still very much in possession of traditions, historical discourses, and organizational resources to fuel popular protest.[17] However, resistance was not limited to peasant subalterns. In some places—central and northern Jalisco, southern Veracruz—it was opposition and threats of violence from relatively large, politically well-connected commercial ranchers and dairymen that stymied the campaign (although these men tended to avoid censure in the press). Many rural people objected to the campaign simply because it became a feeding frenzy of extortion and profiteering by federal and local officials and their allies.[18]

Most important for our purposes is how popular protest merged with expert dissent. Most of Mexico's small group of professional veterinarians joined the campaign, attracted by the rare offer of steady employment, but many remained critical of slaughter. At the Veterinary School of the Universidad Nacional Autónoma de México, Mexico's most prestigious researchers in the field shunned the campaign and openly advocated vaccination, arguing that slaughter, far from the cutting edge of disease control policy, was needlessly costly, unscientific, and backward; their students echoed these sentiments in their newsletter, El Lancet.[19] Indeed, the general idea that vaccination offered another possible model was widely known, and many petitions from farmers, Catholic dissidents, and peasant communities made some reference to it.[20] Such ideas spread through the press and cattle associations, but also probably through the actions of veterinarians themselves. In one dramatic incident, after campaign personnel accepted an invitation to dine in the village of Irimbo, eastern Michoacán, a Mexican veterinarian attached to the commission stood to give a speech in which he condemned the US-imposed slaughter policy, claimed that more humane medical approaches existed, and encouraged villagers not to cooperate with the campaign. After the speech, the startled US officials promptly left for Morelia, while "a good number of the near 200 campesinos present gathered around Dr Chapa at the close of his speech with expressions of agreement."[21]

In the face of opposition, the Alemán administration adopted an awkward, Janus-faced posture, obeying but not wholly complying with the bilateral agreement that founded the joint commission. Mexican funding and political and administrative support for the commission's operations were slow and halting. Alemán angered the BAI by inviting European, Brazilian, and Argentine veterinary experts to offer advice on laboratory techniques and vaccine production, and sent Mexicans abroad to gain expertise.[22] In April 1947 the USDA demanded that Mexican research efforts on the virus cease in case they undermined the slaughter campaign, but Alemán still allowed groups of veterinarians to go on supposedly private trips to European laboratories.[23] According to some accounts, throughout 1947 the Mexican codirector of the campaign, the *chihuahuense* lawyer Oscar Flores, quietly hoped for a turn to vaccination.[24] Thus, the full arsenal of James C. Scott's rural "weapons of the weak"—noncompliance, dissembling, threats, potshots, and occasional riots—were much in evidence and melded with what John Dwyer has called the "diplomatic weapons of the weak."[25] By the autumn of 1947, the campaign had reached a complete impasse. After slaughter operations were suspended in November, President Truman wrote to a friend that the commission had been so unpopular that it "almost created a rebellion down there."[26]

Opened in May 1948, the Palo Alto laboratory was a central component in a new deal struck by the US and Mexican governments to continue the eradication campaign on a new basis: isolated slaughter combined with massive repeated waves of livestock vaccination. Located on the road from Mexico City to Toluca, the new laboratory was initially intended to help with the analysis and typing of field samples, and vaccines were imported from Dutch and Argentine facilities. However, BAI and Mexican scientists argued it would be necessary to make vaccines in Mexico, using Mexican samples collected from the field, which would better respond to the type of virus present and avoid the problem of transporting temperature-sensitive vaccines across continents. The commission soon decided to make the Palo Alto laboratory the hub of a complicated vaccine-production system of unprecedented scale, spread over several other facilities around Mexico City.[27] This system involved purchasing and transporting tens of thousands of disease-free cattle from the "clean" zone in Mexico's north, infecting most of them in controlled conditions, and "harvesting" infective material from them by hand (principally from their tongues), and mixing it with chemicals in centrifuges to create a vaccine; smaller numbers of cattle were kept for purposes of testing the innocuity of vaccines. To fund the laboratory, scientists also developed a controlled system to slaughter these cattle and safely market products in nearby Mexico City.[28]

By the end of 1948, this complex was churning out such quantities of vaccine that it even surprised the commission officials. To administer this vaccine, the campaign organized teams to inspect and vaccinate millions of head of livestock in successive waves, creating original maps and census data, and hauling ice-packed bottles of vaccine by mule train if necessary. This system was similarly innovative not only in its sheer scale and degree of coordination but also in its objective; previous FMD vaccination campaigns in Europe had not been designed with permanent eradication within a national territory as an objective.

This impressive new technical capacity shifted the political dynamics of the campaign. Although popular hostility and sometimes violent resistance did not disappear, vaccination generally proved more acceptable to rural society. The vaccine program also enjoyed greater cooperation from Mexican agencies and professionals, not least veterinarians. Many had supported vaccination from the start, and the campaign now provided them with gleaming, state-of-the-art facilities; greater Mexican government investment in veterinary education and research rapidly followed.[29] Mexico's veterinarians now found their scientific achievements and new laboratory front and center in commission propaganda. (The previous slaughter policy, in which commission-nominated "killers"—often soldiers—drove hundreds of head of livestock into enormous machine-dug pits, shot them, slashed their bodies, and buried them in lime and earth, had lacked for edifying imagery.)

US accounts tended to submerge scientific exchanges in a vague story of bilateral collaboration, whereas Mexican scientists and veterinarians emphasized their debts to European and particularly Latin American knowledge, alongside their independent contributions to the campaign. For example, in December 1946, three Mexican biologists first isolated and identified the "Mexico-Puebla" type of the virus, arranged to have it independently verified in Britain, developed a crude early vaccine, and even tested it on dairy herds in the valley of Toluca. Soon afterward, the US State Department worried that visiting Brazilian and Argentine veterinary scientists were encouraging their Mexican counterparts to reject US slaughter protocols and demand more formal virus research.[30] Dr. Silvio Torres, Brazil's leading veterinary expert, remembered a tense meeting with Mexican and US officials, in which he had warned of the impracticality of slaughter due to the scale of the epizootic and Mexico's low level of education and administrative weaknesses. He claimed that condescending USDA officials had ignored his warnings that imposing slaughter might provoke another "revolution."[31] When the campaign shifted toward vaccination in late 1947, the Mexican scientists Dr. Fernando Camargo and Dr. Alfredo Tellez Girón used their knowledge of the vaccine-production techniques developed by Torres and the Argentine Dr. Francisco Rosenbusch to design Mexico's vaccine production facility.[32] However, the story of knowledge exchanges did not begin or end with the laboratory. Both Mexican and US experts also subtly relied on other kinds of local knowledge to effectively administer the vaccine. Vaccination teams may have crisscrossed central Mexico laden with all manner of ostentatious imported technology—mosquito nets, DDT, syringes, pith helmets—but they also relied on local guides and translators to provide access to isolated communities and locate semi-wild animals; during a grueling campaign in the tropical lowlands around Coatzacoalcos, US veterinarians soon learned that locally made boats of hollowed tree-trunks—*cayucos*—were by far the most appropriate technology for getting around.[33]

The success of the program at Palo Alto allowed Mexican veterinarians to claim a larger national and regional role. In 1950 the Venezuelan military junta invited a party of fourteen Mexican veterinary experts to offer advice on an FMD outbreak; they helped create a replica of Mexico's vaccination-production system and laboratory, which allowed the government to substantially control (but not eradicate) the outbreak. Interviewed by Venezuela's press, the Mexican group argued that their experience had taught them that Latin American countries needed to join together and assert their own expertise rather than just swallow Yankee policy prescriptions.[34]

After 1954, the laboratory at Palo Alto remained the headquarters of the eradication commission's much smaller successor dedicated to disease surveillance—the bilateral Joint US–Mexico Commission for the Prevention of FMD—which retained a small team of Mexican and US scientists at the laboratory. During the 1960s, each year they received and analyzed hundreds of virus samples reported and collected by Mexico's growing corps of regional veterinarians and by local committees of lay inspectors—committees first created during the eradication campaign. Palo Alto also supported numerous other modernizing projects of the Mexican Secretariat of Agriculture, including stock improvement and artificial insemination, and campaigns against rabies and cattle ticks.[35] With the support of Mexico, the USDA hoped to create a secure FMD-free zone across Central America, using the Isthmus of Panama as a geographical barrier and Palo Alto as a hub for surveillance. In the 1960s Palo Alto became the designated laboratory for a Central American system of animal disease surveillance and control created—with US support—by the Organismo Internacional Regional de Sanidad Agropecuaria (OIRSA). In addition to analyzing samples, the laboratory hosted regional conferences, helped to train Central American experts, and sent Mexican veterinary advisers to Central America.[36]

Rio de Janeiro

The FMD crisis in Mexico demonstrated to US officials the enormous economic and political costs involved in improvising a response to a major epizootic, the increasingly sophisticated knowledge of the virus and vaccination that was available, and the need to revamp US policies in response. The clearest illustration of this change in South America was the Panamerican Center for Foot-and-Mouth Disease (PANAFTOSA), a new animal disease laboratory in Rio de Janeiro created in 1951 by the Pan American Sanitary Bureau. It was funded in large part by the Organization of American States (OAS), and also received support from the Brazilian government. In some ways PANAFTOSA's role was similar to Palo Alto's. It received virus samples from across South America for testing and typing. Although the US government was always keen to keep Palo Alto's holdings of live virus and vaccine-production capacity to a minimum after 1954, PANAFTOSA appears to have been permitted to hold larger stores of live FMD virus and create facilities for vaccine production.[37] However, in South America vaccine production generally still continued in a plethora of private facilities—as it had since the 1920s—albeit now with PANAFTOSA's advice and assistance. PANAFTOSA also trained visiting veterinarians and advised national governments on appropriate systems of FMD control. Importantly, the advice dispensed by PANAFTOSA was more flexible and open-ended than the BAI's position before 1947: countries should consider which mix of quarantine, inspection, slaughter, and vaccination was best suited to them, taking into account a host of contextual factors. As in Mexico, the Rio facilities initially set up for FMD control also branched out into research on other animal diseases deemed damaging to national development.[38]

The Rio laboratory also reflected US political and strategic considerations. Rather than leaving South American governments and veterinarians to their own devices, the United States decided that more effective control in the South—by whatever means—could help prevent spread further North. The Rio laboratory could serve as a first line of defense, but also use South America as a vast living archive of different virus strains and refine new vaccination techniques. Various US agencies could agree that Brazil was the obvious choice for the laboratory. The USDA officially blamed Brazilian exports of high-grade zebu bulls as the cause of Mexico's outbreak, and US diplomats probably considered PANAFTOSA a useful way of helping to smooth over the resulting tensions. Along with Argentina, Brazil had one of the most developed centers of veterinary expertise in the region and (unlike Argentina) was a major geopolitical ally. Indeed, the Brazilian location may have made the project somewhat more palatable to US ranching interests and their congressional allies. Many ranchers in the US Southwest feared one day having to compete with cheap, disease-free South American meat, but above all with the high-quality beef of Argentina.

However, PANAFTOSA was hardly a unilateral imposition of US power and knowledge. The laboratory was also an attractive proposition to Brazil's government, ranchers, and veterinary experts. Brazil supplied land and existing facilities and contributed an initial investment of half a million dollars to construct new laboratory facilities. In return, it received US technical assistance and investment channeled through the OAS, and recognition of its regional leadership role.[39] US support for research and possible eradication also carried the vague promise of future access to US and UK markets. PANAFTOSA provided a major stimulus for Brazil's own nascent project of FMD research and control, which had begun in 1943 in Rio Grande do Sul under Torres.[40]

PANAFTOSA thus represented a compromise in US and Latin American perspectives on FMD and exemplified larger trends in the Pan American

Sanitary Bureau of which it was a part. From 1947 to 1960, the bureau grew rapidly in size and engaged in a growing range of ambitious projects. (In recognition of this scope the name was changed to the Pan American Health Organization—PAHO—in 1958.) Under the leadership of Frederick Soper, who had cut his professional teeth in Rockefeller public-health campaigns in 1920s Brazil, the agency also became closely tied to Brazil. Through the 1950s, the Bureau offered prestigious scholarships to Latin Americans to study medicine and veterinary science at US colleges; one of PANAFTOSA's additional roles was to help recruit suitable candidates across South America. And yet, as Marcos Cueto has argued, there was more to the bureau than one-way Americanization. Soper was very keen to avoid accusations of imperial meddling, and jealously defended bureau autonomy from other US agencies. He carefully recruited ambitious young professionals from Latin America and reduced the dominance of US personnel; under Soper, PANAFTOSA was jointly run by a Chilean and a US veterinarian. Soper encouraged bureau staff to see themselves as apolitical experts in progress, relatively autonomous from any national government.[41] Cueto also argues that the bureau's experience in public health campaigns in Haiti from 1950 to 1954 fostered a greater sensitivity to different national contexts and popular culture. For those involved in veterinary medicine and PANAFTOSA, it was clear that the decisive learning experience had happened a few years earlier, during Mexico's FMD crisis.[42]

Such compromise did not guarantee success, but eventually the PANAFTOSA project bore fruit. In the early 1950s USDA officials hoped that the Mexican campaign could be a new model for eradication elsewhere, but they were soon frustrated. In the 1960s all the national eradication drives attempted in South America—in Argentina, Ecuador, Uruguay, Venezuela, and Colombia—failed, having been undermined by political instability, social opposition, and poor-quality vaccines produced in private laboratories. Political support from the United States was also wavering. The Kennedy administration incorporated FMD control into the Alliance for Progress's package of rural modernization, but faced renewed criticism from US ranching interests on this score; in this context, stable funding from the OAS was also uncertain.[43] However, in 1969 the PAHO took over both the funding and operation of PANAFTOSA, and in 1972 it became the headquarters of the Comisión Sudamericana para la Lucha Contra la Fiebre Aftosa, a new multilateral body that provided financial support and planned control policies and information sharing across national borders. As a result of improved coordination and slowly improving oil-based vaccines, in the 1980s and 1990s Chile, Argentina, Uruguay, and Brazil gradually controlled and eradicated FMD through a mixture of slaughter and vaccination.[44]

Long Island Sound, New York

The FMD outbreak in Mexico also reshaped policies and institutions much closer to Washington, DC. The United States had long seen calls for greater research on the FMD virus, but these were generally resisted by those who deemed it unnecessary, uneconomic, or dangerous. The outbreaks of the 1910s caused some scientists, ranchers, and members of the public to wonder why the considerable advances made by the BAI in researching and controlling other diseases could not be replicated with FMD. The FMD outbreak in California in 1924 again led to more calls for research. The USDA sent a committee of three scientists to Europe to investigate the possibilities of vaccination. However, the committee concluded that vaccination was unviable and slaughter remained the most rational US policy. The BAI stood firm behind its slaughter protocols and argued that the virus was simply too dangerous and contagious to risk further research in the mainland United States.[45] Even during World War II the US government refused to endorse FMD research in US territory. It devised a tripartite agreement with the United Kingdom and Canada to divide scientific labor on germ warfare: US scientists focused on rinderpest, Canadian scientists focused on various poultry diseases, and UK scientists worked on FMD. Even then, according to Clinton Anderson (the secretary of agriculture, 1945–1948), FMD research received relatively little support and focused on epidemiological questions rather than vaccination. In a furious private letter written to the editors of the *Farm Journal*, Anderson described the wartime arrangements and claimed that war had allowed Richard Shope—the head of the Rockefeller Institute and US germ-warfare research—to create a crude vaccine for rinderpest; by contrast, US ranching interests and their allies in Congress, worried about removing barriers to the import of Argentine beef, had discreetly obstructed similar advances on FMD.[46]

The Mexican epizootic shifted the balance of forces decisively in favor of those US scientists and politicians—like Anderson—who wanted to develop research on FMD (and other animal diseases considered dangerous) on US territory. BAI officials used to argue that US geographic isolation was similar to that of the British Isles, but the Mexican crisis had discredited that idea. With the advent of the new vaccination program in Mexico in 1948, pressure mounted further. Increasing tensions with the USSR surely also played a role, but it is worth noting that US and UK intelligence agencies had known about the Soviet seizure of German FMD research facilities since 1945.[47] Both Anderson at the USDA and the US army briefed Truman on the need for a US research facility, and Truman signed an order funding it.[48] In May 1948 Dr. Maurice Shahan, cohead of the joint commission in Mexico and one of the BAI's senior researchers, was ordered back to Washington to help make preparations for the US laboratory he would later direct, along with a Colonel Brown, a US army germ-warfare expert who had secretly observed the Mexican campaign.[49] The same year the British managed to evacuate the German germ-warfare and FMD specialist (and Rockefeller Institute alumnus) Eric Traub from Soviet-held eastern Germany, and in early 1949 Traub arrived in the Unites States, a beneficiary of Operation Paperclip. (For their part, in May 1948 Argentina lured Otto Waldmann himself and set him up in an official FMD laboratory.)[50] While the new laboratories in Mexico and Rio de Janeiro focused on surveillance and branched out into a variety of programs aimed at modernizing livestock production, the argument for the US laboratory rested on a more militarized notion of national security. As knowledge of virus and vaccine techniques spread, the US government could not afford to fall behind in its understanding of how to defend itself or weaponize FMD, still less farm out this work to foreigners or be blocked by narrow US ranching interests.[51]

However, the project still faced long delays and resistance. In 1948–1950 the USDA surveyed and considered a large number of possible sites, particularly in the states of Washington, Rhode Island, and New York. Some congressmen condemned the plans and vowed to block research in their states, while others pushed hard for the project. For example, Rhode Island politicians wrote to Truman arguing that the federal investment would help cement the Democratic Party in the state for years. The US army was impatient to establish a laboratory as soon as possible, while the navy—asked to report on the possibility of using one of its facilities in Rhode Island Sound— dragged its feet.[52] The US government invited Ian Galloway, the British head of FMD research during World War II, to advise on the laboratory. Galloway was strongly in favor, but warned that the island location, preferred by the USDA, would bring unforeseen practical difficulties. Based on his experiences in Britain and visiting the German laboratory on Riems, research on an island could work for a short time, but quickly the isolation sapped morale and caused researchers to "develop nomadic tendencies."[53] Despite considerable opposition to the project voiced in town-hall meetings and local newspapers, eventually the government settled on an old army base on Plum Island, in Long Island Sound. Still, the USDA recognized that refitting the decayed facility and designing the elaborate security and waste disposal protocols required would take several years.[54]

Pirbright Institute, Surrey, United Kingdom

To compensate for the delay, US agencies also renewed and bolstered the old alliance with UK animal disease research at the Pirbright Institute, Surrey. Ironically, FMD research at Pirbright was itself the product of struggles in the UK very similar to those around Plum Island. In 1912, an early attempt to conduct research in British India failed because the native breeds showed few clinical symptoms and some had developed long-standing immunity to strains of the virus; research with animals on a disused warship moored off the coast at Harwich proved utterly impractical. Slaughter during the 1922–1924 epizootic provoked such a wave of criticism that the Ministry of Agriculture (MAG) grudgingly allowed for the establishment of permanent FMD research at Pirbright, but retained tight control. Thereafter, Pirbright scientists found themselves in an awkward relationship with the public. Many citizens assumed that the ultimate goal of research was to produce a viable vaccine to replace slaughter, but the MAG remained firmly wedded to "stamping out" and prioritized typification and epidemiology. Scientists were encouraged to downplay the possibility of a vaccine even as they reported findings to the public.[55] Pirbright emerged from World War II as one of most prestigious animal disease laboratories in world, and an authority on typing virus strains. In 1945–1946, Pirbright received dozens of virus samples from Africa, Europe, and the Americas for analysis.

Pirbright also seems to have been perceived by many countries as enjoying some independence from US agencies, perhaps more than it really had. Ian Galloway was invited to advise many different countries on disease control; Venezuela invited him in 1950 during a period of tense relations with the United States, and he briefly accompanied Mexico's team of veterinary scientists.[56] In mid-1947, as the difficulties of the slaughter program became obvious, Mexico also approached Pirbright for independent advice and asked for permission to send two scientists to visit. Galloway and his colleagues initially agreed to the request, assuming that it had received the backing of the USDA and the State Department, but then found out that both agencies had not been informed. Placed in an awkward position, Pirbright settled on a diplomatic fudge: it decided to receive the two Mexican scientists, give them a very perfunctory tour, and restrict discussion to laboratory techniques. Much to Galloway's relief, when the two Mexicans arrived they were very tight-lipped anyway, and uninterested in broaching larger geopolitical or policy questions.[57]

Despite Pirbright's international standing, increased US support for it came at an opportune time for the institution. In 1947–1948, the laboratory faced a tightening budget, struggled to deal with all the viruses it accepted for analysis, and confronted critics who could see little use for the facility in peacetime given its lack of progress (or even hostility) toward vaccination. In 1950, the US government asked the UK to engage in a major expansion of Pirbright for the purposes of joint germ-warfare research. The UK chiefs of staff were delighted with the request, and considered it an important way of improving US-UK relations.[58] The UK Ministry of Defence and MAG proposed a seven-year expansion program; after further US encouragement, in 1951 plans were accelerated and by 1953 were completed, having been funded in part by US loans channeled through the Ministry of Defence. Pirbright scientists, led by Galloway, also eagerly embraced expansion, although the project was not without problems. The expansion ran five years behind schedule, hampered by infighting among the various agencies and officials involved in the laboratory, only some of whom were aware of the military dimension of its work. In 1952, Ernest Gowers, who chaired a committee of inquiry into FMD research, described the situation to the MAG's parliamentary secretary: "You ought to look at the Pirbright problem personally. The scientists there are splendid people doing splendid work. But the system of control is just chaos . . . the governing body itself is quite incapable of controlling Galloway [who has] been charged (so he says) with highly secret work which he cannot possibly tell his governing body about because they have not been passed by MI5!"[59] Along with problems of secrecy, expansion at Pirbright also heightened long-standing tensions between competing understandings of its role and purpose. The MAG's unwavering support for slaughter in yet another epidemic in 1951–1952 became even harder to justify juxtaposed to the ostentatious investment in Pirbright, and news of innovations in vaccination in Europe and Mexico. Managing these tensions apparently placed Galloway, an able scientist but prickly man and poor administrator, under considerable strain, and officials at the MAG began to worry about his psychological well-being.[60]

Nevertheless, military investment and integration into US security policy benefited Pirbright in the long term. Once Plum Island was opened in 1954, it gradually took a larger share of biological warfare research, but Pirbright remained prominent.[61] In 1957, the FAO nominated it the "world FMD Reference Laboratory." To the delight of the MAG, this secured the laboratory's position as the scientific center of a network of multilateral commissions dedicated to FMD surveillance and control in the Americas and in Europe. Indeed, Pirbright scientists continued to visit and advise on FMD in Europe and the Americas. In 1957 Dr. William Henderson, a veteran British researcher at Pirbright, accepted the PAHO's invitation to head PANAFTOSA, held the post in Rio de Janeiro for nine years, and visited and advised most countries in South America on the testing of virus samples and control techniques.[62]

Several broader points emerge from this story. Most obvious, perhaps, are the multiple scales necessary to understand the history and politics of expertise. The category of Latin America is certainly a defensible framing; inter-American debates about FMD were particularly intense, and the notion of

Latin America informed the perception of the interests at stake and the institutions built to address this problem. However, this history was shaped by local and national dynamics, and embedded in a larger global—and particularly transatlantic—context. The conflicts unleashed and lessons taught by Mexico's FMD epizootic reverberated across Latin America, into supposedly domestic US institutions, and reached across the Atlantic and reshaped relations with a key Cold War ally.[63]

Closely related, we can also see how power and scientific knowledge did not simply flow from a US center to a Latin American periphery. Indeed, the neglected history of animal health illuminates Latin American strategies for coping with the postwar US government's enormous power and scientific authority. As in human medicine and public health, we see how Latin American societies—with their particular geopolitical location, historical trajectory, and sociopolitical structures—engaged with foreign expertise and produced competing, regionally inflected modernisms. There was certainly something inflexible, scientifically authorized, and "high-modernist" about the first year of Mexico's FMD campaign; the US government imposed a slaughter policy on the commission, which then struggled mightily to make rural Mexico legible and compliant.[64] Expert and lay demands for vaccination and research—informed by other Latin American and European models—show how the crisis also produced a competing scientific modernism with what we might call a bifocal perspective: in James C. Scott's terms it was lower—more amenable to local (or at least subnational) sociopolitical and epidemiological contexts—but also much higher—promoting and celebrating the production of laboratory-based scientific knowledge.[65] Just as they did in the better-studied fields of diplomacy and political economy, Latin American states and societies resisted and deflected US authority in various ways, and also pushed for the creation of multilateral institutions that were, at least in theory, inclusive.[66] Spurred by the Mexican crisis, the United States decided to build a new international institutional infrastructure to control animal disease for the purposes of national security. All parts of the infrastructure were not equal, and publicly acknowledged research for the purpose of surveillance, defense, and rural development coexisted with a well-funded and highly secretive transatlantic program of offensive germ warfare. However, in creating this system the United States adopted a policy position on FMD control that was more flexible and context-dependent than previously, incorporated the views and fostered the careers of Latin American experts, benefited from knowledge of the virus and vaccination techniques produced—at least in part—by Latin Americans, and funded facilities and veterinary education that would be of use in many other national modernizing projects.

NOTES

1. For an overview, see Gilbert M. Joseph and Jürgen Buchenau, *Mexico's Once and Future Revolution: Social Upheaval and the Challenge of Rule since the Late Nineteenth Century* (Durham, NC: Duke University Press, 2013), 87–165.

2. For an insightful discussion of the historiography of the Green Revolution, see Tore C. Olsson, *Agrarian Crossings: Reformers and the Remaking of the US and Mexican Countryside* (Princeton, NJ: Princeton University Press, 2017), 1–11. Efforts by US agencies and foundations to reshape livestock and animal husbandry are less well-known, but were considerable. For example, Juan Manuel Cervantes Sánchez, Cristián López Montelongo, and Ana María Román de Carlos, *La Medicina veterinaria mexicana, 1853–1985: Vista desde sus instituciones* (Mexico City: Universidad Nacional Autónoma de México, 2012), 187–189.

3. M. S. Shahan, "The Control of Foot and Mouth Disease in Mexico," *Canadian Journal of Comparative Medicine* 17:9 (1953): 369–374.

4. Bruno Latour and Steve Woolgar, *Laboratory Life: The Construction of Scientific Facts* (Beverly Hills: Sage, 1979).

5. By far the best historical account is Abigail Woods, *A Manufactured Plague: The History of Foot and Mouth Disease in Britain* (London: Earthscan, 2004). On rinderpest, see Clive Spinage, *Cattle Plague: A History* (New York: Springer, 2003).

6. Woods, *Manufactured Plague*. On continental Europe, particularly the Netherlands, see Joanna Swabe, *Animals, Disease and Human Society: Human-Animal Relations and the Rise of Veterinary Medicine* (London: Routledge, 2002). For the United States, see Alan L. Olmstead and Paul W. Rhode, *Arresting Contagion: Science, Policy, and Conflicts over Animal Disease Control* (Cambridge, MA: Harvard University Press, 2015), 115–137. On the spread of FMD in Argentina and Brazil in the late nineteenth century, see Manuel A. Machado, *Aftosa: A Historical Survey of Foot-and-Mouth Disease and Inter-American Relations* (Albany: State University of New York Press, 1969), 3–19.

7. Jaime Torres Bodet, *La victoria sin alas: Memorias* (Mexico: Porrúa, 1970), 36–37.

8. For Britain, see Abigail Woods, "Why Slaughter? Cultural Dimensions of Britain's Foot and Mouth Disease Control Policy, 1892–2001," *Journal of Agricultural and Environmental Ethics* 17, no. 4 (2004): 341–362.

9. Mulhern, Coatzacoalcos, Veracruz, to Noyes, Mexico City, November 23, 1947, National Archives and Records Administration (hereafter NARA), Record Group (hereafter RG) 17, USDA, BAI, US–Mexico Commission for Eradication of FMD (hereafter NARA/CFMD), box 29, "Veracruz." For metaphors likening the campaign to military conquest and US stereotypes of Mexican ignorance, superstition, and inefficiency, see also James Porter, *Doctor, Spare My Cow!* (Des Moines: Iowa State College Press, 1956).

10. Bryan L. McDonald, *Food Power: The Rise and Fall of the Postwar American Food System* (Oxford: Oxford University Press, 2016).

11. Woods, *Manufactured Plague*, 87; Anderson to Farm Journal, January 1948, Truman Library, Clinton P. Anderson Papers, box 7, "foot and mouth."

12. *National Intelligence Estimate 31*, September 4, 1951, NARA, RG 263, 9.

13. Transcript of oral history interview with Samuel A. Montague, Independence, Missouri, October 30, 1992, Truman Library, 21.

14. Olsson, *Agrarian Crossings*, 129–158.

15. José Carmen Soto Correa, *El rifle sanitario, la fiebre aftosa y la rebellion campesina* (Mexico City: Instituto Politécnico Nacional, 2009).

16. Bodet, *La victoria sin alas*, 33; oral history interview with Samuel A. Montague, 20–21.

17. Thomas Rath, *"Que el cielo un soldado en cada hijo te dio:* Conscription, Recalcitrance and Resistance in Mexico in the 1940s," *Journal of Latin American Studies* 37, no. 3 (2005): 507–531; Paul Gillingham, "Maximino's Bulls: Popular Protest after the Mexican Revolution," *Past and Present* 206 (2010): 175–211; and Tanalís Padilla, *Rural Resistance in the Land of Zapata: The Jaramillista Movement and the Myth of the Pax Priísta, 1940–1962* (Durham, NC: Duke University Press, 2008). On autonomy, see John Tutino, "The Revolutionary Capacity of Rural Communities: Ecological Autonomy and its Demise," in *Cycles of Conflict, Centuries of Change*, ed. Elisa Servín et al. (Durham, NC: Duke University Press, 2007), 211–268.

18. Confidential Monthly Reports, October–November 1947 in NARA/CFMD, box 1.

19. See also interviews in the special issue of *Imagen Veterinaria* 1, no. 4 (2001); and various clippings, 1947, NARA/CFMD, box 5, "information reports."

20. See numerous petitions in Archivo General de la Nación (AGN), Ramo Presidentes, Alemán Valdés, 545.1/31.

21. Saulmon, Morelia, to Shahan, Mexico City, November 23, 1947, NARA/CFMD, box 29, "Michoacán."

22. Bodet, *La victoria sin alas*, 32.

23. Monthly reports, April–May 1947, CFMD, box 1.

24. Teresa Williams Irvin, *Let the Tail Go with the Hide: The Story of Ben F. Williams* (Bloomington, IN: Unlimited Publishing, 2001), 210.

25. John Dwyer, "Diplomatic Weapons of the Weak: Mexican Policy making during the U.S.-Mexican Agrarian Dispute, 1934–1941," *Diplomatic History* 26, no. 3 (2002): 375–395.

26. Truman to M. Wallgren, Governor, Washington State, December 27, 1947, President Secretary's File, box 183, Truman Papers, Truman Library.

27. Monthly reports, January–May 1948, CFMD, box 2.

28. Monthly reports, January–May 1948, CFMD, box 2.

29. Larissa Adler de Lomnitz and Leticia Mayer, *La nueva clase: desarrollo de una profesión en México* (Mexico: UNAM, 1988), 88.

30. Cervantes Sánchez, López Montelongo, and Román de Carlos, *La medicina*, 183; and Copy of Thurston, Embassy, to State Department, February 18, 1947, NARA/CFMD, Weekly reports, box 1.

31. *Anais da I conferência de febre aftosa: realizada na cidade do Rio de Janeiro D.F., de 5 a 11 de setembro de 1950* (Rio de Janeiro: n.p., 1950), 55.

32. For example, see Alfredo Tellez Girón, "Iniciación del brote de Fiebre Aftosa en México e investigaciones llevadas a cabo durante los años 1946–1952," *Veterinaria Mexicana* 9 (1978): 31–36.

33. Various correspondence, Mulhern, Coatzacoalcos, to Mexico City, December 1947–April 1948, NARA/CFMD, box 29, "Oaxaca."

34. Machado, *Aftosa*, 66; and various press clippings, personal collection of Dr. Juan Manuel Cervantes Sánchez.

35. I discuss these campaigns in detail in "Agrarian Ghost in the Machine: Veterinarians, Animals and Ejidos in an Industrializing Countryside," unpublished paper.

36. Various reports, 1960–1964, AGN, Secretaria de Agricultura e Recursos Hidráulicos (SARH), box 012, "OIRSA."

37. Edgardo Seoane and Carlos Palacios, *Informe sobre la aftosa, problema presente y futuro del continente Americano y la importancia del centro Panamericano de fiebre aftosa* (Washington, DC: Unión Panamericana, 1967), 1–12.

38. Seoane and Palacios, *Informe sobre la aftosa*, 1–12.

39. Machado, *Aftosa*, 74.

40. *Anais da I conferência de febre aftosa.*

41. Marcos Cueto, *The Value of Health: A History of the Pan American Health Organization* (Rochester, NY: University of Rochester Press, 2007), 95–108.

42. Cueto, *Value of Health*, 110.

43. Machado, *Aftosa*, 77–107.

44. Woods, *Manufactured Plague*, 135.

45. Georges W. Corner, *A History of the Rockefeller Institute, 1901–1953* (Princeton, NJ: Rockefeller Institute Press, 1965), 196.

46. Anderson to Farm Journal, January 1948, Clinton P. Anderson Papers, box 7, "foot and mouth," Truman Library. Anderson never received a reply, and it is possible that he decided against sending this explosive letter.

47. "State Research Institute at Riems, Microbiological Research," May 13, 1948, NARA, CREST, CIA-RDP83-00415R000900020012-6.

48. Various correspondence, February–November 1948, Truman Presidential Secretary Files, Truman Papers, box 161, "foot and mouth," Truman Library.

49. Monthly reports, October 1947, CFMD, box 29, "Querétaro."

50. Linda Hunt, *Secret Agenda: The United States, Nazi Scientists, and Project Paperclip, 1945–1990* (New York: St. Martin's Press, 1991), 344; Galloway memo, September 1949, National Archive (UK), MAF 245/3331; and "Otto Waldmann, German Chemist," October 4, 1948, CREST, CIA-RDP82-00457R001900380002-2.

51. Michael Christopher Carroll, *Lab 257: The Disturbing Story of the Government's Secret Germ Laboratory* (New York: William Morrow, 2004), 41–70.

52. Various correspondence, February–November 1948, Truman Presidential Secretary Files, Truman Papers, box 161, "foot and mouth," Truman Library.

53. Galloway, Report on Progress and International Collaboration, December 12, 1947, National Archive, MAF 117/107.

54. Christopher, *Lab 257*, 44–45.

55. Woods, *Manufactured Plague*, 68–80.

56. Machado, *Aftosa*, 66.

57. Pirbright Monthly Reports, 1947, National Archive, MAF 240/77.

58. Defence memo, August 23, 1951, National Archive, DEFE 10/30.

59. Cited in Woods, *Manufactured Plague*, 89–90.

60. Cabot to MAF, ca. 1952, National Archive, MAF 240/565.

61. Brian Balmer, "The Drift of Biological Weapons Policy in the UK 1945–65," *Journal of Strategic Studies* 20, no. 4 (December 1997): 115–145.

62. Obituary of Sir William Henderson, *Guardian*, December 19, 2000.

63. On the effect of imperial and neocolonial relationships on US domestic institutions, see Alfred W. McCoy and Francisco A. Scarano, eds., *Colonial Crucible: Empire in the Making of the Modern American State* (Madison: University of Wisconsin Press, 2009).

64. James C. Scott, *Seeing Like a State: How Certain Schemes to Improve the Human Condition Have Failed* (New Haven, CT: Yale University Press, 2001), 4.

65. For an argument for "low modernism" in the US New Deal, see Jess Gilbert, *Planning Democracy: Agrarian Intellectuals and the Intended New Deal* (New Haven, CT: Yale University Press, 2015), 60–79.

66. On multilateralism and postrevolutionary Mexico, see Christy Thornton, "Sovereignty and Solidarity: The Mexican Revolution and the Origins of the Postwar Order, 1919–1948" (PhD diss., New York University, 2015).

7

NASA IN CHILE

Technology and Visual Culture

Pedro Ignacio Alonso and Hugo Palmarola

This chapter transforms National Aeronautics and Space Administration (NASA) design history into an archaeological subject, highlighting the role of graphic design in the creation of a scientific image that is associated with operations of a military and strategic nature. We argue that the design of this logo, although not in itself a technology, was key for NASA's tracking mission to operate in foreign territory, supporting wide-ranging diplomatic efforts to justify the United States' presence in Latin America. In March 1958 the Soviet Union had placed an item on the agenda of the upcoming regular session of the United Nations General Assembly, titled "The banning of the use of cosmic space for military purposes, the elimination of foreign bases on the territories of other countries, and international cooperation in the study of cosmic space," which confronted the United States with the issue of responding to and preempting this question in the General Assembly.[1] The timely creation of NASA, the design of its insignia, and the general role graphic design played within the agency's operations were not just accessory, but structural to the success of the offshore distribution of an entire technological system. We aim to show that the NASA logo—in Chile and Latin America—was not only part of a branding campaign intended for political propaganda or image building, but that it was part of the overall design of an intricate system whose components included satellites, buildings, technicians, equipment, infrastructure, radio signals, and the diplomatic and media strategies that made it possible to cross national borders—an endeavor nearly as complex as overcoming gravity.

FIGURE 7.1. NASA insignia at former satellite tracking station, Peldehue, Chile, 2015. Dating from the 1960s, this is a rounded concrete slab of 207 centimeters in diameter covered with tiles. Photo by Hugo Palmarola, 2015.

This chapter offers new insights into the role played by visual culture in the promotion and use of technologies. Specifically, it demonstrates how the graphic design of the NASA insignia was crucial in the preservation of the United States' network of satellites overseas. By creating a desirable imaginary about space exploration, it promoted the acceptance of NASA's physical facilities in Chilean and Latin American territories.

A Satellite for the US Army

Within the context of the political, ideological, and economic disputes of the Cold War, a number of technological exchanges took place between Latin American countries and the United States, including the installation of a satellite tracking station in Chile in 1957, as part of the Minitrack Network. This state-of-the-art project, a chain of nine stations within Latin America, aimed to track radio signals from the United States and was developed by the Naval Research Laboratory (NRL). Under the direction of Dr. John P. Hagen, the program was based on novel technologies devised by the engineer John T. Mengel for satellites crossing the seventy-fifth West Meridian on each orbit. Cutting through Latin America, this initial North–South line received the nickname "the fence" from its creators at the NRL. Despite the fact that they were built and managed by the US army, the stations were established in 1957 under the banner of science in the context of the International Geophysical

FIGURE 7.2. NASA's satellite tracking station, Peldehue, Chile, circa 1980s. Courtesy of the Swedish Space Corporation.

Year (IGY), which took place between July 1, 1957, and December 31, 1958. As the IGY came to a close, the stations were transferred to a civilian scientific agency that had just been established in October 1958: the National Aeronautics and Space Administration.

A long-forgotten physical reminder of this story is a round concrete slab, 207 centimeters in diameter and 16 centimeters thick that holds on its surface a mosaic of small tiles representing the NASA acronym and logo, with a red slash representing aeronautics, stars representing outer space, an orbit path representing space travel, and a sphere representing a planet. Fragments of concrete and tiling that are scattered near the discarded sign belonged to the portion of the design that extended outside the circular geometry of the emblem, which broke into pieces when the logo was removed from its original location at the rural site of Peldehue, 41 kilometers northeast of Santiago, Chile (33°,08" South, 70°,40" West).

The Peldehue site had been chosen by the NRL and was granted to the United States in a 1956 agreement with the Chilean government (through the agency of the University of Chile) to serve as the second (and final) satellite tracking station installed in the country by the US army in 1957. The other facility, located in the Salar del Carmen in the Atacama Desert, was dismantled in 1963, when the increased capacities of new satellites and the Peldehue station made it redundant. Peldehue soon became the largest NASA base in Latin America, with a support staff of over three hundred people, including one hundred resident engineers and technicians, who occupied an enclosed

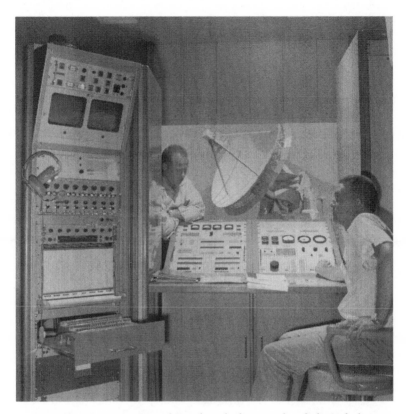

FIGURE 7.3. Antenna command console in the foreground, with the 40 ft. diameter antenna in the background at NASA's satellite tracking station, Peldehue, Chile, circa 1960s. Courtesy of the Swedish Space Corporation.

and self-sustaining site of more than one hundred hectares. Besides the various types of antennas positioned in its fields, monitoring equipment and computers were housed in single-story prefabricated buildings. The station was equipped with an electricity generator, medical facilities, ambulance, fuel supply, and fire station. After operating for more than thirty years, it was finally closed in 1989, when US strategic satellite tracking needs were able to be commercially outsourced or no longer required earthbound facilities. The site was then donated to the University of Chile, where it served as the Center for Space Studies until it was sold to the Swedish Space Corporation in 2008.[2]

The United States, Chile, and Latin America

During the postwar period, in the 1940s and 1950s, US policy toward Latin America aimed to contain the expansion of communism in the region. In

FIGURE 7.4. Chilean "huaso" (cowboy) and NASA technicians standing beside a 40 ft. diameter antenna at NASA's satellite tracking station. Peldehue, Chile, circa 1966. Courtesy of the Swedish Space Corporation.

Chile, President Gabriel González Videla (1946–1952), who was especially receptive to this mission, signed the Pact of Rio in 1947, the Pact of Bogotá in 1948, joined the Organization of American States (OAS) in 1948, and signed a military pact with the United States in 1952. In addition, pressured by the United States, González Videla passed the "Law of Permanent Defense of Democracy" in 1948, which outlawed the Communist Party. This alignment around a regional bloc, as a principle of collective continental security, committed the countries of Latin America—such as Chile—to the plans the United States had against the Soviet Union. In this context, according to Stefan Rinke, "Chile's strong integration into the inter-American system of the post-war period was manifested, amongst other things, in the degree of use that the country made during the 1950s of US military aid, including military missions and training of Chilean officers in US institutions. Simultaneously, the CIA established a network of operations in Chile."[3]

In this political context, it is no coincidence that in 1951, Chile and the United States signed their first Basic Agreement for Technical Cooperation between their two governments, which facilitated the installation of US technicians and technologies—including those from the future NASA—in the country.[4]

Thus, contacts between Chile and the United States increased significantly from the 1950s, although the discursive alignment with the United States underwent certain changes when Carlos Ibáñez del Campo was elected president in 1952, with a majority of the People's Socialist Party. The Chilean Left maintained that the influence and the pacts entered into with the United States subjected Chile to the complete domination of that country. The most powerful Latin American response to curb this type of influence was the creation of the Economic Commission for Latin America in 1948, where dependency theory was developed. This theory explained underdevelopment as the result of domination by external powers—the United States being the main dominator of Latin America—which kept the region in a condition of permanent dependency.

The US economic crisis of 1957 caused great economic and social agitation in Latin America, and although the United States founded the Inter-American Development Bank (IDB) in 1959, it was not possible to solve the structural problems in the region. Representing a radical alternative to these problems, the Cuban Revolution began in 1959, a situation that led to the rupture of relations in 1960 and an embargo against the island by the United States, one of the last activities undertaken by Dwight D. Eisenhower before leaving power. That same year, Eisenhower visited Chile, and in his speech before the Senate he requested greater participation of both US investments and counterinsurgency. The containment of the revolution in Latin America was initiated in 1961 with the financial assistance of the Alliance for Progress promoted by John F. Kennedy. The presence of the United States in the region then became even more important. The outcome of the Cuban Crisis of October 1962 underscored the Soviet Union's recognition of US hegemony in Latin America.[5] Until the end of the 1960s, Chile and the United States remained within the margins of a basic coincidence of interests.

Chile perceived itself as a solid member of the Western world, to the point of becoming a model country for the Alliance for Progress, especially during the government of Eduardo Frei Montalva (1964–1970).[6] However, toward the end of his term, Frei criticized US policy in order to get rid of Chile's image as a US vassal. "By 1970," Rinke writes, "no-one took the development aid thesis seriously. It was simply considered as a screen for imperialism . . . aid for progress and other forms of cooperation, both economic and technological, began to be interpreted as strategies to strengthen the dependence . . . of Chile and other countries of the Third World with respect to knowledge."[7]

The expected development with the Alliance for Progress did not occur. On Kennedy's death, Lyndon B. Johnson increased cooperation with the security forces, creating the School of the Americas in 1963, which aimed to step up the fight against communism and the protection of US investments in Latin America, as well as to support right-wing dictatorships, economic pressure, political interference, and secret CIA actions in the region. These facts, in addition to the progressive crisis of the Alliance for Progress, increased anti-Americanism in Latin America during the second half of the 1960s.[8]

One of the highest points of anti-Americanism arrived during the socialist presidency of Salvador Allende (1970–1973). A few months before Allende took office, the US ambassador in Chile, Edward M. Korry, reported to the White House the following NASA situation in Chile: "The tracking station, because of its relationship with the University of Chile and the nature of its activities, has a certain amount of built-in protection. Nevertheless, an eventual campaign of harassment and charges of improper activities would not be surprising."[9] In spite of Allende's rise to power, NASA in Chile managed to overcome any type of aggression and surprisingly it was not questioned by the government or the population. The University of Chile, as well as its supposed civil and scientific orientation, played a key role in making this American institution an "invisible point" in the hectic political map of the period in Chile.[10] It also remained out of the controversy during the violent military dictatorship (1973–1989) that overthrew Allende.

US Satellite Tracking Stations Overseas

On October 4, 1954, the Special Committee for the International Geophysical Year recommended the launching of earth satellites by countries across the globe in the interest of science.[11] On July 28, 1955, the White House announced that President Eisenhower had approved plans for the launching of small, earth-circling satellites as part of the United States' participation in the IGY. "The president expressed personal gratification that the American program will provide scientists of all nations this important and unique opportunity for the advancement of science."[12]

By October 1957, a year before the establishment of NASA, the Minitrack network was fully operational. The project had begun in March–April 1955. Under the direction of Captain Winfred Berg, the senior navy officer assigned to the Project Vanguard,[13] a team of NRL and army personnel traveled through Latin America seeking possible sites and negotiating the necessary agreements with the countries that were involved.[14] The date and scope of this tour coincides with a report issued by the Technological Capabilities Panel in Washington, DC, one month before Berg's trip, titled "Meeting the Threat of Surprise Attack," also known as the Killian Report (after James F. Killian, president of the Massachusetts Institute of Technology).

According to Walther A. McDougall, and in the context of the Cold War, this report advised that "if continuous surveillance of Soviet installation and exact targeting of Soviet bases were to be assured, the solution was to spy from outer space [using] camera-toting satellites, circling the earth south to north in polar orbit" and doing so "under the legal cover of the freedom of space—if such legal cover could be established."[15] And it was.

Eisenhower's announcement on July 28, 1955, was not surprising, given his hesitation about the use of manned high-altitude reconnaissance aircraft (a concern ultimately proven correct when the Soviet Union shot down such a plane in 1960).

On September 9, 1955, the NRL was tasked with setting up the Minitrack stations. One year later, the US Army Corps of Engineers initiated construction at the six identified sites at the request of the NRL: Havana, Panama City, Quito, Lima, Antofagasta, and Santiago. The task was assigned more specifically to the specially created Project Vanguard Task Force.[16] Although the entire operation belonged to the US military space program, Eisenhower's creation of NASA allowed government officials, engineers, and aerospace executives, in the words of the historian Jennifer Light, to "eschew the public rhetoric of war in favor of the language of scientific planning and management."[17] There is clear evidence of this overlap not only in the exchange of personnel between the newly created agency and the US Army but also in the operation of the NASA Space Operations Control Communication Network.

One diagram from NASA's Communication Standing Operating Procedures shows that information gathered at the tracking facilities in Chile, Peru, Ecuador, and Panama was delivered first to the Pentagon (abbreviated WAR in the diagram) before being forwarded to NASA's Operations Con-

FIGURE 7.5. Some of Project Vanguard's key staff with a map of South America in the background. Left to right, Commander W. J. Peterson, planning coordinator; Leopold Winkler, engineering consultant; Homer E. Newell Jr., science program coordinator; Milton W. Rosen, technical director; Mrs. Lillian M. Campbell, secretary to the director; Hagen; James M. Bridger, Vehicle Branch; John T. Mengel, Tracking and Guidance Branch; and Joseph W. Siry, Theory and Analysis Branch. From Constance McLaughlin Green and Milton Lomask, *Vanguard: A History* (Washington, DC: National Aeronautics and Space Administration, 1970), 74.

trol Center, then located in Washington, DC.[18] It was not an accident that the first signal ever tracked by the Peldehue station belonged to Sputnik 1, the satellite successfully launched by the Soviet Union on October 4, 1957 (the same month this station began its operations). The Soviets' space body caused a major impact in military circles, which were concerned about the possibility that the Russians had other outposts in orbit that they could not detect through a tracking beacon.[19] In response, the US government quickly invested in an expanded network of stations scattered throughout five continents, which were flexibly added and removed according to the requirements of the program.[20] Between 1957 and 1972, the US government invested approximately $1 billion in tracking and data acquisition facilities.[21] From 1957 to 1989, more than twenty-two stations were built around the world, from the seventy-fifth meridian "fence" to its global dissemination in the enlarged Satellite Tracking and Data Acquisition Network, Satellite Automatic Tracking Antennas, and NASA Ground Communications System networks.

As the physicist William Corliss noted, these stations were not static by any means.[22] They were installed, closed, dismantled, or transferred from one site to another depending on strategic needs and technological improvements. Hence, attempting to determine the full, accurate number of US sat-

FIGURE 7.6. Dr. John P. Hagen, director of Project Vanguard, holding a model of a rocket and explaining a cutaway of the satellite to members of the press at the US Naval Research Laboratory in Washington, DC. The Minitrack Network of stations cutting across Latin America is visible in the background map. Washington, DC, December 13, 1956. Courtesy of ArtNotch.

FIGURE 7.7. John T. Mengel, chief of the Tracking Section for Navy's Project Vanguard shows the press a map with the diagram of the Minitrack network, with the chain of stations strewn along the seventy-fifth meridian. November 13, 1957. Courtesy of International News Sound Photo.

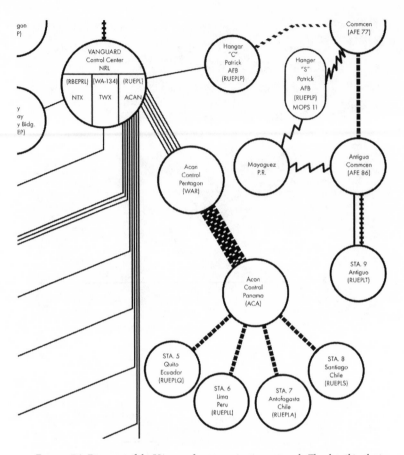

FIGURE 7.8. Diagram of the Vanguard communication network. The detail in the image shows that Quito, Lima, Antofagasta, and Santiago (Peldehue) are connected to Panama, then to the Pentagon, and finally to the Vanguard Control Center NRL, by means of ACAN (Army Command and Administrative Net). From William R. Corliss, *The Evolution of the Satellite Tracking and Data Acquisition Network (STADAN)* (Greenbelt, MD: Goddard Space Flight Center-National Aeronautics and Space Administration, 1967), 25.

ellite tracking stations is an elusive task, and to a certain extent even an irrelevant one (for instance, their names were often changed and were subject to their locations).

A Visual History of the NASA Insignia

The logo that would come to grace Peldehue station was created by James Modarelli in 1959 as a revision of the first NASA seal designed by the US Heraldic Branch. When T. Keith Glennan, the first director of NASA, asked

Modarelli for a new insignia, he made it clear he was asking for something intended to become an image that would be widely distributed to the mass media. After the Commission of Fine Arts received Modarelli's version from the Quartermaster Corps for comments and approval, the commission only reluctantly approved it, stating that it was essentially a pictorial conception very reminiscent of designs that were common in current commercial advertising.[23] This reception reflects the intention of Modarelli to give NASA an image that was more contemporary and marketable than those of traditional heraldic institutions. Modarelli's plan primarily aimed at differentiating the new insignia from the traditional coats of arms of institutions such as the various public departments or branches of the army.

The logo has been a matter of controversy ever since its conception. For instance, in 1961 it was strongly criticized by *Time* magazine, which described it as lackluster, childish, and appalling after its being featured on the medal awarded by President John F. Kennedy to Alan Shepard, the first astronaut ("One side of the medal shows a planet and satellite—a motif that any schoolboy might have thought up").[24] This criticism did not dwindle even after the NASA insignia gained high visibility and popularity in the United States and abroad during the height of the space program, whose climax was the successful moon landing in 1969. At that point, NASA seemed to have achieved complete support from Americans,[25] a task previously seen as impossible, and its insignia was consequently used to brand important manned missions such as the Mercury and Gemini projects, the Apollo program, the Space Shuttles, and the International Space Station.

However, in 1975, NASA decided that a more modern logo was needed and switched to a design by the firm Danne and Blackburn that became known as the "worm," with a red stylized rendering of the NASA acronym.[26] The emergence of a new insignia demonstrates NASA's unstable nature and continuous efforts to come up with a proper image for itself, constantly attempting to better fulfill its function as a model of advanced science and technology. Compared to the old logo, called the "meatball," the new "worm" logo was designed to project a simpler, more direct idea, with the energy of the flat red color. In addition, the horizontal bars on the two letters "A" were removed, possibly to form two triangles that resemble two rockets pointing to the sky. This shift also seems apposite to our discussion of the obsolescence of the icon in Chile, given that it had been conceptually discarded as an image for the agency years before the logo had fallen into ruin at Peldehue.

The bicentennial celebration of 1976 appears to have been a key impetus for the new design, as the US government initiated the Federal Graphics Improvement Program that resulted in more than forty-five government agencies replacing their logos with a more contemporary image between 1971 and 1981. (Coincidentally, in 1974 the same firm responsible for designing a new

FIGURE 7.9. NASA insignia at the satellite tracking station. Peldehue, Chile, circa 1970s. The flags of Chile and the United States are visible within the picture. Courtesy of the Swedish Space Corporation.

logo for NASA developed the logo for the bicentennial celebrations.)[27] The Space Shuttle took the new NASA worm into space on its fuselage, while also being included on the astronauts' suits. While many younger staff members appreciated the new design, NASA veterans strongly resisted what they saw as an imposition from central NASA headquarters.[28] This resistance toward

FIGURE 7.10. NASA insignia at the satellite tracking station. Commemorative photograph in celebration of the Independence Day of the United States, Peldehue, Chile,
July 4, 1980. Courtesy of the Swedish Space Corporation.

the new logo was evident in several NASA centers, particularly at Langley.
After the *Challenger* disaster, the *Endeavour, Discovery, Columbia,* and *Atlan-
tis* returned to using the old meatball in 1988. The old logo was again at the
center of an event of immense media coverage with the relaunch of the Space
Shuttle *Discovery* in 1988. Hence, when the NASA administrator Dan Gol-
din brought the meatball back officially in 1992, it appears that he did so "to
invoke memories of the one-giant-leap-for-mankind glory days of Apollo."
This successful comeback was accomplished even though the meatball was
considered by many as a design nightmare. According to one graphics manager, "It doesn't print well on laser printers because of the gradations on the
airfoil, and it can't be used at less than 5/8 inch because the stars disappear
and the type becomes illegible."[29] Moreover, it was hard for color printers to
match its blue background accurately, and the lettering and airfoil did not
contrast enough on black-and-white copiers. In addition, its round shape
made it difficult to artfully place type around or near it.[30] Richard Danne
and Bruce Blackburn, the designers of the worm, disapproved of the return
to the meatball and were angered by a design they considered a throwback to
Buck Rogers in terms of its sophistication. They claimed that, simply put, "it
didn't look like a modern space agency."[31] Thus, the derelict logo finds itself
in a situation of vicissitude and controversy, recipient of a seemingly double
ruination and redemption, both material and conceptual.

FIGURE 7.11. Abandoned NASA access cards at the Swedish Space Corporation (NASA's former satellite tracking station), Peldehue, Chile. Photo by Hugo Palmarola, 2015.

A Strategic Insignia in Chile

The archaeology of graphic design presented in this case study conveys an attempt to unveil the history of the Cold War in Latin America from non-traditional sources. These visual sources are immersed in the imageries of popular culture, especially the imageries imported from the United States into the region. The history of NASA has been extensively studied, and it has already been widely shown that, for the United States, space exploration was primarily developed with its possible military uses in mind.[32] However, from a design perspective, this article uncovers the efforts of the United States to portray the Peldehue station—and the Minitrack Network in general—as a scientific venture, thereby (according to Light) "diverting attention from the nation's other growing space program dominated by military and intelligence data-gathering concerns."[33] Regardless of the tangible scientific breakthroughs achieved by these satellite tracking networks,[34] an examination of the actual and rhetorical transition from the military-industrial complex to NASA reveals that its insignia was, in fact, an integral cog in a well-staged US strategy that used design to shape the agency's desired image for international mass consumption. This examination of the abandoned mosaic of the NASA logo attempts to advance our understanding of the Chilean station in terms of its role in a much larger global network by analyzing it at the intersection of design, technicians, military economies, technologies, ideologies, and cultural and geospatial considerations.

FIGURE 7.12. Archaeological study of the NASA insignia at the former satellite tracking station in Peldehue, Chile, by the authors and the archaeologist Amalia Nuevo
Delaunay. Photo by Hugo Palmarola, 2015.

In fact, the complex, shifting, and paradoxical nature of the icon as a
charged image can only be grasped if we understand how it relates to a more
complex system of historically charged communication. If the design of the
meatball logo does make NASA look unmodern, then the ruined mosaic in
Chile would seem to represent the least modern image available to the space
agency. The logo not only abandoned the rules of a supposedly higher technology linked to automation or mass production, but its very construction as
a mosaic employed a distinctly ancient form of craftsmanship. Turned into
an archaic monument, it therefore betrayed the aspirations of new technology, while simultaneously betraying all that it stood for—namely, US science
and technology as both highly advanced and scientific. The ruined logo thus
signals the unexpected reversals that technology and expertise often experience when confronted by the realities they encounter on foreign soil. Considered both as a document, and as evidence, this apparently unimportant mosaic disc, with a long-discarded insignia, can tell us what traditional sources
cannot.

NOTES

1. Proposal for U.S.-U.S.S.R. Cooperation in Outer Space, Confidential Memorandum
from John Foster Dulles to Dr. James R. Killian Jr., Special Assistant to the President, White

House, Washington, DC, July 23, 1958. Unclassified document no. 911.802/7–2358 (National Archives and Records Administration [NARA], Washington, DC).

2. The Swedish Space Corporation holds stations in Chile, Australia, and Canada. It is engaged in all business areas related to satellite management, development of rockets and balloons, launching services, and flight tests.

3. Stefan Rinke, *Encuentros con el Yanqui: Norteamericanización y cambio cultural en Chile, 1889–1990* (Santiago: Centro de Investigaciones Diego Barros Arana-DIBAM, 2013), 292.

4. This agreement was signed in Santiago on January 16, 1951, and entered into force on July 27, 1951.

5. Alfredo Riquelme, "Chile y la Guerra Fría en Chile: Los intrigados nexos entre lo nacional y lo global," in *Chile y la Guerra Fría Global*, ed. Tanya Harmer y Alfredo Riquelme (Santiago: Instituto de Historia Pontificia Universidad Católica de Chile-RIL, 2014), 17.

6. Rinke, *Encuentros con el Yanqui*, 300.

7. Rinke, *Encuentros con el Yanqui*, 385.

8. Stefan Rinke, *América Latina y Estados Unidos* (Mexico City: El Colegio de México-Marcial Pons, 2015 [2012]), 185.

9. "Contingency Paper ('Fidelism without Fidel') 1970: August," report in *Chile in the Archives of the U.S.A. (1970) Documents From the Archives of Former U.S. Ambassador to Chile Edward M. Korry (1967–1971)*, *Estudios Públicos* 72 (Spring 1998): 18.

10. Looking back, in 2008 the tracking stations were proudly described by Charles T. Force (NASA's former associate administrator for the Office of Space Communications) as "invisible." Charles T. Force, foreword to Sunny Tsiao, *Read You Loud and Clear! The Story of NASA's Spaceflight Tracking and Data Network, Part 1* (Washington, DC: National Aeronautics and Space Administration, 2008), xvii.

11. Walter A. McDougall, *The Heavens and the Earth: A Political History of the Space Age* (Baltimore: Johns Hopkins University Press, 1985), 118.

12. McDougall, *Heavens and the Earth*, 121.

13. "Project Vanguard" was the large, original project that was committed to the geopolitics of US satellite tracking for the space program, which was planning to launch satellites. Therefore, all tracking stations in Latin America were the result of the Vanguard endeavor.

14. William R. Corliss, *The Space Tracking and Data Acquisition Network (STADAN), the Manned Space Flight Network (MSFN), and the NASA Communications Network (NASCOM)* (Maryland: NASA, 1974), 23.

15. McDougall, *Heavens and the Earth*, 116.

16. McDougall, *Heavens and the Earth*, 20–23.

17. Jennifer S. Light, *From Warfare to Welfare: Defense Intellectuals and Urban Problems in Cold War America*, (Baltimore: Johns Hopkins University Press, 2003), 96.

18. Document in the John T. Mengel Papers, held at the NASA Historical Archive, Washington, DC.

19. Corliss, *Space Tracking and Data Acquisition*, 33.

20. To count the initial set of Minitrack stations, we refer to those that were already built and in operation by October 1957: Blossom Point (Maryland), 1956–1966; Coolidge Field

(Antigua Island), 1957–1961; Batista Field (Havana, Cuba), 1957–1958; Pampa de Ancón (Lima, Peru), 1957–1969; Paramo de Cotopaxi (Quito, Ecuador), 1957–1981; Salar del Carmen (Antofagasta, Chile), 1957–1963; and Peldehue (Santiago, Chile), 1957–1988. See Corliss, *Space Tracking and Data Acquisition,* and Tsiao, *Read You Loud and Clear!*

21. Corliss, *Space Tracking and Data Acquisition,* 3.

22. Corliss, *Space Tracking and Data Acquisition,* 24.

23. L. R. Wilson, Secretary of the Commission of Fine Arts, letter to Lt. Col. James S. Cook Jr., Chief, Heraldic Branch of the Army Office of the Quartermaster Corps, February 25, 1959, Files of the Institute of Heraldry, Department of the Army, Fort Belvoir, VA, to be deposited in the NASA HRC. Quoted in Joseph R. Chambers and Mark A. Chambers, *Emblems of Exploration: Logos of the NACA and NASA* (Washington, DC: NASA, 2015), 63.

24. "Lackluster Medals," *Time,* May 19, 1961, 84.

25. Chambers and Chambers, *Emblems of Exploration,* 75.

26. Steve Garber, "NASA Meatball Logo," accessed May 3, 2016, http://history.nasa.gov/printFriendly/meatball.htm.

27. Chambers and Chambers, *Emblems of Exploration,* 89.

28. Chambers and Chambers, *Emblems of Exploration,* 92.

29. Garber, "NASA Meatball Logo."

30. Garber, "NASA Meatball Logo."

31. Kenneth Chang, "$79 for an Out-of-Date Book about a Modern NASA Logo," *New York Times,* September 1, 2015.

32. See Adam Yarmolisnky, *The Military Establishment: Its Impacts on American Society* (New York: Harper and Row, 1971); McDougall, *Heavens and the Earth;* and Light, *From Warfare to Welfare.*

33. Light, *From Warfare to Welfare,* 102.

34. The network was initially employed for physical research such as the Lyman Alpha experiment, the cosmic ray experiment, and environmental studies regarding temperature, pressure, and surface erosion measurements. NRL Report 4700, Project Vanguard Report No. 1: Plans, Procedures and Progress. Unclassified Secret document (Washington, DC: Naval Research Laboratory, January 13, 1956), 48–50.

PART III

INFRASTRUCTURES
OF THE BUILT
ENVIRONMENT

8

PLANNING, POLITICS, AND PRAXIS AT COLOMBIA'S INTER-AMERICAN HOUSING LAB, 1951-1966

Mark Healey

In May 1957, when the military government of Colombia fell, a group of students were busy putting up an odd structure on the campus of the National University in Bogotá. After a decade of brutal strife had displaced millions and killed hundreds of thousands, many groups were pushing for a return to civic peace and civilian rule. Yet the conflict had shattered communities and revealed pervasive social needs. How to rebuild? The structure rising on the campus suggested one model: this was a new form of rural home, modest yet modern, whose construction was a community effort and whose design reflected careful thought and austere innovation. The structure was a model peasant home built from bricks of stabilized dirt that had been compressed with a new metal device; with the use of this tool, the poor could build their own homes at very low cost as a community endeavor. But those building this model house were not peasants: they were Colombian and international students at the Centro Interamericano de Vivienda y Planeamiento (CINVA), or Inter-American Housing and Planning Center, working with blueprints they had drawn up themselves, a device invented by a Chilean professor at CINVA, and a model for community building developed by other CINVA professionals. This model home promised a better future for the rural poor of Colombia, and a more prominent role in building that future—but it also highlighted the importance of new kinds of experts in bringing this future to pass.

In contrast to the patrician partisan leaders of the past or the brutal military officers of the present, the students and professors at CINVA modeled in their actions and their building a new democratic sensibility, one that would become characteristic of the civilian government of the National Front that would come to power the following year. It is not hard to see this sample structure going up in such a visible location as a model for the new Colombia. Yet CINVA was also very much a product of the Violencia, and its leaders had worked closely with the military. The model house was the product of an innovative series of experimental rural housing projects CINVA had conducted over the previous five years. In bringing this work into the city, it highlighted the needs of the countryside and even subtly suggested that some of the tools to meet those needs might even find urban applications. But it also undercut a key insight of those experiments, which had always rethought housing in the context of whole communities, by isolating this individual structure and focusing attention on the ingenious device, the CINVA-RAM block press, which would soon become a ubiquitous feature of community development projects worldwide. Drawing many visitors and receiving ample coverage in the press, the model house nicely captured the achievements and ambivalences of this novel space of Cold War social reform.[1]

This chapter examines the first decade of this crucial but forgotten institution, CINVA. As its name suggests, this institution was part of the Organization of American States, and although it did most of its work in Colombia, it drew in scholars, practitioners, and professionals from across the Americas. Powerfully shaped by US experiences and priorities, it was nonetheless inflected by Latin American experts and activists, and would have a significant impact on debates about housing and citizenship across the hemisphere. It would also play an important role in reshaping the political culture of the middle class, and especially professionals, in Colombia during and after the Violencia. This is thus an examination of what the historian Leandro Benmergui has called a "transnational contact zone" of discourses and practices of housing and development.[2]

This institution was also in another contact zone, between projects for urban renewal and for rural development. Although CINVA did do work on large-scale housing projects, its efforts and attentions were most focused on the urban fringe and, surprisingly, on rural development. Thus this chapter, like some intriguing work on postwar architecture and planning, is focused particularly on connections between the urban and the rural, and between the formal, state-sanctioned city of modernizing discourses and the two worlds that seemed to threaten it, the rapidly growing urban periphery and the declining world of rural settlements.[3] In particular, CINVA was an important early space for thinking about the now-familiar practices of autoconstruction, and in ways historians are only beginning to explore, an early forum for attempts to deploy autoconstruction as a state-promoted strategy for development.[4]

The field experiences of CINVA trainees and experts might well be classified as "development encounters," in the suggestive phrase of the Colombian anthropologist Arturo Escobar.[5] And this chapter fits squarely within the substantial body of critical work on development produced since the 1990s. Yet this literature has, on the whole, paid relatively little attention to housing, or institutions like CINVA. Indeed, even Escobar's pioneering work gave short shrift to the specific institutions and complex politics of development in the decades before 1970. Yet as this chapter will show, CINVA was a key space in the making of a developmentalist state and, more specifically, in forging a generation of activist professionals. Looking more closely at this history is thus useful in thinking about the transnational histories of experts, housing, and development, and particularly about their trajectories within Colombia itself.

This account begins with two events in April 1948 in Bogotá. The first is the international congress that founded the Organization of American States (OAS), as a transformation of the old Pan American Union, under the leadership of its first secretary general, the Colombian statesman and Liberal Party stalwart Alberto Lleras Camargo. In the creation of the new institution, there were numerous attempts to strengthen and expand the limited institutions of international cooperation that had existed under the Pan American Union. More than fifty new centers or programs were proposed, but CINVA was the first to be approved, in September 1951, a clear indication of the rising importance of housing as a political problem. Various countries offered to host it, but Colombia prevailed, surely in part because of the influence of Lleras Camargo, but also thanks to the promise of a new building on the campus of the National University and subsidies and resources from the Instituto de Crédito Territorial (ICT), the lead government housing agency. In short, CINVA was an institution of modernizing, technocratic social reform, powerfully shaped by dominant US visions of what modernization should look like.

The second event stands in stark contrast to this tidy history of progressive institutions: the assassination of the Liberal leader Jorge Gaitán on April 9, 1948, in the midst of the OAS conference, and the massive protest and revolt that sparked, first in Bogotá itself, but later all across the country. The Bogotazo did not begin the massive partisan slaughter that would become known as the Violencia, but it did dramatically accelerate it.[6] Over the following decade, hundreds of thousands would lose their lives in a dizzying outbreak of social violence between Conservatives and Liberals, and the police, army, and the peasantry. Although this essay will not delve deeply into that experience, the dark shadow of the Violencia haunts all the modernizing practices and attempts at rethinking society examined here.[7] The Conservative administrations of Mariano Ospina Peréz (1946–1950) and Laureano Gómez (1950–1953), as well as the military regime of General Gustavo Rojas Pinilla (1953–1957) would see the high point of the violence, and also the launching of numerous modernization initiatives. After the Bogotazo, the

Violencia was overwhelmingly concentrated in the countryside, which both accelerated urban growth and narrowed and urbanized the everyday power of the state.

The Violencia tore apart the stability and legitimacy of the Convivencia, rule by the small republic of notables who headed the Conservative and Liberal parties. In the aftermath of the Bogotazo, the cities would largely settle into an uneasy quiet, and the state would slowly and partly reassert its control over the larger cities (and certain departments relatively unaffected by partisan violence). But outside that circumscribed urban reach, the state's legitimacy and authority were gravely weakened, as certain state agencies (notably the police) became active agents of slaughter, while other state agencies weakened and collapsed. If a characteristic of the republic of notables had been its lettered, gentlemanly air, one feature of Colombian cultural life in these years was the broad questioning of the wisdom of these leaders and of the suitability of such salon intellectuals for the exercise of power.

Paradoxically, then, Colombia in these years of murderous state collapse was also a laboratory for ambitious programs of state-led modernization. The two most prominent were dramatic schemes for urban and economic development.

Shortly after the Bogotazo, three prominent architects declared that the destruction had "frankly cleared and partly resolved" problems in the crowded city center, and launched a campaign to transform the city.[8] Within a year, the leading international modernists Le Corbusier, José Luis Sert, and Paul Wiener had been hired to draft a plan for remaking Bogotá. Over four years, they produced two ambitious proposals, a more general Pilot Plan authored by Le Corbusier and a more detailed Development Plan authored by Sert and Wiener. The effort foundered at the height of the Violencia, when General Rojas Pinilla overthrew the civilian government and scrapped the plan, but it suggests the internationalist ambitions of the Bogotá elite.[9]

The program for economic modernization had a more lasting impact. In 1949 the World Bank sent a team to Colombia to conduct a full country study. This came at a moment of transition for the Bank, as it turned away from financing the reconstruction of Europe toward promoting the development of the Global South. Colombia was the first country study and a crucial test case. The head of the mission, the US-Canadian economist Lauchlin Currie, produced a plan for broad-based, comprehensive development, including investments in housing and other social programs. This sparked an intense debate about the best strategy for promoting economic development, which led the Bank to reject the plan and break with Currie, turning instead to a narrower, more project-centered vision. Unlike the failed urban plan, though, this early controversy only led to closer ties between the Bank and the Colombian government, as a series of subsequent missions produced grand, top-down proposals for economic growth.[10]

Despite strong claims for comprehensiveness, each of these attempts at planning proved incomplete and poorly integrated with the others, even on their own terms. Curiously enough, after Currie fell out with the World Bank, he was hired by the government of Colombia to work on various projects, including a social development plan for Bogotá, which the Sert–Wiener architectural team only discovered when a friend sent them a press clipping about it—an attempt to integrate the two was foiled by the military coup that led to the canceling of all travel, and eventually of both plans.[11]

Whatever the political vagaries of high-level planning, it is worth stressing how easily these novel forms of knowledge fit into established schemes of political authority, with foreign experts having familiar figures of the republic of notables as their major interlocutors—the various iterations of national councils for economic planning, for example, were all staffed with leading politicians of the past decade.

Yet alongside these top-down schemes for modernization, Colombia was a staging ground for smaller-scale US technical assistance programs in agriculture, health, and education under the Point Four aid scheme launched by President Truman in 1949. Some built on earlier cooperation programs, others were new, but all were marked by a growing attempt to strengthen the state on a community level, particularly later in the 1950s. The most prominent was the Corporación del Valle del Cauca, established in 1954 to promote integrated river basin development on the Tennessee Valley Authority model. Several also produced a new kind of political leadership, more technically proficient than in the past, and also, crucially, concerned with exercising power in more "democratic" ways across the social distances still characteristic of Colombia.

In its mandate and general approach, CINVA bore a strong resemblance to these sectoral programs, and worked alongside many of them, notably the Cauca Valley Authority. But despite many shared assumptions, CINVA would be led in a different direction by its institutional design, multinational personnel, and greater commitment to experimentation.

Why was housing chosen for the first OAS institution based outside of the United States? In part, this was a response to the dramatic growth of cities and the very mixed success of housing initiatives designed to address it. The possible consequences of inaction were made starkly clear at the founding conference of the OAS in 1948. But there was also a long-standing tradition of Pan American conferences on housing and social reform, including a major conference on popular housing in Buenos Aires in 1939, which had issued a formal call for founding a hemispheric agency to study housing, repeated

at numerous conferences of architects, municipal officials, and engineers in
the years since.

A third influence, though little appreciated at the time, was the cadre of
housing experts in the new institutions of international development in the
United States and Europe. As the historian Nancy Kwak and the historical
geographer Richard Harris have recently shown, a tightly knit group of housing experts, a mix of New Deal veterans and European exiles, had taken up
strategic positions in several new institutions in the late 1940s to develop
a strategy for housing in former colonies and the Global South. This group
included figures such as Ernest Weissman, head of the small housing office
at the UN, and particularly Jacob Crane, at the Home Housing Finance Authority in Washington, DC. An ally of theirs, the architect Anatole Solow,
was named the first head of a small Housing and Planning Division at the
Pan American Union in Washington, and then advocated for establishing a
center in Latin America. Although none of these experts controlled sufficient
resources to actually build projects, they played key roles in shaping policy
debates about housing, designing the new housing agencies founded by governments worldwide and, later, the approaches to providing international
funding for housing.[12]

Crane in particular was a quiet figure with broad influence in shaping the
field of housing discourse. In contrast to the dominant emphasis on industrialization and large-scale state-built housing, he advocated a different approach. Drawing on a series of small-scale programs in Puerto Rico during
the 1940s, where he had been a housing official, he proposed instead what
he termed "aided self-help"—schemes for community development in which
the state provided sites, materials, and basic infrastructure, but the housing
itself was built by the group labor of community members.[13] Unmentioned
in the first comprehensive discussion of low-cost housing initiatives in the
Americas published in 1949 under OAS auspices, the idea of "aided self-help"
would quickly become a centerpiece of the new strategy when CINVA was
created two years later.[14]

CINVA as an Institution

For its first two years, CINVA functioned in borrowed offices on the fifteen-
year-old campus of the Universidad Nacional. But by 1953, its new building
was finished, an elegant work in concrete, brick, and glass, with innovative
vaulted concrete roofs. Laid out around an informal courtyard, with ample
offices and large open laboratories along common walkways, it was intended to provide a new ambience for research and design.[15] It was designed by
Eduardo Mejía, the dean of the architecture school, and Herbert Ritter, who
five years earlier had waxed enthusiastic about remaking the city after the

Bogotazo, and later had headed the municipal office coordinating the Le Corbusier–Sert–Wiener plan. While the plan itself was losing support by 1953, the fact that the new CINVA building was designed by one of its major advocates underscored how closely the center was tied into a broad front of modernizing initiatives.

There was a confident tone of Latin American modernism about CINVA, however appalling the social statistics invoked to justify its work. Photos from the early years show custom touches such as a grand donut-shaped table for trainee seminars that would look quite at home at the UN,[16] or students talking and reading while lounging in BKF (or Butterfly) chairs, the Argentine-designed seats that were Latin America's sole contribution so far to the furnishings of international modernism.[17]

Leonard Currie, the first director of CINVA, was a Harvard architect who had trained and later worked under Walter Gropius, the former director of the Bauhaus. He had spent World War II building airstrips in Central America and later the Pacific. This work had given him an interest in Latin America and an appreciation for the complexities of managing construction, while deepening his Bauhaus-derived commitment to interdisciplinary teamwork as the basis of research and design. He set the tone for the work of the center, recruiting a diverse range of professionals, from architects and engineers, naturally, to economists, sociologists, anthropologists, and social workers. Architects were the leaders, but these were architects whose interests ran less to individual structures than to collective questions of community development and planning.

Formally, the center had four missions: training, research, scientific exchange, and direct consulting with government agencies. As Currie noted, if the center's entire budget were solely dedicated to building houses, it could produce at most fifty per year. Instead, its task was to train "housing technicians," carry out research, publish the latest results, and help to evaluate or reorient the policies of housing agencies. This was thus a center of training and experimentation, a think tank rather than an executor of policies.[18]

Most important, CINVA offered a yearlong graduate course on all aspects of housing, centered on a field project up to six months long. From the start, this was to be a transnational, interdisciplinary team who would learn by doing. As Currie put it in an early flyer, at CINVA the "research program is carried forward in the field, in the workshop, the laboratory and the library."[19]

The emphasis on field research, the integration of different disciplines, and even graduate education were new to Colombia. Until then, Colombian universities only offered undergraduate degrees. CINVA thus served as a training ground for the country's first generation of professional social scientists, as well as many architects, planners, and engineers.

At the time, the sociologist Orlando Fals Borda later remembered, "There was no research of any kind, no trips into the field for anyone, except one from the Institute of Natural Sciences." This changed with CINVA, which represented "a fundamental challenge to how the academy functioned in Colombia." For Fals Borda in 2001, CINVA's three key contributions were its commitments to research, to interdisciplinary teams, and to a common Latin American identity. As he put it, "CINVA started to make us think about the rest of the world, especially the world of Latin America."[20]

Over the next decade, CINVA brought nearly three hundred young professionals from across the region to Bogotá, sending them back, as the secretary general of the OAS said in 1956, with "the spirit of crusaders and missionaries in the social field of housing."[21]

Beyond the yearlong course, CINVA also offered specialized courses for staff of state agencies, such as social workers from the Colombian-American Agricultural Service, building inspectors from the ICT, and others. Although less directly tied to the research program, these courses too would contribute to reshaping the technical staff of the Colombian state.

CINVA's commitment to field research had significant consequences. Particularly in the rural housing program, CINVA projects were experimental from the outset, intended to be explorations and pilot programs, designed as experiences in learning for trainees, instructors, and the communities themselves. In several cases, the first year of a program would entice local officials to sign up themselves for later CINVA courses. Whatever the practical limits and conceptual narrowness of these experiments, this would make CINVA into a model for how to forge a new knowledge and state authority after the Violencia.

CINVA undertook a range of projects, including urban housing and various initiatives to rationalize and standardize the construction industry, but its most innovative work, which soon became the heart of the project, was in rural housing.

In some ways this is not surprising: it was in the countryside where the needs were obviously most urgent. But given the level of violence there, the intensity of the CINVA program is remarkable. While it is difficult to discern why particular sites were chosen, they covered much of the country, and especially the Cauca River Valley after 1954. Reports are entirely silent on the Violencia, or politics more generally, except for occasional remarks on working with the local priest or comments about how community-building projects were simplified by the fact that everyone belonged to the same party. The international staff at CINVA was quite aware, however, of the political allegiances of the Colombian staff, and of the role the center played for many Liberals to practice a kind of politics in internal exile. But while CINVA projects clearly focused on areas where there had been little violence or where, as in Boyacá, the worst of the violence had subsided, they displayed a central concern for the underlying structural causes of poverty and inequality and how housing might play a role in addressing them.

Rural Housing

In Colombia, unlike other Latin American countries, housing reform had begun with the countryside. The Instituto de Crédito Territorial was established in 1938, with the mission of building proper rural homes. Working alongside the cooperative housing program established by the Coffee Growers Federation, the ICT carried out a significant program of rural construction over the following two decades. In 1942, the ICT was reorganized to become the lead state housing agency overall, and began building projects in the cities as well. After another reorganization in 1957, it turned entirely to urban projects, and wound down its lingering rural commitments. Through 1957, however, the ICT had built over fourteen thousand rural houses, mostly during the early years, with the Coffee Growers Federation contributing a few thousand more.[22]

Significant as these numbers were, they paled in the face of the challenge. ICT rural housing, moreover, was designed on standard lines by urban architects, built by outside labor, and paid for by mortgage loans. These houses were a matter of transplanting urban models into the countryside, rather than building on the traditions, experiences, or capabilities of rural communities. Their outside design, expensive labor, and quality materials made them too costly for the vast majority of the rural population. Indeed, by the time the ICT turned to urban projects, it was beginning to make this explicit. In 1947, for example, the ICT held a design competition for a standardized "economical home." Though the ICT specified attached housing, each home was also two stories, with multiple bedrooms and a carport. The winning entries came from all the leading young Colombian modernists; as the carport suggested, these "inexpensive" homes were not cheap, and they were destined for the growing urban middle class.[23]

The rural housing program at CINVA struck out in a different direction. It would be shaped above all by two figures, the Argentine architect Ernesto Vautier and the Colombian sociologist Orlando Fals Borda.

At first glance, Ernesto Vautier was an unlikely choice. He was certainly distinguished, with a stream of publications dating back thirty years and built works across Argentina, ranging from stylish apartment blocks to large-scale housing developments. Three years after graduating from university, he and his fellow architect, Alberto Prebisch, had produced a prize-winning design for a model sugar plantation and mill town in the Northwest and then gone on to author a series of polemical articles in the avant-garde literary magazine *Martín Fierro* introducing the key principles of modernist architecture to Latin America. In the years since, Vautier's ardor for functionalism had cooled, but he had remained interested in comprehensive planning. Alongside his private practice, he had been active in debates about urban planning and had been a lead designer on many state projects, from a pioneering neighborhood for military families to housing for a new Argentine steel mill and plans for a new city of fifty thousand outside Buenos Aires. At his most ambitious, he and a colleague had led the team that proposed to rebuild the city of San Juan on a new site and an entirely different design after it was destroyed by an earthquake in 1944. From his strident early modernism to his enthusiasm for top-down transformation, he seemed out of step with the vision of CINVA. Except for a single article nearly two decades earlier, he had little direct experience with rural housing. But his frustrations in Argentina, and perhaps his experience in San Juan, drew him toward a different approach to architectural practice.[24]

In 1952 Vautier left Argentina, exchanging his professorship in urbanism in one of Latin America's most dynamic cities for a post teaching and studying rural housing in the impoverished Colombian countryside. He did not renounce his comprehensive vision or his sometimes plodding attempts at incorporating multiple disciplines into design: surviving syllabi and lecture notes testify to the eclectic breadth of theoretical writings on dwellings and planning that he assigned and to his insistence on basic questions such as temperature and solar orientation.[25] Colombia would even provide him with a final chance at comprehensive planning, when CINVA was tasked with developing a project for the rural hamlets surrounding Colombia's first steel plant, in Sogamuso. In this 1956 project, just as in his 1944 project for rebuilding San Juan, we can see Vautier's determination to find a balanced, stable, and just arrangement for development, a careful integration of all elements into the countryside, a highlighting of social concerns as a central feature of the project.[26]

Despite these continuities, his work in Colombia showed a change in direction. Back in 1944, he had proposed abandoning the ruins of San Juan to build an entirely new city and a reshaped countryside designed by architects, with the fallen adobe homes replaced by robust new concrete structures. Now he would revisit—and reverse—this earlier approach.

In this effort, Orlando Fals Borda would be his key ally and interlocutor. Fals Borda was a brilliant young sociologist, with a heterodox disposition and a disarming manner. Raised a Protestant in Barranquilla, he came from outside the elite circles and had almost by chance won a scholarship for undergraduate study in the United States. Moving to Bogotá on his return, he found a job with an American company building a dam north of the city and, befriending some of the workers, forged a strong connection with their village. Intrigued by the rapid social change the workers were undergoing, he discovered sociology, and while continuing to work for the company at their home office in Minnesota, he earned a masters degree and then went on to gain a doctorate in rural sociology from Florida. Throughout, his major concern was the transformation of rural lives by the forces of modernization that he himself had come to embody. This connection gave him a strong sense of empathy and a powerful drive to analyze and intervene, fully evident in the flurry of rural research initiatives he launched with Vautier.[27]

After two years at CINVA, Vautier wrote a short article for a business magazine about the project. He began with a brief tour of the profound short-comings of shelter in the countryside, where 95 percent of homes had dirt floors, 98 percent lacked toilets, and virtually 100 percent lacked potable water. This quick survey showed that the ICT, for all its efforts, had barely begun to address the problem, and given the cost of its units, could never do enough. With nearly all campesinos left "to resolve the problem of housing as in the past," with their own hands, the challenge was a question of "improving techniques and aspirations . . . of educating and developing capabilities." Instead of focusing narrowly on "producing more and better houses," interventions should aim more broadly at "producing better men and communities, capable of producing such houses." The ICT should transform itself from a credit institution into an agency of social service and technical assistance.[28]

This new program started with "existing social reality," with learning about "local materials, techniques, habits, and economies." It was flexible, attentive to geographic variation, and part of a broader program to address all aspects of campesino life, especially health and education. Vautier envisioned new "cultural missions" working in the countryside on "experimental and critical . . . pilot projects."[29]

Vautier broke these "pilot projects" down into five steps: socioeconomic survey of living conditions, critique of local housing, design of possible improvements, evaluation, and building of a possible model. Throughout, the idea was to work with the community rather than for the community and to rethink all designs from the standpoint of locals. Any designs should be locally reproducible, every project for a new home should be achievable in stages, "according to the most urgent needs," and any technical innovation had to be simplified so it could be reproduced by others. In short, this was a program of targeted, reflexive interventions. The work might be "less direct," but it was ultimately likely to have a broader and "growing" impact than would building a handful of new structures.[30]

In a longer article published a year later, Fals Borda offered a more comprehensive rethinking of rural housing from the standpoint of campesinos, systematically taking apart how the focus on producing modern, hygienic, and functional houses had misunderstood the conditions of rural life and the meaning of shelter. Taking an ethnographic view, Fals Borda developed a different conceptual structure for thinking about housing, one sympathetic to reform but grounded in an appreciation of the range of solutions and depth of thinking of campesinos themselves.[31]

Following this approach, the teams led by Vautier and Fals Borda undertook a dozen community studies in six years, involving over a hundred students from across the continent. These projects were in the spirit if not the letter of the new thinking on "aided self-help." The original Puerto Rican projects had involved building cement block housing in new villages formed after agrarian reform and resettlement. In the Colombian countryside, there had been little reform, there were few resources, and the state was weak. What the CINVA teams retained from the vision, however, was the central idea that remaking housing involved activating the energies and visions of communities themselves, and it needed to be grounded in the desires and capabilities of campesinos. Thus these projects began with an exploration of rural lifeways, from the meanings of neighborliness to the reasons that rural settlements were so often strung along the length of roads rather than clustered into small hamlets. In their careful drawing and surveying, their close listening, the architects and social scientists were learning a different means of professional practice, and trying, however tentatively, to forge a different future for Colombia and for their own countries.

What is notable about these studies is how they deploy the rhetoric of modernizing design and social science, only to undercut many of its foundational assumptions. A particular obsession of architects, for instance, was the functional separation of spaces. But these rural missions gradually demonstrated how single spaces could and should serve multiple functions, and thus misguided architectural efforts to simplify would render "improved" housing nearly unusable. These were also lessons that would be developed further in the projects some of these same teams undertook in informal settlements on the rapidly expanding edge of cities, notably Cali.[32]

Throughout, they paid close attention to the possibilities of technical improvement. The Chilean engineer Raúl Ramírez developed a new device for compressing a mixture of soil and cement into hardened blocks, suitable for producing high-quality, low-cost building materials for rural housing. This was a refinement of earlier ICT experiments with soil cement, but it reached wider application with Ramírez's more resilient design, the CINVA-RAM block press. Vautier and Fals Borda carried out extensive testing with Ramírez, trying to find ways to make the technology as simple and flexible as possible. Test structures of soil cement went up in nearly all their field projects. Most prominently, they built an improved rural house of soil cement on the campus of the National University itself, right across from the CINVA building. Embracing vernacular building techniques as the basis for better construction, with the possible supplement of soil-cement blocks, was a break with previous housing proposals, working in finished industrial materials, or even from the previous works of Vautier himself, for example, his push a decade earlier to entirely eliminate adobe housing from San Juan. In the published reports on the pilot projects, Vautier and his colleagues also made clear not only the possibilities of soil cement but also its limitations, most notably in the subtle ways it sometimes continued to strengthen the authority of urban experts they were trying to undermine. Here too the pursuit of technical innovation led to a rethinking of the social conditions of their professional practice.

One of the last projects Fals Borda would undertake at CINVA tied together his two commitments in the previous years, by bringing the techniques for collectively erecting structures and building communities to the town he had lived in and studied for his dissertation, Saucío. Taking the tools developed with CINVA projects back to Saucío, Fals Borda and two others helped to organize the community to build a school, form an agricultural cooperative, and establish a new set of community organizations, including a soccer team. This was a first case of community building in post-Violencia Colombia, and Fals Borda quickly wrote up the case as a model for how to create the kind of democratic public he believed the country needed.[33]

Legacies of CINVA

Fals Borda was not a program leader at CINVA, but he was intensely involved with many of its research projects, especially in rural settings. This experience deeply shaped his thinking about how to build a new democratic Colombia by creating a new body of state officials and the development of new community capacities. This would be his central project after the return to civilian rule under the power-sharing agreement known as the National Front (1958–1974), and particularly the administration of Alberto Lleras Camargo (1958–1962). In many ways, the frenzied and ambitious agenda he launched in the first years of the National Front can be traced directly to his experiences at CINVA. At the Universidad Nacional, he established sociology as a discipline and major for the first time, becoming the first head of the department, placing a strong emphasis on research, and dedicating a substantial budget to publishing a flurry of early investigations.[34] Like the parallel work of Gino Germani in Argentina, he aimed to put sociology on the map with a combination of training, research, and publication. His work for the Colombian state led him to push successfully, along with other CINVA veterans like the Bogotá mayor Jorge Gaitán, for the passage of a participatory planning law, forming Juntas de Acción Comunal, that, though initially limited, would transform the local practice of politics over the coming decades. More broadly, he was key to a range of initiatives to expand and professionalize staffing for the state and to promote new forms of action, notably including agrarian reform. His deep engagement with rural Colombia in the 1950s, for his dissertation research and CINVA projects, also drew him into frontally addressing the Violencia in the landmark collective study published in 1962.[35]

This agenda of social reform and democratic professionalism was certainly not a product of Orlando Fals Borda alone; he was joined by figures such as the anthropologist Roberto Pineda, who had worked with CINVA in the 1950s and would later become its director, and a range of other heterodox thinkers in the new professional middle class. They won the ear and support of Alberto Lleras Camargo, the first president under the National Front, and the partial achievement and broader frustration of their agenda would profoundly reshape Colombian politics in the next decade, as A. Ricardo López and Robert Karl have suggested.[36] But it is worth restating just how much of this agenda specifically crystallized in the experience of CINVA in the 1950s.

After 1958, the experience of CINVA was nationalized, in a positive and negative sense. In a positive sense, Fals Borda and a cluster of other young heterodox professionals carried this spirit into a transformation of the policies and personnel of the state. In a negative sense, within CINVA itself, this experimental spirit would largely be shut down. What had become a somewhat free-wheeling multinational space would be trimmed into a narrower and more disciplined binational institution, aimed at training Colombian functionaries along the lines US development experts preferred.

Just as the experimental spirit of CINVA was reshaping the Colombian state, a new leadership was putting an end to this experimental spirit within CINVA. This began with a 1959 review of CINVA commissioned by the OAS and written by the US architect Walter D. Harris. A Yale professor who had been working on a US-funded aided self-help housing scheme in postcoup Guatemala, Harris criticized the CINVA program for its dispersed program and lack of academic rigor. In response, the OAS signed a six-year consulting agreement with Yale to raise the academic profile of the center, and Harris became the new director.

Under Harris, CINVA shifted away from its multinational research program to become a binational institution focused on technical training. Harris was broadly knowledgeable about Latin America, having published several articles and a recent book on urban growth. But he was less interested in exploring new methods than in applying those already developed. Above all, he thought CINVA should become a more prestigious and focused graduate program in architecture and planning, abandoning its fieldwork, research, and consulting. Thus his arrival coincided with the departure of much of the international faculty, a decline in research projects, and a drop in publications.[37] One minor indication of the new direction, for instance, could be found in a short study, "The Community Planning Concept," prepared in 1961. The first half of the study, authored by the Colombian architect Jorge Rivera Farfán, offered an overview of the disorderly present of Latin American cities, a brief summary of the importance of the "neighborhood unit" concept in planning, and a final remark on the valuable experience CINVA was getting in working on this "forgotten area." The second half of the study, authored by a US scholar Harris had specifically brought in as a leading expert, was a grab bag of definitions from functionalist sociology and generalizations about cities in the North Atlantic. There was no attempt to grapple with what CINVA had learned by actually carrying out dozens of studies. The experience of the past decade was discarded in favor of a flat recital of orthodoxies.[38]

From this point forward, CINVA would become more of an instruction program in applied knowledge than a generator of new research. When the Alliance for Progress was launched in 1961, Harris was replaced by the Puerto Rican economist Rafael Mora-Rubio, and CINVA assumed an important but distinctly secondary role in the ambitious new development initiatives. The center became an important tool in the massive US-funded housing project in Ciudad Techo, Bogotá. Unlike the roughly parallel initiatives launched in Rio de Janeiro and Buenos Aires, this project was centered on aided self-help, in a partial vindication of the approach CINVA had developed over the previous decade. But the center itself had little role in shaping the development; instead, it focused primarily on training social workers to supervise the selection of new residents and guide their adaptation to their new homes. In turn, the rural housing program abandoned pilot projects, in favor of training extension agents for the new agrarian reform agency. Increasingly, CINVA no longer generated new ideas or approaches, but simply transmitted those developed by others, including some of its former leaders.[39]

Even so, the ideas CINVA had generated were key to the policies and self-representation of the new political class. A fitting sense of this transformation could be found in the pages of *Revista Proa*, the modernist architecture and planning journal, in early 1961. The opening editorial celebrated the recent appointment as mayor of Bogotá of the Yale-trained architect Jorge Gaitán Cortés, a CINVA veteran who had been one of the strongest advocates for Le Corbusier's plan for the city a decade earlier. But the rest of the issue was dedicated to a single long article by Germán Samper, a prominent architect who from 1948 to 1954 had worked for Le Corbusier in Paris on the Bogotá plan and many other projects. In his piece, Samper offered a "new vision of the social role of the professional" that he had gained over the previous six years while working to design, coordinate, and usher to success an aided self-help housing project on the capital's outskirts.[40] Samper included not only the usual section and elevation drawings but also a complete chronicle of the ups and downs of the project, with cameo appearances by most of the major figures from CINVA, as well as several from the ICT and the municipal government. The project had begun with a request for help from Samper's driver. For the architect, the project suggested how professionals might bridge social distances and forge a broader sense of democratic community, urgent tasks in Colombia under the National Front. This article was an especially powerful condensation of the vision of the progressive middle class as the key builder of a democratic Colombia that Ricardo López has incisively analyzed.[41] Samper marked a distance from his past aristocratic bearing, stressed his sympathy for the poor, described a participatory and mobilizing process, and brought it all together in a synthetic view of his own modernized, up-to-date authority. This was an authority that would reshape Colombian politics and society in the coming years, both forging a new state and then rebelling against that state. Yet even for someone who had spent the mid-1950s drawing in a studio in Paris rather than exploring the shattered countryside, it was an authority forged in key ways by CINVA.

NOTES

1. *Casa Campesina de Suelo Cemento* (Bogotá: CINVA, 1957).

2. Leandro Benmergui, "The Alliance for Progress and Housing Policy in Rio De Janeiro and Buenos Aires in the 1960s," *Urban History* 36, no. 2 (2009): 303–326.

3. See, for example, the essays in Brodwyn Fischer, Bryan McCann, and Javier Auyero, eds., *Cities from Scratch: Poverty and Informality in Urban Latin America* (Durham, NC: Duke University Press, 2014); and Brodwyn Fischer, *A Poverty of Rights: Citizenship and Inequality in Twentieth-Century Rio de Janeiro* (Stanford, CA: Stanford University Press, 2009).

4. See in particular, the excellent work of Nancy H. Kwak, *A World of Homeowners: American Power and the Politics of Housing Aid* (Chicago: University of Chicago Press, 2015).

5. Arturo Escobar, *Encountering Development: The Making and Unmaking of the Third World* (Princeton, NJ: Princeton University Press, 1994), esp. 85–89.

6. Herbert Braun, *The Assassination of Gaitán* (Madison: University of Wisconsin Press, 1985).

7. See Mary Roldán, *Blood and Fire: La Violencia in Antioquia, Colombia* (Durham, NC: Duke University Press, 2002).

8. Jorge Arango, Herbert Ritter, and Gabriel Serrano, "La reconstrucción de Bogotá" *Revista Proa* 13 (1948): 11–20.

9. On the plan, see Maria Cecilia O'Byrne Orozco, ed., *LC BOG: Le Corbusier en Bogotá* (Bogotá: Universidad de Los Andes, Facultad de Arquitectura y Urbanismo, 2010); and Doris Tarchópulos, "Las huellas del plan para Bogotá de Le Corbusier, Sert y Wiener." *Scripta Nova* 10, no. 218 (2006): 1–13.

10. For a striking and archivally rich account of this first mission and its place in the emergence of development economics and the consolidation of the World Bank, see Michele

Alacevich, *The Political Economy of the World Bank: The Early Years* (Stanford, CA: Stanford University Press, 2009).

11. Michele Alacevich and Andrea Costa, "Economic Policies and Urban Development in Latin America," in *Open Economics: Economics in Relation to Other Disciplines,* ed. Richard Arena, Sheila Dow, and Matthias Klaes (Hoboken, NJ: Taylor and Francis, 2009), 190–208.

12. On the emergence and influence of this cluster of experts, see Richard Harris and Ceinwen Giles, "A Mixed Message: The Agents and Forms of International Housing Policy , 1945–1973," *Habitat International* 27 (2003): 167–91.

13. On Crane and "aided self-help," see Richard Harris, "The Silence of the Experts: 'Aided Self-Help Housing,' 1939–1954," *Habitat International* 22 (1998): 165–189.

14. In the overview written in 1947, there is no mention of "aided self-help": Francis Violich with Anatole Solow, *Low-Cost Housing in Latin America* (Washington, DC: Pan American Union, 1949). By contrast, this is the central emphasis of Anatole Solow and Rodrigo Masís, *Cooperación Interamericana en el campo de vivienda y urbanismo* (Washington, DC: Pan American Union, 1950).

15. "Centro Interamericano de Vivienda Bogotá," *Revista Proa* 74 (1953): 16–20.

16. Leonard Currie, *Inter-American Housing Center* (Washington, DC: Pan American Union, 1954), 2.

17. *Prospectus 1956 Inter-American Housing Center* (Bogotá: Centro Interamericano de Vivienda, 1956), 21.

18. *Prospectus,* 6, 8.

19. Currie, *Inter-American,* 3.

20. Quoted in Jorge Rivera, "El CINVA: Un ejemplo de cooperación técnica" (MA, Universidad Nacional de Colombia, 2002), 18–19.

21. Quoted in Juan Molina y Vedia, *La ciudad dulce: Ernesto Vautier* (Buenos Aires: Nobuko, 2010), 40.

22. Between 1942 and 1957, the ICT also built over eighteen thousand urban homes. Rivera, "El CINVA," 84.

23. "Resultados del concurso de vivienda económica," *Revista Proa* 7 (1947): 12–18.

24. On Vautier's work in San Juan, see Mark Healey, *The Ruins of the New Argentina* (Durham, NC: Duke University Press, 2011). On his overall trajectory, see the reflections in Molina y Vedia, *La ciudad dulce,* and the exhibition catalog *Ernesto Vautier: Un arquitecto con compromiso social* (Buenos Aires: CEDODAL, 2005).

25. See, for example, Ernesto Vautier, *El hombre y su vivienda frente al clima* (Bogotá: Centro Interamericano de Vivienda y Planeamiento, 1958).

26. *Proyecto Sogamuso—Paz De Río: Ensayo de una metodología* (Bogotá: Centro Interamericano de Vivienda, 1956).

27. See Alexander Pereira Fernández, "Fals Borda: La formación de un intelectual disorgánico," *Anuario Colombia de Historia Social y de la Cultura* 35 (2008): 375–411.

28. Ernesto Vautier, "El problema de la vivienda rural en Colombia," *Economía colombiana* 2 (1955): 59, 60, 62.

29. Vautier, "El problema," 61.

30. Vautier, "El problema," 61–62.

31. Orlando Fals Borda, "Aspectos psico-sociológicos de la vivienda rural colombiana," *Revista de psicología* 1 (1956): 206–229.

32. See particularly Orlando Fals Borda and Ernesto Vautier, *La vereda de Chambimbal: Estudio y acción en vivienda rural* (Bogotá: Centro Interamericano de Vivienda y Planeamiento, 1958); and Orlando Fals Borda, Ernesto Vautier, and Josephina Albano, *Manual de investigación y acción en vivienda rural* (Bogotá: Centro Interamericano de Vivienda y Planeamiento, 1958). For their work in other contexts, see also Orlando Fals Borda and Ernesto Vautier, *Urbanización Boyacá: una experiencia de práctica interprofesional en vivienda* (Bogotá: Centro Interamericano de Vivienda y Planeamiento, 1959), the rural sections of *Proyecto Sogamuso— Paz de Río*, and the urban project in *Siloé: un proceso de desarrollo comunal aplicado a un proyecto de rehabilitación urbana* (Bogotá: Centro Interamericano de Vivienda y Planeamiento, 1958).

33. Orlando Fals Borda with Nina Chaves and Ismael Márquez, *Acción Comunal en una vereda colombiana* (Bogotá: Universidad Nacional de Colombia, Departamento de Sociología, 1961).

34. This is the "Monografías sociológicas" series. See, for example, Orlando Fals Borda, *La teoría y la realidad del cambio sociocultural en Colombia* (Bogotá: Universidad Nacional de Colombia, Departamento de Sociología, 1959).

35. Germán Guzmán Campos, Orlando Fals Borda, and Eduardo Umaña Lima, *La violencia en Colombia: Estudio de un proceso social*, 2 vols (Bogotá: Tercer mundo, 1962).

36. See Robert Karl, *Forgotten Peace* (Oakland: University of California Press, 2017) and A. Ricardo López, "Conscripts of Democracy: The Formation of a Professional Middle Class in Bogotá during the 1950s and Early 1960s," in *The Making of the Middle Class: Toward a Transnational History*, ed. A. Ricardo López and Barbara Weinstein (Durham, NC: Duke University Press, 2012), 161–196. More broadly, see A. Ricardo López, *Makers of Democracy: A Transnational History of the Middle Classes in Colombia* (Durham, NC: Duke University Press, 2019), 21–108.

37. On the change under Harris, see Rivera, "El CINVA," 140–141.

38. Jorge Rivera Farfán and George Cardis, *The Community Planning Concept* (Bogotá: Inter-American Housing and Planning Center, 1960), 9, 11, 20.

39. On CINVA after 1961, see Rivera, "El CINVA," 152–178.

40. Germán Samper Gnecco, "Casas por ayuda mutua y esfuerzo propio en el Barrio 'La Fragua' Bogotá," *Revista Proa* 147 (1961): 3–16.

41. Ricardo López, *Makers of Democracy* and "Conscripts of Democracy."

9

DAMS AND HYDROELECTRICITY

Circulation of Knowledge and Technological Imaginaries
in South America, 1945–1970

Fernando Purcell

This chapter explores the triumph of the "concrete revolution," the phenomenon that led to the construction of fifty thousand large hydroelectric dams around the world during the twentieth century.[1] The analysis focuses on South America during the early Cold War, when the construction of hydroelectric plants surged to its greatest magnitude in the region. In order to explain the success of this revolution, the chapter studies the roles that experts and technical knowledge, as well as the circulation of ideas and cultural representations, had in terms of constituting imaginaries favorable to the dam-building process.[2]

Although the concrete revolution in South America had important pre-1945 antecedents, because of the national efforts toward industrialization and import substitution,[3] it materialized during the global Cold War, when world superpowers and developing nations focused on the challenge of modernizing countries such as Chile, Colombia, and Peru through comprehensive development plans. Emblematic hydroelectric projects such as Bajo Anchicayá in Colombia (1955), Cañón del Pato in Peru (1958), and Rapel in Chile (1968) were developed in precisely this context and are excellent representative examples of broader phenomena playing out in South America overall.[4]

The Bajo Anchicayá dam was completed in 1955 and is located near the city of Cali, in Valle del Cauca, Colombia. It was Colombia's first big dam, and its construction lasted from 1944 to 1955, although the major advances occurred between 1950 and 1955. Municipal, departmental, and national authorities drove this project that had important international collaboration.

In fact, the United States supported the project through different means, just as it did for other developmental projects in Colombia, including housing, as addressed in this volume by Mark Healey (chapter 8).[5] The project developed at a time when Colombia confronted political and economic instability, which both configured a fertile ground for communism. This is why US collaboration with Colombia increased over the years and became even stronger under the dictator Gustavo Rojas Pinilla (1953–1957), who was opposed by communists in Colombia and who received support from the United States.[6] Numerous high-ranking US officials and private consultants such as David Lilienthal, the former head of the Tennessee Valley Administration (TVA) in the United States, visited the country in the late 1950s and supported the building of this dam.

Cañón del Pato in Perú was a hydroelectric plant originally conceived by the Peruvian engineer Santiago Antúnez de Mayolo in 1915.[7] However, the project became feasible only at the beginning of the Cold War with the important participation of US engineers, including Barton M. Jones, a former engineer of the TVA.[8] Located in the Department of Ancash, the run-of-river hydroelectric plant was inaugurated in 1958 by President Manuel Prado, but its major impulse came from President Manuel Odría, who governed between 1948 and 1956. Odría's government was clearly procapitalist and anticommunist, and he helped promote vital US economic and political interests in Peru.[9] Odría fervently opposed communism and even outlawed the Communist Party during his authoritarian government. During his presidency, he promoted a liberal economy seeking to diminish the state's participation in the economy and gave an important push to the development of infrastructure in order to promote development.[10] His government's slogan was "Not Words but Facts.[11] His successor, Manuel Prado (1956–1962), the president who inaugurated Cañón del Pato, sought a more democratic society but continued being allied with the United States, an important characteristic of US-Peruvian relations, at least until the late 1960s.[12]

The Rapel dam was inaugurated in Chile in 1968 and even though the initial soil prospects were conducted in the mid-1940s, its construction started in 1961 by the National Company for Electrical Development in Chile (ENDESA), a state-owned company during the right-wing presidency of Jorge Alessandri (1958–1964). It was finished in 1968 when Eduardo Frei was president (1964–1970). Rapel became popularized as a project during Frei's presidency, which had a reformist tone and was marked by a close relationship with the United States. In fact, Chile received some of the most important economic and political support from the Alliance for Progress, especially after Frei was elected.[13] Frei tried to avoid the marginalization of poor people and to integrate dispossessed people to full citizenship; he was also a fervent anticommunist. Unlike right-wing politicians in Chile who were reluctant to make structural changes, Frei coined the idea of a "Revolution in Liberty" as a way to fight communism. It meant reformism instead of armed struggle to confront problems including agrarian reform and political inclusion, and was seen as a very interesting program by the United States within the Cold War framework.

An Energetic Cold War Weapon

Both the United States and the Soviet Union regarded the development of hydroelectric energy as an important Cold War "weapon." Energy was the basic source for development, potential economic growth, stability, and success, and hydroelectricity proved to be a cheaper and safer way to generate electricity in developing countries, compared to oil or coal-operated plants and nuclear power.

The Soviet Union limited its energy-development technology to its sphere of direct influence, whereas the United States established a different model that combined a vast plan of dam construction both in the United States and in dozens of developing countries.[14] The spread of high dams was an important strategy to contain communism during the Cold War.[15] Dam building was promoted by the United States to bring progress and modernity, when countries including Chile, Colombia, and Peru had high poverty rates, weak economies, and low percentages of electric coverage that reached less than 50 percent of the population.[16] All these factors provided fertile ground for communism. Yet influential Americans were convinced that the disposition of enough energy could trigger economic prosperity and become a crucial tool for modernization and democracy, instead of communism.[17]

The building of dams was also an important strategy to establish or strengthen diplomatic relationships because of the technology transfer and assistance that usually persisted for decades, not to mention spare replacement parts that linked countries with their suppliers. As Gabrielle Hecht and Paul N. Edwards argue, exports of technical expertise to the developing world became a major means of establishing alliances and forms of dependency for the United States and the Soviet Union.[18] In addition, these mega constructions involved important fluxes of money through international loans provided by American or international banks that moved along ideological lines during the Cold War.[19] This is why dams became part of geopolitical strategies that, as the historian Richard Tucker points out, "were a driving motivation for the locations of a series of these dams."[20]

For the United States, dams were extremely relevant to contain communism. When conflict with the Soviet Union escalated after 1945, the United States was in a better position to promote hydroelectricity in developing countries. The United States already played a dominant role at a global level in the so-called domestication of river systems, thanks to the accumulation of expertise through institutions such as the Bureau of Reclamation, from 1902 on, and the TVA, established in 1933 in the context of the Great Depression.[21] Convinced of the universal value of the "domestication" of hydraulic resources and the "industrialization of nature,"[22] these institutions deployed dozens of highly qualified technical specialists and hydrotechnocrats around the world to provide technical assistance, contributing to a revolutionary phenomenon: the politicization of expertise. At the same time, hundreds of foreign visitors attended trainings in their offices and in the field. As the TVA chief David Lilienthal pointed out in 1944: "Our foreign visitors see with particular clarity that TVA speaks in a tongue that is universal, a language of things close to the lives of people: soil fertility, forests, electricity, phosphate, factories, minerals, rivers. No English interpreter is needed when a Chinese or a Peruvian sees this series of working dams, or electricity flowing into a single farmhouse."[23]

Together with the political interest of containing communism through development, this conviction regarding the universal applicability of technology and expertise was the legitimizing foundation for vast technical assistance programs throughout the world in areas such as agriculture or hydraulic resource management. Although these programs were created before the end of World War II, they took on a powerful strategic dimension for the United States in the early Cold War, during the presidency of Harry Truman and the implementation of the principles of foreign relations expressed by the Point Four Program of 1949.[24]

Circulation of Knowledge and Experts

The historian Christopher Sneddon argues that US government agencies such as the Bureau of Reclamation spread large-dam technologies and the ideologies that guided them across the globe. However, this US-centric view overlooks the actions of South American societies and states in this "revolutionary" global process. In order to explain the success of this technological revolution, we also need to consider regional spaces, such as South America, and their national particularities. This is necessary to contribute to current trends on Cold War studies that have been paying attention to the developing world and its role in this global conflict.[25]

In South America, the Cold War coincided with an urgent demand for energy needed to fuel the post-Depression developmentalist industrialization policies and with a series of efforts that promoted import substitution in Latin America. Notwithstanding the asymmetry between the United States and South America in terms of highly complex technology, South American engineers and technicians began to discuss and execute national electrification projects earlier in the century, especially in the 1930s and early 1940s. In this context, they became part of global circuits of training, transfer, and discussions of hydroelectricity and related technology. But in order to participate in these circuits, they needed projects and institutional apparatuses. Hence, the state played an important role in engineers' actions by creating institutions that promoted electrification such as the Institute of Water Use and Electrical Development in Colombia (Electraguas) and ENDESA in Chile, by designing and financing works, and, at the same time, by promoting the insertion of their engineers in global circuits.

As they designed electrification plans and hydroelectric projects with the support of their states, South American engineers were not isolated within their countries. Through universities, international exhibitions, congresses, and engagement with specialists from other countries, many formed part of complex webs of expertise. A good example of the latter is the case of the Colombian engineer Carlos Sanclemente, a representative of the generation of "técnicos" in his country: pragmatic researchers who developed "modern" public policies. Sanclemente graduated as an engineer from Colombia's National University in 1944 before specializing in hydroelectric plants. He became the submanager of Electraguas in 1949 and then went on a long tour in Europe to see "all" of the continent's hydroelectric plants. He then enrolled in MIT before returning to Colombia, where he maintained permanent contact with American and European hydroelectricity specialists, which were strengthened once he became the manager of Electraguas.[26]

The Bureau of Reclamation archives show that engineers from South America consistently visited the bureau's agencies and laboratories.[27] Some stayed several months, including the Chilean engineers Juliet and Matus who received training in hydroelectric "project planning, design, construction, and operation maintenance" in the early 1940s.[28] From its headquarters in Denver, Colorado, the bureau's Foreign Cooperation Department managed requests to visit its offices and plants, provided logistical assistance to visitors, and facilitated the spread of technology, especially after 1945.[29] David Lilienthal notes that in 1944 the TVA had "served as training ground for foreign technicians," including "two-score engineers and agriculturists from a dozen republics in South America."[30] Furthermore, the TVA sold equipment and provided technical assistance for the development of perforations in Peru's Cañón del Pato and Chile's Rapel project, among many other places in South America during the 1950s and 1960s.[31]

These processes of interaction among experts underscore the importance of the generation of knowledge. The circuits of expertise helped generate global technological knowledge that circulated regardless of language or cultural barriers. The Bureau of Reclamation, for instance, early on established a team of translators to record the proceedings of conferences related to hydroelectricity organized in places including the Soviet Union, Italy, Germany, Norway, and China.[32] Moreover, technicians from the United States who provided technical assistance in other countries gained crucial knowledge from their experiences. The expertise consolidated in these American institutions derived from their accumulation of data throughout their country and the world, leading to what I would refer to as a *dense internalization of local knowledge* that was generated in different parts of the world; it was then spread in a universal sense through technical assistance.

We need to examine the role of local knowledge in the creation of a global phenomenon. As Emily S. Rosenberg reminds us, these "circuits of expert knowledge" allowed for a series of "localized facts to be compared, tested, confirmed, and connected together."[33] Likewise, Tina Loo and Meg Stanley, referring to case studies in North America, draw on the idea that big dams were deterritorialized and globalized "by turning situated knowledge about locales into work experience, problems, and case studies that travelled, informing development in other parts of the world."[34] But who generated this knowledge? How was it accumulated and internalized most densely in countries like the United States? Local knowledge about hydroelectric plants was not generated by local residents only, but by engineers and technicians of diverse nationalities operating within myriad locales. Local spaces are not fixed. Their meaning, characteristics, and identity are constantly reconfigured through the circulation and actions of peoples.[35] Thus, engineers and technicians became part of and influenced the local spaces they visited. They also contributed to the creation of local knowledge related to hydroelectric projects that later circulated to important institutions in the United States, where the accumulation of local reports and its synthesis created room for universal proposals during the Cold War. Engineers and technicians moved around the world, connecting spaces; they constituted the gears of a machinery in which credit institutions, governments, diplomats, entrepreneurs, contractors, and workers all participated. Although these actors were part of the global phenomenon of transference and use of hydroelectric technical knowledge, they mostly operated at local levels, in limited spaces and environments.

Not all engineers played the same role. Although we should avoid simple notions of core–periphery diffusion and pay attention to the interactions between South Americans and North Americans—and to the historical forces and initiatives generated in South America—it is also important to recognize the clear asymmetry in the handling of complex technological knowledge that has to do with power imbalances. Yet, even in light of this, it is necessary to appreciate how the knowledge of local engineers contributed to the success of the "concrete revolution." Working for their respective national states, figures such as Santiago Antúnez Mayolo in Peru, Carlos San-

clemente and Espíritu Santo Potes in Colombia, and Reinaldo Harnecker in
Chile played extraordinary roles in the construction of hydroelectric works
and electricity planning, in addition to bringing together complementary
instances of local knowledge. This knowledge included relationships with
geography, climate, geology, soil, and idiosyncrasies of the multiple local actors involved in the hydroelectric projects, including the residents of often
remote construction areas who understood, better than anyone, rivers and
the flow of water.

Imaginaries

The success of the "concrete revolution" was not due only to the role of engineers, the circulation of technological knowledge, and the execution
of projects. Civil society and the ways in which hydroelectric plants were
"imagined"—the links between the nation and progress, the efforts of the
engineers, the environmental context, and the social benefits, despite the environmental disruptions—all came to form a scaffolding that allowed for the
construction of massive projects that enjoyed widespread support.

Paradoxically, most of the people who created this sociocultural scaffolding of imaginaries had never seen a hydroelectric plant in their lives; moreover, they had little understanding of physics, mathematics, or technical
knowledge. They did not necessarily understand angles, resistance, variabili-
ty of water flow, transmission networks, and they did not speak the technical
language prevalent in engineering circuits. Nonetheless, South American
societies that favored such projects predicated their positions on imaginaries
that were related, directly or indirectly, to hydroelectric technology.

Imagining the Industrialization of Nature

As a result of vast and numerous projects related to the environment, the
Cold War profoundly altered humans' understanding and appreciation of
the biosphere, leading to ambitions that ranged from efforts to "industrial-
ize nature,"[36] as in the case of hydroelectric dams, to attempts to control the
weather as President Lyndon Johnson sought to do in India in order to "mit-
igate drought, prevent famine, and firmly anchor South Asia in the United
States' sphere of influence by bringing precipitation to India's parched lands
courtesy of weather control."[37] Although the desire to control and manipulate nature did not begin with the Cold War, authors such as J. R. McNeill
and Corinna R. Unger emphasize that the Cold War added "a special urgency
to the centuries-old effort to overcome humanity's subordination to the environment. Modern technology offered new, increasingly effective ways of
doing so. Faith in science and technology, moreover, encouraged bold environmental interventions."[38]

During the Cold War, both the United States and the Soviet Union, despite their deep ideological differences, promoted models of progress and modernization predicated on the exploitation of natural resources through the manipulation and control of nature. As Richard P. Tucker has noted, "the most massive projects for transforming nature to suit Cold War strategies were river basin development programs centering on high dams."[39] It is no coincidence, then, that Cold War–charged American media outlets such as the Spanish-language versions of *Reader's Digest* and *Life*, which both had high readership in Latin America, offered information, images, representations, and even publicity related to hydroelectric plants.[40] These reinforced notions of humans' capacity to transform nature for their own benefit.[41] These ideas consistently emphasized human activities that yielded "construction." Discussion and activism derived from the destruction or disruption of the environment increased in the 1960s in the United States and only much later in Latin America.

The history of hydroelectric development during the early Cold War had a profound effect on the environment. All the projects analyzed here were built over several years, which entailed prolonged alterations in the environment. The first geological studies in Rapel were conducted in 1943 but the dam itself was not inaugurated until 1968. Likewise, construction on Bajo Anchicayá began in 1944 and the project began functioning in 1955, after two years of stoppages due to lack of funding. The work for Cañón del Pato lasted from 1944 to 1958, when the plant was inaugurated; meanwhile, it faced economic problems as well as floods and other natural disasters of big proportions, including the outburst flood of October 1950.[42]

These projects affected not only the flow of rivers that were redirected (Cañón del Pato) or contained (Bajo Anchicayá and Rapel) but also riparian terrains and distant areas that were opened up with new roads that altered territorial and environmental realities. Landscapes were significantly altered by the emergence of new settlements and camps, transmission lines, and electricity substations. In the Rapel project, 80 square kilometers of arable land were flooded to create an artificial lake able to hold 700 million cubic meters of water. This altered not only the landscape but also the fauna and the productive economic activities related to agriculture and tourism. At the same time, hundreds of people, mostly poor campesinos, were displaced from Rapel—precisely at a time in which agrarian reform sought to strengthen campesinos' ties to the land, not to displace them.[43] In Cañón del Pato, construction entailed the perforation of rock and the construction of several tunnels with dynamite; in addition to the profound environmental effects, the construction caused several deaths.

The negative impact on the environment and on local residents and workers was largely elided by discourses that minimized damages and emphasized regional and national development with strong patriotic messages. Hydroelectric plants were in remote sites and conceived to serve interests that were located elsewhere. The Rapel plant supplied the city of Santiago with electricity; Cañón del Pato was linked to Chimbote and its steel mill; and Bajo Anchicayá, to the city of Cali.

Despite the negative environmental impact of these hydroelectric projects, what prevailed among South American societies was strong support because of the positive stance toward the human domination of nature for the progress and development of societies. In a 1957 issue of *Selecciones* (the Spanish-language version of *Reader's Digest*), Coca-Cola took out a full-page ad in homage to hydrodynamic engineers who, as the text declared, "dominate the river to man's benefit," by using dams to transform the strength of rivers into light and electricity and, therefore, "transform arid sites into blossoming countryside and industries." Thus, the ad explicitly established a direct relationship between engineers, control of nature, and human progress.[44] Such acknowledgment certainly resonated in South America, where engineers began to engage more actively in society, even in the realm of politics. On the occasion of the inauguration of the hydroelectric plant in Cañón del Pato and the steel mill in Chimbote in 1958, the magazine *Caretas* celebrated the engineer Max Peña Prado. The magazine defended the idea that "what Peru needs, now more than ever, are men of action, captains of industry, engineers and mathematicians, men who are able to build. In sum, leaders who combine intellectual and constructive capacities. They are the conductors of the economic revolution of our time."[45]

The industrialization of nature, then, was a job for engineers. It was highly valued; it represented the triumph of human interests over the environment. Accordingly, when the hydroelectric plant of Bajo Anchicayá was inaugurated in Colombia in 1955, the press noted that the river had been "corrected, channeled, reformed," transformed into "a power arm in the service of economic interests" in the Cauca Valley. The accompanying photo offered uncontestable proof of the human triumph over nature.[46]

In his book written on the eve of the long-dreamed-of inauguration of the Cañón del Pato hydroelectric plant in 1958, Santiago Antúnez de Mayolo also emphasized the epic and heroic triumph of humanity over nature: "The fast-flowing waters of the Santa River" were now "tamed by man's genius and hand in the Cañón del Pato" in order to "generate electrical current."[47]

In the mid-twentieth century, the admiration provoked by the very construction of plants—those "temples of modernity"—strengthened the link between control and industrialization of nature.[48] The news, information, and images of grand engineering feats that circulated in the press further exalted humanity's capacity to overcome "the obstacles of nature" in order to benefit society. Numerous articles written in the United States circulated in South America and reinforced the magnificence of these human accomplishments. The article titled "The Seven Wonders of North American Engineering," for example, featured two hydroelectric dams (Grand Coulee and Hoover), as well as the Colorado River aqueduct. Grand Coulee, the article noted with pride, is the "most powerful generator of hydroelectric power in the world." The Hoover dam, in turn, "rises—formidable and rotund in its majestic beauty—over the border between Nevada and Arizona. . . . The astonished spectator wonders, what type of men could have believed themselves capable of building such a work." The article predicted that although the Swiss were building even higher dams, "the Hoover will remain a proud testimony to the inventiveness and audacity of our time."[49] Other US outlets with wide circulation in South America, such as the Spanish-language version of *Life*, constantly referred to hydroelectric mega-projects,[50] water and energy,[51] and included publicity from different companies involved with dams. The accompanying photographs and drawings unequivocally symbolized for the admiring reading public the highest levels of technological development reached by North American companies.

In several South American countries, magazines, newspapers, and even film series and documentaries gave wide coverage to hydroelectricity and featured plant inaugurations, thus reinforcing these links for the public in South America.[52] As was the case in the United States, the media emphasized the benefits of industrial control over natural resources, the grandeur of the projects, and their huge positive impacts on development.

National Imaginaries

If technological imaginaries of global projection were created in and spread from countries such as the United States, in South America nationalist and patriotic imaginaries linked hydroelectric projects to the national.

When Colombia's first hydroelectric dam was built in Bajo Anchicayá in 1955, the dictator Rojas Pinilla "nationalized" it by making David Lilienthal, now a consultant after leaving the TVA, a Knight of the Order of Boyacá, the main recognition for foreigners in Colombia.[53] For Rojas Pinilla, Anchicayá was central to the Lilienthal Plan that sought to replicate the Tennessee Valley Authority in the Cauca Valley, with hydroelectric development as its central goal. The Cauca Valley Corporation—still in operation today—emerged from this project in 1954, having the TVA as a model, just as in the Mexican case presented by Tore Olsson in this volume (see chapter 2). Taking a clearly strategic approach, Lilienthal himself loaded his technical assistance in Colombia with nationalist language, despite his explicit view that the expertise he had built over the decades since leading the TVA had universal validity. In his first report to the president of Colombia, Lilienthal argued that the proposal would contribute to the "second liberation of Colombia." In the first, of course, Simón Bolívar "opened the door of political independence and freedom." The weapons of the new liberation, Lilienthal insisted, were neither cannons nor swords, but rather "highways, and railroads, electrification, dams for irrigation and flood control and power." The fruits of victory "can be as glorious as those won in the battles fought by Bolívar and his fellow patriots," Lilienthal declared, adding, "The Colombians who lead their countrymen toward this 20th Century Liberation will surely be as highly honored and as long-remembered as those who, following Bolivar more than 100 years ago, offered their lives to win their country's independence."[54]

On the inauguration of the Bajo Anchicayá plant near the cities of Cali and Buenaventura, the newspaper *El Relator* described the celebrations in which "Cali appears like a veritable luminaria of the nation." President Rojas Pinilla participated in the impressive six-hour parade throughout the city.[55] For his part, the engineer and president of Peru, Manuel Prado, declared that the 1958 inauguration of the Cañón del Pato plant and the Chimbote steel mill fulfilled "one of the greatest permanent longings in his life, satisfying a vital aspiration of the nation." Before symbolically pushing the button that turned on the hydroelectric plant and the steel mill, he proclaimed, "Seized by feelings of intense patriotism, I now start up heavy industry in Peru, and offer it to the present and future generations as an invaluable patrimony of *peruanidad*."[56] The Chilean press similarly tended to highlight the actions of Chileans much more than the permanent interaction between Chilean engineers and those of other parts that yielded hydroelectric projects such as that in Rapel in 1968.[57] The nationalist pride provoked by the great hydroelectric accomplishments in the country traversed Chilean society. Workers from the Rapel plant wrote in their newspaper in 1967 that the working class in general needed to appreciate what was being done for a better tomorrow: "Conscious of the importance and magnitude of our obligations, upon completing the construction of our cathedral [the dam], that rises from the splendorous green of the mountain forests, we can go home with the satisfaction of having fulfilled, of giving an important part of our lives to this valuable project, the summit of the Nation's technological patrimony."[58]

The inauguration ceremonies at projects such as Bajo Anchicayá in Colombia, Cañón del Pato in Peru, and Rapel in Chile leave traces of the constitution of these works as patriotic emblems and foundations of pride for national technological accomplishments. In each case, national flags undulated, people marched in magnificent parades, and regional and national authorities attended. This manner of celebrating and imagining the hydroelectric works and technological progress in nationalist codes was fundamental to the success of these huge undertakings. Moreover, it helped attenuate the destruction that these projects entailed: the tragic death of workers in Cañón del Pato when an outburst flood destroyed everything in its path, the flooding of villages and campsites in Rapel, and the displacement and relocation of hundreds of people whose houses were flooded by the artificial lake created by the Rapel dam. Such were the necessary sacrifices made to progress and the nation.[59]

Imagining Electricity

Written, visual, and audiovisual representations of the hydroelectric plants and related technologies circulated through popular culture and the media, allowing people to *imagine uses* of technology with which most had never been acquainted. Regarding the concept of *imagined uses*, Simone M. Müller and Heidi J. S. Tworek point out that "while previous scholars have focused on actual, physical uses of technology, we argue that imagined uses, as part of or beyond such contexts, were just as important."[60] This view points to an appreciation of the social appropriations of technology and of the social and cultural construction of technology—and hence, to the site of the scaffolding of the concrete revolution led by engineers.

The technologies that made hydroelectricity possible must be understood from a *sociotechnical systems approach*, which implies that technologies should be considered as interdependent networks of "artifacts, institutions, people, and social systems."[61] Thus, the examination of imaginaries opens perspectives not only on hydroelectric plants but also on the electricity they generated and their impact on everyday life.

Unlike petroleum, coal, or wood, the flow of electricity—the direct consequence of hydroelectric technology—is not a form of stored hydrocarbon energy and does not exist in nature. As the anthropologist Akhil Gupta reminds us, electricity "cannot be seen, smelled, or heard, and for all practical purposes, it cannot be tasted or touched without lethal consequences. There is thus no sensual way to experience electricity." Therefore, as a product of hydroelectric plants, electricity is abstract, always mediated, "and thus is from the very beginning a social and cultural thing, not something that belongs to the natural world."[62] An editorial published in Cali, Colombia, a few days after the inauguration of the Bajo Anchicayá plant in July 1955, provides a good example of how people anthropologically approached electricity and its abstract quality. The writer noted critically that although the plant was functioning, the "electric fluid is not yet visible throughout the city because it has nowhere to go." This "visibility" of the "electric fluid" is an interesting abstraction since it is impossible to "see" electricity. In fact, the same article resolved the abstraction with the help of an analogy that played with the two meanings of the word *aterrizar*: "to ground" or "be grounded" and "to land." "Hydroelectric fluid needs to be 'grounded,' but 'grounded' in lightbulbs, reflectors, and decorative lights." The article referred to the lack of public light ing, light, and "lamps and lightbulbs" in the sector of San Fernando where whole sections of urban streets remained "in the dark, like the good times when the moon was the only streetlamp."[63]

In the period under review here, electricity was mediated socially and culturally by a series of actors such as entrepreneurs, publicists, and editors of the press and the media who had an important role in the creation of imaginaries that linked electricity to the domestic sphere through the promotion of household appliances such as irons, refrigerators, radios, and stoves. Moreover, this kind of consumption was important in political and ideological terms. Propaganda from the United States during the Cold War gave a special place to the consumption of electric appliances as a way to promote American-style modernity and to counter communist allegations that capitalism served only rich people. This explains the effort by the United States to sell the idea of widespread use of electric appliances across social classes in their country and the Westernized world.[64]

By the mid-twentieth century, the level of electrification of South American homes was still below 50 percent.[65] Therefore, in the decades of the 1940s and 1950s, the entrance of electric appliances into the household was an intensely lived phenomenon, especially after the inauguration of new hydroelectric plants. The universe of people who managed to acquire appliances gradually expanded, even though the phenomenon had begun in the 1920s. Marketing strategies related a series of electrical appliances to modernity through positive significations. The time that these appliances supposedly saved for those doing household chores would lead to the "liberation of women" and enhance family comfort, although the real story was different from that.[66] Nonetheless, electric appliances became extremely attractive to all sorts of people, including criminals. Cali's *El País* newspaper included the headline, "Mrs. Graciela Rodas suffered a severe head injury from Roberto Azarías with her own electric iron." Mrs. Rodas explained to the authorities that Azarías "came to the small establishment she runs in her house and ordered two beers. When she was distracted, Azarías tried to steal her electric iron from inside her house; when she intervened, the aforementioned attacked her."[67]

It could be argued that the publicity about and consumption of electric products conferred a modern sensuality to something so immaterial as electricity and indirectly to technologies such as hydroelectric plants. Of course, most never saw any actual hydroelectric plants in person; rather, they imagined them through their appearances in the mass media.[68] However, the impact was much greater. It also reached people who, without ever purchasing new devices or products, "consumed" hundreds of representations in ads published in their countries, in showcases, on the street, at fairs, and in public spaces. Day to day, all these representations reinforced a discourse that directly associated these devices with modernity in order to make them more attractive, which occurred between 1920 and 1950.

As the consumption of electric appliances spread, people in these societies demanded more energy. They criticized the blackouts while rationing progressively began to alter everyday life as electrical coverage and consumption expanded.[69] Complaining about the instability of electricity in Cali, a reader using the pseudonym of "España" wrote to *El País*. He mentioned that a blackout in the middle of the American Park Circus show had almost killed a person doing high-wire pirouettes. "España" drove home this point with an analogy between women and the availability of electricity in the city: "With this feminine whim of the electric grid, there can be no calculations, no budgets, no planning. Everything is useless." He continued: "What bothers me most about this blessed light is its perfidiousness. Imagine that it 'goes away.' Housewives run to buy candles. We light one candle in the dining room, another in the bedroom, another in the kitchen and yet more for Saint Zita's daughters' room. 40 pesos spent on 'incineration.' As if we were in a golden age to splurge in such a manner. And when the four or five candles are halfway through their quiet suffering and sacrifice, the blessed light reappears, smiling. How long will we continue like this?"[70]

These realities were common in South America during the early Cold War years. They generated a fertile environment for citizen support for the construction of new hydroelectric projects that, ideally, guaranteed that people could fully experience modern life not only in public spaces but also in the domestic sphere. And for all these, new hydroelectric plants were required, which increased support to build them.

The success of the "concrete revolution" that led to the construction of dozens of hydroelectric dams in South America sprang from the development of complex technologies and the expert knowledge of engineers and technicians, both from the United States and South America, who traveled around the world. It also grew from the existence of sociocultural scaffoldings that, expressed through diverse imaginaries, helped launch this revolution in the early Cold War. This leads us to think about the relevance of studying social and cultural aspects that mediate and influence the ways in which different societies receive, appropriate, or discard new technologies, and at the same time validate or condemn the expert knowledge that makes them possible. The success of expertise and the technology it yields is by no means guaranteed, regardless of the efficiency, utility, and value that experts ascribe to them. Their triumphs and failures differ depending on the social-cultural imaginaries with which they interact in each context.[71]

Although, at first glance, the development of hydroelectricity may seem rather circumscribed, I hope to have shown how it opens up perspectives on central aspects of the Cold War: the efforts to modernize and develop, and the geopolitical implications that sprang from the United States' relationships with South American national governments. The examination of hydroelectricity also allows us to observe the Cold War's impact from an environmental perspective—an angle that has remained largely unexplored in Latin America. The sociocultural dimension of the conflict appears through the different imaginaries created during the period through the circulation of ideas, knowledge, and representations of technologies and their uses. The global characteristics of the conflict likewise become visible through the circulation of experts and technical expertise, which were closely related to the technical assistance promoted by Harry Truman's 1949 Point Four Program. Finally, the hydroelectric plants and their impacts allow us to observe the movement and relevance of state actors as well as engineers, workers, entrepreneurs, publicists, and people who, from the perspective of domestic consumption, influenced the development of the Cold War. This chapter thus contributes to studies of the Cold War through an integration of varied historiographic vistas that are usually analyzed in isolation. As such, my study seeks to bring together innovations in recent Cold War historiography that have remained fragmentary. I combine a global approach to understanding the Cold War in Latin America, taking into account perspectives that deal with the generation and circulation of technical knowledge through regions, the environment, the consumption of modern artifacts, and nationalism.

NOTES

The research for this chapter was made possible by financing from Project Fondecyt Number 1170055 in Chile.

1. Christopher Sneddon, *Concrete Revolution: Large Dams, Cold War Geopolitics, and the US Bureau of Reclamation* (Chicago: University of Chicago Press, 2015). What constituted a "large dam" has changed over time, but the International Commission on Large Dams defines it as a dam that is higher than fifteen meters. International Commission on Large Dams (ICOLD), *Dams and the World's Water* (Paris: ICOLD, 2007), 28.

2. A more encompassing explanation of this global process would require a study of financial aspects; the current chapter contemplates political, institutional, diplomatic, and cultural aspects, focusing on technology and its actual and imagined uses.

3. Alan M. Taylor, "On the Costs of Inward-Looking Development: Price Distortions, Growth, and Divergence in Latin America," *Journal of Economic History* 58, no. 1 (1998): 1–28.

4. This chapter focuses on three South American countries that (1) shared the Andes as their water source, (2) experienced active intervention from the United States regarding the promotion of hydroelectricity, and (3) had economic precariousness, relative to other coun-

tries such as Argentina and Brazil. Other factors in the selection of these three countries included the diplomatic and cultural proximity with the United States during the period under review, as well as their respective governments' concern with developing these projects, which yielded support for technicians and engineers and the development of specialized bureaus. The list of big hydroelectric plants during this period is much more extensive. Plants in Chile include Abanico, Cipreses, Sauzal, Canutillar, Isla, El Toro, and Colbún-Machicura. Those in Colombia include Calima, Lebrija, Caldas, and Alto Anchicayá. In Peru, they include Mantaro, Huinco, Paucartambo, Callahuanca, and Moyopampa.

5. Colombia was a country that preoccupied US authorities early during the Cold War, especially after the Central Intelligence Agency discovered Soviet support for the leftist politician Jorge Eliécer Gaitán. He was a leading figure of the Liberal Party in Colombia during the 1940s and was shot in April 1948. This caused disturbances all over the country, intensifying violence between conservatives and liberals, which caused thousands of deaths between 1946 and 1958. See Stephen J. Randall, *Colombia and the United States: Hegemony and Interdependence* (Athens: University of Georgia Press, 1992), 193–194.

6. Ricardo Arias Trujillo, *Historia de Colombia contemporánea (1920–2010)* (Bogotá: Uniandes, 2011), 110–111.

7. Neydo Hidalgo Minaya, *55 años de Cañón del Pato: Una proeza en los Andes: Historia de la Central del Cañón del Pato* (Lima: Duke Energy Perú, 2013), 69.

8. Santiago Antúnez de Mayolo, *Relato de una idea a su realización ó la central hidroeléctrica del Cañón del Pato* (Lima: Editora Médica Peruana, 1957), 57.

9. Lawrence A. Clayton, *Peru and the United States: The Condor and the Eagle* (Athens: University of Georgia Press, 1999), 170.

10. Carlos Contreras and Marcos Cueto, *Historia del Perú Contemporáneo* (Lima: IEP-PUCP-Universidad del Pacífico, 2014 [1999]), 311.

11. Contreras and Cueto, *Historia del Perú*, 313.

12. Richard J. Walter, *Peru and the United States, 1960–1975: How Their Ambassadors Managed Foreign Relations in a Turbulent Era* (University Park: Pennsylvania State University Press, 2010), 1–5.

13. From 1961 to 1969 Chile received $743 million in US economic aid, equivalent to 11.8 percent of the program. See Jeffrey F. Taffet, *Foreign Aid as Foreign Policy: The Alliance for Progress in Latin America* (New York: Routledge, 2007), 67.

14. Paul Josephson, *Industrialized Nature: Brute Force Technology and the Transformation of the Natural World* (Washington, DC: Island Press, 2002). See also Paul Josephson, "War on Nature as Part of the Cold War: The Strategic and Ideological Roots of Environmental Degradation in the Soviet Union," in *Environmental Histories of the Cold War*, ed. J. R. McNeill and Corinna R. Unger (New York: Cambridge University Press-German Historical Institute, 2010), 21–49.

15. Richard P. Tucker, "Containing Communism by Impounding Rivers: American Strategic Interests and the Global Spread of High Dams in the Early Cold War," in McNeill and Unger, *Environmental Histories*, 39–163.

16. Organización Latinoamericana de Energía (OLADE), *Cobertura eléctrica en América Latina y el Caribe* (Quito, June 2012), 40, 43, 106.

17. David Lilienthal, *TVA: Democracy on the March* (Westport, CT: Greenwood Press, 1977 [1944]), 77–92.

18. Gabrielle Hecht and Paul N. Edwards, "The Technopolitics of Cold War: Toward a Transregional Perspective," in *Essays on Twentieth-Century History*, ed. Michael Adas (Philadelphia: Temple University Press), 286.

19. Tucker, "Containing Communism," 142. See also W. H. Becker and W. M. McClenahan Jr., *The Market, the State, and the Export-Import Bank of the United States, 1934–2000* (Cambridge: Cambridge University Press, 2003).

20. Tucker, "Containing Communism," 139.

21. David Ekbladh, "'Mr. TVA': Grass-Roots Development, David Lilienthal, and the Rise and Fall of the Tennessee Valley Authority as a Symbol for U.S. Overseas Development, 1933–1973," *Diplomatic History* 26, no. 3 (Summer 2002): 335–374.

22. Universality was a mental conception among engineers and technicians not only from the United States; rather, it transcended borders and became embedded in the culture of development in many international institutions. The United Nations, the World Bank, and the Export-Import Bank (Eximbank) all played important roles in financing these projects. They further reinforced the asymmetric logic between developed and underdeveloped countries by commissioning experts (and drawing on the expertise of engineers and technicians) from the United States and Europe to develop technical viability studies and give approval for credit. Moreover, the Cold War was a conflict characterized by the effort of the United States and the Soviet Union in order to prove the universal applicability of their ideologies. See Odd Arne Westad, *The Global Cold War* (Cambridge: Cambridge University Press, 2007), 4.

23. Lilienthal, *TVA*, 198.

24. Stephen Macekura, "The Point Four Program and US International Development Policy," *Political Science Quarterly* 128, no. 1 (2013): 127–160.

25. See, for example, Westad, *Global Cold War*; David Ekbladh, *The Great American Mission: Modernization and the Construction of an American World Order* (Princeton, NJ: Princeton University Press, 2010); Matthew Connelly, *Fatal Misconception: The Struggle to Control World Population* (Cambridge, MA: Belknap Press of Harvard University Press, 2008); and Arturo Escobar, *Encountering Development: The Making and Unmaking of the Third World* (Princeton, NJ: Princeton University Press, 1995). For Latin America, see Gilbert M. Joseph and Daniela Spenser, *In From the Cold: Latin America's New Encounter with the Cold War* (Durham, NC: Duke University Press, 2008); Benedetta Calandra and Marina Franco, eds., *La guerra fría cultural en América Latina: Desafíos y límites para una nueva mirada de las relaciones interamericanas* (Buenos Aires: Biblos, 2012); and Alfredo Riquelme and Tanya Harmer, *Chile y la Guerra Fría global* (Santiago: RiL Editores-Historia UC, 2014) I would include here my own work on the Peace Corps: Fernando Purcell, "Connecting Realities: Peace Corps Volunteers in South America and the Global War on Poverty during the 1960s," *Historia Crítica*, Bogotá, no. 53 (May–August 2014): 129–154.

26. *La Semana*, Bogotá, February 27, 1961.

27. On the visit by the Peruvian Luis Soldi, see National Archives, Denver (henceforth, DEN), "Letter of S. O. Harper to Commissioner," Denver, October 11, 1944, General Correspondence File 1930–1945, box 109, folder "Foreign Activities: Peru." On the visit by the Chil-

ean engineers Juliet and Matus, see DEN, "Letter of William E. Warne, Assistant Commissioner to Commissioner BOR," December 23, 1943, General Correspondence File 1930–1945, Box 104, Folder "Foreign Activities: Chile." In Colombia, Nicolás del Castillo's visit in the 1960s was especially important. See DEN, "Various Documents Colombia," Foreign Cooperation, box 80, folder "Colombia 66–68."

28. DEN, "Letter of William E. Warne, Assistant Commissioner to Commissioner BOR," December 23, 1943, General Correspondence File 1930–1945, box 104, folder "Foreign Activities: Chile."

29. DEN, "Various Documents Chile," Foreign Cooperation, box 80, folder "China 5–6-66–8-28–68." The folder says "China" by mistake. It should say "Chile."

30. Lilienthal, *TVA*, 197.

31. Neydo Hidalgo Minaya, *55 años*, 122.

32. DEN, "Letter of Commissioner BOR to Chief Coordinator," December 11, 1931. General Correspondence File 1930–1945, box 113, folder "Correspondence: Translation of Foreign Languages."

33. Emily S. Rosenberg, "Transnational Currents in a Shrinking World," in *A World Connecting 1870–1945*, ed. Emily S. Rosenberg (Cambridge, MA: Belknap Press of Harvard University Press, 2012), 919.

34. Tina Loo and Meg Stanley, "An Environmental History of Progress: Damming the Peace and Columbia Rivers," *Canadian Historical Review* 92, no. 3 (September 2011): 421.

35. Tim Cresswell and Peter Merriman, Introduction, *Geographies of Mobilities: Practices, Spaces, Subjects* (Burlington, VT: Ashgate, 2011), 1–15.

36. Josephson, *Industrialization of Nature*.

37. Kristine C. Harper and Donald E. Doel, "Environmental Diplomacy in the Cold War: Weather Control, the United States, and India, 1966–1967," in McNeill and Unger, *Environmental Histories*, 116–117.

38. J. R. McNeill and Corinna R. Unger, "Introduction: The Big Picture," in McNeill and Unger, *Environmental Histories*, 16.

39. Tucker, "Containing Communism," 139.

40. An article in the Peruvian magazine *Caretas* in 1960 stated that *Selecciones* of Reader's Digest had the country's largest readership with publication of 125,000 issues, followed by *Caretas*, and then *Life en español*. *Caretas*, Lima, May 25–June 8, 1960.

41. For such publicity, see: *Selecciones del Reader's Digest*, October 1952, 135; *Selecciones del Reader's Digest*, February 1953, 168; *Selecciones del Reader's Digest*, September 1959, 141.

42. *El Comercio*, Lima, October 21, 1950. For a complete analysis of this outburst flood, see Mark Carey, *In the Shadow of Melting Glaciers: Climate Change and Andean Society* (New York: Oxford University Press, 2010), 67–96.

43. *Diario Oficial*, Santiago, May 2, 1960.

44. *Selecciones del Reader's Digest*, July 1957, 105.

45. *Caretas*, Lima, May 1–15, 1958.

46. *La Semana*, Bogotá, week of May 23, 1955.

47. Antúnez de Mayolo, *Relato de una idea*, 5.

48. About the famous analogy between dams and temples attributed to Jawaharlal Nehru see Daniel Immerwahr, *Thinking Small: The United States and the Lure of Community Development* (Cambridge, MA: Harvard University Press, 2015), 66–68.

49. *Selecciones del Reader's Digest*, February 1956.

50. See, for example, *Life en español*, December 7, 1953; *Life en español*, October 25, 1954, 34–35.

51. *Life en español*, February 15, 1954.

52. The documentary *Electrificación Nacional* debuted in Peru in 1958. As Lima's *El Comercio* noted, the film "shows the main electricity projects that have been carried out by private companies such as Empresas Eléctricas Asociadas e Hidroandina as well as the huge hydroelectric plant of the Paucartambo de Cerro de Pasco Corporation and other companies of Provincias. The fifteen-minute film also shows the new Cañón del Pato plant and the important Machu Picchu project. *El Comercio*, Lima, April 24, 1958 (Morning ed.). For Chile, the projects by ENDESA were particularly salient; several were carried out by the documentary filmmaker Rafael Sánchez at the Pontificia Universidad Católica de Chile.

53. *Diario Gráfico*, Bogotá, July 8, 1955.

54. David Lilienthal, *Recommendation on the Establishment of Regional Development Authorities by the Republic of Colombia* (Cali: Imprenta Departamental, 1954), 17.

55. *El Relator*, Cali, July 21, 1955.

56. *El Comercio*, Lima, April 22, 1958 (Morning ed.).

57. *El Sur*, Concepción, May 2, 1955.

58. *Acontecer Rapelino*, October 1967.

59. On the circumstances and difficulties in the construction and destruction of the Cañón del Pato project, see Mark Carey, *In the Shadow*, 67–96.

60. Simone M. Müller and Heidi J. S. Tworek, "Imagined Use as a Category of Analysis: New Approaches to the History of Technology, *History and Technology* 32, no. 2 (2016): 106.

61. Hecht and Edwards, "Technopolitics of Cold War," 273. See also Wiebe Bijker, Thomas P. Hughes, and Trevor Pinch, eds., *The Social Construction of Technological Systems* (Cambridge, MA: MIT Press, 1987).

62. Akhil Gupta, "An Anthropology of Electricity From the Global South," *Cultural Anthropology* 30, no. 4: 556.

63. *El País*, Cali, July 24, 1955.

64. Laura A. Belmonte, "Selling Capitalism: Modernization and US Overseas Propaganda, 1945–1959," in *Staging Growth: Modernization, Development, and the Global Cold War*, ed. David C. Engerman, Nils Gilman, Mark H. Haefele, and Michael E. Latham (Amherst: University of Massachusetts Press, 2003), 114–115.

65. According to the registers of the Organización Latinoamericana de Energía (OLADE), in 1970 Colombia had 51.08 percent electric coverage. Chile had 53.7 percent and Peru just 31.98 percent. OLADE, *Cobertura eléctrica*, 40, 43, 106.

66. Pedro Alvarez, *Mecánica doméstica: Publicidad, modernización de la mujer y tecnologías para el hogar, 1945–1970* (Santiago: Ediciones UC, 2011).

67. *El País*, Cali, March 14, 1955.

68. On links between electricity and modernity, see David E. Nye, *Electrifying America: Social Meanings of a New Technology, 1880–1940* (Cambridge, MA: MIT Press, 1990); and Graeme Gooday, *Domesticating Electricity: Technology, Uncertainty and Gender, 1880–1914* (Pittsburgh: Pittsburgh University Press, 2016).

69. On the rationing of electricity in Santiago de Chile, see Ángela Briones, "El racionamiento eléctrico en la zona de concesión eléctrica de la Compañía Chilena de Electricidad Limitada (1946–1949)" (Thesis, Pontificia Universidad Católica de Chile, 1994).

70. *El País*, Cali, November 15, 1950.

71. A good example of the importance of these sociocultural aspects for the development of new technologies can be found in Chile. When electricity arrived in this country in 1883, the newspaper *El Ferrocarril* commented on the first two streetlamps installed in the city's plaza. In defense of the traditional use of gas, the editorialist identified electricity as an "evil" that was spreading "faster than good." Everything, he concluded was the idea of a "naive Yankee named Edison." *El Ferrocarril*, Santiago, February 16, 1883, 2.

10

PLANNING THE SANTIAGO METRO IN COLD WAR CHILE

Andra B. Chastain

On September 4, 1964, Eduardo Frei Montalva was elected president of Chile under the slogan "Revolution in Liberty." He promised an ambitious slate of structural reforms that would redistribute resources to the poorest in society and lift the country out of its chronic underdevelopment. Among his most prominent policies were agrarian reform, social housing, national control over the copper industry, and the strengthening of grassroots organizations. Although these signature programs have attracted much attention, both from observers at the time and historians since, the Frei government also spearheaded a far-reaching urban transportation plan for Santiago, the nation's capital and largest city. The centerpiece of this program was a five-line metro system that was to cover ninety kilometers, both above- and belowground, by 1990.[1]

Much was riding on the success or failure of Frei's Revolution in Liberty. His party, the Christian Democrats, had rapidly gained influence as a reformist, centrist party that promised a third way between capitalism and communism. For US policymakers, Frei appeared to be the "last, best hope" to prevent communist revolution from spreading in Latin America.[2] This mission was especially urgent by the early 1960s, after the Cuban Revolution had swept into Havana in 1959, and Salvador Allende, the candidate representing Chile's Marxist parties, had nearly won the presidency the year before. To combat revolutionary appeals, the United States had in 1961 launched the Alliance for Progress, a massive aid program for Latin America that sought to foster political reform and long-term economic development. Chile was a top target and received more aid per capita than any other country in the program.[3]

At first glance, it seems surprising that Frei would champion a project like the metro. His key policies on agrarian reform, copper, and housing all required major state spending, and Chile was already burdened by heavy foreign debt. On top of these challenges, he was determined to control the country's chronic inflation. Moreover, Frei depended on significant US aid and welcomed US–Chile partnerships through the Alliance for Progress. The metro, for its part, was expensive, ambitious, and reliant on French funding and expertise. This chapter asks how and why the project came to be, particularly in the context of rapid urban growth, sharpening political conflict in Chile, and a shifting Cold War funding landscape. It explores the place of national and international expertise, highlighting the pivotal role of a French-trained Chilean urbanist who rallied support for the metro in the face of dwindling state resources and bitter political conflict.

By the end of the 1960s, the metro had been transformed from a paper dream that prompted skepticism to a busy excavation site with dedicated resources and staff. In charting this story, I examine how the Cold War raised the stakes of expert knowledge and how technical and political criteria became entangled. Technical arguments that the metro was the "best" or "correct" solution to Santiago's traffic problem obscured the complex negotiations needed to make the project a reality. I contend that the metro was a hybrid system, a result of French prestige and funding as well as decades of Chilean research and promotion. Moreover, this was not a story of foreign experts parachuting in and ignoring local needs. In fact, the metro initially responded to urgent needs for better services to keep pace with rapid urban growth. Yet the form it took by the end of the decade did not entirely align with the original vision of its planners.

This study adds to our understanding of how technologies have been used to further political projects in the global Cold War. Some large-scale technological projects, such as nuclear programs or satellite systems, were clearly tied to geopolitics.[4] Green Revolution programs to increase food production, with their goal of undercutting potential revolutions in the Third World, also illustrate the use of technological innovation for political ends.[5] In some cases, technological systems were designed for explicitly revolutionary aims, as we see in the cybernetics program to control the national economy during Allende's Chile.[6] The Santiago metro, however, was not explicitly political in its origins. Instead, planners justified the project as a neutral and apolitical necessity for the expanding metropolis.[7] Yet, as we will see, technical disputes over the project's design spilled over into political battles.

Transportation in Crisis

The Santiago metro was not a new idea. In fact, a subway had been proposed many times since the 1920s in response to the city's worsening traffic congestion that had developed as the urban area expanded. Santiago had grown rapidly since the early twentieth century, driven by migration from mining areas during economic downturns and from the countryside as rural working conditions declined. In addition, industries and government services were concentrated in Santiago, bolstering the city's primacy. By 1960, over one in four Chileans lived in Santiago, which had reached a population of nearly two million.[8]

Meanwhile, rising numbers of motorized vehicles competed for space on an outdated colonial street grid. Santiago was severely centralized, with government offices, schools, and commerce squeezed into the city center. Most residents relied on public transit, which by the 1960s typically meant a long, crowded journey on a bus. Dozens of private bus operators had proliferated since the 1940s while the state-owned bus company struggled. Few residents owned a car, with most car use concentrated in the affluent eastern suburbs.[9] Nonetheless, experts predicted that the number of cars in the capital would skyrocket in the coming years.

Santiago's geography of residence and employment meant that transit demands were, for decades, highest along the north–south corridor. This was confirmed in early subway studies carried out from the 1920s through the 1950s.[10] Most working-class neighborhoods and industries were located in southern, northern, and western Santiago. The city's middle and upper classes, by contrast, settled in eastern Santiago, known as the *barrio alto*. Studies showed that the city's popular sectors endured long waits for public transit and spent as much as three hours or more commuting each day.[11] All this added up to valuable lost time for workers and lost productivity for the national economy. These losses were compounded by the public health danger posed by Chile's high accident rates.[12] Transportation problems thus caused not only economic losses due to time spent in traffic but also losses due to death, injury, and disability.

Transportation problems also acquired greater urgency due to the rising political tensions and security fears sparked by the Cold War. In 1965, the US planner Melvin Webber stressed that "popular discontent" with Santiago's transit service was "real" and that the "deep dissatisfaction" was "potentially explosive."[13] In fact, fare hikes had sparked major urban uprisings in the past. In 1949 an increase in student fares had set off a popular revolt that paralyzed Santiago until army troops restored order.[14] Another uprising oc-

FIGURE 10.1. Juan Parrochia Beguin pointing at a model of urban transportation in Santiago, circa 1967–1969. Note the cutout showing where the subway would run. He is flanked by officials from the Ministry of Public Works and Transportation. Courtesy of Juan Antonio Parrochia.

curred in 1957, when fare increases set off protests, riots, and police violence that killed at least twenty people and injured many more.[15] Webber was right, then, that discontent with transit service had the potential to spark protests and undermine national security. In the face of these multiple challenges, many transportation experts concluded that a crisis was looming unless serious measures were taken.

The Haussmann of Santiago

The widely acknowledged expert behind the metro was Juan Parrochia Beguin, a Chilean urbanist with grand visions for remaking Santiago. Over the course of his career, which began in the late 1950s and blossomed in the 1960s, Parrochia became known for his expertise in all matters concerning urban transportation and his determination to enact his plans. His outsized role in the remaking of Santiago earned him comparisons to Baron Haussmann, the powerful prefect of the Seine who had remade Paris under Napoleon III.[16]

Born in 1930 in southern Chile, Parrochia came from a prosperous land-holding family with European roots. He learned French as a boy from his father, who used a map of the Paris Métropolitain to teach his son to read. Parrochia attended high school at the Alianza Francesa, and in 1947 he began studying architecture at the University of Chile, graduating in 1953.[17] He spoke French fluently throughout his life, a skill that would serve him well in his later negotiations for metro funding.

Parrochia was shaped by his extensive time abroad between 1953 and 1957. On graduation, he sailed to France, where he made contacts in the French Ministry of Reconstruction. Over the next five years, he traveled the world—much of it by motorcycle—to soak up as much knowledge about architecture and urbanism as possible. Parrochia was awestruck by Vienna and admired the Catholicism of France, but he also traveled with communist companions and ventured into Eastern Europe and the Soviet Union. He traveled down the Nile River and explored the Middle East; in Syria, he was arrested and beaten by the police, who accused him of espionage. He toured the modernist city of Chandigarh, India, and he was impressed by China's large, modern factories. His final tours took him to Australia and Japan, followed by Canada, the United States, Mexico, and Central America. Interspersed among these journeys, he found time to work in the French Ministry of Reconstruction and earn a graduate diploma in urbanism in Brussels.[18]

On his return to Chile in 1957, Parrochia set out to remake Santiago. By the mid-1960s, his career revolved around urban transportation planning, which he conceived of as an unbreakable trilogy: metro, roadways, and street transit. The guiding idea was to coordinate these three elements, so that roads and bus lines complemented the metro, the backbone of the system. For Parrochia, the architect's role was to harmonize these into one whole. "It's a trilogy. It's very presumptuous to say it, but it's like—God has three parts. What he did was integrate these different problems into one," his wife explained. Like the Father, the Son, and the Holy Spirit, transportation was, for Parrochia, simultaneously three and one. This trilogy—or trinity—would take graphic form in the metro's logo of three red diamonds.[19]

As a Christian Democrat, spirituality infused Parrochia's life and vision. His work was his calling, and he felt an "immense responsibility" to serve multiple "totalities": "our civilization, our era, our epoch, our *patria*, our city." As his wife emphasized, a "social sensibility" guided his work, which he shared with Frei. Indeed, Parrochia greatly admired Frei and believed that transportation planning could "improve accessibility and thus tend to smooth out our radical economic and social segregation."[20] One might even see a parallel between Parrochia's vision of integrated transportation and the Christian Democratic vision of an integrated, communitarian society. In Parrochia's ideal city, buses, cars, and metro would harmonize with one another, rather than compete, not unlike the Catholic communitarianism that sought to replace ruthless capitalism and avert class conflict.

Parrochia prized expertise and made this known to all who encountered him. He often grew irritated with nonspecialists and expressed scant interest in democratic planning processes. His world travels had steeped him in the rarified world of urban planning and architecture and made him impatient with the opinions of nonexperts. Journalists described him as rude and haughty; he would curse at them or dismissively close his eyes when speaking.[21] He advanced his long-term vision through an "exhaustive knowledge of bureaucracy" and willingness to make creative use of legal tools.[22] Parrochia had once confided to his colleague that "the fun is doing things without money"; he would later convince ministers to fund his projects. He was a "bulldozer," a man of action who was reportedly capable of "wiping an entire city off the map if the construction of the metro required it."[23] He disdained politics and avoided the limelight, yet he was a Christian Democrat with a direct telephone line to Frei's ministers. His clarity of vision inspired his students and staff, but his conviction also made him enemies.[24]

Parrochia was, in sum, a man of multiple influences, both national and international. He was deeply shaped by his training at the University of Chile as well as his graduate studies in Belgium, work in the French Ministry of Reconstruction, and world travels on both sides of the iron curtain. He had a personal affinity for France, but his vision was global. He was also deeply rooted in Santiago, where he made his home with his wife and their five children. By 1965, when Frei tasked him to begin studies for a metro, Parrochia was poised to turn his early education and experiences into a far-reaching plan for remaking the city.

Early Optimism and Challenges, 1965–1966

Parrochia was assisted by a crucial ally in the presidential palace: shortly after taking office, Frei declared his strong support for a metropolitan railway. In 1965 he oversaw the creation of a transit commission, headed by Parrochia, and ordered it to work at an "extraordinarily rapid" pace. This commission would spearhead the complex metro negotiations in the coming years.[25] The plans for a metro were also bolstered by the optimism and economic growth that characterized the early years of the Frei administration, before the political and economic troubles that would erupt after 1967.

Despite these promising signs, Parrochia's plans for Santiago ran into an immediate roadblock: scarce funding. Frei's other priorities, such as agrarian reform, housing, and grassroots programs, also required significant funding and political capital, while the fight against inflation necessitated tight control on state spending. "Government spending is at its limit, and if we go over by a millimeter," inflation will become "unstoppable" and "we will have failed," Frei told his cabinet in 1965.[26] Concerns about cost spurred the transit commission to consider an elevated monorail, which would avoid expensive excavations, but this option was discarded over worries about the constraints it would put on future urban development.[27] In addition to scarce funding, there were political troubles: the Christian Democrats' bid to govern alone, rather than form a coalition with parties on the Right or Left, sparked hostility in Congress and slowed the passage of key reforms. But these political and economic challenges were mitigated by several factors that would set the metro apart from the Christian Democrats' other programs. First, unlike agrarian reform or copper legislation, the project did not need congressional approval. Second, Parrochia was at the helm, committed to bringing the project to fruition regardless of the controversy it might generate. And third, the government could turn to foreign aid and investment as an alternative to limited state resources.

On this last point, the metro was not alone. From the beginning, the Frei government had high hopes that foreign aid and investment, combined with domestic savings, would spur growth and provide resources for reforms. The Cold War funding landscape at first seemed auspicious: the United States wanted to ensure that Chile did not go the way of Cuba, and it offered aid to Frei during his campaign and in the early years of his administration. Frei also sought to strengthen Chile's relationship with Western Europe: in July 1965, hoping to negotiate a European version of the Alliance for Progress, he toured Italy, France, West Germany, and England.[28] He was generally disappointed by aid offers on this trip, however, and by the following year, the potential for US aid was also worsening. This was due, in part, to Washington's waning interest in the Alliance for Progress, with Vietnam a bigger concern now than Chile's political future. Under the Christian Democrats, Chile also struck a more independent diplomatic stance, reopening ties with the Soviet Union and repudiating the US invasion of the Dominican Republic.[29] This independence irritated US policymakers, but it resonated with the broader nonaligned movement in Latin America, Asia, and Africa. It also resonated in France, where de Gaulle was seeking to project independence from the

United States and portray France as the champion of the Third World.[30] This diplomatic affinity would soon prove useful in negotiating support for the Santiago metro.

Even with the possibility of foreign aid and investment, a massive infrastructure project like the metro still required the state to take a guiding role. From early metro proposals in the 1940s and 1950s to Parrochia's plans in the 1960s, the assumption was that the state would oversee the construction and operation of the system; this made sense given that the Christian Democrats, like most experts in Chile and throughout Latin America, viewed state planning as central to economic growth and reform.[31] The question of state involvement in the project, however, opened a fraught political debate that revealed intense domestic opposition to Frei's reforms. According to right-wing critics of the project, the failure of past metro proposals lay with "outmoded nationalists and myopic statists" who insisted that the project be carried out with "Chilean engineers, Chilean plans, and Chilean money." Conservative commentators repeatedly insisted that an underground railway should be built via concession to a private operator—despite the fact that the prospect of private profit was dubious.[32] The insistence by Frei's right-wing opponents that state involvement would spell failure for the metro would grow more strident as political polarization intensified later in the decade.

Transnational Planning and the Discourse of Crisis, 1966–1968

In 1966, still riding a strong economy and popular support, the Frei government announced an international competition for a comprehensive transportation study, the crucial precursor to a metro. Ten companies made offers, with Canada, Sweden, France, Japan, Chile, and the United States represented.[33] The winning contract went to a Chilean–French consortium composed of CADE (Consultores en la Administración de Empresas), a Chilean administrative engineering company; BCEOM (Bureau central d'études pour les équipements d'outre-mer), a French infrastructure agency working in France's overseas territories; and SOFRETU (Société française d'études et de réalisations de transports urbains), the export arm of the Paris transit authority that had just done similar studies in Montreal and Mexico City and was collaborating on the construction of metro systems in those cities. Dozens of French specialists soon began to arrive, including engineers, demographers, and economists. Working closely with Chilean experts and drawing on studies already completed by the Chilean government, they would gather data on land use, employment patterns, family income, traffic patterns, and many other factors. The data would then be brought to France, where it would be processed by computers to derive an "automatic model" of future transportation demand in Santiago.[34]

For Parrochia and most observers across the political spectrum, the metro was justified by the discourse of an impending disaster. "We must prepare ourselves to confront an urban transportation crisis," Parrochia told local mayors and city councillors.[35] This was an idea that he repeated to the press and reiterated in his writings. In 1968, Parrochia warned that Chile would soon face the same "transportation crisis" that Europe confronted in the postwar reconstruction years, caused by an influx of cars into dense, rapidly growing cities. This was the same crisis that the United States faced in the 1930s and 1940s, he said, and the same crisis that Mexico, Argentina, Brazil, and Venezuela were beginning to suffer. Chile was only "a bit behind" them, and he urged the country to deal with the issue while there was still time. The prospect of waiting, he said, would be grim. Without decisive action to remake the city, it would suffer worsening congestion and, ultimately, total paralysis.[36]

Implicit in this discourse of crisis was a linear narrative of global development. The assumption was that all countries would experience the same crisis, and that "backward" nations should be alert to the arrival of the automobile age and act now, before the cost of remaking the urban fabric rose. Rather than arguing that developing societies should learn from the mistakes of industrialized nations by steering clear of car culture altogether, Parrochia embraced cars and public transit as necessarily dependent on one another. In fact, Parrochia was a strong supporter of urban highways and believed Chile could not modernize without an extensive network of ring roads and expressways.

After two years of research, the Chilean–French consortium released its report. The hefty four-volume study outlined two alternatives: either the city could continue building roads to serve its transit needs or it could build an "independent transportation network"—that is, a metro—accompanied by a complementary road system. This report found that a metro would have higher up-front costs but would ultimately save money over the long run.[37] In late 1968, Frei's transit commission formally endorsed the metro plan, which would entail the construction of five lines over the next two decades. This announcement marked a critical milestone in the project.[38]

In the time it had taken to carry out this study, however, the political landscape in Chile had shifted. The government's popular support had dropped, and Frei's opponents were reaping the benefits. On the Right, Chile's traditional conservative parties had dissolved and founded the National Party. On the Left, new and more radical forces had emerged: the Socialist Party declared its Marxist-Leninist objectives, and the recently formed Revolutionary Left Movement called for armed guerrilla struggle. Moreover, the leftist wing of the Christian Democrats had gained control of the party, causing further complications for Frei. Social mobilizations were now widespread, including among the urban poor, who organized to seize land, set up self-built communities or *campamentos*, and push for revolutionary change.[39]

With political divides deepened by Cold War hopes and fears, the moment did not seem propitious for a metro. Indeed, the public reaction to the metro report, especially from the Right, was intense skepticism. After decades of empty government promises that a subway would be built, why would this time be any different? The right-wing press attacked the idea of a state-run metro and claimed that the government, for lack of funds, would never be able to finish the project. The "national custom of initiating numerous projects simultaneously without concentrating efforts and funds on completing any of them," would spell disaster for the metro, they complained.[40] Above all, observers noted that the biggest hurdle was financing.[41] Without funding, this report would gather dust just as previous proposals had.

Construction and the Negotiation of French Aid, 1969

For all its mounting troubles, the Frei government oversaw significant progress on the metro in its final two years in office. In fact, the speed of the project seemed to increase in relation to the intensity of the opposition that the government faced. As Frei's support crumbled and critics assailed the government from all sides, the metro occupied an increasingly important place in national political debates.

In June 1969, in the wake of further electoral losses and the split of the Christian Democratic Party, the government announced that construction would begin on the first line of the metro. Whereas prior studies had shown the importance of the north–south corridor, the minister of public works and transportation, Sergio Ossa, announced that the first line would run east–west, into the *barrio alto*. The official reason was that demand was marginally higher along this corridor. But Ossa was defensive about this choice, saying that it was not "capricious" and responded to a "real need." Why was the east–west route (Line 1) chosen, if all earlier signs had pointed to the north–south corridor (Line 2) being most urgent? A generous reading was that Line 1 was cheaper to build, since it ran beneath a wide public thoroughfare, the Alameda, and thus did not require expropriations. A less generous reading was that prioritizing Line 1 was simply another instance of government resources flowing to the middle class and neglecting the poor. This was precisely the critique leveled by some on the Left: "Let the *rotos* go screw themselves for eternity, piled up in buses, risking their lives every day and spending two hours going a distance that takes a rich person only fifteen minutes."[42]

Shortly after Ossa's announcement, and with funding not yet secured, workers broke ground on the western stretch of Line 1. Eager to cement the project's future, Parrochia, Ossa, and Eduardo Arriagada, an influential engineer from CADE, took matters into their own hands and began discussing a foreign loan directly with the National Bank of Paris. This broke with protocol, as it left Chilean diplomats in the dark.[43] Yet the move was typical of Parrochia's style: he forged ahead, determined to carry out the project even if by unorthodox means. The French, meanwhile, were determined to win the metro contract. The French ambassador, René de Saint-Légier, believed they could beat the competition, which included a Japanese team and an American–Canadian team. French experts had several factors on their side: Chilean officials had seen the success of the Mexico City metro in person, French firms had now been conducting studies in Santiago for over two years, and, not least, the French were offering extensive technical assistance.[44]

Gabriel Valdés, Frei's foreign minister, picked up where Parrochia had left off and began discussing financing directly with the French government. At a meeting in November 1969, he made a strong case to Saint-Légier for Chile's commitment to the metro and to working with the French. Chile's decision had been made "at the highest level" and was "irrevocable," Valdés declared. Indeed, the Chileans wanted the project to be discussed at the highest governmental levels, not merely between private businesses or public agencies. Saint-Légier came away from this meeting impressed by the Chileans' "keen desire" to work with the French.[45] As evidence of this desire, Valdés put the metro on the agenda for the upcoming meeting of the Franco-Chilean Mixed Commission to be held in Santiago in late November.[46]

The Mixed Commission provided an important forum for Chile and France to cement their political solidarity and economic ties. President Georges Pompidou expressed his government's friendship toward Chile, and Chilean and French representatives affirmed their shared principles, including the right to self-determination, the principle of nonintervention, and the rejection of bloc politics.[47] Highlighting Chile's commitment to democracy, French Secretary of State Jean de Lipkowski declared that "Chile appears as a moral reserve in a world convulsed."[48]

Chilean and French delegates also sought to strengthen their economic ties. For Chile, French investment and foreign aid seemed to offer an antidote to dependent development via import-substitution industrialization. Specifically, Chile sought to bolster its national industrial capacity by importing French capital goods. Chilean delegates were particularly interested in foreign investment that provided for greater national participation in industry and manufacturing. French delegates, for their part, wanted to increase their exports to Chile.[49] They were also interested in filling the gap in US aid to Latin America, which was on the decline since Nixon had taken office.[50] France was also eager to counterbalance US cultural hegemony in Chile by, for example, ensuring French language teaching in schools.[51]

Not least, the Chilean team stressed its interest in securing funding for the metro. Their efforts to win financing were successful: during the Mixed Commission, French officials promised to ensure up to 275 million francs, or approximately $50 million, to cover French goods and services for the first line.[52] This was a major sum, almost triple the amount Frei had unsuccessfully solicited from France at the start of his presidency.[53] The Franco-Chilean Mixed Commission thus appeared to be an important success for both sides: France came closer to clinching its role in the project, and the Chilean government could celebrate a political and economic victory at an increasingly contentious time.[54] In October, Frei had put down a brief but ominous military insurrection, and by the end of the year the country was fully swept up in the three-way presidential campaign for the following year. The Christian Democrats' candidate, Radomiro Tomic, would face off against Jorge Alessandri, the former president and candidate on the Right, and Salvador Allende, the veteran leader of the Marxist Left. As the campaign heated up, metro debates would become ensnared in Chile's increasingly intense political battles.

Technopolitical Controversies Erupt

For years, conservative skeptics had argued that a metro was a good idea in principle that would nonetheless never happen because of scarce funding and the state's inability to follow through on such a large undertaking. However, once the government seemed capable of carrying it out, opposition from the Right emerged stronger than ever. In late 1969 and early 1970, during the run-up to the September 1970 presidential elections, the National Party spearheaded an all-out effort to stop the metro. In heated congressional sessions, one senator attacked the project, alleged that the French must have bribed the Christian Democrats, and demanded a formal inquiry into the project, which was soundly defeated.[55] In an open letter to the press, another National Party senator complained that it was unfair for Frei to commit to such expensive contracts at the end of his term. The metro was "one of the largest public works contracts ever envisaged in Chile," he wrote, with a total sum "higher than the investments made in the copper mines."[56]

The Christian Democrats described these attacks as thinly veiled attempts by the right-wing opposition to discredit the government. In an open letter, the public works minister Eugenio Celedón defended the government's metro plans. First, he noted that the project had long been publicized and debated, as the government had held many meetings with engineers, architects, planners, and builders, and the official Chilean–French report had been made public. Second, he noted that the studies were exceedingly thorough and emphasized that the transportation plan comprised both a metro and a complementary highway system. Third, Celedón pointed out that the metro would be less expensive over the long term than a transit system based solely on buses and cars. In sum, the total "social costs" of the project were "extremely low" compared to the social benefits that would be reaped by citizens.[57]

The National Party doubled down in its opposition. It openly warned Chilean business owners against investing in the metro, claiming that the studies were "absolutely incomplete" and that the project would never be finished because of the huge sums needed in the future.[58] The timing, which coincided with metro loan negotiations in Paris, was likely designed to damage Chilean efforts to secure funding.[59] The implication was clear: if the Right won the presidential elections in 1970, it would halt the project. The opposition's complaints were disingenuous, since dozens of metro studies had been carried out over the years, and conservatives had, until this point, complained about the *excess* of studies and the lack of decisive action from politicians. The truth was that they recoiled at the idea of a state-built metro, particularly if their political opponents could take credit for it.

Alongside this political opposition to the project, a technical conflict brewed among experts. Chilean engineers were broadly supportive of the metro, agreeing that the long-term savings would more than justify the initial investment. However, they were alarmed by the government's plans to use pneumatic wheels in place of traditional steel rolling stock. Rubber tires were touted as being quieter and smoother, but engineers warned that they would increase maintenance costs, require imported materials, and be incompatible with Chile's existing railroads due to their narrower gauge.[60] In April, French and Chilean metro experts faced off with a crowd of engineers and architects in a meeting lasting over five hours. Rubber-tire supporters—including Parrochia, the French–Chilean consortium, and most government officials—pointed to the success of the new rubber-tired metros in Montreal and Mexico City and noted that the greater friction generated by tires meant faster starting and stopping times and the ability to negotiate greater inclines and tighter turns. Supporters of traditional metal traction—including the Chilean Institute of Engineers—countered that other modern metros used metal, including in Toronto, Hamburg, and Berlin, and argued that steel rolling stock would be cheaper to acquire and maintain, since the technology was more widespread.[61]

This technical debate about rolling stock soon spilled over into the political arena and provided additional ammunition for the metro's opponents. Technical differences of opinion became a pretext for conservatives to air their political differences and call for the entire project to be halted until after the September elections. The editors of El Mercurio, for example, admitted that a metro was the best solution, but seized on the rolling stock dispute to argue that any construction should be postponed until "definitive studies" were carried out. Thus, they concluded, "It seems prudent to leave the final decision pending until the next government assumes office."[62] Observe the slide from technical to political criteria: if the issue were in fact technical, why delay the decision based on a political timetable?

The root of the issue for conservatives was the fact that the metro was tied to the state. It would involve public investment, public operation, and eventually the birth of a new public enterprise. This was unconscionable to most on the Right, who declared that only the private sector should be tasked with such a project. One former state transportation engineer, for example, alleged that the metro would lead to a state monopoly on transportation. He claimed that the costs would be higher than anticipated, require state subsidies, and drain the national economy; he pointed to the struggling state bus company as evidence that state enterprises could not be trusted. His arguments then turned ideological: the metro, he said, portended a "socialized state" and would "fundamentally threaten the survival of the regime of liberty."[63]

The conservative editors at *El Diario Ilustrado* echoed this idea, alleging that the technical polemic had been fabricated in order to distract from what was, in their view, the real issue: the role of the state versus private investors. The editors claimed that the government ought to seek out concessionaires, rather than paying for it with the national budget. They accused metro supporters of having misguided "nationalist" ideas and insinuated that a bloated bureaucracy was already forming at the metro. In fact, the government was carrying out a public works program, just as it also built roads and ports, and the private sector would be heavily involved through the provision of construction contracts. The press suggested that the ties between the French experts and the Christian Democrats were suspect, and that even the choice of calling it a "metropolitano" rather than an "underground railway" showed that the planners were "thinking in French."[64] Thus, for conservatives, the metro seemed both alarmingly nationalist *and* suspiciously foreign. With fears that Allende might come to power in September, the metro came to stand in both for the specter of socialism and the threat of the foreign.

Meanwhile, the Left was cautiously divided regarding the metro. *El Siglo*, the newspaper of the Communist Party, was generally supportive and emphasized that the project would ultimately free workers' time.[65] But *Puro Chile*, a leftist tabloid, hit the nail on the head in its critique of the metro: it noted that working-class residents tended to travel North–South in Santiago, and the wealthy tended to move East–West. Because Line 1 would be built first and was at that point the only line with financing, the editors were skeptical that the project would ever benefit Santiago's poorest residents.[66]

Amid heated opposition from the Right and caution from the Left, the Frei government pushed forward. Overriding the debate among engineers, the transit commission unanimously approved the choice of rubber rolling stock.[67] Construction bidding began on Line 1, and, with the elections fast approaching, the government opened a bid for the purchase of metro trains.[68] Eleven companies expressed interest, including five French firms and two companies each from Chile, Japan, and Canada.[69] Government officials strove to present an image of a fair, open international bidding process on this sensitive issue. They noted that rubber rolling stock was manufactured in Canada, not just in France. In addition, the bidding process had the option of excluding the pneumatic bogies, allowing more firms to compete.[70]

However, this image of fair and open competition did not square with contracts signed behind the scenes. In February 1970, the government had signed a loan with France for 285 million francs, or about $50 million, the majority of which would go to fund the purchase of the metro cars. Crucially, over 85 percent of the loan had to be spent on French goods and services. Moreover, if it accepted this loan, Chile could spend only a limited amount on goods from third-party countries.[71] In essence, this contract protected French manufacturers. The government did not announce this loan agreement in the press, and did not acknowledge that the decision to opt for rubber traction was in fact "eminently favorable" to French companies.[72]

In September, Allende won a tight three-way race to become the first democratically elected Marxist leader in the hemisphere. Though Parrochia was removed from his role as metro director, his replacement, the socialist Eduardo Paredes, maintained Parrochia's original vision. The five-line design and choice of rubber rolling stock remained, and construction on Line 1 continued. Allende also spearheaded construction on Line 2, conscious that it would have a greater impact on the city's popular sectors. Yet neither line would open until after the 1973 military coup that ushered in the brutal dictatorship of General Augusto Pinochet.

The history behind the metro's planning and financing demonstrates that foreign aid from France was significant. Although others have concluded that European aid was a disappointment for the Frei government, this study finds that, in fact, the sum secured for the metro was substantial; without it, the project would have remained little more than a good intention. This loan is all the more surprising in that it came precisely at the moment when the Christian Democrats were facing a political crisis: by 1969, their party had splintered, electoral support had eroded, and both the Right and Left were gaining ground.

The extent to which foreign aid for the metro contributed to national development was murky, however. The level of national industrial participation was not as high as Chilean leaders wanted, and the loan terms benefited French commercial interests. This was particularly concerning to the Allende administration, which sought to renegotiate the French loan in favor of Chilean industry. Yet the metro served as a monumental material embodiment of Chile's dreams of modernization and development in the late 1960s. The project was not a French imposition on Chile, but a local initiative that had been decades in the making. The metro was a hybrid system, both Chilean and French. It arose out of decades of Chilean studies and debates about the need for a subway. Conservatives claimed that Frei was "thinking in French" and indeed, foreign aid was crucial. Yet this was a Chilean project with deep roots in the national community of engineers, architects, and planners. With his training that was both local and international, and his commitment to remaking Santiago along the lines of the global cities that had inspired him, Parrochia himself embodied the hybrid nature of the project.

This study further illustrates how the Latin American Cold War raised the stakes of expert knowledge. The growing polarization within Chile, incited by Cold War dynamics that were simultaneously domestic and global, engendered resistance to the project from both sides of the political spectrum. Despite acknowledging the metro's technical merits, the Right attacked the project for its ties to the state and alleged power to hasten the arrival of socialism. Conservative commentators also seized on the technical rolling stock dispute in an effort to halt the project until after the 1970 elections. The Left, meanwhile, criticized the project for not going far enough to serve the popular classes. This position echoed its broader critiques of the Frei government, which it criticized for not moving fast enough on its program of structural change. Although planners spoke of the metro as a purely technical solution—as the best or correct answer to a technical problem—the debates underlying the project indicate otherwise. In fact, historical contingencies and political calculations were central to the metro's survival. In this Cold War climate, the consequences of technical choices reached far beyond the domain of engineers and experts and spilled over into the increasingly intense social and political conflicts of the day.

NOTES

1. On agrarian reform, copper, and housing, see Heidi Tinsman, *Partners in Conflict: The Politics of Gender, Sexuality, and Labor in the Chilean Agrarian Reform, 1950–1973* (Durham, NC: Duke University Press, 2002); Florencia E. Mallon, *Courage Tastes of Blood: The Mapuche Community of Nicolás Ailío and the Chilean State, 1906–2001* (Durham, NC: Duke University Press, 2005); Thomas Miller Klubock, *La Frontera: Forests and Ecological Conflict in Chile's Frontier Territory* (Durham, NC: Duke University Press, 2014); Angela Vergara, *Copper Workers, International Business, and Domestic Politics in Cold War Chile* (University Park:

Pennsylvania State University Press, 2008); Mario Garcés, *Tomando su sitio: El movimiento de pobladores de Santiago, 1957–1970* (Santiago: LOM, 2002); and Edward Murphy, *For a Proper Home: Housing Rights in the Margins of Urban Chile, 1960–2010* (Pittsburgh: University of Pittsburgh Press, 2015).

2. Leonard Gross, *The Last, Best Hope: Eduardo Frei and Chilean Democracy* (New York: Random House, 1967).

3. On the Christian Democrats, see Michael Fleet, *The Rise and Fall of Chilean Christian Democracy* (Princeton, NJ: Princeton University Press, 1985); and Cristián Gazmuri, *Eduardo Frei Montalva y su época*, 2 vols. (Santiago: Aguilar, 2000). On US-Chilean relations, see William F. Sater, *Chile and the United States: Empires in Conflict* (Athens: University of Georgia Press, 1991); Jeffrey F. Taffet, *Foreign Aid as Foreign Policy: The Alliance for Progress in Latin America* (New York: Routledge, 2007); and Tanya Harmer and Alfredo Riquelme, eds., *Chile y la guerra fría global* (Santiago: RIL, 2014).

4. See, for example, Gabrielle Hecht, *The Radiance of France: Nuclear Power and National Identity after World War II* (Cambridge, MA: MIT Press, 1998) and *Being Nuclear: Africans and the Global Uranium Trade* (Cambridge, MA: MIT Press, 2012); and Pedro Ignacio Alonso and Hugo Palmarola, chapter 7 in this volume.

5. Nick Cullather, *The Hungry World: America's Cold War Battle against Poverty in Asia* (Cambridge, MA: Harvard University Press, 2013); and Timothy W. Lorek (chapter 3) and Reinaldo Funes-Monzote and Steven Palmer (chapter 5), in this volume.

6. Eden Medina, *Cybernetic Revolutionaries: Technology and Politics in Allende's Chile* (Cambridge, MA: MIT Press, 2011).

7. Aníbal Mardones interview, March 12, 2015; María Mercedes Bravo interview, October 25, 2015; Lautaro Cárcamo interview, January 28, 2015. All interviews were conducted by the author in Santiago, Chile, unless otherwise noted.

8. "Población del país: Características básicas de la población (censo 1960)," Dirección de Estadística y Censos, Santiago, 1964, 1–3.

9. Ministerio de Obras Públicas y Transportes and Programa Chile-California, "Encuesta de origen y destino del movimiento de personas en el Gran Santiago," Santiago, November 1966, 3, 46–48.

10. Luis Lagarrigue Alessandri, "Metropolitano de Santiago," Santiago, 1924; Karl H. Brunner, "Seminario de Urbanismo," *Comuna y hogar: Boletín de las municipalidades de Chile* 18 (December 1930); Gabriel Quirós, "Estudio acerca del servicio de movilización colectiva de Santiago," *Anales del Instituto de Ingenieros de Chile* (April–May, June 1944); Leopoldo Guillén B., "El Metropolitano de Santiago y la movilización colectiva," Dirección General de Obras Públicas, Departamento de Ferrocarriles, Santiago, October 1952.

11. "Encuesta de origen y destino," 43–46; "Santiago conquista su metropolitano," *Revista AUCA* 2 (1966).

12. "Reunión constitutiva de la Comisión Coordinadora Nacional de Planificación en Transporte y Tránsito," ODEPLAN, Santiago, September 2, 1971.

13. Melvin M. Webber, "Mejoramiento del servicio de transportes en el área metropolitana de Santiago," Programa de Cooperación Técnica Chile-California (September 1, 1965), 24.

14. Marcelo Mardones, Simón Castillo, and Waldo Vila, *Micrópolis: Historia visual del transporte público de superficie en Santiago, 1857–2007* (Santiago: Consejo Nacional de la Cultura y las Artes, 2011), 55.

15. Pedro Milos, *Historia y memoria: 2 de abril de 1957* (Santiago: LOM, 2007), 77–99, 358, 365.

16. Lautaro Cárcamo interview, January 28, 2015.

17. Peter Himmel interview, March 3, 2015; María Isabel Pavez Reyes, ed., *En la ruta de Juan Parrochia Beguin* (Santiago: Universidad de Chile, 2003), 304.

18. Pavez Reyes, *En la ruta*, 186–230.

19. María Mercedes Bravo interview, October 25, 2015; Peter Himmel interview, March 3, 2015; Juan Parrochia Beguin, *Santiago en el tercer cuarto del s. XX: El transporte metropolitano en Chile, realización de Metro y Vialidad Urbana* (Santiago: Universidad de Chile, 1979), 41–65.

20. Parrochia Beguin, *Santiago*, 21, 23; María Mercedes Bravo interview, November 29, and December 22, 2015.

21. See, for example, Hernán González Valdebenito, "Juan Parrochia," *La Segunda*, March 26, 1970.

22. Mauricio Muñoz, "Vocación y creatividad en el servicio público," in Pavez Reyes, *En la ruta*, 44.

23. Peter Himmel interview, March 3, 2015; Rosario Guzmán, "Juan Parrochia," *Qué Pasa*, September 11, 1975.

24. Vicente Acuña interview, December 22, 2015.

25. "S.E. ordenó acelerar estudios para la construcción del metropolitano," *El Mercurio*, February 18, 1965; "Estudios para construcción de ferrocarril metropolitano," *Revista de la Construcción*, no. 34 (March 1965): 41.

26. Acta resumida de la sesión de gabinete del 9 de marzo 1965, Carpeta 95, Casa Museo Eduardo Frei Montalva, 3–4.

27. Telegram from Saint-Légier to Diplomatie Paris, October 21, 1969, file DE.3.8, box 164, L'Ambassade de France à Santiago du Chili (hereafter AFSC), Centre des Archives Diplomatiques de Nantes (hereafter Nantes).

28. Joaquín Fermandois, *Mundo y fin de mundo: Chile en la política mundial 1900–2004* (Santiago: Universidad Católica de Chile, 2005), 309–311; Taffet, *Foreign Aid as Foreign Policy*, 80–82; Fleet, *Rise and Fall of Chilean Christian Democracy*, 82, 89–90.

29. Taffet, *Foreign Aid as Foreign Policy*, 82–92.

30. Tyler Stovall, *Transnational France: The Modern History of a Universal Nation* (Boulder, CO: Westview, 2015), 411–412.

31. The importance of state planning was manifest in the work of Chile's Office of National Planning (ODEPLAN), founded in 1965, and the UN Economic Commission for Latin America and the Caribbean (CEPAL), headquartered in Santiago. Simon Collier and William F. Sater, *A History of Chile, 1808–2002*, 2nd ed. (Cambridge: Cambridge University Press, 2004), 317–318.

32. See, for example, "Ferrocarril subterráneo," *El Diario Ilustrado*, February 18, 1965; "El ferrocarril subterráneo," *El Diario Ilustrado*, March 8, 1965.

33. BCEOM-SOFRETU-CADE, *Estudio del sistema de transporte metropolitano de Santiago de Chile* (Santiago: Ministerio de Obras Públicas y Transportes, May 1968), iv–v.

34. "Investigaciones sobre el transporte metropolitano," *El Mercurio*, July 21, 1967; "Transporte rápido dará a Santiago el metropolitano," *La Nación*, August 18, 1967. Meanwhile, a Japanese engineering team carried out a free metro study. They recommended two lines in western and southern Santiago. However, the government did not pursue their proposal. See "Misión japonesa estudiará transporte metropolitano," *La Nación*, March 17, 1967; "Dos recorridos iniciales para el metro santiaguino," *La Nación*, December 12, 1967.

35. "Transporte urbano: problema que une a todos los alcaldes," *La Nación*, August 5, 1967.

36. "Informe sobre el transporte metropolitano," *La Nación*, March 8, 1968; Parrochia also dramatized the impending paralysis in an allegorical fairy tale titled *Los tres pastores*, written in 1974.

37. BCEOM-SOFRETU-CADE, *Estudio del sistema de transporte metropolitano*.

38. "Gobierno aprobó construcción de ferrocarril metropolitano," *El Mercurio*, October 14, 1968.

39. Collier and Sater, *History of Chile*, 320–324.

40. "Transporte metropolitano," *El Diario Ilustrado*, October 18, 1968. The conservative *Diario Ilustrado* ran countless editorials in this vein during Frei's presidency. Skepticism was not confined to its pages; see, for example, "El metropolitano," *La Tercera de la Hora*, February 7, 1967.

41. "Problemas del transporte," *El Diario Ilustrado*, March 19, 1967.

42. *Roto* ("broken") was a pejorative term for a lower-class Chilean. "¿Un metro para los ricos?" *Puro Chile*, April 21, 1970; "El 'metro' será, en primer lugar, para los pijes del barrio alto," *Puro Chile*, May 22, 1970.

43. Telex 342, Enrique Bernstein to Ministerio de Relaciones Exteriores de Chile, October 2, 1969, vol. 44/FRA, Archivo Histórico—Ministerio de Relaciones Exteriores (hereafter MinRREE).

44. Telegram from Saint-Légier to Diplomatie Paris, October 21, 1969, file DE.3.8, box 164, AFSC, Nantes.

45. Telegram from Saint-Légier to Diplomatie Paris, November 12, 1969, file DE.3.8, box 164, AFSC, Nantes.

46. The Franco-Chilean Mixed Commission was first held in 1967, in Paris, and would be held biannually, alternating between Paris and Santiago.

47. "Comunicado" from Saint-Légier to Maurice Schumann, December 5, 1969, box 150, AFSC, Nantes.

48. Letter from Saint-Légier to Maurice Schumann, December 5, 1969, box 150, AFSC, Nantes.

49. "Acta de la subcomisión de asuntos económicos y financieros," 1969, box 84QO 64, Amérique Chili 1964–1970, Centre des Archives diplomatiques de La Courneuve (hereafter La Courneuve).

50. Dossier économique 1969, box 84QO 64, Amérique Chili 1964–1970, La Courneuve; and Sater, *Chile and the United States*, 153–154.

51. "Procès-verbal, Sous-commission des Relations culturelles, scientifiques et techniques," November 26–28, 1969, box 150, AFSC, Nantes; and "Communiqué franco-chilien," November 25–27, 1969, box 150, AFSC, Nantes.

52. "Acta de la subcomisión de asuntos económicos y financieros," 1969, box 84QO 64, Amérique Chili 1964–1970, La Courneuve; and "Comunicado de prensa," 1969, box 150, AFSC, Nantes.

53. Fermandois, *Mundo y fin de mundo*, 309.

54. Press coverage of the Mixed Commission was favorable across the political spectrum. Letter from Saint-Légier to Maurice Schumann, December 5, 1969, box 150, AFSC, Nantes.

55. "Comisión investigadora acerca de la decisión del ejecutivo de construir el ferrocarril metropolitano de Santiago" [summary of Senate session], *El Mercurio*, December 26, 1969; and "Construcción del ferrocarril metropolitano de Santiago" [summary of Senate session], *El Mercurio*, January 10, 1970.

56. "El Senador Pedro Ibáñez se refiere al metropolitano," *El Diario Ilustrado*, December 25, 1969; and "El PN y el metro," *La Segunda*, December 26, 1969.

57. "Nuevos antecedentes sobre el metropolitano da el Ministro de Obras Públicas," *El Mercurio*, January 23, 1970.

58. "Advertencia sobre los contratos del metropolitano," *El Mercurio*, January 23, 1970.

59. Telex 1 from Enrique Bernstein to Ministerio de Relaciones Exteriores, January 6, 1970, vol. 54/FRA, MinRREE.

60. "Ferrocarril metropolitano de Santiago y el Instituto de Ingenieros de Chile," *El Mercurio*, January 23, 1970.

61. "Ruedas de goma o metálicas para el metro de Santiago," *La Nación*, April 14, 1970; "El metropolitano de Santiago," *El Mercurio*, May 10, 1970; for a detailed account of this controversy from the perspective of an engineer who supported metal traction, see Mauricio Froimovich, *La verdad sobre el metropolitano de Santiago de Chile* (Santiago: n.p., 1971).

62. "Precisiones sobre el metropolitano," *El Mercurio*, January 30, 1970.

63. Patricio Huneeus Salas, "Observaciones al metropolitano," *El Mercurio*, April 11, 1970.

64. "Ferrocarril subterráneo," *El Ilustrado*, April 25, 1970. The term *metropolitano* alluded to the Paris *métropolitain*.

65. "Santiaguinos esperan construcción inmediata de metropolitano," *El Siglo*, March 20, 1968; and "El Metro," *El Siglo*, April 7, 1970.

66. "¿Un metro para los ricos?" *Puro Chile*, April 21, 1970; "El 'metro' será, en primer lugar, para los pijes del barrio alto," *Puro Chile*, May 22, 1970.

67. "Ruedas de goma tendrá el metro," *La Nación*, April 16, 1970.

68. "Se abrieron las propuestas para el metropolitano," *El Mercurio*, January 16, 1970; and "Inscripción de contratistas para el Metro," *La Nación*, April 27, 1970.

69. Letter to the Compagnie Française d'Assurance pour le Commerce Extérieur, June 2, 1970, file DE.3.8, box 164, AFSC, Nantes.

70. "'Metro' con ruedas neumáticas," *El Mercurio*, April 16, 1970; and "El 'Metro,' una vía que conduce hacia el futuro," *La Nación*, September 24, 1970.

71. Nineteen percent of this loan would come from the French Treasury, with the remainder from private French banks. "Protocolo financiero entre el Gobierno de la República de Chile y el Gobierno de la República de Francia," February 2, 1970, vol. 7478, Fondo Ministerio de Obras Públicas, Archivo Nacional de la Administración; and "Protocole financier entre le gouvernement de la République Française et le gouvernement de la République du Chili," February 2, 1970, file DE.3.8, box 164, AFSC, Nantes.

72. Telegram to Diplomatie Paris, April 16, 1970, file DE.3.8, box 164, AFSC, Nantes.

PART IV

TOWARD NEW REGIMES OF EXPERTISE

11

MIDDLE
MODERNISMS

Collecting and Measuring Nature in the Peruvian Amazon

Emily Wakild

Peru came late to conservation. Neighboring states in South America created national parks as early as 1903, but it was not until the late 1960s that Peruvian bureaucrats began to feel pressure, both politically and ecologically, to set aside particular landscapes as distinct from development plans and modernization schemes.[1] The general places to do so seemed obvious—one each in the three paradigmatic regions of the coast, the sierra, and the jungle—but where precisely to situate a new program of parks was not clear. In order to decide this, a Kenyan wildlife consultant, Ian Grimwood, was invited by the elite Peruvian conservationist Felipe Benavides Barreda to provide expertise to the government courtesy of the British Ministry of Foreign Development. Grimwood's report became a template for Peru's rapid creation of conservation areas during the Cold War, which included the creation of seven national parks by 1988.

Among the parks Grimwood's report recommended was Manu. Located in the far western Amazon basin in the departments of Madre de Dios and Cusco, and officially created in 1973, the park and Cocha Cashu, the scientific field station within it, are widely recognized in international ecological circles for the field-changing science that emerged from there.[2] The accumulation of systematically deduced patterns, observations, and syntheses about tropical nature simultaneously created compelling arguments for the protection of large, contiguous natural areas. Tropical ecology developed as a place-specific discipline in conjunction with remote, sparsely populated natural areas rather than inside museums and laboratories of Western institutions. Therefore, the practice of natural field science (including the breth-

ren disciplines of conservation biology, tropical ecology, zoology, and so on)
evolved interdependently with the creation of conservation areas at Manu,
and in many parts of Latin America.

In addition to the larger trends of conservation biology and tropical field
research development, the Manu area provides particular insight into the
connection between expert and popular forms of science by exposing different ways of knowing nature exemplified in individual lives. To understand
these connections, I borrow from the historian of science, Robert Kohler,
who has articulated the importance of *residential knowledge* as a lens through
which historians might understand the accumulation of expertise in one
place over a long period of time.[3] The intertwining of wild places, curious
investigators, and space for knowledge-gathering endeavors altered specific
understandings of how species evolved, of the ways organisms coexist, and of
the often chaotic processes of natural change over time.[4]

The construction of natural field stations within national parks in the
Peruvian Amazon constitutes an example of how scientific research became
influential and self-legitimizing within the broader Cold War context. The
range of available knowledge about tropical nature changed dramatically
between the 1950s and the 1980s as parks—rather than museums, laboratories, or zoos—became the premier repositories of expertise, much of which
came to be philosophically articulated as biodiversity. These activities took
place in what can be considered Latin America's between and betwixt *middle* landscape, socially, politically, and ecologically. By middle landscapes,
I refer to geographical places such as parks and reserves with a public and
nonextractive charge that also occupied middling ideological realms in the
sense that they were not places seen as valuable by Spanish colonial projects or nationalist development schemes, but they also were not uninhabit-
ed or unknown places. Parks and field stations expanded greatly in this era,
but they are complicated spaces that do not fit into either high modernist
schemes seeking authoritarian control over nature and society (that largely
failed), or low modernist schemes of more democratic and grassroots social
reorganization.[5] Instead, parks and field stations form a middle modernism of politics and society, one intimate to many states that vacillated from
democratic to authoritarian rule and yet subservient to these regimes' more
pressing political needs in agriculture, land reform, or urban development.
This middle landscape of public land unavailable for exploitation provided
a setting that did not easily fit into developmentalist tropes for private enterprise or land reform efforts to manage specific community lands through
state institutions. The power of parks to convey modernizing sentiments for
protecting nature was often contradicted by weak protection on the ground
and routine confusion over just what a park should do. Although some scholars have argued that conservation came to be a force so powerful that it cre-

ated hundreds of thousands of refugees globally, the reality in Latin America was much milder.[6] Rarely did conservation have the political cachet, let alone the budget or boots on the ground, to effectively displace people or reorient land use patterns. But neither was conservation useless as parks' cumulative footprint grew to include vast areas that remain refuges for large animals and sites without seriously destructive industries.

Middle also refers to middle actors, usually middle-class folks with some, but not a lot of power that obtained higher-than-average levels of education and generally advocated for conservation. Conservation's actors rarely fit nicely into a Cold War binary of local or global, expert or resident; many resided comfortably in the middle space between these categories. Biologists often fit into a middle space between state managers obligated to service particular programs and private researchers investigating potential markets or development schemes. This is not to say that the middle provides a pure space, simply that as sites of expertise and premier locales for experts, parks provided a place for middle-class individuals to engage in producing knowledge not directly tied to projects of low or high modernism.

Continuing the theme of a middle position, natural field science disciplines attracted many women scientists. Unlike engineering, medicine, or computer science, the lack of lucrative career prospects for biologists meant more space for women to pursue their passions in this arena. The scientists, who came from a mixture of European, US, and Peruvian institutions, began to set up repetitive and longitudinal studies rather than engage in expeditionary adventures. Their expertise differed from knowledge gleaned from traditional practices or customary uses, although it was not uncommon to incorporate such insights into species lists or nomenclature. To understand the historical creation of these parks and the science within, we must set aside the mythic straw men of pristine nature and wilderness, the manufactured competition between conservation and development, and the skewed disciplinary historiography highlighting only cosmopolitan elites or enlightened native people; we must instead probe the center where scientists, collectors, and residents lived and contributed to the process of understanding how the natural world works.

From this vantage point, it becomes apparent that in a Cold War context where experts largely proselytized development, conservation's scientists were resisters.[7] Resistance to the gospel of development was waged not only by those people who experienced the violent or repressive effects of socioeconomic or political dislocations; it was also waged by scientists who saw themselves as voices for nature, some of whom also experienced the violence of the Cold War.[8] Neither science nor scientists can be considered apolitical during the antagonistic bipolar atmosphere of the struggle between superpowers, and yet neither were all scientists merely pawns of their home country's pol-

itics. Sometimes studying a monkey was just a search for direct knowledge
about a monkey. For many field scientists, the more they could prove as new
knowledge about monkeys, birds, plants, or the forest itself, the more they
could speak for nature and morally resist development at all costs. The methods of speaking for nature were many, but by far the most effective was the
language of biodiversity and the creation of parks. Not all scientists thought
of themselves as resisters—many preferred to claim to exist outside politics—
but by using the lens of resistance to understand their work, we become able
to see the ways some people went about their lives and accumulated expertise
to make compelling claims for nature itself, despite geopolitical schisms.

Peru's Cold War

The Cold War had contradictory effects on conservation in Peru during the
1970s and 1980s. Peru was neither a clear case of leftist struggle, such as
Cuba, Chile, or Nicaragua, nor did its politics embody the reactionary regimes of Brazil or Argentina. Rather than a right-wing military dictatorship,
Peru was ruled by a left-wing military dictatorship from 1968 to 1980, itself
a peculiar event.[9] Beyond this, the 1980 emergence of the Maoist insurgency
known as the Shining Path (Sendero Luminoso) resulted in a battle with the
Peruvian state until more than 69,000 people were killed, adding another
layer of political complexity. For many, the Shining Path was the Peruvian
experience of the Cold War, although it was at its most intimate level an internal rivalry rather than a battle between superpowers. In a smaller sense, despite the rhetoric of and principles of communism, the Shining Path had less
to do with the Cold War than with lingering inequalities and philosophies of
colonialism.[10] But the violence and trauma of the conflict was the experience
of the time for Peruvians. The development of place-situated research and the
ascension of conservation areas as the main strategy for national wildlife and
forest policy may appear tangential, or at least less overtly connected to development or strategy than industrial programs or militarization. Certainly,
many conservationists saw their work as existing outside political allegiances, and yet the Shining Path conflict did not spare conservationists, most dramatically in their 1989 murder of the Peruvian journalist Bárbara D'Achille
who oversaw a regular ecology forum in the Lima newspaper, *El Comercio*.[11]

Though relatively new to Peru, the creation of conservation areas rode
a crest of internationalization globally driven by increased activity from international institutions, growing sophistication of scientific justifications for
conservation, and changing domestic sentiments for and management over
natural landscapes.[12] The consolidation of the International Union for Conservation of Nature (IUCN); the support of the United Nations and its various ministries, especially the Food and Agricultural Organization (FAO);

Second bear 1955 June

FIGURE 11.1. Celestino Kalinowski and spectacled bear, June 1955. Courtesy of the Field Museum GN9266d. Reprinted with permission.

and employees of the Pan American Union played a large role in this ascension. So, too, did the work of national agencies such as the US Peace Corps, German development agencies (BMZ), and institutions such as the Frankfurt Zoo, the Smithsonian Institution, and the Nature Conservancy. The 1970s were a key decade for regional conservation, a time when countries that had done little to conserve before, such as Colombia and Costa Rica, joined emphatically in the process. These developments rode the crest of the first regional meeting for conservation, held in San Carlos de Bariloche, Argentina (the site of South America's first national park), in 1968, and the participation of various domestic scientists in this and other exchanges.[13] Nationally, ministries for managing natural resources were created as well, formalizing the state presence in the oversight of nature.

Conservation, therefore, was an activity both tangential to the Cold War and wrapped up in it. For instance, US Peace Corps volunteers who worked in parks and wrote management plans made ineffective cold warriors although their activities did much to develop institutional capacity for conservation.[14] But certainly conservation was never neutral, as the Shining Path guerrillas who assassinated the journalist Barbara D'Achille likely suspected. The cumulative intervention of various international institutions could be interpreted by some as compromising national sovereignty. Yet a purely bureaucratic or institutional look at the rise of conservation does not fully capture the role of expertise or the varieties of knowledge that contributed to conservation's impressive footprint.[15] A closer look at the production and circulation of scientific knowledge that contributed to conservation thus helps to both contextualize expertise and present the Cold War through another prism, one that captures the middle status of many actors that mediated the relationship between nature and society.

From Extractive Collections to Conservation in Place

The spectacled bear (*Tremarctos ornatus*) was pulled into an upright position with rope tied around his wrists and suspended around wooden scaffolding. Fully erect, the animal's outstretched arms extended more than six inches above the head of the hunter, Celestino Kalinowski. Posed in pale clothing with one arm around the dark bear's back, and the other cocked onto his hip, Kalinowski struck a pose for the photograph taken with each of the male specimens he collected. At first glance, the photographs appear an unbridled parade of masculine prowess displayed in the serial trophies of several successful hunting escapades. Yet the mechanics of the photograph, including the formulaic exhibition, the uniform scaffolding holding the bear, and the hunter's pose and subdued and unemotional expression suggest that external expectations, such as those articulated by the Chicago Field Museum of Natural History who received the bears, shaped the performance of this ritual. Most likely, the photographs expose a middle path that includes both of these interpretations.

Full-grown spectacled bears, the only bear in South America, were uncommon by 1955, the year Kalinowski shot, skinned, and prepared three males and one female for museum quality display. He collected these animals in the land where he was born, just outside the place he would help to become Manu National Park. In addition to the four bears, he also shot a puma on this June hunting expedition. This was likely Kalinowski's last major gathering of large animals from the region and the eerily humanlike bears posed in the pictures illuminate the size of a void these missing animals created in the landscape. The late 1940s and 1950s, peak years of collecting by Kalinowski, straddled a rebounded abundance in the forest after the catastrophic human and animal toll the rubber boom had ravaged on the region three and four decades before.

Kalinowski was the son of a Polish hunter, Jan Kalinowski, sent by a Polish count in 1887 to Peru to collect exotic birds. Jan soon discovered he preferred Peru and with his Peruvian wife had eighteen children whom they raised in the remote Marcapata Valley, seventy-five miles from Cuzco. The family lived both isolated and connected, mainly farming and selling taxidermy animals to collectors around the world.[16] Born in 1922 and taught these trades by native peoples and his father, Celestino developed keen skills for hunting and honed the techniques of taxidermy for the animals he collected. This enterprise was not without its risks; Celestino developed a severe hernia in 1955, which contributed to his changing ideas about animal extraction, but the autonomy and lucre of special arrangements with museums allowed the Kalinowskis to inhabit several interlocking and changing scientific worlds.[17]

Kalinowski was a first-rate hunter and partial naturalist. He preferred to collect at night, when the animals came to him as he imitated their calls perfectly.[18] He could identify species, often by their Latin names, and he made observations of animals' habits, behavior, feeding preferences, defensive techniques, and population fluctuations. This mixture of formal and informal scientific knowledge came across in his letters describing the collections he sent to Chicago.[19] Colin Sanborn, the curator of mammals at the Chicago Field Museum of Natural History, eagerly awaited shipments from Kalinowski, whom he adored. The shipments came regularly, once or twice a year for the nearly ten years of Kalinowski's employment by the museum, and their contents filled halls and galleries with rainforest animals from tiny squirrels and bats to the human-sized spectacled bear. "Your collection from the lowlands now totals 54 different kinds of mammals, many new to Peru, some rare, and two new species," wrote Sanborn to Kalinowski in 1951. "It is a wonderful collection and you have certainly done a very first class job of collecting. We are all proud of you," he continued.[20] In keeping with naturalist customs, Kalinowski collected specimens, then preserved them for storage in museums. Although he observed each animal's living practices, Kalinowski's objective, and the aim of his employers, was to remove the animals from the place in which they lived to further study them in conjunction with similar animals. Kalinowski often answered questions of habitat and location for the museum staff, such as when Sanborn requested a porcupine and Kalinowski reported that they lived in another region and could be harvested only in the dry season.[21]

Kalinowski's skills were recognized by Sanborn and others at the Field Museum. They invited him to Chicago and promised him employment there, offering a more than fourfold increase in his current wage, a pension plan, life insurance, and frequent field trips and expeditions.[22] He chose instead to remain in Peru and tried his hand at the lumber business in addition to collecting.[23] Sanborn visited Peru, assisted with arranging Kalinowski's collections in Lima at the Javier Prado Natural History Museum and even collected with him around Cuzco.[24] Kalinowski practiced a technical profession on which the more academic scientific community relied. He was an intermediary between animals of the remote western Amazon and the metropoles where animal bodies were gathered and stored.

Kalinowski is recognized in histories of the park as the "father of Manu," and his role opens up questions about the circulation of conservationist sentiments among residents.[25] His practice, which included nighttime hunting, animal calls, shotgun use, and more, indicated a transitional era between extractive collecting and observation in place. Species abundance was at a level where his harvesting did not fully compromise the larger population in the region.[26] Though hundreds of animals were collected, extraction of this level did not decimate the region, as it was checked by the capacity and desire of a few collectors. Kalinowski's work took place in specific locales, ones he knew by season, altitude, and terrain. But the scientific enterprise he participated in centered on removing those animals from that larger context (which importantly he understood) and isolating them into taxonomic pieces of a puzzle. By the end of his career, Kalinowski began to fear for what would happen if the rugged lands where the animals resided became subject to other extractions—logging, gold mining, and farming. He sensed a connection between the place and its value despite the dispersion of his collections worldwide.

Animals captured, killed, preserved, and distributed by the Kalinowski family ended up in museums around the world. Residents of Chicago, Washington DC, Paris, and London gazed on the vast array of tropical wildlife in carefully controlled museum rooms, with intimate lighting and interpretive signs. Ironically, in the early 1960s, a Peruvian elite with a budding interest in animals and conservation, Felipe Benavides Barreda, laid eyes on a spectacular collection of Peruvian birds at the Smithsonian museum. Benavides asked the museum director where the animals originated so that he, too, might acquire a collection. He was given Kalinowski's name.[27] It was under these circumstances, years after Kalinowski had given up collecting, that he was called to Lima to meet with Benavides. By this point, Kalinowski had a change of heart about collecting and voiced larger concerns about rapid transformations under way in his native region. Logging camps had begun to move into the Manu River, long Kalinowski's favorite place to collect due to the incredible abundance of wildlife.[28] Kalinowski explained to Benavides that commercial hunting and logging would destroy the integrity of Peru's magnificent fauna and that this region alone retained intact suites of animals.[29]

Kalinowski's meeting with Benavides coincided with the arrival of another expert on wildlife, called to Peru by Benavides, and the rise of an increas-

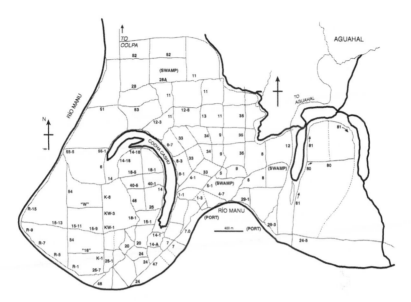

FIGURE 11.2. Reproduction of sketch map of trail system at Cocha Cashu Biological Station in 1984. Original outline by Louise Emmons, details added by Carol Mitchell and other researchers. Map courtesy of Cesar Flores and San Diego Zoo Global. Map reproduction by Andrew Chastain.

ingly committed group of scientific conservationists working for the national government. Ian Grimwood, a British wildlife specialist from Kenya, arrived in 1967 to do a survey of Peruvian wildlife and make recommendations for locations for national parks in each of the country's distinct ecological regions. Grimwood's report and his recommendations have become foundational documents for Peruvian conservation despite the fact that Grimwood merely confirmed and repeated recommendations developed by Peruvians.[30] Individuals like Kalinowski provided the initial work that raised the profile of the region, a profile confirmed by the international expert Grimwood, when he wrote his final report in 1967. The Manu reserve was first declared in 1968 and officially became a national park in 1973. Among other prohibitions, the creation of the park meant animals could no longer be hunted for collection in the park area. This meant that if scientists wanted to study the animals, those scientists had to go to where the animals lived.

A Place to Study Animals

In 1973 Cocha Cashu stood out to John Terborgh because the animals made the forest whole. He had traveled throughout Peru and South America for more than a decade and had never before seen "a place in the lowlands that was utterly pristine."[31] Terborgh's research to that point concentrated on birds since it seemed impossible to find animals in populations worthy of study in situ that were unconditioned to flee all humans. Terborgh, a Harvard-educated biology professor then working at the University of Maryland, was not the first or the only scientist to work at Cocha Cashu, but the corps of scientists and field assistants he collaborated with and trained over the next forty years would transform the way biologists looked at field research in remote conservation areas. In particular, they reformulated scientific expertise about neotropical primates.

When Terborgh arrived in 1973, Manu was on the cusp of meaningful federally protected status, and it already had a skeleton of a research station.[32] The 1968 declaration reserved 1.4 million hectares for the investigation of the possibility of a park, and the field station resided deep inside.[33] As for the building of the actual station, a pair of scientists, Paul Pierret, a professor of wildlife at the National Agrarian University in Lima, and Rudolf Hoffman from Frankfurt, Germany, set out in search of black caimans. The largest and commercially most valuable of South American crocodilians, these animals had become increasingly rare and difficult to study in their rapidly disappearing natural habitats of lowland tropical rivers. In 1969 Hoffman and Pierret recruited the students Augosto Tovar and Manuel Ríos to help build a station on a spot they identified on an oxbow lake in order to study the caimans. Ríos described the initial canoe trip to find the station as a complete adventure, "All we could do was count the number of bends in the river to find the right location."[34]

The Manu River region was remote for many reasons, but from a practical viewpoint, transportation was the largest impediment to scientific research. Obstacles could be overcome, but, as Terborgh explained, "One must pay to enjoy the pleasures and benefits of the pristine environment—in added time, inconvenience, and expense."[35] The long journey to the station began with two to three days on a one-way road from Cuzco that crossed two ranges of the Andes and descended more than three thousand meters, just to get to the Madre de Dios River. At that point all roads ended and supplies had to be transferred to dugout canoes, which were sturdy vessels twelve to fourteen meters long with outboard motors. The Madre de Dios was a formidable river; one hundred kilometers (or two days' travel) downstream, its confluence with the Manu River marked the turn to the biological station. Another two days on the river past log jams, tree litter, and muddy banks brought Cocha Cashu into view. This treacherous journey meant a driver, a river guide, and boat hands were essential members of any trip. By most accounts, the boat ride was made pleasant by watching macaws, herons, kingfishers, and terns glide along the water, and travelers gazed toward the banks in anticipation of rarer capybaras, anteaters, and jaguars.

Once off the river, in order to begin to study the animals, scientists needed to cut trails through the forest, an activity only permissible at the biological station and nowhere else in the park. Manu's lowlands are densely covered by tropical forest characterized by the range and varied size of the flora. At the level of the human eye, the landscape is dark, dense, and moist, covered with leaves, lichens, and branches, but the canopy itself reaches up to towering fig trees, keystone species that form the crown of the forest at as much as sixty meters.[36] Most of the botanical specimens have lianas, or woody vines that twist and climb on hosting trees and branches, and a large suite of smaller trees that make up the understory. This vegetation can be virtually impenetrable—especially if you are attempting to follow a tiny primate such as the pygmy marmoset (*Cebuella pygmaea*). As a result, researchers spent the 1974 field season cutting a series of trails set on a compass course to be able to rapidly move through the otherwise foreboding forest. Building the trails revealed many mysteries of the forest as scientists were often surprised when the seemingly uniform vegetation abruptly changed and they encountered swamps, canebrakes, uplands, or other features contoured into the complex mosaic of habitats. Once the trail system was in place, the scientists could begin conducting a census of the animals and familiarizing themselves with the animals' habits.

In order to follow the troops of monkeys and observe their behavior, the primate study led by Terborgh transformed the trails at Cashu. Monkeys were ideally suited to ecological study because their lives included a range of daily activities well within human abilities to observe. Swinging, chasing, howling, chirping, slurping, defecating—monkeys revealed their lives in patterns. Unlike birds or bats, people could follow and distinguish troops of monkeys and even develop fond feelings for them. For instance, the primate researcher Debra Moskovits cultivated a knack for recognizing individual monkeys and perceiving subtleties in their behavior.[37] Fifteen primate species inhabited the park, eleven could be found at Cashu, and five were the focus of the Terborgh team's study. Potential species ranged in size from the pygmy marmoset, affectionately known as the "pocket monkey," which is the world's smallest monkey, weighing about 100 grams or about the size of a chipmunk, to the largest, black spider monkeys, which weighed up to 13.5 kilograms and regularly traveled by swinging their long arms from branch to branch.[38]

Although primates gave way to study, their habits were best witnessed through continuous observation, which scientific teams accomplished by taking turns. The team protocol allowed intensive study without individual exhaustion. The primate researchers included Terborgh, Moskovits, Grace Russell, Charles Janson, and Barbara Bell. The botanist Robin Foster also contributed expertise and time in the field.[39] Working as a team, the group

logged more than 2,700 contact hours with mixed troops of monkeys between August 1976 and August 1977. This amounted to more than 540 hours
of observation per species. A scientist would observe and record, using a systematic reference code, the behaviors witnessed. The scientist could then follow, noting direction and speed, as the monkeys moved through the forest.
For reasons of safety, primates generally remained in a single place after dark,
so the researcher would then "put the monkeys to bed" where she could return to find them there before dawn. The ability to follow the monkeys and
systematically observe them meant that for the first time, scientists had a clear
picture of the interaction of each species with its environment including diets,
foraging techniques, ranging, time budgets, and use of resource trees across
the four annual seasons of wet, dry, and the transitions between them. Life
histories of animals and their behavior are the building blocks of larger scientific insights, and Cashu proved a perfect place to compile these histories.

In the end, the book and papers in this study contributed to a growing
set of ideas about the evolutionary importance of species diversity.[40] There
was not one main contribution, a silver bullet of scientific discovery that Terborgh's team or Cocha Cashu's researchers contributed.

Rather, they accumulated a set of insights that allowed scientists to see
with new emphasis the role of animals as seed dispersers and thus shapers
of the forest. Having animals in the forest meant that the flora of the forest
grew in a particular way. They learned new aspects about the relationships
among these animals, such as that some species often forage in mixed species
flocks for particular advantages. The study contributed to the understanding
of keystone species, including fruiting fig trees that helped smaller animals
make it through the dry season's times of dearth.[41] In addition to the raw value of these observations for comparisons, such insights have potential management implications for protecting large reserves and wild animals. It is out
of these insights that fields such as conservation biology and terms such as
biodiversity emerged.

In addition to the expansive findings of this and other studies, the benefits and obligations of team research brought an accompanied spirit of ca-
maraderie—where everyone took turns cooking, including lead scientists.
Although Terborgh would go on to publish numerous papers and books, it
was this teamwork and collaboration that allowed Cashu to develop into an
"alma mater" for a corps of Peruvians who came to understand the biological
processes of wild nature in this spot.[42] The Peruvian conservationist Enrique
Ortiz and the wildlife photographer Walter Wust got their start as field assistants to Terborgh and other scientists.[43] The rigors of work in the tropics
involved a spectrum of hard labor such as cutting trails or setting up nets,
which required fit and able team members. Scientists often recruited Peruvians for these jobs and paid them to work for months on end in the remote

forest. This allowed scientists to economically staff the station while providing young Peruvians opportunities to learn English, biology, and scientific research protocols. Whether or not they went on to become field scientists themselves (some, such as Ortiz studied with Terborgh in the United States), their lives were changed. Terborgh included administrators and the people who enforced policy as part of his team. He recognized the labor of park guards, mentioning eight of them by name in the acknowledgments of his book, and he also frequently credited Peruvian scientists and bureaucrats, especially Marc Dourojeanni and Carlos Ponce del Prado, for their work in establishing and managing the park, without which the research could scarcely have taken place.

More than anything, the reason Manu's nature remained wild by any classification was its maintenance of a full suite of animals. In comparison to most other places in Peru in the 1960s, Manu's animals had the space to interact with each other without extreme pressures from human developments. That is how Kalinowski found them in the 1940s and 1950s, and that is how Terborgh and his team observed them in the 1970s. Manu was neither empty nor untouched, but the scale of incursion was not enough to overpower non-human systems. Beyond disruption to human communities, the shattering effects of the rubber boom had provoked as yet unexplored effects on the forests and on the populations of animals encountered half a century later. Yet these incursions did not trigger a full-out collapse, due to the many obstacles still at play.

Scientists and Resisting Development in the Amazon

Scholarship on science in South America has long been shaped by the work of high-profile expeditions and the characterization of these expeditions as evocative of a particular imperial gaze.[44] More recently, scholars have begun to consider the ways in which scientists worked in networks, both horizontally with other scientists and vertically with informants, assistants, and collectors. The nature of the tropics and tropical science in the late twentieth century shares certain characteristics with these expeditions, but the practice of doing science in the same place while gathering residential knowledge adds layers of meaning to an actual place. The biological station, with set trails and predictable stability meant questions could be repeated, adding iterative insights. During the Cold War, tropical research shifted from extractive practices, exemplified by the taxidermy of Kalinowski, to study in place, epitomized by the research station at Cocha Cashu. This meant scientists could withdraw knowledge without extracting animals and also without facilitating explicit geopolitical or economic goals, thus opening a new chapter for the region.

The tropical rain forests of Amazonia were, in the 1960s, one of the least understood biomes on the planet. (Many researchers would say that this dearth of knowledge remains true today, but it was even more severe fifty years ago.) Despite centuries of keen interest by naturalists and explorers, vast areas remained unstudied and simple questions about what species and how many lived there and how they were distributed remained wide open. Logistical challenges of simply getting to areas stood in the way of many curious researchers, but a new generation of eager young scientists emerged from universities after World War II, primed by debates about how to define species and explain their development. It was a heady time for ecology, when notions of equilibrium were shaken and many scholars began to seek explanations for diversity in quantitative population and community ecology studies.[45] Some of them turned their attention to these basic and fundamental—but still extremely difficult and complex—questions that sought to understand whether animals inhabited the Amazon in a predictable pattern. Where species lived mattered to the question of how they might be protected.

David Cleary has pointed out that there is no reliable estimate of the percentage for the total protected area in the Amazon because of the definitional problems of the area itself, but the vast matrix of conservation classifications far exceeded other large regions such as the American West or the African savannas.[46] Brazil alone has nearly 24 percent of its Amazon territory designated in the form of a conservation unit.[47] This amounts to more than 124 million hectares or an area greater than the combined states of Texas, California, and New York (or the country of Peru).[48] Add to this the indigenous lands designated in the same region, and the amount of territory set aside for protection from aggressive development nearly doubles.[49] Indeed, one of the most surprising and radical effects of the transfer of land designations in Amazonia over the past forty years has been the partial union of traditional groups' historical claims to territory based on the past and conservationists claims to territory based on visions of the future.[50] The size of these designations is as staggering as how rapidly this came about.

In 1959 there were virtually no conservation areas in the region and twenty years later, Amazonian conservation seemed triumphant.[51] Conservation's quantitatively dramatic rise provides a useful metric: South America had 76 protected areas in 1974 and ten years later, there were 253.[52] Both international and domestic actors leaned on science and scientists for justification, explanation, and even motivation. Scientists were at work figuring out just why the Amazon was so diverse in order to understand species evolution but also to provide justification for leaving much of the Amazon alone so that evolution could proceed. Marc Dourojeanni, a Peruvian scientist and conservation expert, has argued that creating a park is "a manifestation of political will" and has advocated well-constructed proposals and publicity campaigns emphasizing species at risk, exceptional biodiversity, and the value of environmental services.[53] Regimes across the region found these scientific arguments compelling, despite their apparent contradiction with developmentalist programs.

What scientists did with their new knowledge also provides new interpretations of Cold War regimes. During this era, expertise was seen as a good thing, a justification, a modern attribute. New scientific language, such as the term *biodiversity*, gave lay people a way of talking about the richness of nature, the inequality of its distribution, and a recognition of difference as positive. It also gave some scientists the authority to use conservation as a brake on development in strategic locations, especially ones unlikely to be developed for economic reasons.[54] Resistance is not only reserved for the powerless. One lens through which to see the rise of conservation and the increase of scientific research in the tropical Americas is as scientific resistance to developmentalist tropes. Scientists, with some degree of power, crafted increasingly convincing arguments for the protection of nature amid developmental mandates. Scientists provided expertise for nature, which alone had none. They advocated parks, which prevented roads, and they both subtly and overtly accumulated understandings of animals and thus created sympathy for the wild world. Their efforts did not thwart development or human population growth and resource use, but by strategically defending particular places they provided an important use of their expertise.

New interpretations of conservation areas have abounded in recent years due in part to the impressive global footprint they occupy.[55] These critiques have largely dispelled the notion that nature conservation is benign or neutral, a perception that likely made park creation possible in so many national contexts. Some argue that parks are outdated relics of the past in an increasingly anthropogenic world, others use them as democratic and nationalist propaganda, and still more critics claim that parks serve only as tools of capitalism used for land grabbing.[56] This much is clear: national parks transformed the land tenure and occupation patterns of the Amazon in the twentieth century, and natural field science evolved as a path to help this transformation. That the largest contiguous swaths of tropical forest exist in these refuges and that native population numbers are rebounding for the first time in a century on these same lands points to some of the results from the residential knowledge that advocated for and led to the creation of these parks.

Relations of dependence, exchange, and curiosity characterize the middle habits of expertise that more fully contextualize the process of doing science within a national park. Although all the lives that have passed through Manu cannot be accounted for, a few highlight these forces. Celestino Kalinowski accumulated knowledge as an immigrant's son, a lifetime local resident, and a skilled professional hunter; he developed transnational exchanges with premier natural history institutions. John Terborgh, by contrast, built a repertoire of understanding as a US academic who spent more than forty years conducting research in the park. He developed firsthand relationships with other scientists (nearly a third of whom were women), park officials, boat drivers, and Peruvian assistants.[57] Scientists at Manu have trained more Peruvians in tropical field science than any Peruvian institution. Nevertheless, the knowledge is not secretive or hidden and it was often used by the government itself.

In its 1987 application for UNESCO World Heritage status, the Peruvian government noted that in the less than fifteen years since Manu National Park had been created, more than two hundred scientific publications based there contributed to the global understanding of tropical ecosystems. The nomination continued, "Manu is consequently the most exclusive and representative park in the Amazon basin. Some botanists claim that Manu has more plant species than any other protected area on earth."[58] Manu's story is frequently told through similar statistics and superlatives. Any description of the location in a newspaper, magazine, or photography book incorporates both quantitative and qualitative indications of value. From "Peru's Amazonian Paradise" or "Planet Earth's greatest ecological jewel," to even the simpler "repository of biodiversity," the landscape is replete with promise.[59] Allegories of Eden, paradise, and alternatively a green hell, are common in literature and imagery of the Amazon, and yet Manu's superlatives have a unique quality in their persistence and how they are lifted wholesale from scientific literature or crafted by scientists to have translatable qualities.[60] Cocha Cashu is the site of most of these confirmed superlatives. It is neither a museum nor a laboratory, but a place where science unfolds and can be continually confirmed, refined, and deepened, thus carving out an important middle space within a Cold War context.

Notes

1. After two reserved zones were created in the early twentieth century (Cordillera Huayhuash in 1902 and Humedales de Puerto Viejo in 1908), there were no further conservation units until the creation of National Parks Tingo María (1961) and Cutervo (1965); both originated with local enthusiasm and neither met the international criteria for national parks. See International Union for Conservation of Nature, World Database of Protected Areas, wdpa .org, June 2017. Between 1961 and 1988, thirty-eight protected area designations were created in Peru, including seven national parks.

2. International Union for Conservation of Nature and Natural Resources, "World Heritage Nomination: IUCN Summary 402: Manu National Park (Peru)," Gland, Switzerland:

UNESCO, 1987; James Fenner, "IUCN Study Pinpoints World's Most 'Irreplaceable' Protected Areas," *The Guardian*, November 7, 2013.

3. Robert E. Kohler, *All Creatures: Naturalists, Collectors and Biodiversity 1850–1950* (Princeton, NJ: Princeton University Press, 2006), and Kohler, "History of Field Science: Trends and Prospects," in *Knowing Global Environments: New Historical Perspectives on the Field Sciences*, ed. Jeremy Vetter (New Brunswick, NJ: Rutgers University Press, 2010), 212–240.

4. For an introduction to some of these findings from Cocha Cashu, see John Terborgh, "An Overview of Research at Cocha Cashu Biological Station," paper presented at Association for Tropical Biology, at the Conference of the American Institute of Biological Sciences Conference, Columbus, Ohio, August 10–12, 1987; Nigel C. A. Pitman, Miles R. Silman, and John W. Terborgh, "Oligarchies in Amazonian Tree Communities: A Ten-Year Review," *Ecography* 36, no. 2 (2013): 114–123; Miles R. Silman, John W. Terborgh, and Richard A. Kiltie, "Population Regulation of a Dominant Rain Forest Tree by a Major Seed Predator," *Ecology* 84, no. 2 (2003): 431–438; and Louise Emmons, "Comparative Feeding Ecology of Felids in a Neotropical Rainforest," *Behavioral Ecology and Sociobiology* 20 (1987): 271–283.

5. James C. Scott, *Seeing Like a State: How Certain Schemes to Improve the Human Condition Have Failed* (New Haven, CT: Yale University Press, 1998); and Jess Gilbert, *Planning Democracy: Agrarian Intellectuals and the Intended New Deal* (New Haven, CT: Yale University Press, 2015). For Mexico, Michael A. Ervin introduced the concept of "middle politics" as a way of examining statistics and data collection by the Mexican state. See Michael A. Ervin, "The 1930 Agrarian Census in Mexico: Agronomists, Middle Politics, and the Negotiation of Data Collection," *Hispanic American Historical Review* 87, no. 3 (2007): 537–570. What I am concerned with here is distinct, in that field biologists were not working for state-based data-gathering projects and their data did not primarily concern people but rather ecological systems.

6. Mark Dowie, *Conservation Refugees: The Hundred-Year Conflict Between Global Conservation and Native Peoples* (Cambridge, MA: MIT Press, 2009). Dowie's chapter 6 on Manu in particular is a stretch, dealing with theoretical displacement. Stephan Amend and Thora Amend estimated 85 percent, in *National Parks without People? The South American Experience* (Gland, Switzerland: IUCN, 1995); and Janis B. Alcorn, "Noble Savage or Noble State? Northern Myths and Southern Realities in Biodiversity Conservation," *Etnoecologica* 2, no. 3 (1994): n.p. Others argue that displacement rarely occurs; see Alejandro Velazquez and David Bray, "From Displacement-based Conservation to Place-based Conservation," *Conservation and Society* 7, no. 1 (2009): 11–14.

7. On experts proselytizing development, see Chastain and Lorek, Introduction to this volume.

8. Daniela Spenser, "Epilogue," in *In from the Cold*, ed. Gilbert M. Joseph and Daniela Spenser (Durham, NC: Duke University Press, 2008), 394.

9. Carlos Aguirre and Paulo Drinot, eds., *The Peculiar Revolution: Rethinking the Peruvian Experiment under Military Rule* (Austin: University of Texas Press, 2017). The dictatorship was first under the leadership of General Juan Velasco Alvarado until an internal coup resulted in Velasco's removal and replacement by General Francisco Morales Bermúdez in 1975.

10. Recent studies of the Shining Path have differentiated the experiences of the conflict. See especially Miguel de la Serna, *The Corner of the Living: Ayacucho on the Eve of the Shining Path Insurgency* (Chapel Hill: University of North Carolina Press, 2012); Jaymie Heilman, *Before the Shining Path: Politics in Rural Ayacucho, 1895–1980* (Stanford, CA: Stanford University Press, 2010); and Arthur Scarritt, "First the Revolutionary Culture: Innovations in Empowered Citizenship from Evangelical Highland Peru," *Latin American Perspectives* 40, no. 4 (July 2013): 101–120.

11. The reserve at Pampa Galeras that was built to conserve vicuña, a species D'Achille was investigating at the time of her capture and assassination, was renamed in her honor in 1993. See http://www.sernanp.gob.pe/pampa-galeras-barbara-d- achille.

12. Wilko Graf von Hardenberg, Matthew Kelly, Claudia Leal, and Emily Wakild, eds., *The Nature State: Rethinking the History of Conservation* (London: Routledge, 2017).

13. International Union for Conservation of Nature and Natural Resources, "Proceedings of the Latin American Conference on the Conservation of Renewable Natural Resources," San Carlos de Bariloche, Argentina, 1968, IUCN. For more on comparative examples of conservation in the region, see Claudia Leal, "Behind the Scenes and Out in the Open: Making Colombian National Parks in the 1960s and 1970s," in Hardenberg et al., *Nature State*, 135–157; Frederico Freitas, "Ordering the Borderland: Settlement and Removal in the Iguaçu National Park, Brazil, 1940s–1970s," in Hardenberg et al., *Nature State*, 158–175; and Emily Wakild, "Protecting Patagonia: Science, Conservation, and the Pre-History of the Nature State on a South American Frontier, 1903–1934," in Hardenberg et al., *Nature State*, 37–54.

14. For instance, Gary Wetterberg served in the Peace Corps in Chile and wrote the first management plan for Vicente Pérez Rosales National Park. He went on to a career with the FAO supporting parks worldwide. Stanley Taft, a cowboy from Texas, contributed to the first management plan at Pampa Galeras in Peru as a Peace Corps volunteer.

15. For an overview of conservation in Latin America, see Emily Wakild, "A Panorama of Parks: Deep Nature, Depopulation, and the Cadence of Conserving Nature," in *A Living Past: Environmental Histories of Modern Latin America*, ed. Claudia Leal, José Augusto Pádua, and John Soluri (New York: Berghahn Books, 2018), 246–265.

16. Kim MacQuarrie, *El paraíso Amazónico del Perú: Manu Parque Nacional y Reserva de la Biosfera* (Barcelona: Francis O. Pathey, 1992), 42.

17. C. C. Sanborn, June 30, 1955, Field Museum of Natural History Archive, Chicago, Zoology Corres/Sanborn 1946–1955/Folder Kalinowski (hereafter FMNHA-ZC-Sanborn/ Folder Kalinowski). His father's name is sometimes Hispanicized to Juan.

18. As recounted by his son, Bronislaw, in MacQuarrie, *El paraíso Amazónico*, 63.

19. See, for instance, his description of a new species of opossum, Kalinowski to Sanborn, July 15, 1950, FMNHA-ZC-Sanborn/ Folder Kalinowski.

20. Colin Campbell Sanborn to Celestino Kalinowski, February 8, 1951, FMNHA-ZC-Sanborn/Folder Kalinowski.

21. Kalinowski to Sanborn, May 14, 1951, FMNHA-ZC-Sanborn/Folder Kalinowski.

22. Sanborn to Kalinowski, April 10, 1951, FMNHA-ZC-Sanborn/Folder Kalinowski.

23. Sanborn to Kalinowski, March 27, 1951, FMNHA-ZC-Sanborn/Folder Kalinowski.

24. Sanborn to Kalinowski, March 27, 1951, FMNHA-ZC-Sanborn/Folder Kalinowski.

25. MacQuarrie, *El paraíso Amazónico*; Eleana Llosa Isenrich and Luis Nieto Degregori, *El Manu a través de la historia* (Lima: Proyecto Pro-Manu, 2003).

26. Although this is difficult to confirm, for similar assessments, see Harald Sioli, "La colonización de la Amazonia puede provocar un desequilibrio ecológico," *Boletín de la Sociedad Geográfica de Lima* 92 (1973): 119–21; Paul Pierret and Rudolf Hofmann, "Informe de viaje en la reserva nacional del Manu," 1967, in Centro de Datos de Conservación, Universidad Nacional Agraria-La Molina, Lima, Peru (hereafter CDC-UNA-LM). The volume of trade in wildlife in these years was intense on the level of sheer exports, although it is not well studied. Certain areas of the Amazon are more accessible than others, allowing greater harvesting of wildlife. Dourojeanni notes that the export of skins and animal products produced more economic value than any other Amazonian extraction, although the bulk of this trade came and went in the northern Amazonian city of Iquitos, with quicker access to the Atlantic via Manaus and the Amazon River. Marc Dourojeanni, "Fundamentos y ejecución del programa de parques nacionales y reservas equivalentes del Perú," *II Taller Internacional sobre el manejo de áreas silvestres, Parque Nacional de Iguazú, Argentina*, 1973, CDC-UNA-LM—Informes.

27. PRODENA—WWF, "Donación hecha al Parque Nacional de Manu, 1977," Frankfurt Zoological Society Archive (hereafter FZSA).

28. MacQuarrie, *El paraíso Amazónico*, 63.

29. "Crearán Gran Parque Nacional del Manú," March 13, 1968, FZSA.

30. Marc Dourojeanni, *Crónica forestal del Perú* (Lima: Universidad Nacional Agraria la Molina, Editorial San Marcos, 2009), 208.

31. John Terborgh, *Five New World Primates: A Study in Comparative Ecology* (Princeton, NJ: Princeton University Press, 1983), ix.

32. Dourojeanni, *Crónica*, 142, 223–224.

33. "Crearán Gran Parque Nacional del Manú," March 13, 1968, FZSA. Funds from the International Union for Conservation of Nature and World Wildlife Fund were secured to make the park function.

34. Oral history interview with Manuel Ríos Rodriguez, June 29, 2013, author's collection.

35. Terborgh, *Five New World Primates*, v.

36. John Terborgh, "Community Aspects of Frugivory in Tropical Forests," in *Frugivores and Seed Dispersal*, ed. A. Estrada and T. H. Fleming (Dordrecht: Dr. W. Junk, 1986), 371–384.

37. The gendered aspects of female monkey researchers have been well explored in the Old World; see Julie des Jardins, *The Madame Curie Complex: The Hidden History of Women in Science* (New York: Feminist Press at City University of New York, 2010), esp. chap. 7.

38. Louise Emmons, *Neotropical Rainforest Mammals: A Field Guide* (Chicago: University of Chicago Press, 1997 [1990]), 105, 142.

39. Terborgh, *Primates*, xiii.

40. For an overview of some of these changes, see David Quammen, *The Song of the Dodo: Island Biogeography in an Age of Extinction* (New York: Scribner, 1997).

41. John Terborgh and Margaret Stern, "The Surreptitious Life of the Saddle-backed Tamarin," *American Scientist* 75 (1987): 260–269.

42. Enrique Ortiz, "Manu 40 años," *El Comercio* (Lima), May 26, 2013. Oral history interview, Walter Wust, July 2, 2013, author's collection.

43. Wust, interview; Servicio Nacional de Áreas Naturales Protegidas, *Manu National Park, 40 años* (Lima: Wust Ediciones, 2013).

44. Most notably, Mary Louise Pratt, *Imperial Eyes: Travel Writing and Transculturation* (London: Routledge, 1992).

45. Sharon E. Kingsland, *The Evolution of American Ecology, 1890–2000* (Baltimore: Johns Hopkins University Press, 2005); Megan Raby, *American Tropics: The Caribbean Roots of Biodiversity Science* (Chapel Hill: University of North Carolina Press, 2017).

46. David Cleary, "Extractivists, Indigenes, and Protected Areas: Science and Conservation Policy in the Amazon," in *Global Impact, Local Action: New Environmental Policy in Latin America*, ed. Anthony Hall (London: Institute for the Study of the Americas, 2002), 199–216; and José Augusto Drummond, "From Randomness to Planning: The 1979 Plan for Brazilian National Parks," in *National Parks beyond the Nation: Global Perspectives on "America's Best Idea,"* ed. Adrian Howkins, Jared Orsi, and Mark Fiege (Norman: University of Oklahoma Press, 2016), 210–234.

47. Conservation units have strict protected areas such as national parks and units for sustainable development including extractive rubber reserves. Accurate as of October 2014, split nearly evenly between state and federal units. Instituto SocioAmbiental has the most accurate maps and assessment, see www.socioambiental.org.

48. Peru = 128,000,000 hectares and Brazilian conservation areas, 124,986,091 hectares.

49. Instituto Socio Ambiental map, 111,401,207 hectares in indigenous lands. This includes all stages of legal-administrative ratification but 93 percent of this figure has been confirmed.

50. Paul E. Little, *Amazonia, Territorial Struggles on Perennial Frontiers* (Baltimore: Johns Hopkins University Press, 2001), 232.

51. On Brazil setting an unprecedented new standard for the way science could infuse conservation policy, Emily Wakild, "Jaú and Pleistocene Refuges," manuscript in preparation. Ronald A. Foresta, *Amazon Conservation in the Age of Development: The Limits of Providence* (Gainesville: University Press of Florida, 1991), 94.

52. Roderick P. Neumann and Gary E. Machlis, "Land-use and Threats to Parks in the Neotropics," *Environmental Conservation* 16, no. 1 (1989): 13–18, 15.

53. Marc Dourojeanni, "Political Will for Establishing and Managing Parks," in *Making Parks Work: Strategies for Preserving Tropical Nature*, ed. John Terborgh, Carel van Schaik, Lisa Davenport, and Madhu Rao (Washington, DC: Island Press, 2002), 327.

54. Terborgh et al., *Making Parks Work.*

55. Bernhard Gissibl, Sabine Höhler, and Patrick Kupper, eds., *Civilizing Nature: National Parks in Global Historical Perspective* (New York: Berghahn Books, 2012), 1–27; and Howkins, Orsi, and Fiege, *National Parks beyond the Nation.*

56. For some important avenues in this dense literature, see the polemic, Peter Kareiva, Michelle Marvier, and Robert Lalasz, "Conservation in the Anthropocene: Beyond Solitude and

Fragility," Breakthrough Institute (2012). See also Charles Geisler, "A New Kind of Trouble: Evictions in Eden," *International Social Science Journal* 55: 175 (2003): 69–78; Arun Agrawal and Kent Redford, "Conservation and Displacement: An Overview," *Conservation and Society* 7 (2009): 1–10; Dan Brockington, Rosaleen Duffy, and Jim Igoe, *Nature Unbound: Conservation, Capitalism and the Future of Protected Areas* (London: Earthscan, 2008); and Dowie, *Conservation Refugees*. The idea of America's exceptionalism is greatly stressed in the documentary by Ken Burns, *The National Parks: America's Best Idea* (Arlington, VA, PBS, 2009).

57. Cocha Cashu Research Log, Center for Tropical Conservation, Duke University. The log shows 113 women out of the 315 researchers registered at Cocha Cashu between 1975 and 2009.

58. IUCN, "World Heritage Nomination," 1987.

59. MacQuarrie, *El paraíso Amazónico*; John Terborgh, *Requiem for Nature* (Washington, DC: Island Books, 1999), 23; and "Manu: 40 años," *El Comercio*, Lima, May 26, 2013.

60. Nancy Leys Stepan, *Picturing Tropical Nature* (New York: Reaktion Books, 2001), is among the best studies of this contradiction.

12

PRIVATIZING EXPERTISE

Environmental Scientists and Technocrats in Chile's Transition to Democracy

Javiera Barandiarán

On September 11, 1973, Chile's military deposed the socialist president Salvador Allende and instituted a conservative military government. A decade into this repressive regime, scientists began gathering in large public meetings to discuss how they, as experts, might better serve society and the state. At one such meeting, the biologist Ernst Hajek asked rhetorically, "Often scientists are accused of being stuck in their ivory towers, facing the academy and with their backs to the country's real problems. . . . But scientists could also ask, and how do you enter that other ivory tower, the organizations where decision makers work?"[1] In the context of Chile's authoritarian military regime, many scientists felt shut out of decision making by this "other ivory tower"—the state.

Nonetheless, scientists have long been active participants in government and state-led projects in both democratic and authoritarian regimes, a fact that has been amply documented by historians.[2] As this volume argues, the Cold War only raised the stakes of expertise for government. Scholars have long considered Chile as following this tradition.[3] Nineteenth-century Chilean intellectual and political leaders championed a "scientific government" that resonated with positivist ideals.[4] Positivist ideals guided policies through the 1920s, including during the Carlos Ibañez administration, which relied on engineers to increase efficiency and eliminate "petty politics."[5] Experts continued to be influential after 1973 under Augusto Pinochet's military regime, but they differed in training as economists displaced engineers as the technocrats of choice.[6]

If experts held sway in Chilean government, why then did Hajek feel they did not? Was there something about natural and physical scientists—Hajek's audience that day—that led the military regime to shun them as trusted technocrats? If so, why then would an authoritarian regime allow meetings with hundreds of participants to take place? What influence, if any, did these meetings have on the democracy that followed? This chapter recounts the history of these meetings, organized by the Center for Environmental Research and Planning (Centro de Investigación y Planificación del Medio Ambiente or CIPMA), to reflect on the meaning of technocrats or experts in Chilean government during and after the dictatorship. Technocrats are individuals with "a high level of specialized academic training which serves as a principal criterion on the basis of which they are selected to occupy key decision-making or advisory roles in large, complex organizations."[7] Scholars sometimes use the terms *technocrats, experts,* and *scientists* interchangeably to identify people who have political influence by virtue of their training, credentials, or affiliation with activities considered to be scientific.[8] However, the Chilean experience does not fit this pattern. This case is interesting because, although scientists desired to participate actively in public policy, their efforts were unsuccessful for reasons that illuminate how neoliberal ideology shapes knowledge production and public expertise.

Many natural and physical scientists, including Hajek, were left out of the government's ivory tower not for lack of funding or institutional opportunities, but because of a shift in the organization of knowledge production brought about by the Chicago Boys, who became Pinochet's technocrats of choice. Named in reference to the university where many completed their studies, the Chicago Boys convinced the military government to implement neoliberal reforms that included, among other things, the creation of a market for scientific knowledge. This market transformed the foundations of public expertise, from a relationship between state officials and scientists based on trust and a kind of intimate privilege, to a transactional one guided by supply and demand.

The exclusion of natural and physical scientists from the cast of potential technocrats has had consequences for environmental governance, the focus of this chapter. Studies of Chilean environmental governance have found that excluding scientists from policymaking precluded an "authentic pluralism" in favor of business interests.[9] Those experts who are affiliated with the state, moreover, are seemingly confident to the point of arrogance, preferring to find solutions to policy problems rather than admit ignorance or that something cannot be done.[10] By contrast, in public Chilean scientists often appear unsure of themselves and emphasize the fallibility of science over its usefulness as a reliable form of knowing.[11] Meanwhile, the advisory gap left by scientists has been filled by environmental consultants. They have profited from the booming market for environmental impact assessments, and they shape legislation and institutions as advisers to political parties.

This chapter first introduces the term *technocrat* as used in Chile during the dictatorship years. The second half of the chapter focuses on scientists, first while they participated in CIPMA meetings and later when some worked to build a National Center for the Environment (Centro Nacional de Medio Ambiente), known as CENMA. The analysis relies on several sources, including scientists' published writing, the legislative history, official documents found in libraries or given to the author by the participants in these events, and interviews conducted by the author.

Technocracy in Dictatorship

Although many quarters supported the military coup of 1973, making it increasingly foreseeable, what would follow the coup was far less clear to the Chilean public and to those involved in the military junta. As recounted by the historian Verónica Valdivia, subversive civilian and military officials agreed on the need to remove their common enemy—Salvador Allende and the Marxist groups his government had empowered—and on their policy priorities. At the top of this list was the need to address a severe economic recession and acute poverty that some academics, generals, and political elites believed was driving support for Marxism. Stabilizing the economy, lowering inflation, and increasing production were thus understood by members of the military junta to be crucial to their success. How to achieve those goals, however, was far less clear.[12]

On usurping office, Pinochet moved to consolidate his power through violence and by cultivating advisers whom he could draw on for support but also pit against each other. The coup itself met little resistance. Nevertheless, Pinochet and the junta unleashed what they called a "war against the Marxist cancer," an internal enemy that needed to be eradicated. They created a violent secret police and unleashed terror campaigns to intimidate the population. In parallel, Pinochet surrounded himself with legal and constitutional scholars, former presidents, conservatives, and the Chicago Boys.[13] Legal and political experts were institutionalized through the high-ranking Council of State and the committee tasked with drafting a new constitution. Meanwhile, *gremialistas* like Jaime Guzmán and Miguel Kast exercised influence through myriad channels. Guzmán was the regime's principal adviser, Pinochet's speechwriter, and the spirit behind *gremialismo*, a conservative ideology that advocated for circumscribed civic organizations, rather than liberal democracy, to mediate between individuals and the state. Guzmán recruited thousands to his ideas, and this support was crucial to the military regime.[14] Kast, also a well-known *gremialista*, directed social and economic policy at the influential National Planning Office (ODEPLAN). Kast recruited like-minded professionals and created a state apparatus capable of implementing social and economic programs throughout the country that reflected the military government's values. Having studied economics at the University of Chicago, Kast helped integrate the economists and *gremialistas*.

The Chicago Boys were a group of young men affiliated with the Catholic University of Chile's economics department who completed graduate training at the University of Chicago or at other like-minded economics departments. They believed that markets were superior in every way to state action and redefined the role of the state in this light.[15] Like other conservatives, their opposition to Allende had deep roots: they first became outspoken in 1967 in opposition to the University Reform launched by Allende's predecessor, President Eduardo Frei. Their discontent growing during Allende's government, a small group prepared an economic reform plan for a future, conservative government, contained in a book known as "the brick." Through a contact in the navy, the same day of the coup they delivered "the brick" to the military junta.

The Chicago Boys were able to sway Pinochet for several reasons. First, as argued by the political scientist Carlos Huneuus, they had what the military government most needed: a coherent plan for economic recovery that they confidently promoted and substantiated with appeals to scientific authority. Second, as academics they were political outsiders, unaffiliated with any of Chile's traditional political parties. This appealed to Pinochet and the *gremialistas*, who disdained parties, seeing them as a source of inefficiency and petty politics and to blame for politicizing universities, the military, and other organizations during the Frei and Allende years. Their political detachment also mirrored a programmatic nonalignment: the Chicago Boys' policy recipes did not appear to benefit any specific group, such as small or large business, agribusiness, and others, which were then clamoring for reforms that would protect their access to state subsidies and protections. When Pinochet took power, he needed an economic recovery plan that would roll the state back from economic activity after decades of expanding state intervention. This is what the Chicago Boys promised to deliver, exceedingly confident in their expertise and claims of political and economic neutrality.[16]

Scientists as Technocrats? CIPMA's Meetings

In 1979, some academics set up CIPMA as a nongovernmental organization (NGO) focused on environmental issues. Starting in 1983, CIPMA organized three large town-hall-style meetings to kick-start public debate about environmental degradation and provide scientists with a platform to influence public policy. CIPMA's cofounder, Guillermo Geisse, an architect and urban planner who did graduate studies at the University of California, Berkeley, wrote that the first meeting demonstrated that "the scientific community is ready to contribute solutions to the country's environmental problems, provided they find adequate channels through which to communicate their research to society and, especially, to decision makers."[17] Eager to create these channels, for the next decade CIPMA organized meetings and workshops and published a journal, *Ambiente y Desarrollo*, to disseminate environmental research and provide a forum for scientists to debate policy issues.

The response to CIPMA's call in 1983 was overwhelming; three hundred attended the first meeting, five hundred attended the second meeting in 1986, and even more attended the 1989 meeting—the last before the transition to democracy. Geisse recalled that their aim in making CIPMA was to generate a dialogue around environmental issues to contribute, in some way, to rebuilding democracy.[18] They did not support a specific concept, like sustainable development or set of policies. Rather, the goal was to create a conversation outside of military-controlled spaces about a development plan focused on quality of life, instead of the Chicago Boys' neoliberal ideas. The environment was strategically selected. Remembering the environmental movement he witnessed while studying in Berkeley, California, in the 1960s, Geisse believed that concern for the environment challenged the military emphasis on growth, in which pollution was treated like an indicator of wealth, and poverty was best tackled by fostering export-oriented industries. An environmental perspective required instead a commitment to quality of life and social equity.

Scientists provided ideas, knowledge, and—crucially—political protection. The National Academy of Sciences sponsored the meetings, and renowned scientists were actively involved: the educator Juan Gómez Millas, the physiologist Hector Croxatto, the economist Osvaldo Sunkel, and many others. In Geisse's view, the government would not put the Academy of Sciences in prison. As scientists doing "technical" things, government officials considered them unthreatening and even granted CIPMA researchers visas to travel abroad to attend conferences.

At the meetings, participants discussed many ideas that touched on all sectors of Chilean economic life: forestry, conservation, oceans, energy, and mining. Articles published in *Ambiente y Desarrollo* testify to broad-ranging discussions, including how to improve scientists' relationships with the state, industry, or communities; what environmental policies in use outside of Chile might be adapted for local use; and which proposals specific industries should consider to foster sustainability.[19] Scientists also shared their research results. For example, *Ambiente y Desarrollo* dedicated an issue to findings from a UNESCO-funded project on biodiversity, and published articles on new environmental science initiatives.[20] CIPMA was politically influential and captured the attention of dozens of scientists and professionals. However, scientists never positioned themselves as trusted government advisers, serving society through science, for three reasons: Cold War tensions, transitional moderations, and the triumph of neoliberal ideals.

Cold War Tensions

The physicist Igor Saavedra, then president of the Academy of Sciences and a national science prize winner, delivered the keynote at the 1983 CIPMA meeting. His talk, titled "Our Scientific Community and Its Local and Global Responsibilities," aimed to inspire scientists into action while recognizing the magnitude of the challenges they faced.[21] He described this challenge as unique to scientists working in a Third World country: their circumstances required them to reconcile two seemingly contradictory goals—to produce science that was both "universal" and "excellent" and also "locally relevant." In the First World, Saavedra explained, two scientific communities existed, one dedicated to universal and the other to applied science. But in Third World countries like Chile, every scientist had to fulfill both roles simultaneously. "Science is always universal," Saavedra explained, and "we should never simply do 'science good enough for Chile.' We must insist on cultivating universal science, that which is inventing the future."[22] Yet circumstances forced the Third World scientist to renounce research on the "great scientific questions" that bring international recognition, in order to help build the nation.

These statements reflect several controversies that raged during the Cold War among Chilean and Latin American scientists. These had to do with the region's intellectual and material dependence on First World or developed nations. Material dependence was straightforward. National spending on scientific research had always been low—around half a percentage point of gross domestic product—and dropped even further during the military regime. In 1986 the national science budget was reportedly just US$2 million.[23] This translated into a litany of material grievances: poorly equipped offices and libraries, excessive costs and administrative burdens for imported books and research materials, and faculty salaries that attracted few to the profession and left researchers facing financial problems. To maintain a simple middle-class life, faculty had to work either multiple jobs or find an independent source of wealth.[24] The dictatorship years aggravated these conditions and ended a period of relative wealth for Chilean science. The Cold War motivated the US government and foundations to generously fund research; in Chile, academics embraced this funding and set about producing "science of excellence." New labs and institutes were created and unprecedented numbers of Chileans completed graduate studies abroad.[25]

Unfortunately, foreign funding seemingly accentuated the region's intellectual dependence. Many academics in Chile and in neighboring countries argued that foreign funding directed scientists' attention away from problems of local concern toward questions set by researchers in First World countries.[26] US policies supported science, but had other objectives as well. President Kennedy's Alliance for Progress, for instance, aimed to foster economic growth to reduce the appeal of communism. Project Camelot, funded by the US military, raised fears among local scientists of being unwitting participants in US efforts to intervene against Allende. Intellectual dependence operated also at a smaller, more diffuse scale. This included the pressure to publish in indexed journals, in English, with results that answered questions derived from theories and research conducted in the United States or European countries.[27] Spending time abroad was an opportunity and a dislocation, prompting potential conflicts between those who left and those who stayed. In short, as expressed by Saavedra, Chilean scientists felt torn between pursuing the best scientific opportunities available to them and their commitments to improving Chilean society. In a roundtable discussion hosted by Saavedra, one successful scientist concluded that they survived thanks to a "quixotic mindset" that led highly motivated people to persist despite their poor working conditions.[28]

The Cold War and 1967 University Reform brought these tensions to a boiling point. Although some academics supported the University Reform as conducive to more democratic, just, and plural universities, others opposed it because it introduced electoral politics into universities. Political fighting and polarization soon dominated university life. After the 1973 coup, the military quickly took control of universities and detained, disappeared, or forced into exile thousands of students, faculty, and staff. Throughout the 1970s, faculty left universities for "safe spaces" where they could work uncensored.[29] This was the origin of CIPMA: Guillermo Geisse created it once he could no longer tolerate the rarefied atmosphere at the Catholic University.[30] Many other similar institutes were created by the Catholic Church and foreign donors to protect academics. These provided a fruitful home for the prodemocracy opposition.[31]

In this context of censorship and surveillance, CIPMA's founders identified the environment as a strategic opportunity for scientists to participate in public policy. According to Saavedra: "The inter-disciplinary discussion of Chile's environmental problems should serve to formulate concrete solutions to the problems that affect us, and who else but [scientists] to detect and solve these. If this occurs we will show the man on the street the value of science and technology, its capacity to solve problems and define quality of life. A social consensus will emerge with respect to the importance of science and technology, indispensable to make these activities permanent and significant in the country."[32] The environment thus bridged First and Third World science that could meet universal scientific standards as well as help solve issues of local concern. CIPMA's approach, however, differed in crucial ways from that of the Chicago Boys. Whereas the economists were intellectually coherent and confident, CIPMA fostered an interdisciplinary dialogue among a plurality of concerns and interests. This structure ultimately facilitated the rise of more moderate and promarket voices in environmental policy.

Transitional "Moderations"

By 1989, when the third CIPMA meeting was held, Chilean politics had changed significantly: in a referendum held the previous year, just over half of Chileans denied Augusto Pinochet another eight years in power. The military government had almost two years to prepare to hand over power to democratically elected leaders. During this transitional period, CIPMA worked to transform the conversations and networks it had built into policies and laws the new democracy might adopt. The organization's events were increasingly dominated by powerful groups, including conservatives seeking an influential role in the new democracy and representatives from recently privatized companies eager to help shape the new environmental regulations.

Scientists prevailed at the first CIPMA gathering in 1983, but the group's 1986 meeting was dominated by industry, and by 1989, industry and political actors predominated.[33] CIPMA was penetrating into policymaking circles, but its proposals were becoming increasingly tempered. For Guillermo Geisse, it was clear that policy change would occur only "within realistic parameters" (*dentro de lo posible*). CIPMA's meetings were always open to industry and—whether they participated from their own initiative or were invited by CIPMA organizers hoping to broaden support for their proposals—their participation increased over time. Most legislators and politicians at the time had superficial and simplistic views of the environment. By contrast, and given Chile's integration into global markets, industry was developing at that time a more strategic understanding of environmental harms and regulations. The North American Free Trade Agreement, signed in 1988, signaled that global free trade would increasingly require industry and governments to adopt environmental policies. For all these reasons, Geisse saw in industry a potential ally. For instance, in 1990 CIPMA organized five industry-specific seminars to produce concrete legislative proposals. In the mining sector group, five of the seven participants came from industry, as did eight of the ten participants in the forestry seminar. Neither group included representatives from communities, workers' unions, or environmental NGOs, and at most one or two academics joined each group.[34]

CIPMA thus took a technocratic turn.[35] The themes guiding each meeting bear witness: whereas in 1986 the theme was "quality of life" and in 1989 "sustainable development," two themes that raised thorny issues like inequality and injustice, in 1992 CIPMA adopted the uninspiring cry of "environmental management." CIPMA shaped the environmental framework law, a priority for the first democratic administration of Patricio Aylwin. Between 1990 and 1992, under the direction of Rafael Asenjo, CIPMA guided the drafting of this law and, in 1993, published it as a book. Asenjo, a lawyer and longtime participant in CIPMA, became the nation's first environment secretary. The framework law reflected support among moderate and conservative individuals for a small coordinating agency, called CONAMA (Comisión Nacional de Medio Ambiente, National Environmental Commission). They believed a coordinating agency that could lobby sectoral ministries to incorporate environmental perspectives into their work was preferable to an Environment Ministry because the latter risked "becoming a Ministry of No," that is, an obstructionist and therefore isolated entity.[36] The proposal became associated with technocratic views, particularly after the economist Edgardo Boeninger—described as a "technocrat par excellence"[37]—was tasked with negotiating the law with legislators.

At these meetings one of the leading voices representing industry and the *gremialistas* was that of Ricardo Katz, an engineer who had worked at ODEPLAN and the National Energy Commission during the dictatorship. He was an expert on urban pollution and had, since the late 1970s, directed a team led by Juan Escudero at the University of Chile's engineering school, which studied and monitored air pollution in Santiago.[38] At CIPMA, Katz advocated for market-based and rational choice policies for pollution control.[39] The future environmental law, he wrote in *Ambiente y Desarrollo*, should be fair, nondiscriminatory, based on checks and balances, and provide a large role for *gremios*—the professional associations that *gremialistas* like Guzmán and Kast had championed.[40] He also argued that in a poor country such as Chile, environmental protections are regressive, insofar as the poor ultimately pay for reducing pollution and suffer most from any slowing in economic growth. Katz's ideas were influential among conservatives; he reportedly wrote the speech delivered by the right-wing presidential candidate, Hernan Büchi, at the 1989 CIPMA meeting.[41]

These negotiations led to an environmental framework law that environmentalists considered conservative.[42] The law privileged market-based principles like gradualism and efficiency. Legislators gave CONAMA few tools with which to regulate industry. The agency was understaffed and underresourced and did not have a legal mandate to enforce environmental quality or emission standards. Its tasks were instead limited to proposing broad policies, lobbying sectoral ministries, managing the process by which new quality and emission standards were drafted, and overseeing environmental impact assessments. Little environmental leadership could be expected from CONAMA's advisory council, which included one representative of the president and two members each from academia, NGOs, business, labor, and environmental consulting companies. Scientists thus lost their best opportunity to gain institutionalized influence, as the framework law gave consulting companies an equal voice.[43] In practice, environmental consulting companies flourished and learned to use their influence wisely: they became financially important due to environmental impact assessments and began to operate like think tanks in that each political party developed a privileged relationship with a specific consulting company. For example, at that time, Ricardo Katz founded his company, GAC (Gestión Ambiental Consultores), which advises right-wing parties on environmental policy.[44]

CIPMA was not alone in shifting from a seemingly subversive, large-tent organization set up to challenge the military government toward an increasingly moderate group.[45] Rather, as Daniel Levy argues, the transition had a "moderating" effect on independent institutes created during the dictatorship. Like CIPMA, several shifted toward applied work done at the behest of political parties. The democracy that reemerged after the dictatorship thus reflected a new organization of public expertise: linkages between government agencies and university-based academics were either replaced or dwarfed in importance by the influence of a new generation of think tanks. A lasting effect of the military intervention in universities was thus a privatization of expertise; as independent institutes created to house academics fleeing universities became think tanks, political parties came to rely increasingly on these for expert-based policy advice.[46] These became the new, post-Pinochet technocracy.

A Market for Science Triumphs

The shift to a private market for expertise, and the parallel erosion of publicly funded knowledge, is vividly demonstrated by the struggles faced by an environmental science center called CENMA. The center was spearheaded in the early 1990s by Juan Escudero, an engineer and expert on urban air pollution who, together with Katz, had advocated for market-based solutions to environmental problems. The original mission of CENMA was to serve as a laboratory that could provide state agencies with environmental data and analysis. In 1992 the Japanese Aid Agency (JICA) offered to support such a laboratory so as to replicate Japan's approach to scientific advice, where federal and regional environmental agencies have in-house expertise. Japanese investments and trade were growing quickly, particularly for Chilean forestry and fish products.[47] Some interests were threatened by environmen-

tal degradation; indeed, around this time, a few prospective Japanese investments were blocked due to environmental concerns.

Even with Japanese financial assistance, Escudero and his colleagues worried that CENMA would be too expensive for the Chilean state to support.
The Japanese aid agency envisioned CENMA within CONAMA, to provide
the new environmental commission with privileged, strategic expert advice
and in-house capacities to produce environmental information to support
regulation. But Chilean officials argued this was not possible under Chilean law; the state cannot by law have a privileged relationship with any one
group.[48] CONAMA was, moreover, very small: guided by neoliberal principles, right-wing legislators capped CONAMA's staff and budget to avoid
bloating the state. They also rejected earmarking funds for environmental
research, arguing that all issues had to compete for funding from the nation's
general budget, "as if on a level playing field."[49] Opposition to funding environmental research reflected an unwillingness to protect the environment,
as well as neoliberal principles privileging market competition over state-led
actions, particularly regarding the state's access to information. If the state
was to have a limited role in public life, it was neither necessary nor desirable
for it to have access to expert information.[50]

The solution was to constitute CENMA as a private foundation on lands
ceded by the University of Chile, although CONAMA had "legal attribution
to assume overall responsibility for the project."[51] This arrangement resonated with Escudero's experience; for twenty years, he had worked on air pollution at the university's School of Engineering, in close cooperation with
ODEPLAN. CENMA would replicate this experience, particularly since the
lab was focused on analyzing urban problems such as air pollution and waste
management. Japanese experts supported these efforts; for example, the
person who developed Tokyo's air pollution forecasting models spent three
years designing a model for Santiago. Under Escudero's directorship, CEN-
MA staff collected data, developed models, analyzed results, and prepared
reports that they presented to CONAMA and state agencies responsible for
water, public health, and waste management.[52] They also trained dozens of
state officials in environmental impact assessments.

Five years after its founding, however, support for CENMA began to
crumble. In 2000, shortly after signing an agreement to extend Japanese aid
funding for two years, CONAMA and then the University of Chile withdrew
their financial contributions, without a public explanation.[53] CONAMA cut
its contribution by two-thirds, and the University of Chile soon after appointed a director to CENMA recruited to "close the center down."[54] Henceforth CENMA's budget fluctuated wildly; it fell to less than US$1 million a
year, then tripled a few years later after CONAMA signed a multiyear agreement for services.[55] In 2011 the budget again fell and dozens of scientists

left. In 2017 CENMA remained in limbo, slowly losing its talent and seeing its equipment fall into disrepair.[56] The second floor remained closed due to structural damages to the building caused by the 2010 earthquake.

What accounts for CENMA's demise and how do its struggles illuminate the structural challenges faced by environmental experts during the apparent triumph of the market that characterized the end of the Cold War in Chile and beyond? At an institutional level, CENMA's troubles reflected poor coordination with the University of Chile. For the university, hosting the center was expensive and the benefits diffuse; the university's initial support for CENMA had been dependent on state funding. The relationship between CENMA and the School of Engineering was informal, and no provisions were made for the center to cultivate a cooperative relationship with the School of Natural Sciences or the ecology department. Given the scarcity of resources within the university, some natural scientists saw in CENMA opportunities to fund their own work. The center's structure thus set it up to fail; although CONAMA had legal responsibility and defined its priorities, CENMA's director was chosen by the university chancellor from among tenured faculty. Changes at the university combined with lack of funding for research as well as long-standing intellectual rivalries conspired to force CENMA to veer sharply between two kinds of science—one set by CONAMA to produce regulatory or "applied" science, such as that done by engineers on pollution, and one set by the university to produce "basic" science of interest to natural scientists, for publication in indexed journals.[57]

Beyond the university, CENMA was also crippled by the weaknesses inherent in Chile's environmental legislation, and specifically by the limitations placed on the new environmental commission, CONAMA. At most, the agency could do office-desk enforcement. CONAMA could not do surprise inspections or take samples of effluent for an independent analysis; under the environmental framework law, it had no mandate to enforce environmental quality and emission standards. For this reason, and as anticipated by right-wing legislators, CONAMA had no need for data about pollutants, emissions, or the environmental quality of air or water bodies—the kind of information that CENMA was designed to collect.

At a more fundamental level, CENMA's troubles also reflect shifting views of scientific credibility as Chile transitioned to a market society. In the 1980s, Igor Saavedra distinguished First from Third World science. The former he described as basic, of excellence, and oriented at answering the "big questions" of life and the universe. The latter was, by contrast, applied and aimed at finding solutions to development problems related to poverty, disease, or hunger. Twenty years later, CENMA found itself torn between similar categories, with few people in CONAMA or the University of Chile sympathetic to the potential for CENMA to produce a kind of "Third World knowledge." Their lack of sympathy might have reflected CONAMA's limited mandate. Neither could they respect CENMA as a First World scientific center—its support did not come from the United States and its outputs did not seem destined for publication in top-tier academic journals.[58] CENMA seemed ideally placed to answer the hopes articulated by scientists at the CIPMA meetings, when the environment seemed an opportunity for scientists to "prove their worth to the man on the street." Instead, in the 1990s, scientists largely turned their backs on CENMA and saw no useful role for this kind of center in environmental management.[59]

After 2000, CENMA tried to reinvent itself as a national reference center. Assisted by Canada's environmental agency, the center purchased equipment and trained to obtain International Organization for Standardization (ISO) 17.025 certification, which certifies that a lab is competent to test and calibrate equipment and materials, thus ensuring the traceability of data. Global mining companies often require ISO 17.025, making this a seemingly ideal opportunity—it could have provided a valuable social service and generated revenue for CENMA. But the weakness of Chilean environmental regulations again undermined the center; because Chilean law does not require ISO 17.025, mining companies were unwilling to pay a premium for laboratory work that met international standards.[60]

CENMA then followed the path outlined by legislators: to compete for funding as if on a level playing field. The center's scientists were forced to compete against consultants and university-based scientists for contracts disbursed through a highly regulated "public market" that all state agencies are required to use.[61] These tenders are widely perceived to privilege price over quality; the cheapest science always wins, with negative consequences for data collection efforts over time or analysis that requires specialized equipment or robust, interdisciplinary teams. A former CENMA director minced no words in criticizing public tenders for environmental information, calling them "the greatest imbecility the world has ever seen." He also denounced a global double standard; multilateral organizations advise the Chilean government "that the market is the only thing that works and to get rid of everything else . . . but look how [the US government] funnels money into the Environmental Protection Agency and all its scientific capacity, all paid for by the state."[62] In 2019, after resisting earlier attempts, CENMA was forced to close.

Reflections on Neoliberalism and Science

Without stable public funding, CENMA had to reinvent itself—as a state-run lab providing strategic advice for regulation, as a national reference center, and as the provider of contract-based consulting services for industry.

Yet in all these visions, CENMA never tried to become a public interest lab committed to protecting the environment. Instead, as CENMA invested in ISO certifications and turned to contract work, it became more like any other commercial laboratory without the special status a public institution might have. Since the military coup of 1973, the University of Chile has faced a parallel crisis, and public support for science—whether applied, basic, environmental, or something else—has not improved. Despite paying lip service to the importance of science and technology, no democratic government has increased funding for scientific research beyond half a percentage point of gross domestic product.[63] For the University of Chile, the situation is dire; at a time when rival private universities have been investing in high-tech, scientific campuses on Santiago's outskirts, the University of Chile has lacked the financial, human, and political resources to even envision such a project.

Compared to the 1980s, when scientists championed the possibilities that "interdisciplinary" environmental science might create, scientists have adopted increasingly narrow understandings of what constitutes worthy and credible science. In interviews, many scientists dismissed CENMA as "too applied," "too technical," or "not able to attract the best scientists because it is not sufficiently academic." They complained they did not know what CENMA was—a think tank, a consulting company, a scientific center or something else.[64] In a census of Chilean scientists, the Academy of Sciences defines scientists as people publishing their work in indexed academic journals, a definition that resonates with Saavedra's First World science ideals, but ignores the possibilities for Third World science such as that produced by CENMA. It is also a definition that puts scientists far from the world of policymaking and the realm of technocrats. In the period analyzed here, technocrats included different professionals who subscribed to neoliberal, moderate, free-market principles and were able to translate their ideas into coherent policy proposals. One major shift involved political parties: during the dictatorship technocrats were unattached to traditional political parties whereas in the new democracy their status depended on developing an intimate relationship with a specific party. By contrast to technocrats, scientists were divided along disciplinary lines (engineers vs. ecologists) and cultural lines (applied vs. basic science). These divisions, alongside the structural conditions detailed above, held back scientists' public influence.

At the same time, the role of environmental scientists—and their potential to influence policy—was clearly conditioned by the Chilean state's embrace of free-market principles during the dictatorship and transition to democracy. The itineraries of the experts discussed in this chapter were shaped by the constrained political landscape during the Concertación years as, for example, industrial representatives and private consulting companies shared a seat at the table with professional scientists. They were also impacted by the economic landscape that severely limited public funding for scientific research and pushed the work of knowledge creation from universities and government agencies to private think tanks and consultancies. If the Latin American Cold War was characterized, to a significant extent, by the increase in international funding for targeted, strategic research to promote development and modernization, the end of the conflict—together with the accompanying entrenchment of neoliberal ideology—brought with it a shift from public to private funding of expertise. As this case and other chapters in this volume demonstrate, expertise is not a "pure, disembodied set of principles" that travel from place to place, but a body of knowledge deeply tied to local practices and political processes.[65]

Notes

1. Erns Hajek, "Medio Ambiente, Desarrollo y Academia," *Ambiente y Desarrollo* 3, no. 1–2 (1987): 11–16, quote on 13.

2. See the introduction to this volume for many relevant works.

3. María Angélica Illanes, *En el nombre del pueblo, del Estado y de la ciencia: Historia social de la salud pública en Chile, 1880–1973* (Santiago: Colectivo de Atención Primaria, 1993); Thomas M. Klubock, *La Frontera: Forests and Ecological Conflict in Chile's Frontier Territory* (Durham, NC: Duke University Press, 2014); and Heidi Tinsman, *Buying into the Regime: Grapes and Consumption in Cold War Chile and the United States* (Durham, NC: Duke University Press, 2014).

4. Patricio Silva, *In the Name of Reason: Technocrats and Politics in Chile* (University Park: Pennsylvania State University Press, 2009); Patricio Silva, "Lastarria, Letelier and 'Scientific Politics' in Chile," *Bicentenario. Revista de historia de Chile y América* 5, no. 2 (2006): 85–114.

5. The term *petty politics* is used by Daniel Levy, "Chilean Universities under the Junta: Regime and Policy," *Latin American Research Review* 21, no. 3 (1986): 95–128. See also Eden Medina, *Cybernetic Revolutionaries: Technology and Politics in Allende's Chile* (Cambridge, MA: MIT Press, 2011).

6. Manuel Tironi and Javiera Barandiarán, "Neoliberalism as Political Technology: Expertise, Energy, and Democracy in Chile," in *Beyond Imported Magic: Essays on Science, Technology, and Society in Latin America*, ed. Eden Medina, Ivan Costa Marquez, and Christina Holmes, (Cambridge, MA: MIT Press, 2014), 305–330; Patricio Silva, "Technocrats and Politics in Chile: From the Chicago Boys to the CIEPLAN Monks," *Journal of Latin American Studies* 23, no. 2 (1991): 385–410.

7. P. Silva, "Technocrats and Politics," 385.

8. See, for example, Ann Campbell Keller, *Science in Environmental Policy: The Politics of Objective Advice* (Cambridge, MA: MIT Press, 2009); Abby Kinchy, *Seeds, Science, and Struggle: The Global Politics of Transgenic Crops* (Cambridge, MA: MIT Press, 2012); Sheila Jasanoff, *The Fifth Branch: Science Advisers as Policymakers* (Cambridge, MA: Harvard University Press,

1990); and Roger Pielke, *The Honest Broker: Making Sense of Science in Policy and Politics* (Cambridge: Cambridge University Press, 2007).

9. David Carruthers, "Environmental Politics in Chile: Legacies of Dictatorship and Democracy," *Third World Quarterly* 22, no. 3 (2001): 343–358; Eduardo Silva, "From Dictatorship to Democracy: Business-State Nexus in Chile's Economic Transformation, 1975–1994," *Comparative Politics* 28 (April 1996): 299–320; and Javiera Barandiarán, "The Authority of Rules in Chile's Contentious Environmental Politics," *Environmental Politics* 25, no. 6 (July 11, 2016): 1013–1033.

10. P. Silva, *In the Name of Reason*; and Sebastián Ureta, *Assembling Policy: Transantiago, Human Devices, and the Dream of a World-Class Society* (Cambridge, MA: MIT Press, 2015).

11. Javiera Barandiarán, *Science and Environment in Chile: The Politics of Expert Advice in a Neoliberal Democracy* (Cambridge, MA: MIT Press, 2018).

12. Verónica Valdivia Ortiz de Zárate, *El golpe después del golpe: Leigh vs. Pinochet* (Santiago: LOM Editores, 2003). See also Arturo Valenzuela, "The Military in Power: The Consolidation of One-Man Rule," in *The Struggle for Democracy in Chile*, ed. Paul Drake and Iván Jaksic (Lincoln: University of Nebraska Press, 1995), 21–72.

13. Valdivia, *El golpe*. On the importance of terror, specifically the Caravana de la Muerte, to the consolidation of Pinochet's power, see Carlos Huneeus, *El régimen de Pinochet* (Santiago: Editorial Sudamericana, 2000).

14. Huneeus, *El régimen de Pinochet*, chap. 7 explains *Gremialismo* and the power of its leader, Jaime Guzmán. Of particular importance, in 1970 *gremialistas* won control of the student federation at the Catholic University. They used this platform to oppose Allende's government and promote adherence to Pinochet's government.

15. Huneeus, *El régimen de Pinochet*, chap. 8 identifies four different policy phases the Chicago Boys went through. In Chile and beyond, neoliberal thought is heterogeneous and dynamic. See, for instance, Philip Mirowski and Dieter Plehwe, *The Road from Mont Pelerin: The Making of a Neoliberal Thought Collective* (Cambridge, MA: Harvard University Press, 2009).

16. Many within the government opposed the Chicago Boys; see Valenzuela, "Military in Power"; and Valdivia Ortiz de Zárate, *El golpe después del golpe*.

17. Guillermo Geisse, "Presentación," *Ambiente y Desarrollo* 1, no. 1 (1984): 7–11, quote on 7.

18. Interview with Guillerno Geisse, December 10, 2010.

19. See, for instance, *Ambiente y Desarrollo* 3, no. 1–2 (1987) and 7, no. 1 (1991).

20. Alberto Gyhra Soto, "Universidad, medio ambiente y desarrollo," *Ambiente y Desarrollo* 5, no. 1 (1989): 79–83; José Valencia, "La organización internacional del programa El Hombre y la Biosfera (MAB)," *Ambiente y Desarrollo* 2, no. 1 (1986): 107–110. The UNESCO biodiversity project was so important that it is mentioned in Vivian Montecino and Julieta Orlando, eds., *Ciencias ecológicas 1983–2013: treinta años de investigaciones chilenas* (Santiago: Editorial Universitaria, 2015).

21. Igor Saavedra, "Nuestra comunidad científica y sus obligaciones locales y globales," *Ambiente y Desarrollo* 1, no. 1 (1984): 15–18.

22. Saavedra, "Nuestra comunidad científica," 16.

23. Igor Saavedra, "El regreso de los científicos," *Ambiente y Desarrollo* 2, no. 3 (1986): 133–148.

24. Saavedra, "El regreso"; see also the life story of the physiologist Hector Croxatto, in Maria Roblero, *Promesas del asombro: Hector Croxatto: Un pionero de la ciencia experimental en Chile* (Santiago: Ediciones Universidad Católica de Chile, 1995).

25. Fernanda Beigel, ed., *The Politics of Academic Autonomy in Latin America* (Surrey: Ashgate, 2013); Federico Vasen, "What Does a 'National Science' Mean? Science Policy, Politics and Philosophy in Latin America," in *Science Studies During the Cold War and Beyond*, ed. Elena Aranova and Simone Turchetti (New York: Palgrave Macmillan, 2016), 241–265; Montecino and Orlando, *Ciencias ecológicas*; and Geisse interview.

26. Beigel, *Politics of Academic Autonomy*; Vasen, "What Does a 'National Science' Mean?"; Hebe Vessuri, *"O inventamos o erramos": La ciencia como idea-fuerza en América Latina* (Bernal: Universidad Nacional de Quilmes Editorial, 2007).

27. Beigel, *Politics of Academic Autonomy*; and Roblero, *Promesas del asombro*.

28. Saavedra, "El regreso."

29. Pamela Constable and Arturo Valenzuela, *A Nation of Enemies: Chile under Dictatorship,* (New York: W. W. Norton, 1991); Jorge Nef, "Environmental Policy and Politics in Chile: A Latin American Case Study," in *Environmental Policies in the Third World: A Comparative Analysis*, ed. O. P. Dwivedi (Westport, CT: Greenwood Press, 1995), 145–174.

30. Geisse interview.

31. Daniel Levy, *Building the Third Sector: Latin America's Private Research Centers and Nonprofit Development* (Pittsburgh: University of Pittsburgh Press, 1996); and P. Silva, *In the Name of Reason.*

32. Saavedra, "Nuestra comunidad científica," 15; Hector Croxatto echoes this sentiment in "La miseria y el ingenio: Comentario al discurso inaugural del Segundo Encuentro Científico del Medio Ambiente," *Ambiente y Desarrollo* 3, no. 1–2 (1987): 24–25.

33. This shift is borne out in several *Ambiente y Desarrollo* articles, and by Geisse. He recalled that the first meeting attracted human rights groups, students, and political journalists, mining industry representatives, and "at least one" *gremialista*. The second meeting was sufficiently high-profile to attract the US ambassador and be reported in the *Wall Street Journal*.

34. *Ambiente y Desarrollo* 7, no. 1 (1991). This special issue contains detailed proposals from each group convened by CIPMA. I am including as "industry representatives" individuals who worked for public organizations that were dedicated to promoting industry such as the State Development Corporation (Corporación de Fomento a la Producción, also known as CORFO). Representation was more balanced in the groups on fisheries and agriculture. The detailed proposal for the group on "industrial and urban environments" is not available.

35. Eduardo Silva, "Democracy, Market Economics, and Environmental Policy in Chile," *Journal of Inter-American Studies and World Affairs* 38, no. 4 (1996): 1–33; and Levy, *Building the Third Sector.*

36. Geisse interview, and interview with Patricio Rodrigo, December 28, 2010.

37. Alfredo Joignant, "The Politics of Technopols: Resources, Political Competence and Collective Leadership in Chile, 1990–2010," *Journal of Latin American Studies* 43, no. 3 (2011): 517–546.

38. Interview with Juan Escudero, June 9, 2011.

39. Ricardo Katz, "El rol de las empresas en la conservación ambiental: Sector industrial: una visión económica," *Ambiente y Desarrollo* 4, no. 1–2 (1988): 107–109; and Katz, "Incentivos y regulación: Una coexistencia necesaria," *Ambiente y Desarrollo* 6, no. 3 (1990): 76–80.

40. Ricardo Katz, "Diálogo entre empresarios e investigadores: El caso de la contaminación," *Ambiente y Desarrollo* 4, no. 1–2 (1988): 137–150.

41. Geisse interview.

42. Rodrigo interview; Carruthers, "Environmental Politics in Chile"; E. Silva, "From Dictatorship to Democracy"; Barandiarán, "Authority of Rules"; David Tecklin, Carl Bauer, and Manuel Prieto, "Making Environmental Law for the Market: The Emergence, Character and Implications of Chile's Environmental Regime," *Environmental Politics* 20, no. 6 (2011): 879–898.

43. Barandiarán, *Science and Environment in Chile*; Legislative History 19.300, pp. 435, 500–507 and 923; Law 19.300, article 78(c). Legislative histories are compiled by Chile's National Library and include the congressional discussion leading up to an approved law, in this case Environmental Law 19.300, approved in 1994.

44. Similarly, Jaime Illanes (also active in CIPMA on behalf of industry) founded Gestión Ambiental, S.A. The other major consulting agency, Geotecnia (today Arcadis), has been close to the Christian Democrats and Socialist parties. During the Piñera administration, several GAC employees took high-profile positions, including the environment minister, María Ignacia Benítez, who had worked with Katz since ODEPLAN in the 1980s. In 2015, the socialist president Michelle Bachelet appointed a committee to advise on reforms to environmental impact assessments. Two-thirds of its members came from consulting firms, particularly Arcadis. See *Informe final de la Comisión Asesora Presidencial para la evaluación del SEIA* (2016), http://portal.mma.gob.cl/wp-content/doc/35877_Informe-MMAF_FINAL.pdf.

45. See also Tecklin, Bauer, and Prieto, "Making Environmental Law." This shift mimics that of the US environmental movement, as described by Robert Gottlieb, "Beyond NEPA and Earth Day: Reconstructing the Past and Envisioning a Future for Environmentalism," *Environmental History Review* 19, no. 4 (1995): 1–14.

46. Levy, *Building the Third Sector*; P. Silva, *In the Name of Reason*.

47. Neantro Saavedra-Rivano, "Chile and Japan: Opening Doors through Trade," in *Japan, the United States, and Latin America*, ed. Barbara Stallings and Gabriel Szekely (Baltimore: Johns Hopkins University Press, 1993), 191–209.

48. Escudero interview; interview with Toshimi Koyabachi, June 24, 2011; interview with Eugenio Figueroa, June 7, 2011; "Terminal Evaluation: The National Center for the Environment Project [Chile]" (2002), available from JICA; and "Letter" (June 23, 1993), from Jaime Lavados (Chancellor of the University of Chile) to Enrique Silva (Minister of Foreign Relations) noting JICA's opposition to putting the center within the university. Available from the author.

49. Legislative History 19.300, pp. 1002–1013.

50. Neoliberals believe that the market is the best information processor available, far superior to any human organization. See Mirowski and Plehwe, *Road from Mont Pelerin*; and for an application to the Chilean case, see Barandiarán, *Science and Environment in Chile*.

51. "The minutes of meeting between the Japanese implementation survey team and the authorities concerned of the Government of the Republic of Chile on the Japanese technical cooperation for the National Center for the Environment project," January 18, 1995, signed by Hiroshi Goto (JICA), Goñi (CONAMA), Lavados (U. Chile), and Soler (AGCI Chile). Available from the author.

52. Escudero interview; "Curriculum institucional del Centro Nacional de Medio Ambiente," July 2014, available from CENMA; and "CENMA Annual Report" (1999), available at the Environment Ministry library.

53. "Funding Agreement" (August 11, 2000), signed by Adriana Hoffman (CONAMA), Juan Escudero (CENMA), Luis Bahamonde (University of Chile), and Jumpei Watanabe (JICA). Available from the author.

54. Figueroa interview; "Letter," November 17, 2000, from Luis Riveros (chancellor of the University of Chile) to Pablo Ulricksen (CENMA), complaining that CONAMA's contribution to CENMA was cut to one-third of CENMA's needs; and "Letter," November 2, 2000, from Riveros to Adriana Hoffman (director of CONAMA) complaining of budget cuts. Both available from the author.

55. CONAMA–CENMA Agreements 2008, 2009, and 2010, available from Environment Ministry library.

56. Interviews with CENMA scientists and site visits by the author in June 2011, September 2014, and September 2015; "Letter," July 9, 2013, from Victor Perez (chancellor University of Chile) to CENMA informing them the university will close the center; "Letter," August 6, 2013, from CENMA's workers union protesting this decision; and Manuel Merino, "Inminente cierre del Centro Nacional del Medio Ambiente de la U. de Chile," in *Diario U Chile*, September 4, 2017, http://radio.uchile.cl/2017/09/04/inminente-cierre-del-centro-nacional-del-medio-ambiente-de-la-u-de-chile/.

57. Figueroa and CENMA scientists interviews; "Prof. Eugenio Figueroa es el nuevo Director Ejecutivo del CENMA," in Archivo de Actividades del Rector, April 2, 2003, http://www.uchile.cl/acerca/rectoria/noticias/02abril2003.html; "CENMA Annual Report" (1999). Available from Environment Ministry library.

58. These attitudes are examined in greater depth in Barandiarán, *Science and Environment in Chile*.

59. Scientists' disregard is evident, for example, in that CENMA is not mentioned in a history of ecology and biology at the University of Chile, written by Montecino and Orlando, *Ciencias Ecológicas*, or in *Ambiente y Desarrollo*.

60. Figueroa and CENMA scientists interviews and site visit.

61. For more on the Chilean case, see Barandiarán, *Science and Environment in Chile*, and Beatriz Bustos, "Producción de conocimiento en Chile y el caso de la crisis salmonera," in *Ecología política en Chile: naturaleza, propiedad, conocimiento y poder*, ed. Beatriz Bustos, Manuel Prieto, and Jonathan Barton (Santiago: Editorial Universitaria, 2014), 193–212. For a description of parallel transformation in the United States, see Philip Mirowski, *Science-Mart: Privatizing American Science* (Cambridge, MA: Harvard University Press, 2011).

62. Figueroa interview.

63. Jorge Allende et al., *Análisis y proyecciones de la ciencia chilena* (Santiago: Academia Chilena de Ciencias, Consejo de Sociedades Científicas de Chile, 2005); and Juan A. Asenjo, *Una integración real de Chile a la sociedad del conocimiento: el incremento de la inversión en ciencia y tecnología es condición para el desarrollo del país* (Santiago: Academia Chilena de Ciencias, 2013).

64. These views are explored in more detail in Barandiarán, *Science and Environment in Chile.*

65. Chastain and Lorek, Introduction to this volume.

CONCLUSION

NEW NARRATIVES OF TECHNOLOGY, EXPERTISE, AND ENVIRONMENT IN LATIN AMERICA

The Cold War and Beyond

Eden Medina and Mark Carey

At the opening ceremony of the 2016 summer Olympic games in Rio de Janeiro, the Brazilian organizers sent a luminescent airplane flying from the stadium into the night sky, a stunning spectacle that also challenged the conventional history of technology. The person in the cockpit represented the Brazilian, Alberto Santos-Dumont, who in 1906 became the first person to fly a heavier-than-air machine that achieved liftoff on its own propulsion. The history of flight told in the opening ceremony spectacle positioned Brazil as a world technological leader by toppling the traditional prominence of the Wright Brothers at Kitty Hawk. Brazilians have long held Dumont's accomplishment as evidence that Brazil invented the airplane, a claim they now repeated with the world watching, telling a national story of technological prowess that linked Brazil to one of the most important technological marvels of the twentieth century. Such emphasis on Brazilian, and by extension Latin American, contributions to technology history is essential to making the history of technology a global one by decentering traditional understandings of innovation and invention and putting Latin American accomplishments on equal scientific and technological footing with those of their neighbors to the north. Yet the story of Dumont also represents a trope that limits the ways people understand the technological past: it takes a moment of technological invention, views it in the context of national capability, and then evaluates the modernity of that nation in relation to that of a more industrialized nation, in this case the United States. It also repeats a narrative that defines progress as humans building machines to conquer limitations imposed by the environment.[1]

This volume helps overcome and dismantle these types of national boundaries and the binaries of traditional core–periphery and North–South framings, which continue to exist in the popular imagination even when new narratives emerge to push back against US-centrism as in the case of Dumont at the 2016 Rio Olympics. The book's focus on the Cold War period is apt for these discussions of the history of technology and environmental history. The Cold War period, after all, gave rise to popular stories about science, technology, and the environment in Latin America that framed scientific and technological prowess largely as they were understood in the North and universalized these understandings during that period as hallmarks of modernity. The stories often positioned highly developed regions of the world (such as the United States) in the center, placed peoples from Latin America on the periphery, and described global dynamics in terms of the nation state with people and organizations operating within its bounds or on its behalf. Notions of expertise within these framings privileged certain kinds of knowledge and experts: those from the Global North (e.g., the United States and Western Europe) or, less often, those in Latin America working with—but subordinate to—foreign experts with access to Western knowledge, engineering, and technology. Such frames also viewed physical, nonhuman environments as sources of raw materials for production or consumption or as obstacles to progress that should be overcome. The recent historiographies on the history of technology and environmental history of Latin America, of which this volume is part, have begun to overturn these simplistic narratives by adding nuance through ground-level analyses of Cold War historical processes and actors.

Despite historiographical advances, the problematic popular narrative of a technologically advanced United States and the less developed Latin America continues to persist in the twenty-first century. Even cases that celebrate Latin American technical prowess, like that of Dumont, or the Incas who built Machu Picchu, or the Maya who constructed Tikal, can also carry an underlying message of amazement because, evidently, architectural and engineering leadership were not supposed to emerge from Latin America. These celebratory accounts reify the flip side of the binary, too, in which the media circulates stories of migrant trains with "hordes" clamoring to abandon the economically unstable, technologically backward, and environmentally impoverished Central America and Mexico for the promised

land of the United States. Such racist and historically uninformed portray-
als persist, necessitating a need for new narratives of technology and the
environment.

Much of the scholarship we discuss in the following sections—including
the work in this volume—addresses the need for stories about technology
and expertise that do not present Latin American experiences as peripheral
or as needing to be measured in relation to those of nations with greater economic or geopolitical power. This body of scholarship works to refine narratives of Latin American landscapes, natural resources, and environments
to show that the region was not simply the "backyard" for the imperialists
from the North to conquer, contaminate, extract, and destroy—but rather
were landscapes constructed and produced through complex interchanges
among a host of historical actors, even when imperialism did, in fact, deplete
physical environments. This volume, in particular, makes important strides
in challenging the center–periphery dichotomy by giving greater attention to
the complex ways that technologies, experts, and ideas travel and change in
the course of their travels. Moreover, it puts forth a frame of historical analysis that focuses on multiple actors and processes, not just the state. Four
key themes stand out in this volume regarding the ways we tell the history
of technology and the environment in Latin America during the long Cold
War. The book (1) helps dismantle core–periphery frameworks; (2) redefines
technology, nature, and expertise; (3) decenters the state; and (4) further
uncovers a diversity of expertise and multiple knowledges. After some historiographical and historical background, we discuss each of these four themes
and the relevant literature that these chapters engage, align with, and help
advance. Through this discussion we show how this volume builds on recent
historiographical developments to create a richer understanding of Latin
American expertise during the Cold War.

Historiographical Background and Context

The Cold War era helped generate new stories of environment and technology that spread widely during the period, even though such ways of telling
history had existed before 1945. For example, the modernization theories
that emerged in the 1950s and 1960s, such as Walt Rostow's well-known theory of economic growth, presented technologies of industrial manufacture
as both representations of and conduits to the pinnacle of human progress.[2]
In his 1967 article, "The Spread of Western Science," George Basalla further
applied such economic thinking to science and technology, suggesting that
knowledge and expertise could only develop in Europe and then subsequent-
ly flow into places such as Latin America.[3] These theories posited the industrialized nations in the North, especially the United States and Britain, as a

universal ideal and influenced how those in both the North and the South understood the historical development of Latin America and its relation to Western technology. To assert the role of Latin American experts and expertise is therefore to interrogate not only how expertise was employed on the ground but also the kinds of stories we tell about these efforts.

In the 1960s and 1970s, however, Latin American economists from the United Nations Economic Commission for Latin America (ECLA) began articulating an alternative theory that connected technological capability with economic development, which became known as dependency theory.[4] Replacing the universal path to modernity put forth by scholars such as Rostow and Basalla, dependency theory categorized nations as either developed or developing, drawing attention to inequalities that permitted more-developed nations to amass wealth at the expense of developing nations and providing a theoretical underpinning for understanding why Latin American nations could not follow the same trajectory of economic development as the United States. Yet it too defined Latin American development in terms of increased industrialization and the acquisition of technologies and expertise from elsewhere.

Dependency theory also divided the world into a series of connected dichotomies: developed–underdeveloped, urban–rural, North–South, center–periphery. Although it allowed for a greater diversity of experiences, it also continued to position parts of the world as having less status than others. The classic representation of these themes was Eduardo Galeano's 1971 book, *The Open Veins of Latin America*, which exposed the severe political, economic, human, and environmental impacts of centuries of European and US exploitation of Latin America.[5] But Galeano also reinforced the binary positions of developed–underdeveloped and exploiter–exploited while offering a universal declensionist narrative, which is a history characterized by human suffering, Western intervention, and environmental catastrophe in Latin America, leading to worsening decline.

These tropes, exemplified by Galeano and reinforced by many during the 1970s and 1980s, had an enduring influence on the ways in which the general public and scholars portrayed expertise, foreign presence, and environmental change in Latin America. The accounts from the Cold War and immediate post–Cold War period tended to depict power, knowledge, expertise, technologies, and environmental management as flowing from the Global North and as inflicted on relatively passive or naive Latin Americans.[6] By the 1980s, however, dependency theory had begun to shape histories of technology and create new stories that were less Eurocentric. For example, scholars began to focus on how the specificities of Latin America's past created a different context for science and technology, including studies of how Latin Americans received and developed ideas from elsewhere, developed local and national scientific and technological capabilities, and worked under conditions of adversity and scarcity.[7]

These historiographical moves throughout the 1980s and 1990s helped reject the idealization of Western Europe and North America and the positioning of Latin American technological capabilities as lagging behind those of more industrial nations. As scholars began to rethink simplistic core-periphery Cold War frameworks, they also began to more fully recognize the role of Latin Americans in the production of knowledge and to chronicle environmental initiatives and impacts by Latin Americans and within Latin America. As Thomas Glick observed, "One problem with the conceptualization of peripherality is that it cannot explain how pockets of 'central' science emerge on the periphery."[8] Marcos Cueto further argued that scientific expertise and technologies could emerge in sophisticated ways on the periphery, such as the high-elevation studies of human physiology conducted in Peru, thereby decentering the focus on Europe and the United States.[9] This scholarship on Latin America fit into a larger historiographical trend of uncovering the geography of science, knowledge, and technology; demonstrating how place influenced the production of knowledge; and showing that scientific knowledge and expertise were not universal. Indeed, claims of universality in science often served to perpetuate power imbalances that privileged those from Western Europe and the United States.[10] As part of this shift in scholarship on Latin America, researchers underscored important contributions made by those in Latin America to the history of science and technology from the colonial period to the present—whether through the recognition of indigenous knowledge systems that preexisted the arrival of Western science, the development of successful research programs despite conditions of adversity, or indigenous people's contributions to early European scientific studies and the Scientific Revolution.[11] Other strands of research examined the role of science, engineering, and expertise to processes of nation-building and state formation.[12]

By the twenty-first century, scholarship on expertise was already challenging and dissecting the binaries reified during the Cold War period—particularly in studies of knowledge, technology, and environment.[13] Scholars have clearly been showing, for example, that public health commissions from the United States intended to bring medical enlightenment to Latin America brought with them knowledge and expertise that already existed in Mexico, Central America, and South America, and sometimes even irrelevant medical knowledge and technologies that represented a step backward.[14] Scholarship on the geography of knowledge and expertise has persistently decentered the role of Europe and North America, such as in Stuart McCook's conceptualization of "creole science" or Pablo Gómez's study of how members of black Caribbean communities in the long seventeenth century created authoritative knowledge of the natural world.[15] At the same time, this work has also recognized that new technologies, sciences, and engineering schemes that foreigners took to Latin America were not always exploitative, that local people did not always reject those new experts or technologies, and that Latin American environments were not characterized solely by decline and destruction.[16] Scholars today have been influenced by these historiographical impulses to write more cultural and/or place-based histories of technology and the environment.[17] This work gives heightened attention to analyzing dynamics as they unfold on the ground, where Latin Americans have played an active role, and with messy boundaries and fluid intersections of North–South, nature–culture, and expert–layperson. This volume, to which we now turn, engages with and contributes to these tendencies.

Beyond Dependency and the Core–Periphery Framework

One way in which the chapters in this volume advance our understanding of technology and environment in Latin America is by challenging traditional frameworks that position Latin Americans as passive recipients of technology, knowledge, and expertise from the North. Every author pushes back against deterministic views that overemphasize the role of foreign actors in Latin America and minimize the contributions of Latin American governments, organizations, and peoples. They help further upend narratives that liken technology to a form of "imported magic" that is somewhat mysterious and comes from somewhere else.[18] The Cold War focus of this book brings more nuance to the way we understand the shortcomings of these frames. Recent scholarship on the history of technology and environmental history of Latin America has, of course, also moved away from a core–periphery framework that portrays technological innovation and environmental destruction as emanating primarily from the United States or Western Europe. Indeed, a number of works show the messy and important ways that social groups struggled for power, created technologies, and remade landscapes through contested, ground-level processes.[19] Therefore, the innovation in this volume resides in its numerous case studies, their richness, the explicit focus on examples drawn from everyday life, and the prominent focus on the long Cold War period. It is perhaps even more commendable that the authors eschew core–periphery representations given that the Cold War was a quintessential era for foreign intervention in Latin America. Chapters in this volume also foreground the ways in which Latin Americans from different communities, countries, professional affiliations, and social strata shaped the direction and the form of Latin American material culture, the cultivation and exercise of expertise, the creation of landscapes and environments, and the design of initiatives, policies, and projects in various domains, such as housing, literacy, transportation, science, environmental governance, natural resource extraction, and agriculture.

The works in this volume defy typical dependency and core–periphery constructions in multiple ways, including recognizing the impact of local environments and contexts on the way Latin Americans shaped their technologies and environmental landscapes during the Cold War. For example, Mary Roldán's study (chapter 4) of the Colombian radiophonic school system developed by Father José Joaquin Salcedo ties the successful use of radio technology in rural Colombia to specific local and regional conditions. Andra B. Chastain (chapter 10) similarly traces the way experts constructed Santiago's metro system under President Frei as a local project, addressing Chilean needs rather than simply building from a mold or strict template imposed by foreign experts. The impact of local environments and actors on Cold War histories and historical processes is also illustrated by Emily Wakild's examination (chapter 11) of how the remote Manu National Park environment and the work of middle-level scientists, often women, affected the historical development of tropical ecology and conservation-related sciences in Peru. By revealing how a place-based geography of science and knowledge divulges a greater diversity of objectives, activities, and knowledges in the production of expertise, such analyses argue that expertise must always be understood as a dialogue not only among social actors but between people and nonhuman nature. By emphasizing a diverse range of experts and proposing alternative chronologies and periodizations that decenter the Global North, the examples and arguments found in this book connect environmental history with science and technology studies (STS).

Many of these chapters also recognize that knowledge and expertise flowed not simply from Europe and the United States to Latin America but also within and across Latin America. Timothy W. Lorek (chapter 3), for instance, traces the growth of Colombian agricultural expertise in the 1920s through a partnership between Colombians and Puerto Rican scientists who laid the foundations and innovations of the Green Revolution decades before it officially began after World War II. In fact, Lorek shows, when US agronomists working for the Rockefeller and Ford Foundations appeared in Colombia supposedly to bring technical expertise to South America, they followed in the footsteps of Puerto Ricans and their Colombian partners. Other chapters also offer excellent examples of expertise and knowledge developing within and across Latin America, including Thomas Rath's study (chapter 6) of animal disease laboratories in Mexico, Brazil, the United States, and the United Kingdom that shows how Mexican veterinarians created a "competing scientific modernism" that focused on cattle vaccination for foot-and-mouth disease and pushed back against the slaughter policies advocated by the United States. Collectively, these chapters highlight the many ways

that knowledge and expertise emerged within Latin America and circulated regionally, not just diffusing from Europe and the United States toward
Latin America. These rich examinations of intra- and inter–Latin American dynamics—particularly around histories of technology and technology
transfer—are still unusual insofar as the existing literature often focuses on
exchanges between Latin America and the Global North. The chapters by
Lorek and Rath thus offer new pathways to understand technology and environment within and across Latin America.

Furthermore, several of the chapters in this collection show that expertise can also flow in the reverse direction from the traditional core–periphery
framework, revealing that Latin Americans have offered key technologies,
engineering methods, and knowledge to the rest of the world. This insight is
not new, as researchers have for years been showing how indigenous knowledge contributed to Western science and technology, how Latin American
public health efforts surpassed medical expertise from abroad, how glacier
experts in Peru developed globally applicable engineering practices to prevent natural disasters, and how cybernetic ideas honed under Allende's government in Chile contributed to management ideas in the United States and
Europe, among others.[20] Chapters in this book further advance these ideas,
such as Mark Healey's discussion (chapter 8) of how architects in Colombia during the 1950s built houses and planned urban landscapes with a local
orientation—and with their own innovations, including the CINVA-RAM
block press that "would soon become a ubiquitous feature of community development projects worldwide." His example provides new insight into flows
of knowledge out of the Americas as well as across the region.

Lastly, these chapters situate Latin American technologies, practices,
and expertise not as peripheral to a more industrial metropole but as part of
larger transnational networks of expertise and exchange that cross nations,
communities, and continents. The volume thus contributes to a growing
body of transnational literature in the history of science and technology.[21]
The transnational frame employed in many of the contributions to this volume reveals in new ways how things, living beings, and ideas move in directions that challenge US- or European-centrism and break the North–South
paradigm. Reinaldo Funes-Monzote and Steven Palmer (chapter 5), for instance, delineate networks of exchange between Canada and Cuba that enabled the genetic transfer of bovine stock and the selective breeding of cattle
for more intensive milk production that grew out of Castro's explicit desire
to end Cuba's dependence on the United States and challenge Cold War geopolitics in the Americas. The authors thus draw our attention to less-studied
forms of dependency that arose during the Cold War period, including dependency on the Soviet Union, and the ways that geopolitics reconfigured
independent and dependent relationships among nations. The global satellite

network described by Pedro Ignacio Alonso and Hugo Palmarola (chapter 7)—including aspects of the NASA logo—similarly required the efforts of more than one nation and provides an example of how US technologies were dependent on Latin American support and the efforts of Latin American scientists, engineers, and governments. Fernando Purcell (chapter 9) brings a Latin American perspective to Christopher Sneddon's "concrete revolution" to show how dam construction in Latin America stemmed from the circulation of US experts in Latin America and the circulation of Latin American experts globally.[22] Whereas Cold War strategies to contain communism provided the impetus for US experts to travel south, Latin American experts sought to address national energy needs. Purcell's work thus advances recent work on the history of US engineers and technologies abroad. It shows more dialogue and interaction among experts while simultaneously recognizing the agency of Latin Americans, moves that shift the narrative away from a story of dams and development that center on the actions of those in the Global North, including US engineers and policymakers.

In other cases, Latin American experts fit directly into global trends, such as environmental governance and conservation. In Peru, Wakild argues, "Tropical ecology developed as a place-specific discipline in conjunction with remote, sparsely populated natural areas rather than inside museums and laboratories of Western institutions." Tore C. Olsson (chapter 2) shows how the Tennessee Valley Authority (TVA), "one of the United States' most significant intellectual exports after World War II" influenced two different river valley commissions in Mexico. His analysis shows how the experts and politicians involved in each of these hydraulic projects interpreted the TVA model in different ways and in the service of different Mexican political projects. And as Javiera Barandiarán demonstrates in chapter 12, environmental expertise and management also fit into both national and global networks and trends in Chile, taking on both a Chilean and a transnational nature. These works thus argue that analyses of local, regional, national, and global forces should not disregard but interrogate transnational forces and networks and examine them within social and environmental dynamics operating on multiple and intersecting scales of both space and time.

Redefining Technologies, Nature, and Expertise

Beyond their important contributions to our understandings of technology, nature, and technical expertise in Latin America during the long Cold War, the essays in this volume challenge and expand our usage and definitions of these terms themselves. For example, the term *technology* is often used to refer to machines, artifacts, and tools, a conception that has shaped previous works in Latin American technological history. These studies, which have included such topics as railroad history, industrial manufacture, and agricultural tools ranging from seed plows to mills to the technologies of the Green Revolution, have often viewed the construction, adoption, and use of these machines within the context of economic and labor history.[23] The notion of technology as a tool or mechanical artifact also appears in terms such as *technology transfer* or *appropriate technology*, which frequently surface in discussions of technology and Latin America during the Cold War. Chapters in this volume have furthered our current understanding of large-scale technological systems (such as electrical networks, dams, and metro trains) and consumer goods (such as radios) and examined the history of these machines and artifacts in relation not only to economics and labor politics but also to politics at the local, national, and transnational scale, to different communities of practice, and to ideas of modernity that have varied with time, place, and conditions of possibility.

However, the emphasis on expertise and practice in this volume also builds on other, earlier understandings of technology. As Eric Schatzberg has observed, in the nineteenth century the term *technology* referred to the language of a particular skill or art, including its principles, terminology, and teaching, making the notion of expertise central to how the concept of technology has been historically understood.[24] Indeed, the term derives from the combination of the Greek words *logos* (discourse) and *tekhne* (skill or art). The authors in this volume similarly pay attention to the ways that experts communicate their skills and how their expertise is understood in different contexts. As Alonso and Palmarola's chapter on the design of the NASA logo shows, expertise is performed in different ways and communicated through different linguistic forms: the logo not only formed part of the sociotechnical network of the US space program but also furthered its global presence and contributed to the success of the global satellite tracking system that the United States created for Cold War surveillance from the sky. Language, iconography, and discourse were all central aspects of the construction, circulation, and understanding of technologies and technological systems, thereby indicating a need to recognize and analyze the history of technology in these broad ways.

Other chapters in this volume draw from Latin American experiences to also push for broader and more diverse understandings of technology that extend beyond a simple reference to a machine, artifact, or expertise. A number of the contributors, for instance, actively blur the boundary between what is natural and what is human, thereby challenging the purity of either category. As the chapters by Funes-Mozote and Palmer and by Rath show, cows and viruses function as technologies when modified for milk production and vaccines. As Wakild's chapter illustrates, seemingly mundane practices such as clearing trails in the Peruvian jungle for wildlife observation are also practices that underpin the creation and exercise of scientific expertise. Lorek's chapter shows how trees can function as technologies when planted to shade livestock and smaller coffee and cacao plants. The natural thus becomes technological, and everyday low-tech practices carried out in places far from the laboratory, factory, or construction site, contribute to Latin American expertise and the creation of new knowledge.

Beyond their focus on broadening understandings of technology, the works in this volume further advance conceptualizations of nature and the environment. Understanding nature not simply as trees, rivers, animals, plants, natural resources, and parks, the chapters define environments more broadly, including nontraditional environmental landscapes—from roads and reservoirs to cities, soils, seeds, and fisheries—and hybrid natures, cultural landscapes, and dynamic social-ecological systems. Scholars such as Nancy Stepan and Simon Schama have long argued that nature is culture before it is natural, while others such as Richard White and Mark Fiege have underscored hybrid landscapes as central to the understanding of environmental history.[25] Authors in this volume such as Wakild, Lorek, Purcell, and Barandiarán align with this environmental history scholarship. But their effort to show that environments and landscapes are not just physical environments "out there" but hybrid landscapes adds an important dimension to the bibliography on Latin America: landscapes, they demonstrate, were created through discourse, narratives, and cultural processes. These cultural approaches to the environmental history of Latin America have increased in recent years, showing, for example, how literature, art, and music play important roles in creating and shaping physical environments, too.[26] Less often, however, is the cultural focus integrated into studies of environment, technology, science, and expertise.[27] The chapters in this volume incorporate this approach and thus respond to Stefania Gallini's call to break down nature–culture binaries through efforts that *culturize the natural sciences and naturalize the social sciences.*"[28]

This new cultural and technological focus in environmental history research is revealed in the essays in this volume not simply through the analysis of narratives and discourse but through showing how innovation and expertise have always been about more than just engineering or the practical application of knowledge. As Purcell's contribution illustrates, Latin American expertise in dam building and hydroelectricity generation hinged upon local and regional "imaginaries" of dam building and hydroelectric futures within Latin America. Although these massive infrastructure projects epitomized Cold War projects used by both the United States and the Soviet Union,[29] Purcell contends that Latin Americans played key roles in creating institutions, training experts, providing venues like conferences and exhibitions, developing university programs, and producing the *cultural* space needed for hydroelectricity experts to thrive within South America. Expertise, in other words, needed justification, rationalization, circulation, and cultural approval—and much of that occurred within Latin America, even in cases when the World Bank or foreign companies advocated for the infrastructure projects.

This book's research on historical imaginaries of infrastructures and engineered landscapes across Latin America corresponds with and contributes to other scholarship.[30] As Ashley Carse has argued in his depiction of hybrid environments in the Panama Canal Zone, "engineered canals and highways are surprisingly social and ecological."[31] Other scholarship has helped reframe concepts such as "technology," "the environment," and "nature," broadening critical views beyond machines, rain forests, and natural resources—and also opening opportunities for more collaboration across environmental history and the history of technology.[32] The work in this volume accomplishes this broader conceptualization of nature through the study of livestock exchanges (Funes-Monzote and Palmer), animal diseases (Rath), and dams (Purcell, Olsson), and others, demonstrating intersections among expert knowledge, technology, and environment that blur culture–nature boundaries and conceptualize infrastructure and engineered landscapes as hybrid social-ecological environments. Chapters in this volume show how the Cold War—and its traveling technocrats—ushered in new fantasies and utopian dreams about modernity and ways to remake, control, and harness both nonhuman nature and technologies. Technocrats imagined new urban spaces and housing designs, as in Healey's examination of Colombia's International Housing Lab. Others fantasized about enhanced agricultural productivity that would modernize the countryside in Latin America, which agronomists and other experts hoped could lead to new global configurations of agricultural systems and societies during the Cold War, as Lorek explains regarding Colombia. These changes were not exclusive to the capitalist world. Such ambitious projects for the countryside were also crucial in socialist Cuba after 1959, as Funes-Monzote and Palmer discuss.

As the chapters in this collection show, dialogue, exchanges, and interactions between Latin Americans and foreign experts during the Cold War thus created new understandings and visions of landscapes, environments, technologies, and possibilities. But as these studies also demonstrate, such views were always shaped locally and regionally as well as internationally. These visions of public health, infrastructure, industrial agriculture, livestock production, and urban planning were clearly held not just by technocrats arriving in Latin America from abroad or under the auspices of US and other international development agencies and government institutions. Rather, many Latin American actors held utopian visions of development whose contours were often shaped in subtle or overt ways by Cold War conflicts. This volume and other recent scholarship has helped make those actors' histories part of how we now understand Latin America's environmental and technological past. The focus here on imaginaries, narratives, discourse, and visions of Latin America's environment makes an important contribution by analyzing how people thought about these landscapes and imagined their possibilities. These diverse mental conceptualizations and understandings of the environment, in turn, shaped how peoples, organizations, and governments interacted with, used, and exerted control over the environment in material ways. Broadening the conceptualization of terms such as environment and technology permits this crucial cultural focus in environmental history and opens new directions for future scholarship.

Decentering the Nation-State

A third way the essays in this book advance our understanding of Latin American technology and environment is by challenging the strong grip that state and associated nation-building processes have held on the historiography of modern Latin America. For decades, scholars have illustrated the profound influence the state has had on processes of modernization, industrialization, economic development, infrastructure, natural resource extraction, and environmental governance.[33] Some of this work has illuminated the role of national elites in other parts of the world and how they, and their interlocutors, used science and technology to further programs and policies for social improvement, including programs for economic growth, social welfare, and improved infrastructure.[34] Other recent studies underscore the historical role of the state in landscape management, conservation, and environmental management more broadly.[35] Thus, just as the state has occupied a central role in how we understand the history of science and technology in Latin America, it has also influenced how we understand Latin American environmental history. A recent shift in scholarship, however, has expanded beyond the focus on the state's power in technology, science, and the environment to address, for instance, the private sector, indigenous knowledges, citizen science, and the transnational nature of scientific, technological, and environmental processes.[36]

The essays in this volume demonstrate a further decentering of the nation-state—including the United States and the Soviet Union as well as Latin American nations. They do not simply assume that the state is the dominant force but instead interrogate whether and to what degree the state was a pivotal actor during the Cold War. The chapters in this volume advance scholarship on the state in several specific ways, including our understanding of the relationship of science and technology to nation-building during the Cold War era in areas such as energy (Purcell), transportation (Chastain), and agriculture (Funes-Monzote and Palmer). The chapters also show how these efforts created different national imaginaries. Chapters that take a transnational and comparative approach also shed new light on the operations of the state. Thomas Rath, for example, examines how connections between England, the United States, Mexico, and Brazil shaped the trajectory of veterinary and public health research efforts within each of those nations that intersected with their specific state goals.

As this volume also demonstrates, an examination of the influence of local, regional, and other nonstate environmental forces can reveal other historical processes and drivers of change beyond the state, because physical encounters with animals, plants, rivers, glaciers, and weather cross national boundaries, and influence the production of knowledge. Acknowledging the role of nonhuman actors in the path of history is one way environmental historians have illuminated how human-nature dynamics, infrastructures, technologies, and environmental knowledge emerged outside the bounds of state or imperial structures. Wakild's discussion of tropical science and conservation in Peru, for example, uncovers popular forms of knowledge and a "middle modernism" (an alternative to James C. Scott's state-centric "high modernism"), consisting of complicated spaces and processes that did not fit neatly into either nation-building or grassroots spheres.[37] Indeed, the works in this volume present readers with a diversity of experts unaffiliated or only loosely affiliated with the state, including members of the church (Roldán), partners in private consulting firms (Barandiarán), residents of poor communities (Healey), Latin American veterinary and agricultural scientists (Rath, Lorek), and regional dam experts (Olsson). Considering the ways in which Latin America's historiography has focused so strongly on the role of the state, stronger even than the historiographies of other world regions, the chapters in this volume that focus on nonstate forces open up important pathways for future scholarship.[38]

The chapters in this volume advance the historiography in other ways by challenging conventional state-focused chronologies. In fact, the entire volume embraces the concept of a long Cold War, tracing precursors before World War II and identifying legacies well after 1989. This blurring of state-centered periodization in Latin America is not new among scholars, who have shown that conventional dividing lines, such as independence, can often be arbitrary, artifacts of custom rather than representative of underlying historical forces, issues, and processes. In other words, temporal periodizations that cling to state and political chronologies—not to mention spatial scales that try to restrict environmental processes to nation-state boundaries—may not always be appropriate when analyzing environmental histories.[39] As Christopher Boyer explains, for example, "a close examination of Mexico's modern environmental history leads to a substantially more complicated periodization."[40] In this volume, Lorek is one who challenges Cold War chronologies by rethinking Green Revolution narratives about agrarian development and agroenvironmental processes, thereby destabilizing conventional narratives of nature, decentering Cold War states, and undermining a declensionist narrative of nature in Latin America—all key interventions in Latin American historiography.[41] Barandiarán's chapter also shows the value of adopting a chronology based on shifts in expertise rather than in the state, exploring how the kind of experts with political influence changed markedly during the Pinochet dictatorship, from scientists and engineers to economists, and diminished the influence of Chilean natural and physical scientists.

Although this volume thus demonstrates the value of developing chronologies based on expertise, we should also be mindful of the possible pitfalls of such an approach. As David Edgerton has observed about chronologies based on technology, dividing the past into periods of electrification, motorization, or computerization entails making judgments about significance that are often based on the accomplishments or experiences of richer, more industrialized parts of the world and overlook the highly nuanced ways that technologies are used: technologies may originate well before their moment of peak influence and can continue to exert influence long after they have ceased to be novel, and old and new technologies and technological practices often exist side by side.[42] Applying these observations to the domain of expertise points to the importance of recognizing multiple forms of expertise and knowledge, the ways in which they can come together and exist simultaneously, and the diverse ways in which ideas gain traction and influence in different domains over extended periods of time and take on new kinds of significance.

Histories that focus on expertise can therefore not only push back against state-centered understandings of the past but also shed new light on the complex dynamics of historical processes and the diverse perspectives they contain. The book's analysis of local expertise, such as through the Green Revolution (Lorek) or the "concrete revolution" (Purcell, Olsson), shows a need to depart from a strict Cold War timeline of 1945 to 1989. A ground-level examination of expertise and environment illustrates pre-1945 forces and processes, necessitating this volume's conceptualization of a "long Cold War" that extends back to late nineteenth-century positivism and state expansion efforts into new territories. Whereas science and knowledge of environments and natural resources may have been more strongly tied to the nation-state at the outset of the Cold War, by the 1980s expertise had a more complex relationship with the state and its goals. As Wakild and Barandiarán show in their studies of biologists and environmental scientists, neoliberalism ushered in increased skepticism of scientific expertise.

In this way, the volume's decentering of the state actually has important implications for understanding the contours of the Cold War. Although programs such as the Alliance for Progress and the Green Revolution entered into Latin America with strong US support, everyday forms of Latin American expertise—including that of engineers, policymakers, farmers, and workers—also influenced global trajectories and state agendas. Future scholarship in this vein could perhaps uncover other forms of expertise that are less explored in this volume, including that of women and members of indigenous communities.

Toward a Diversity of Expertise and Multiple Knowledges

A fourth contribution of the work presented in this volume underscores the importance of recognizing, recovering, and analyzing multiple knowledges. Existing scholarship on Latin America has also focused on different knowledge systems, examining local, indigenous, traditional, and other forms of knowledge and expertise in the region that differed from the knowledge coming from Europe and the United States.[43] Scholars previously illustrated how these types of knowledges spanned widely across and throughout Latin America's past—from African slaves' understanding of rice production in Brazil, to indigenous Andean residents' ability to predict El Niño events months in advance by analyzing the brightness of stars in the Pleiades constellation, to the contrast between Spanish and indigenous knowledge of hydrology in Central Mexico.[44] Work in this volume aligns with and advances these insights with a focus on the long Cold War. It shows in particular that expert knowledge during the Cold War did not come just from foreign engineers and scientists exerting their ideas over Latin America. Cold War struggles between capitalism and communism did involve experts who were deployed or engaged to modernize nations in line with the larger geopolitical agendas. In many cases agronomists, engineers, architects, social workers, and others served to further Cold War government policies. However, the chapters in this book also amply demonstrate other ways that multiple knowledges became interwoven and sometimes collided during the twentieth century. From architects, engineers, and NASA technicians to cattle breeders, local planters, road builders, and radio operators, Latin America was home to a vast array of experts—all with unique knowledges—who only sometimes emerged from government agencies and universities.

Numerous chapters also underscore the importance of local knowledges, including knowledge of local materials, techniques, habits, and economies, and the ways local forms of expertise mixed with expertise from elsewhere. For example, Funes-Monzote and Palmer in their study of milk production in Cuba, and Lorek in his study of agricultural science in Colombia, collectively draw attention to the ways that scientists and farmers worked to make livestock and crops resistant to local tropical climates. Purcell looks at how dam-building experts collected a "dense internalization of local knowledge" in different parts of the world, which they then spread in the form of technical assistance. Roldán shows how Catholic priests who worked in the Colombian countryside played an important role as intermediaries between secular experts and members of poor rural communities. The priests used their relationship with the communities to share seeds, scientific growing methods, and news of development resources. Healey shows how architects from the Colombian Inter-American Center for Housing and Urban Planning (CINVA) worked with the communities they served to create housing plans that were informed by local materials, local living conditions, and housing needs.

Yet the contributions in this collection go beyond identifying new experts and new knowledges to also showing experts acting as intermediaries among historical actors and within historical processes. Farmers, ranchers, architects, dam builders, tropical biologists, urban planners, and many others not only developed and spread new knowledge but generated new narratives of nature and the built environment. They envisioned environments not only through their own lenses but also through their interactions, encounters, and discourse with both social actors and physical environments. They also articulated possibilities that went on to shape the lived realities and material conditions of many Latin American peoples and of peoples in other parts of the world. Many times these experts were local residents or other specialists acting outside the state apparatus. But even foreign or government technocrats interacted productively with local residents, indicating that visions of development were often shared or negotiated among grassroots and elite actors. State-sanctioned knowledge, in other words, was not always bad, contested, or negative for Latin American peoples—and this volume clearly shows the complexity of interactions among diverse experts and distinct knowledges.[45] Whether it was dam engineers bringing jobs and electricity to local communities in Chile or cattle-breeding experts remaking bovine culture in Cuba, these diverse and intersecting knowledge systems were never homogeneous or simplistic binary constructions of good–bad, local–national, Latin American–United States.

This suggests that scholarship must analyze technocrats and experts as historical actors who not only shaped the production of knowledge, but whose work was deeply entangled with social, cultural, and political processes. As Mark Carey's work on glacier experts in Peru has shown, engineers, scientists, and technocrats "acted as intermediaries among various social groups and interests, as well as between humans and the physical environment."[46] Their efforts in the Peruvian countryside over many decades during the Cold War thus involved discussions not just about the physical landscape but also about economic development agendas, political authority, race and class relations, and cultural traditions. Chastain and Lorek underscore this same point in their introduction to this volume, observing that its contributors' rendering of experts portrays them as cultural and political intermediaries and historical actors in their own right.

In addition, although experts often act with the authority of institutions (such as those in government, industry, university, and nonprofit sectors), it is important to recognize that their actions do not necessarily align with those of the institution they represent, nor do their beliefs necessarily align with dominant views. Studies of expertise can thus also add nuance to our understanding of these institutions, their actions, and the complexities of the context in which they operate. They can uncover the diversity of opinions and knowledges within institutions, the paths that were not taken, and the significance of the path that eventually prevailed.

This approach consequently offers a different kind of history from below with the potential to add not only new voices and experiences but also debates and disagreements to the historical record due to the ways in which development and modernization were always negotiated at the ground level by numerous actors. By studying the negotiations among different kinds of experts, the ideals of development and modernization cease to appear as universal goals mapped onto the region and instead as processes in the making. Expertise thus emerges in this volume not as monolithic but as evolving knowledge practices. In many cases, the knowledge and expertise generated were informed by experts' personal backgrounds, including their own identities. Other studies on knowledge production and international scholars working in Latin America, such as Ricardo Salvatore's work, have also explored the ways in which the personal histories of the experts themselves shaped knowledge production. Sometimes they are influenced by interactions with physical environments, as Wakild shows in this volume and as Megan Raby demonstrates clearly for biodiversity conservationists working in Latin America.[47] Chastain and Lorek have also identified the "hybrid nationalities of experts" because they often belonged to multiple communities—not only their countries of birth and the nations where they practiced, but also the international arenas, professional societies, cultural roots, and multiple other communities that shaped their professional identities, perspectives, and practices.

In all these ways, this book advances our understanding of how experts shaped historical processes in Latin America during the Cold War in ways that break from earlier stories about nature, technology, and expertise that flourished in the second half of the twentieth century. Instead of evaluating Latin American accomplishments in relation to those of richer, more industrialized nations, the chapters here offer new narratives grounded in the specific experiences of Latin American communities—approaches that also offer compelling frameworks for future research on the history of technology, knowledge, and environment in Latin America. They seek to understand expertise and knowledge production, and by extension technology and the environment, in relation to specific geographical, political, and historical contexts.

The chapters in this volume also do not view Latin American activities as peripheral in the history of science and technology or as politically peripheral to the Cold War struggle between the superpowers. Instead, they put Latin American experiences at the center of analysis and connect the region to other parts of the world in ways that recognize the multidirectional movement of people, ideas, and things. They highlight how multiple kinds of knowledge come together and the ways that the histories of technology, the environment, and expertise operate on multiple spatial and temporal scales, including at the level of local communities, the nation, and in networks of transnational exchange, and on chronologies that depart from traditional nation-state periodizations. They study the actions of elites and non-elites in places that include fields, dams, metro stations, vaccine laboratories, and the Peruvian jungle, to name just a few. Finally, the book's chapters recognize the role of foreign influence but do not view it as the central defining feature of how the region experienced the Cold War.

The volume thus highlights Latin American experiences and changes— and the kinds of stories we tell about them. This is no simple feat. Yet it also draws our attention to the work that remains to be done. Few of the chapters, for example, focus on the expertise or experience of women. Gender is thus barely addressed, here as in research in environmental history more broadly, despite a growing body of literature on women and gender in the history of technology. The experience of indigenous groups and the role of indigenous knowledges are also noticeably absent, as are the specific contributions of peasants, the poor, workers, and those marginalized through other social categories, such as race, ethnicity, or disability. Such absences reflect the limitations of source materials, the judgments of significance made by historical actors, and the decisions of scholars doing the research still today. We draw attention to these absences to issue a challenge for future scholarship and to highlight the need for new methods and source materials to make this kind of historical research possible. Recent scholarship on the history of science and technology in Africa, for example, has examined oral source materials and the meanings found in precolonial African languages as a way to explore knowledge production from an African perspective unmediated by colonial record keeping.[48] As another example, research on the Arctic has increasingly focused on indigenous knowledge, examining it in its own historical, cultural, and political contexts rather than simply as information for Western scientists and engineers to extract and utilize. This research has even inspired new decolonizing methodologies for research that explicitly address and try to overcome the historical politics of knowledge production that delegitimizes or decontextualizes indigenous knowledge.[49]

Pathways of the Past and Future

This essay began by drawing attention to the kinds of narratives about technology, nature, and expertise that emerged during the Cold War period and shaped the ways that we understood Latin American history and the relationship of Latin American nations to the rest of the world. It then drew attention to four significant interventions made by this volume in changing those narratives. Specifically, it moved us beyond center–periphery tropes and the positioning of Latin America as dependent on other parts of the world; it redefined understandings of technology, nature, and expertise; it decentered the state in its analysis without dismissing the nation-building activities that took place during this period; and it drew attention to the diversity of expertise and knowledges at work throughout Latin America during the Cold War period.

As we tell new stories of technology, nature, and expertise—as the authors in this volume do—we improve our understanding of the ways in which people have lived and continue to live in increasingly interconnected and global contexts. We push back against the simplistic understandings that are coded into our popular historical narratives and into our global economic and political relationships. This book thus not only offers a more nuanced understanding of the long Cold War and Latin America's role in it but also shows the ways in which Latin America exists not as a bounded space, but as a porous space that is continuously redefined through the frictions and flows of people, other living beings, ideas, things, and their interactions with dynamic environments.

In so doing, this book underscores novel Cold War *itineraries*, or connected pathways of knowledge circulation that are negotiated on multiple scales, by multiple actors, and with multiple outcomes.[50] Some of these connected paths followed the better known geopolitical and ideological contours of the Cold War, as well as their related modernization schemes. Some of these paths begin and end within the years 1945–1989, the period commonly ascribed to the Cold War. But these are not the only circuits of Cold War travel and exchange. By focusing on the connections made among individuals and groups, rather than nations and the people acting at their behest, this volume illustrates how the Cold War context also served to link cattle breeders in Canada and Cuba; veterinary scientists in Mexico and Brazil; and Catholic priests, secular experts, and members of poor communities in Colombia. It puts forth a new Cold War geography of science, technology, and environment that illustrates how this conflict not only "politiciz[ed] and internationaliz[ed] . . . everyday life" in Latin America, as Gilbert M. Joseph observes in his essay (chapter 1), but also reshaped networks of experts as they worked within and against the constraints of geopolitics. Some of these stories of expertise extend into the 1990s and 2000s, or emerge from activities begun and ideas formed in the late nineteenth and early twentieth centuries. By following the experts, the authors in this volume map out new networks of exchange and new Cold War chronologies. As we tell new stories of the Cold War, we improve our understanding of the global itineraries of exchange that connect diverse technologies, experts, and environments and how they come together to shape historical processes in Latin America and beyond.

NOTES

1. Simon Romero, "A Gilded Olympics Begin with the Opening Ceremony in Gritty Rio," *New York Times*, August 5, 2016, accessed May 16, 2019, https://www.nytimes.com /2016/08/06/sports/olympics/summer-games-opening-ceremony-rio.html. Brazilian pride in Dumont's technological accomplishments can also be seen in the name of the domestic airport in Rio de Janeiro (Santos Dumont Airport) and the name of a supercomputer at the Brazilian National Computer Science Laboratory (LNCC) known as Santos Dumont, or SDumont for short. LNCC, "SDumont," accessed May 16, 2019, https://sdumont.lncc.br/machine .php?pg=machine.

2. W. W. Rostow, *The Stages of Economic Growth: A Non-Communist Manifesto* (New York: Cambridge University Press, 1991).

3. George Basalla, "The Spread of Western Science," *Science* 156, no. 3775 (May 5, 1967): 611–622. A recent reconsideration of Basalla appears in Warwick Anderson, "Remembering the Spread of Western Science," *Historical Records of Australian Science* 29, no. 2 (2018): 73–81.

4. Fernando Henrique Cardoso and Enzo Faletto, *Dependency and Development in Latin America* (Berkeley: University of California Press, 1979).

5. Eduardo Galeano, *Las venas abiertas de América Latina* (Montevideo: Universidad de la República, Departamento de Publicaciones, 1971).

6. As Marcos Cueto and Jorge Cañizares-Esguerra observe, historical interpretations of Western science and its diffusion in Latin America have "overemphasized Latin America's passivity and patterns of cultural and economic dependency to explain the region's stunted scientific development" while also looking for factors, such as the Puritan Reformation and industrialization, that explain why science and technology flourished in the West and not in areas of the so-called Third World. Marcos Cueto and Jorge Cañizares-Esguerra, "History of Science in Non-Western Traditions: Latin America," in *An Introduction to the History of Science in Non-Western Traditions*, ed. Douglas Allchin and Robert DeKosky, History of Science Society, 1999, accessed May 16, 2019, https://hssonline.org/resources/teaching/teaching_nonwest

ern/teaching_nonwestern_latin/. For a discussion of these trends in environmental history, see Mark Carey, "Latin American Environmental History: Current Trends, Interdisciplinary Insights, and Future Directions," *Environmental History* 14, no. 2 (2009): 221–252.

7. For example, see Emanuel Adler, *The Power of Ideology: The Quest for Technological Autonomy in Argentina and Brazil* (Berkeley: University of California Press, 1987); Hebe Vessuri, "The Universities, Scientific Research and the National Interest in Latin America," *Minerva* 24 (1986): 1–38; Jacqueline Fortes and Larissa Adler Lomnitz, *Becoming a Scientist in Mexico: The Challenge of Creating a Scientific Community in an Underdeveloped Country* (University Park: Pennsylvania State University Press, 1994); Mary Louise Pratt, *Imperial Eyes: Travel Writing and Transculturation* (New York: Routledge, 1992); James E. McClellan III, *Colonialism and Science: Saint Domingue in the Old Regime* (Baltimore: Johns Hopkins University Press, 1992); Arturo Gómez-Pompa and Andrea Kaus, "Taming the Wilderness Myth," *Bioscience* 42, no. 4 (1992): 271–279; Kirkpatrick Sale, *The Conquest of Paradise: Christopher Columbus and the Columbian Legacy* (New York: Plume, 1990); Ramachandra Guha, "Radical American Environmentalism and Wilderness Preservation: A Third World Critique," *Environmental Ethics* 11 (Spring 1989): 71–83; and Daniel R. Headrick, *The Tentacles of Progress: Technology Transfer in the Age of Imperialism, 1850–1940* (New York: Oxford University Press, 1988).

8. Thomas Glick, "Science in Twentieth Century Latin America," in *Ideas and Ideologies in Twentieth Century Latin America*, ed. Leslie Bethell (New York: Cambridge University Press, 1996), 356.

9. Marcos Cueto, *Excelencia científica en la periferia: Actividades científicas e investigación biomédica en el Perú 1890–1950* (Lima: Grupo de Análisis para el Desarrollo, 1989); Marcos Cueto, "Andean Biology in Peru: Scientific Styles on the Periphery," *Isis* 80, no. 4 (December 1989): 640–658; and Marcos Cueto, ed., *Saberes andinos: Ciencia y tecnología en Bolivia, Ecuador y Perú* (Lima: Instituto de Estudios Peruanos, 1995).

10. Steven Shapin, "Placing the View from Nowhere: Historical and Sociological Problems in the Location of Science," *Transactions of the Institute of British Geographers* NS 23, no. 1 (1998): 5–12; and David N. Livingstone, *Putting Science in Its Place: Geographies of Scientific Knowledge* (Chicago: University of Chicago Press, 2003).

11. See, for example, Juan José Saldaña, ed., *Historia social de las ciencias en América Latina* (Mexico City: UNAM and M. A. Porrúa, 1996); Brian S. Bauer and David S. Dearborn, *Astronomy and Empire in the Ancient Andes* (Austin: University of Texas Press, 1995); Constance Classen, *Inca Cosmology and the Human Body* (Salt Lake City: University of Utah Press, 1993); Jorge Cañizares-Esguerra, *How to Write the History of the New World* (Palo Alto, CA: Stanford University Press, 2001); Frank L. Salomon, *The Cord Keepers: Khipus and Cultural Life in a Peruvian Village* (Durham, NC: Duke University Press, 2003); Ricardo D. Salvatore, "Local versus Imperial Knowledge: Reflections on Hiram Bingham and the Yale Peruvian Expedition," *Nepantla: Views from the South* 4, no. 1 (2003): 67–80; Jeanette E. Sherbondy, "Water Ideology in Inca Ethnogenesis," in *Andean Cosmologies through Time: Persistence and Emergence*, ed. Rober V. H. Dover, Katharine E. Seibold, and John H. McDowell (Bloomington: Indiana University Press, 1992), 46–66; and Antonio Barrera-Osorio, *Experiencing Nature: The Spanish American Empire and the Early Scientific Revolution* (Austin: University of Texas Press, 2006).

12. Thomas Glick, "Science and Independence in Latin America," *Hispanic American Historical Review* 71 (1991): 307–334; Adolfo Ibáñez Santa María, "Los 'ismos' y la redefinición del Estado: Tecnicismo, planificación y estatismo en Chile, 1920–1940," *Atenea*, no. 474 (1996): 23–50; Peter Gose, *Deathly Waters and Hungry Mountains: Agrarian Ritual and Class Formation in an Andean Town* (Toronto: University of Toronto Press, 1994); and Enrique Mayer, *The Articulated Peasant: Household Economies in the Andes* (Boulder, CO: Westview Press, 2001).

13. For example, Londa Schiebinger and Claudia Swan, eds., *Colonial Botany: Science, Commerce, and Politics in the Early Modern World* (Philadelphia: University of Pennsylvania Press, 2005); D. Graham Burnett, *Masters of All They Surveyed: Exploration, Geography, and a British El Dorado* (Chicago: University of Chicago Press, 2000); Hugh Raffles, *In Amazonia: A Natural History* (Princeton, NJ: Princeton University Press, 2002); and Nancy Leys Stepan, *Picturing Tropical Nature* (Ithaca, NY: Cornell University Press, 2001).

14. For example, Steven Palmer, "Central American Encounters with Rockefeller Public Health, 1914–1921," in *Close Encounters of Empire: Writing the Cultural History of U.S.-Latin American Relations*, ed. Gilbert M. Joseph, Catherine C. LeGrand, and Ricardo D. Salvatore (Durham, NC: Duke University Press, 1998), 311–332; and Mark Carey, "Climate, Medicine, and Peruvian Health Resorts," *Science, Technology, and Human Values* 39, no. 6 (2014): 795–818.

15. Stuart McCook, *States of Nature: Science, Agriculture, and Environment in the Spanish Caribbean, 1760–1940* (Austin: University of Texas Press, 2002); Pablo Gómez, *The Experiential Caribbean* (Chapel Hill: University of North Carolina Press, 2017). We note that describing Latin American science as "creole" is not without complications. In Brazil, for example, the term *creole* has pejorative racial connotations.

16. Eden Medina, *Cybernetic Revolutionaries: Technology and Politics in Allende's Chile* (Cambridge, MA: MIT Press, 2011); Eden Medina, Ivan da Costa Marques, and Christina Holmes, eds., *Beyond Imported Magic: Science, Technology, and Society in Latin America* (Cambridge, MA: MIT Press, 2014); Mark Carey, *In the Shadow of Melting Glaciers: Climate Change and Andean Society* (New York: Oxford University Press, 2010); and Mark Carey, "Mountaineers and Engineers: An Environmental History of International Sport, Science, and Landscape Consumption in Twentieth-Century Peru," *Hispanic American Historical Review* 92, no. 1 (2012): 107–141.

17. For some very recent examples, see, for instance, Eve E. Buckley, *Technocrats and the Politics of Drought and Development in Twentieth-Century Brazil* (Chapel Hill: University of North Carolina Press, 2017); Megan Raby, *American Tropics: The Caribbean Roots of Biodiversity Science* (Chapel Hill: University of North Carolina Press, 2017); Mikael D. Wolfe, *Watering the Revolution: An Environmental and Technological History of Agrarian Reform in Mexico* (Durham, NC: Duke University Press, 2017); Claudia Leal, *Landscapes of Freedom: Building a Postemancipation Society in the Rainforests of Western Colombia* (Tucson: University of Arizona Press, 2018); and John Soluri, Claudia Leal, and José Augusto Pádua, eds., *A Living Past: Environmental Histories of Modern Latin America* (New York: Berghahn Books, 2018).

18. Medina, Marques, and Holmes, *Beyond Imported Magic*, 1–2.

19. For example, Mike Davis, *Late Victorian Holocausts: El Niño Famines and the Making of the Third World* (New York: Verso, 2001); Gastón R. Gordillo, *Landscapes of Devils: Tensions*

of Place and Memory in the Argentinean Chaco (Durham, NC: Duke University Press, 2004); Paul S. Sutter, "Nature's Agents or Agents of Empire? Entomological Workers and Environmental Change during the Construction of the Panama Canal," *Isis* 98 (2007): 724–754; Emily Wakild, "Border Chasm: International Boundary Parks and Mexican Conservation, 1935–1945," *Environmental History* 14, no. 3 (2009): 453–475; Jeremy Ravi Mumford, *Vertical Empire: The General Resettlement of Indians in the Colonial Andes* (Durham, NC: Duke University Press, 2012); Carey, "Mountaineers and Engineers"; Seth Garfield, *In Search of the Amazon: Brazil, the United States, and the Nature of a Region* (Durham, NC: Duke University Press, 2013); Ashley Carse, *Beyond the Big Ditch: Politics, Ecology, and Infrastructure at the Panama Canal* (Cambridge, MA: MIT Press, 2014); Carey, "Climate, Medicine, and Peruvian Health Resorts"; and Raby, *American Tropics*.

20. For example, Schiebinger and Swan, *Colonial Botany*; Saldaña, *Historia social de las ciencias*; Palmer, "Central American Encounters"; Carey, *In the Shadow*; Medina, *Cybernetic Revolutionaries*; Marco Ramos, "Psychiatry, Authoritarianism, and Revolution: The Politics of Mental Illness during Military Dictatorships in Argentina, 1966–1983," *Bulletin of the History of Medicine* 87, no. 2 (2013): 250–278; Gabriela Soto Laveaga, "*Largo dislocare*: Connecting Microhistories to Remap and Recenter Histories of Science," *History and Technology* 34, no. 1 (2018): 21–30; Gabriela Soto Laveaga, *Jungle Laboratories: Mexican Peasants, National Projects, and the Making of the Pill* (Durham, NC: Duke University Press, 2009).

21. For example, see *British Journal for the History of Science* 2012, special issue on transnational or global perspectives in science history, in particular Simone Turchetti, Néstor Herran, and Soraya Boudia, "Introduction: Have We Ever Been 'Transnational'? Towards a History of Science across and beyond Borders," *British Journal for the History of Science* 45, no. 3 (2012): 319–336. See also Lissa Roberts, "Situating Science in a Global History: Local Exchanges and Networks of Circulation," *Itinerario* 33, no. 1 (2009): 9–30; Tiago Saraiva, "The History of Cybernetics in McOndo," *History and Technology* 28, no. 4 (2012): 423–430; Erik van der Vleuten, "Toward a Transnational History of Technology: Meanings, Promises, Pitfalls," *Technology and Culture* 49, no. 4 (2008): 974–994; and Gabrielle Hecht, ed., *Entangled Geographies: Empire and Technopolitics in the Global Cold War* (Cambridge, MA: MIT Press, 2011).

22. Christopher Sneddon, *Concrete Revolution: Large Dams, Cold War Geopolitics, and the US Bureau of Reclamation* (Chicago: University of Chicago Press, 2015).

23. An overview of the literature on technology history in Latin America appears in Michael Lemon and Eden Medina, "Technology in an Expanded Field: A Review of History of Technology Scholarship on Latin America in Selected English-Language Journals," in Medina, Marques, Holmes, *Beyond Imported Magic*, 111–136.

24. Eric Schatzberg, "'Technik' Comes to America: Changing Meanings of 'Technology' before 1930," *Technology and Culture* 47, no. 3 (2006): 486–512.

25. Simon Schama, *Landscape and Memory* (New York: Vintage Books, 1995); Stepan, *Picturing Tropical Nature*; Richard White, "From Wilderness to Hybrid Landscapes: The Cultural Turn in Environmental History," *Historian* 66, no. 3 (September 2004): 557–564; and Mark Fiege, *Irrigated Eden: The Making of an Agricultural Landscape in the American West* (Seattle: University of Washington Press, 1999).

26. See, for example, Susanna B. Hecht, *The Scramble for the Amazon and the Lost Paradise of Euclides Da Cunha* (Chicago: University of Chicago Press, 2013); Michael B. Silvers, *Voices of Drought: The Politics of Music and Environment in Northeastern Brazil* (Urbana: University of Illinois Press, 2018); Barbara E. Mundy, *The Death of Aztec Tenochtitlan, the Life of Mexico City* (Austin: University of Texas Press, 2015); Malcolm McNee, *The Environmental Imaginary in Brazilian Poetry and Art* (New York: Palgrave Macmillan, 2014); and Mark Anderson and Zélia M. Bora, eds. *Ecological Crisis and Cultural Representation in Latin America: Ecocritical Perspectives on Art, Film, and Literature* (Lanham, MD: Lexington Books, 2016).

27. Penny Harvey and Hannah Knox, *Roads: An Anthropology of Infrastructure and Expertise* (Ithaca, NY: Cornell University Press, 2015); Willie Hiatt, *The Rarified Air of the Modern: Airplanes and Technological Modernity in the Andes* (New York: Oxford University Press, 2016); Charles F. Walker, *Shaky Colonialism: The 1746 Earthquake-Tsunami in Lima, Peru, and Its Long Aftermath* (Durham, NC: Duke University Press, 2008); Mark Carey, "Regando el desierto, alimentando la revolución: La influencia de Velasco en las leyes del agua y la agricultura en la costa norte del Perú (Chavimochic)," trans. Fernando Purcell, in *La revolución peculiar: Repensando el gobierno militar de Velasco*, ed. Carlos Aguirre and Paulo Drinot (Lima: IEP–Instituto de Estudios Peruanos, 2018), 319–352.

28. Stefania Gallini, "La naturaleza cultural de la historia ambiental y su rematerialización," in *Historia cultural desde Colombia: Categorías y debates*, ed. Max S. Hering Torres and Amada Carolina Pérez Benavides (Bogotá: Universidad Nacional de Colombia/Pontificia Universidad Javeriana/Universidad de los Andes, 2012), 379.

29. Paul R. Josephson, *Industrialized Nature: Brute Force Technology and the Transformation of the Natural World* (Washington, DC: Island Press, 2002).

30. For example, Harvey and Knox, *Roads*; and Gastón R. Gordillo, *Rubble: The Afterlife of Destruction* (Durham, NC: Duke University Press, 2014).

31. Ashley Carse, *Beyond the Big Ditch: Politics, Ecology, and Infrastructure at the Panama Canal* (Cambridge, MA: MIT Press, 2014), 5.

32. John Soluri, Claudia Leal, and José Augusto Pádua, "Finding the 'Latin American' in Latin American Environmental History," in Soluri, Leal, and Pádua, *Living Past*, 1–22; and Anthony Bebbington and Jeffrey Bury, eds., *Subterranean Struggles: New Dynamics of Mining, Oil, and Gas in Latin America*, (Austin: University of Texas Press, 2013); on environmental history in the history of technology, see Sara B. Pritchard, "Toward an Environmental History of Technology," in *The Oxford Handbook of Environmental History*, ed. Andrew C. Isenberg (New York: Oxford University Press, 2014), 227–258; and Dolly Jørgensen, Finn Arne Jørgensen, and Sara B. Pritchard, eds., *New Natures: Joining Environmental History with Science and Technology Studies* (Pittsburgh: University of Pittsburgh Press, 2013).

33. For example, Gilbert M. Joseph and Daniel Nugent, eds., *Everyday Forms of State Formation: Revolution and the Negotiation of Rule in Modern Mexico* (Durham, NC: Duke University Press, 1994); Stuart McCook, "'Giving Plants a Civil Status': Scientific Representations of Nature and Nation in Costa Rica and Venezuela, 1885–1935," *The Americas* 58, no. 4 (2002): 513–536; and Seth Garfield, "A Nationalist Environment: Indians, Nature, and the Construction of the Xingu National Park in Brazil," *Luso-Brazilian Review* 41, no. 1 (2004): 139–167.

34. See, for example, the 2015 special issue of *History and Technology* edited by John Krige and Jessica Wang as well and their introductory essay to the volume. John Krige and Jessica Wang, "Nation, Knowledge, and Imagined Futures: Science, Technology, and Nation-Building, Post-1945," *History and Technology* 31, no. 3 (2015): 171–179.

35. For example, Wilko Graf von Hardenberg, Matthew Kelly, Claudia Leal, and Emily Wakild, eds., *The Nature State: Rethinking the History of Conservation* (New York: Routledge, 2017); McCook, *States of Nature*; Regina Horta Duarte, *Activist Biology: The National Museum, Politics, and Nation Building in Brazil*, trans. Diane Grosklaus Whitty (Tucson: University of Arizona Press, 2016); and Camilo Quintero, *Birds of Empire, Birds of Nation: A History of Science, Economy, and Conservation in United States–Colombia Relations* (Bogotá: Ediciones Uniandes, 2012).

36. For example, Javiera Barandiarán, *Science and Environment in Chile: The Politics of Expert Advice in a Neoliberal Democracy* (Cambridge, MA: MIT Press, 2018); Wouter Buytaert, Zed Zulkafli, Sam Grainger et al., "Citizen Science in Hydrology and Water Resources: Opportunities for Knowledge Generation, Ecosystem Service Management, and Sustainable Development," *Frontiers in Earth Science* 2, article 26 (2014), http://dx.doi.org/10.3389/feart.2014.00026; Mark Carey, Rodney Garrard, Courtney Cecale, Wouter Buytaert, Christian Huggel, and Mathias Vuille, "Climbing for Science and Ice: From Hans Kinzl and Mountaineering-Glaciology to Citizen Science in the Cordillera Blanca," *Revista de Glaciares y Ecosistemas de Montaña* 1, no. 1 (2016): 59–72; Charles R. Menzies, ed., *Traditional Ecological Knowledge and Natural Resource Management* (Lincoln: University of Nebraska Press, 2006); Soluri, Leal, and Pádua, "Finding the 'Latin American'"; Joana Bezerra, *The Brazilian Amazon: Politics, Science and International Relations in the History of the Forest* (New York: Springer, 2015); Mattias Borg Rasmussen, *Andean Waterways: Resource Politics in Highland Peru* (Seattle: University of Washington Press, 2015); and Luis Mujica Bermúdez, *Pachamama Kawsan: Hacia una ecología Andina* (Lima: Pontificia Universidad Católica del Perú y Instituto de Ciencias de la Naturaleza, Territorio y Energías Renovables (INTE-PUCP), 2017).

37. James C. Scott, *Seeing Like a State: How Certain Schemes to Improve the Human Condition Have Failed* (New Haven, CT: Yale University Press, 1998).

38. Paul Sutter, "What Can U.S. Environmental Historians Learn from Non-U.S. Environmental Historiography?" *Environmental History* 8, no. 1 (2003): 109–129.

39. See, for example, Eric Van Young, "Recent Anglophone Scholarship on Mexico and Central America in the Age of Revolution (1750–1850)," *Hispanic American Historical Review* 65, no. 4 (1985): 725–743; Stuart F. Voss, *Latin America in the Middle Period, 1750–1929* (Wilmington, DE: Scholarly Resources, 2002); Christopher R. Boyer, ed., *A Land Between Waters: Environmental Histories of Modern Mexico* (Tucson: University of Arizona Press, 2012); Soluri, Leal, and Pádua, *Living Past*; Claudia Leal, José Augusto Pádua, and John Soluri, eds., *New Environmental Histories of Latin America and the Caribbean* (Munich: Rachel Carson Center Perspectives, 2013); Stefania Barca, "Laboring the Earth: Transnational Reflections on the Environmental History of Work," *Environmental History* 19, no. 1 (2014): 3–27; and Richard White, "The Nationalization of Nature," *Journal of American History* 86, no. 3 (1999): 976–986.

40. Christopher R. Boyer, "The Cycles of Mexican Environmental History," in *Land Between Waters*, ed. Boyer, 3.

41. See also Prakash Kumar, Timothy Lorek, Tore C. Olsson, Nicole Sackley, Sigrid Schmalzer, and Gabriela Soto Laveaga, "Roundtable: New Narratives of the Green Revolution," *Agricultural History* 91, no. 3 (2017): 397–422.

42. David Edgerton, *The Shock of the Old: Technology and Global History since 1990* (Oxford: Oxford University Press, 2007).

43. For example, D. Graham Burnett, "'It Is Impossible to Make a Step without the Indians': Nineteenth-Century Geographical Exploration and the Amerindians of British Guiana," *Ethnohistory* 49, no. 1 (2002): 3–40; Raffles, *In Amazonia*; Raymond B. Craib, *Cartographic Mexico: A History of State Fixations and Fugitive Landscapes* (Durham, NC: Duke University Press, 2004); David G. Campbell, *A Land of Ghosts: The Braided Lives of People and the Forest in Far Western Amazonia* (New York: Houghton Mifflin, 2005); Yanna P. Yannakakis, *The Art of Being In-Between: Native Intermediaries, Indian Identity, and Local Rule in Colonial Oaxaca* (Durham, NC: Duke University Press, 2008); Wendy Wolford, *This Land Is Ours Now: Social Mobilization and the Meanings of Land in Brazil* (Durham, NC: Duke University Press, 2010); Carey, *In the Shadow*; Kregg Hetherington, *Guerrilla Auditors: The Politics of Transparency in Neoliberal Paraguay* (Durham, NC: Duke University Press, 2011); Andrew S. Mathews, *Instituting Nature: Authority, Expertise, and Power in Mexican Forests* (Cambridge, MA: MIT Press, 2011); Eric D. Carter, *Enemy in the Blood: Malaria, Environment, and Development in Argentina* (Tuscaloosa: University of Alabama Press, 2012); Gabriela Ramos and Yanna P. Yannakakis, eds., *Indigenous Intellectuals: Knowledge, Power, and Colonial Culture in Mexico and the Andes* (Durham, NC: Duke University Press, 2014); Christopher R. Boyer, *Political Landscapes: Forests, Conservation, and Community in Mexico* (Durham, NC: Duke University Press, 2015); and Claudia Leal, *Landscapes of Freedom: Building a Postemancipation Society in the Rainforests of Western Colombia* (Tucson: University of Arizona Press, 2018).

44. Judith Carney, "'With Grains in Her Hair': Rice History and Memory in Colonial Brazil," *Slavery and Abolition* 25, no. 1 (2004): 1–27; Benjamin S. Orlove, John C. H. Chiang, and Mark A. Cane, "Forecasting Andean Rainfall and Crop Yield from the Influence of El Niño on Pleiades Visibility," *Nature* 403 (January 6, 2000): 68–71; and Vera S. Candiani, *Dreaming of Dry Land: Environmental Transformation in Colonial Mexico City* (Stanford, CA: Stanford University Press, 2014).

45. For example, Boyer, *Political Landscapes*; Buckley, *Technocrats*.

46. Carey, *In the Shadow*, 14. In her work on technocrats in the Brazilian Northeast, Eve Buckley takes up similar themes by studying the political conditions that shaped how experts attempted to alleviate poverty in the region. See Buckley, *Technocrats*.

47. Ricardo D. Salvatore, *Disciplinary Conquest: U.S. Scholars in South America, 1900–1945* (Durham, NC: Duke University Press, 2016); Raby, *American Tropics*.

48. Clapperton Chakanetsa Mavhunga, *The Mobile Workshop: The Tsetse Fly and African Knowledge Production* (Cambridge, MA: MIT Press, 2018). See also Kathryn M. de Luna. "Conceptualizing Vegetation in the Bantu Expansion: Reflections on Linguistics in Cen-

tral African History," *Quaternary International* (2016); and Kathryn M. de Luna and Jeffery B. Fleisher, *Speaking with Substance: Language and Materials in African History* (New York: Springer, 2018).

49. Arun Agrawal, "Dismantling the Divide Between Indigenous and Scientific Knowledge," *Development and Change* 26, no. 3 (1995): 413–439; Linda Tuhiwai Smith, *Decolonizing Methodologies: Research and Indigenous Peoples*, 2nd ed. (New York: Zed Books, 2012); Lene Kielsen Holm, Lenore A. Grenoble, and Ross A. Virginia, "A Praxis for Ethical Research and Scientific Conduct in Greenland," *Etudes Inuit. Inuit Studies* 35, no. 1/2 (2011): 187–200; and Shari Fox Gearheard et al., eds., *The Meaning of Ice: People and Sea Ice in Three Arctic Communities* (Hanover, NH: International Polar Institute Press, 2013).

50. Neil Safier, "Global Knowledge on the Move: Itineraries, Amerindian Narratives, and Deep Histories of Science" *Isis* 101, no. 1 (2010): 133–145.

CONTRIBUTORS

Javiera Barandiarán is an associate professor in global studies at the University of California, Santa Barbara. Her work explores the intersection of science, environment, and development in Latin America, and has been supported by the Mellon Foundation, the Social Science Research Council, and the National Science Foundation. Her first book is *Science and Environment in Chile: The Politics of Expert Advice in a Neoliberal Democracy* (MIT Press, 2018).

Mark Carey is a professor of history and environmental studies in the Robert D. Clark Honors College at the University of Oregon, where he specializes in environmental and Latin American history. He coedited *The High-Mountain Cryosphere: Environmental Changes and Human Risks* (Cambridge, 2015) and wrote *Glaciares, cambio climático y desastres naturales: Ciencia y sociedad en el Perú* (IFEA/IEP, 2014) and *In the Shadow of Melting Glaciers: Climate Change and Andean Society* (Oxford University Press, 2010), which received the Elinor Melville Award for the best book on Latin American environmental history. His work has been funded by several National Science Foundation grants, and he has received the Leopold-Hidy Prize for the best article in the journal *Environmental History* (2007), and, more recently, won the King Albert Mountain Award (2018) for lifetime contributions to the world's mountain societies and environments. At the University of Oregon, he runs the Glacier Lab for the Study of Ice and Society.

Andra B. Chastain is an assistant professor of history at Washington State University Vancouver, where she teaches Latin American and world history. Her current book project is a transnational history of the metro system in Santiago, Chile, titled *Chile Underground: The Santiago Metro and the Struggle for a Rational City* (under contract with Yale University Press). She has published articles in the *Journal of Urban History* and the *Revista de Historia Iberoamericana.*

Reinaldo Funes-Monzote is a professor of history at the University of Havana and director of the Geo-Historical Research Program at the Antonio Núñez Jiménez Foundation (Cuba). He is the author of *From Rainforest to Cane Field: A Cuban Environmental History since 1492* (University of North Carolina Press, 2008), which won the Elinor Melville Prize from the Conference on Latin American History. He won the Casa de las Américas award in 2019 for *Nuestro viaje a la luna: Las ideas de la transformación de la naturaleza en Cuba durante la Guerra Fría* (Fondo Editorial Casa de las Américas, 2019). He is currently a visiting professor at Yale University (2015–2020).

Mark Healey is an associate professor of history at the University of Connecticut. The author of *The Ruins of the New Argentina* (Duke University Press, 2011), he is now completing a book on the environmental and political history of water and infrastructure in western Argentina and beginning a new project on the Cold War politics of housing and development.

Pedro Ignacio Alonso, an architect, with Hugo Palmarola, was awarded a Silver Lion in 2014 at the Fourteenth Venice Architecture Biennale. They are the authors of the books *Panel* (Architectural Association, 2014) and *Monolith Controversies* (Hatje Cantz, 2014), and are the curators of the Flying Panels exhibition in 2019 at ArkDes, the Swedish Centre for Architecture and Design.

Gilbert M. Joseph is the Farnam Professor of History and International Studies at Yale University and formerly the president of the Latin American Studies Association. He has written many books and articles on modern Mexican and Latin American history and the history of US-Latin American relations. With Penny Von Eschen he is the editor of the book series American Encounters/Global Interactions, with Duke University Press. In recent years he has edited and contributed to several volumes on the Cold War in Latin America, and in 2019 published a review of the interdisciplinary literature on the Latin American Cold War in *Cold War History.* He is currently working on a volume of essays that examines transnational lives and collaborations at critical moments of US involvement in twentieth-century Latin America.

Timothy W. Lorek is completing a book manuscript tentatively titled *Making the Green Revolution: Agriculture and Conflicted Landscapes in Colombia* (under contract with the University of North Carolina Press). He has been a Mellon Fellow at the New York Botanical Garden and has taught Latin American history, environmental history, and geography at Yale University, Brandeis University, and the University of Hartford, respectively.

Eden Medina is an associate professor of science, technology, and society at MIT. Her research interests span the history of science and technology in Latin America and the history and social studies of computing. She is the author of *Cybernetic Revolutionaries: Technology and Politics in Allende's Chile* (MIT Press, 2011), which received the Edelstein Prize for outstanding book in the history of technology and the Computer History Museum Prize for outstanding book in the history of computing. Her coedited volume *Beyond Imported Magic: Essays on Science, Technology, and Society in Latin America* (MIT Press, 2014) received the Amsterdamska Award from the European Society for the Study of Science and Technology. Her current book project explores how science and technology intertwine with processes of truth, justice, and repair in Chile following the human rights violations committed by the Pinochet dictatorship.

Tore C. Olsson is an associate professor of history at the University of Tennessee, Knoxville. His first book, *Agrarian Crossings: Reformers and the Remaking of the US and Mexican Countryside* (Princeton University Press, 2017), received five prizes including the Latin American Studies Association's Luciano Tomassini Latin American International Relations Book Award and the Agricultural History Society's Theodore Saloutos Memorial Award. He is currently writing a global history of American country music titled "The Global Cowboy."

Hugo Palmarola, a designer from the Pontificia Universidad Católica de Chile (2004), won the Student Essay Prize from the Design History Society in 2018. Together with Pedro Alonso, he was awarded a Silver Lion in 2014 at the Fourteenth Venice Architecture Biennale. They are the authors of the books *Panel* (Architectural Association, 2014) and *Monolith Controversies* (Hatje Cantz, 2014), and are the curators of the Flying Panels exhibition in 2019 at ArkDes, the Swedish Centre for Architecture and Design.

Steven Palmer is a professor of history at the University of Windsor, Canada. From 2006 to 2016 he was the Canada Research Chair in History of International Health. He has published widely on the history of international health in Latin America and on Cuban medical science in the nineteenth and early twentieth centuries. His book, *Medicine and Public Health in Latin America: A History* (Cambridge, 2015), cowritten with Marcos Cueto, was awarded the George Rosen Prize of the American Association for the History of Medicine. Palmer's documentary feature film, *Ghost Artist*, about the maker of a revolutionary medical film from 1967, was released in 2019.

Fernando Purcell is a historian and professor at the Pontificia Universidad Católica de Chile. His research focuses on transnational and global history. He is the author of several books that explore US-Latin American relations, including *¡De película! Hollywood y su impacto en Chile, 1910–1950* (Editorial Taurus, 2012) and *The Peace Corps in South America: Volunteers and the Global War on Poverty in the 1960s* (Palgrave Macmillan, 2019). He currently serves as director of the College UC Program at his home institution in Chile.

Thomas Rath is the author of *Myths of Demilitarization in Postrevolutionary Mexico* (University of North Carolina Press, 2013). He is writing a book about how Mexico's aftosa crisis reshaped state, science, and international relations, and illuminates the history of human-animal relations. He is a permanent lecturer in Latin American history at University College London.

Mary Roldán is the Dorothy Epstein Professor of Latin American History and chair of the history department at Hunter College, City University of New York (CUNY) and a member of the faculty at the CUNY Graduate Center. She has written about drug trafficking, paramilitarism, grassroots peace initiatives to armed conflict, and media in Colombia and is the author of *Blood and Fire: La Violencia in Antioquia, Colombia, 1946–1953* (Duke University Press, 2002), winner of the Fundación Alejandro Ángel Escobar Social Sciences Prize (2003). She is currently completing two monographs, one analyzing the relationship between radio, public opinion, and politics in Colombia, titled "Broadcast Nation: Radio, Politics, and Culture in Colombia, 1930–1962," and another, the history of Latin America's largest Catholic, mass-media based peasant education network (Radio Sutatenza) titled "Cold War Parable: Radio Sutatenza/Popular Cultural Action, 1947–1990."

Emily Wakild is a professor of history and the program director of environmental studies at Boise State University in Idaho. She researches histories of conservation and biodiversity in Latin America and is finishing a work on Patagonia and Amazonia. Her first book, *Revolutionary Parks: Conservation, Justice, and Mexico's National Parks, 1910–1940* (University of Arizona Press, 2011) won the Elinor Melville Prize for Latin American Environmental History from the Conference on Latin American History. She is the author (with Michelle K. Berry) of *A Primer for Teaching Environmental History* (Duke University Press, 2018).

INDEX

Acción Cultural Popular (ACPO)
(Colombia), 114–25; ACPO's
Fundamental Education program,
115; background, 114–18; breakdown
and demise, 129–30; Catholic role in
development, 117–19, 123; Department
of Sociology, 127; Father Salcedo's role,
119–20; funding needs, 117; influence
of and use as model, 122–25; legal
status, 119; measuring effectiveness of,
126–28; public relations for, 120–22;
radio equipment and donations, 122;
statistics evidencing influence, 124
African missions, from Cuba, 38–39
Afro-Colombians, 118–19; legacies of
plantation slavery, 98, 102–3
agrarian development. *See* agricultural
development
agrarian reform, 93; Colombia, 211; Cuba,
137; Mexico, 42, 78
agricultural development in Colombia,
93–109; agricultural research stations,
102–3; Molina Garcés' influence, 97–
101; Durán Castro's influence, 101–5;
extension agents and information
dissemination, 105–8; family-centered
agriculture, 100; and nature, 100;
Puerto Rican influence, 103–4, *106*;
Rockefeller Foundation visits, 96–97.
See also Green Revolution.
agricultural research stations: Chardón's
views on, 104; Durán Castro's visits,
102–3; Puerto Rican model, influence
in Colombia, 105–7. *See also* Palmira
Agricultural Experiment Station
agroecology, 101, 153
aided self-help, 15, 204, 210, 213
Albizia saman (rain tree), 101

Alemán, Miguel, 71–74, 81, 84, 87, 163
Alessandri, Jorge, 218, 248
Allende, Salvador: and anti-Americanism,
184; deposed 1973, 282, 284; elected
1970, 248, 251; and Marxism in Chile,
237; Popular Unity regime, 39
Alliance for Progress: and anti-communism,
288; and Catholic community
development, 108; in Chile, 183–84,
218–19, 237–38; and CINVA, 213;
and foot-and-mouth disease control,
168; formation of, 11, 53; and funding
channels, 15; reduction in funding, 243;
as technical aid mission, 6, 50
Alvarez Pileta, Pío, 143
Amazon rain forest. *See* conservation in the
Peruvian Amazon
Ambiente y Desarrollo, 286, 290
American Foundation for Cultural Popular
Action, Inc., 115, 116, 120, 124–25
Anderson, Clinton, 169
anti-Americanism, 184
Antofagasta, Chile, 185
Antúnez de Mayolo, Santiago, 218, 222–23,
225
appliances, in recently electrified homes,
229–30
Argentina, 20, 39, 40, 167, 208, 264
autoconstruction, 200. *See also* aided self-help
Ávila Camacho, Manuel, 79–81
Aylwin, Patricio, 290

Bajo Anchicayá Dam (Colombia),
217–18, 224–27, see also Cauca Valley
Corporation
Balsas River (Mexico), 86
Basic Agreement for Technical Cooperation
(Chile and United States), 183